TEXTBOOK

Succession:
THE LAW OF WILLS AND ESTATES

Third Edition

EDITOR: VEENA KANDA ROVATI
LLB, MA (Business Law), Barrister

OLD BAILEY PRESS

OLD BAILEY PRESS
200 Greyhound Road, London W14 9RY

First published 1997
Third edition 2001

ISBN 1 85836 418 3

British Library Cataloguing-in-Publication.
A CIP Catalogue record for this book is available from the British Library.

Acknowledgement

The publishers and author would like to thank the Incorporated Council of Law Reporting for England and Wales for kind permission to reproduce extracts from the Weekly Law Reports, and Butterworths for their kind permission to reproduce extracts from the All England Law Reports.

Printed and bound in Great Britain

Contents

iii

9 Legacies and Devises and Their Failure   *111*

Legacies and devises – The doctrine of ademption – The doctrine of lapse – Exceptions to the doctrine of lapse – Failure of gift through uncertainty – Attesting witnesses and spouse – Forfeiture – Lapse by divorce – Disclaimer – The effect of failure

10 Construction of Wills   *137*

General principles of construction – Admissibility of evidence – Equitable presumptions – Section 24 of the Wills Act 1837 – Section 27 of the Wills Act 1837 – Whether gift is absolute or for life – Rules for ascertaining classes – Statutory rules of construction – The Administration of Justice Act 1982

11 Intestate Succession   *165*

Introduction – History – The trust with power to sell – Distribution on total intestacy – Legitimacy, legitimation, illegitimacy and adoption – Partial intestacy

12 Family Provision   *186*

Introduction – Who can apply under the 1975 Act? – Time for making applications – Consideration of an application by the court – What is reasonable financial provision? – The common guidelines – The particular guidelines – Orders – Effect, duration and form of orders – Variation and discharge of orders – Interim orders – Property available for financial provision – Anti-avoidance provisions – Dispositions intended to defeat applications: s10 – Contracts to leave property by will: s11 – Trusts and ss10 and 11 – Choice of court – Deed of variation

13 Executors and Administrators   *232*

Appointment of executors – Transmission of office – Capacity to be an executor – Number of executors – Passing over executors – Renunciation of probate – Appointment of administrators – Capacity to be an administrator – Number of administrators – Passing over administrators – Renunciation of administration – Executors *de son tort*

14 Grants of Probate and Administration   *245*

Distribution of probate business – Obtaining a grant in common form – Caveats and citations – Obtaining a grant in solemn form

15 Types of Grant   *254*

Introduction – Limited grants – Foreign grants; recognition and resealing of grants – Evidence in probate actions

16 Revocation of Grants   *261*

Reasons for revocation – Effect of revocation

17 Vesting, Collection and Realisation of Assets   *265*

Introduction: duties and liabilities of personal representatives – Vesting of property – Mode of vesting of property – Vesting of causes of action – Collection of assets – Inventory and account – Realisation of the estate – Powers of personal representatives – Trustees' powers of investment

Preface

Old Bailey Press textbooks are written specifically for students. Whatever their course, they will find our books clear and concise, providing comprehensive and up-to-date coverage. Written by specialists in their field, our textbooks are reviewed and updated on an annual basis. A companion Casebook, Revision WorkBook and Statutes are also published.

The textbook is designed for use by any LLB undergraduates who have succession within their syllabus. It will also be valuable to CPE/LLDip students and those who are concerned with continuing education. Practitioners should find the material useful to keep abreast of developments, as well as to provide a succinct overview of the law. In addition, students of other professional examinations, including those of the Institute of Legal Executives, as well as students wishing to join one of the accountancy professions, will find the information useful for their respective studies.

This textbook covers and comments further on the recent cases which illustrate modern trends of the court. These include the recent decisions regarding the potential impact of human rights on probate matters in cases such as *Barker* v *Casserly* (2000) and *Camp* v *Netherlands* (2000); a discussion of *Bouette* v *Rose* (2000), indicating the court's approach to an application by a mother as a dependant of her disabled daughter; and the case of *Barrett* v *Kasprzyk* (2000) concerning the nature of the evidence the court is prepared to accept regarding testamentary capacity.

The developments in this edition represent the law as at 1 July 2001.

Table of Cases

Table of Statutes and Statutory Instruments

1

Introduction

1.1 General

When a person dies his assets must be disposed of. It is the function of the law of succession to determine how those assets shall be disposed of. The need for an orderly system for their disposal is essential to the preservation of law and order. There are several methods that might be adopted in disposing of a person's assets.

First, complete freedom on the part of all persons to determine the manner in which their property shall be disposed of after death. Such a system requires a broad framework of rules as to how a person shall set out his wishes as to the disposition of his property. This system was the one used in England from the fourteenth century until 1938. Since 1938 family protection legislation was introduced whereby the testator could be compelled to make testamentary provision for certain family members.

Second, a set of rules or laws may prescribe the manner in which a person's property is to devolve after death. The intestacy rules are an example in English law. Under the Administration of Estates Act 1925 rules are laid down to deal with the distribution of the assets of those who have not taken advantage of the privilege of freedom of testamentary disposition or who have not taken full advantage of it, that is, the will is only effective to dispose of some but not all of their assets. Rules prescribing the manner in which a person's property is to devolve after death usually

1

set out in advance who the property is to devolve upon, for example, the intestacy rules in English law stipulate that the property shall devolve to blood relations. These intestacy rules can, of course, be altered by the use of a valid will left by the testator at his death.

Third, freedom of testation subject to limitations. Modern developments in the law of succession have placed some limitations on a person's freedom of testamentary disposition. A notable example is the Inheritance (Provision for Family and Dependants) Act 1975 which enables the court to provide for the dependants of a person where his will or intestacy or the combination of these do not make adequate provision for the dependant. Thus, the law will, in appropriate circumstances, prevent a widow and young children being left without proper support. The rules against perpetuities and accumulations also impose a restriction on testamentary freedom. See the Perpetuities and Accumulations Act 1964.

Under the rules of public policy certain dispositions are prohibited by will if they serve no useful purpose even though they may comply with the rules of perpetuity. For example, under *Brown* v *Burdett* (1882) 21 Ch 667 a testator was not permitted to devise a house in his will subject to the condition that it was to be locked up and unused for 21 years, as such a gift was contrary to public policy.

It is apparent from the examples given above that all of these methods form a part of the English law of succession.

Finally, for the purposes of this discussion, the following case vividly illustrates the importance of the right of children to be properly supported where a foreign element is involved, and where the widow's own claim is not allowed. In *Black* v *Yates* (1989) The Times 11 May 1989 (QBD) the plaintiff was the widow of the deceased. She was the joint administratrix of his estate, as well as the mother of his adoptive children. The deceased had been killed during his holiday in Spain when he travelled as the defendant's pillion passenger on a motorcycle. English solicitors acted for the plaintiff in respect of her various claims (for herself and for her children) under the Fatal Accidents Act 1976 and the Law Reform (Miscellaneous Provisions) Act 1934. They retained Spanish lawyers to represent her in the Spanish district court hybrid proceedings in respect of the criminal element of the case, in which it the court could award compensation. The English solicitors only sought to establish the defendant's liability: they did not know that they had to expressly decline the exercise by the Spanish court of its powers of disposition where action in another jurisdiction was proposed. A compensation order was made. In the subsequent English proceedings for damages, the defendant raised the defences of *res judicata* and the fact that payment had been made pursuant to the Spanish judgment under the provisions of the Civil Jurisdiction and Judgments Act 1982. In Spanish law the jurisdiction of cases relating to the authority of a parent to act for a minor was a matter for the law of the parent's domicile, in this case the mother.

It was held, as noted above, that the plaintiff failed in her own claim. However, as regards the children's claim the case of *Jeffrey* v *Kent CC* [1958] 1 WLR 927 was cited. Paull J had held that the court had no power to enter into an agreement which compromised the interests of children in an action unless (1) each who was *sui generis* and wished to claim had approved the agreement and (2) the court had sanctioned the agreement as being for the benefit of the infants. The up-to-date position was that O.80 rr10 and 11 governed such a compromise, whether made before or after the institution of proceedings in England. The immediate purpose of s34 of the 1982 Act was to extend the doctrine of merger to foreign decisions. In considering the interests of the children the court went behind the foreign judgment to look at the position at the time of the grant of the power of attorney. In its view this was necessary to protect the interests of the children. Accordingly, judgment was given in favour of the children and the deceased's estate.

In Roman law, the central theory was that of 'universal succession'. This theory drew a distinction between the physical existence and the legal existence of a person and on death the latter still remained. The person upon whom the legal existence devolved was called the 'Heir' and he immediately stepped into all the rights and duties of the dead man. Physical death was not allowed to affect the legal position of the deceased. The distinction between the legal existence and the physical existence of a peson does not appear to have been adopted by English law. However, there are decisions and statutory provisions which appear to lend support to the idea of the deceased's estate being treated as an artificial legal personality. See *Wankford* v *Wankford* (1704) 1 Salk 299. As such artificial concepts are now generally accepted in law, for example, the artificial personality of a company, there seems no reason why a similar concept could not be adopted in the law of succession. However, it might require recasting of many rules as to the powers and duties of personal representatives.

Taxation plays an important role in the law of succession although it is not part of the course for which this book is primarily intended. In English law inheritance tax may be payable on the deceased's estate. One purpose of this tax is to break up concentrations of wealth. Some exemptions and reliefs are given from the tax, especially to a spouse and children. The need to preserve the wealth of a family against such taxes will be important in that a will may be essential in order to take advantage of some of the exemptions and reliefs. Further, the will may require careful drafting and regular review to keep within the limits of the reliefs available and changes in tax law.

1.2 History of succession in English law

It is not proposed to give a detailed history of the law of succession; students who wish to read further than this short statement should refer to Holdsworth, *The History of English Law*; Pollock and Maitland, *The History of English Law*.

The present law of succession can be traced back to the Norman conquest. In 1072 William the Conqueror created the ecclesiastical courts and made them separate from the common law court; this is known as the Ordinance of William the

Conqueror. The separation was carried out at the behest of the church which was seeking to establish itself as an independent institution; the creation of ecclesiastical courts provided an opportunity for the church to introduce the ecclesiastical law of wills into England. This was being developed on the continent at the time.

The ecclesiastical courts gained influence over the disposal of personalty of deceased persons while the common law courts retained control over realty. At first the common law courts stood out against wills of land, declaring that estates of land were not devisable. This was based on military considerations since feudal tenures were essential to the retention of effective military forces. Some exceptions were permitted, such as land subject to burgage tenure. Attempts were made to get round the common law refusal to recognise wills of land. Prior to the Statute of Uses 1535 the use was a popular means of disposing of land by a testator conveying the land to the uses set out in his last will. One of the purposes of the Statute of Uses was to put a stop to devises of land. The Statute led to some revolt and, consequently, the Statute of Wills 1540 was passed which enabled a testator to devise all land held in free and common socage and two-thirds of his land held in knight service. The Statute of Military Tenures 1660 converted land held in knight service into socage tenure thus making the right to dispose of real property by will complete. However, this right remained subject to a number of restrictions, for example, entails, dower and curtesy.

The disposition of personalty by will was controlled by the ecclesiastical courts. As these courts were numerous with each bishop having his own court and also some other ecclesiastical dignitaries having separate courts, different limitations were placed on the power to dispose of personalty in different areas. A common limitation was an entitlement on the part of a testator's surviving spouse and/or issue to a specified portion of the personal estate, usually one-third for the spouse and one-third for the issue. The testator could dispose of the remaining one-third by will, this being described as 'the dead's part' and frequently passing to the church itself. This restriction on testamentary freedom requiring threefold division seems to be derived from the customary law prevailing pre-1066. For example, in Bede's *History of the English Church and People* there is a reference to a similar threefold division as early as AD 735. It is to be noted that the law of Scotland still requires such threefold division (regarding moveable estate) whereby the testator must give at least one-third of his moveable estate to his spouse, another third to his children, leaving one-third to be freely disposed of according to his choice. Where the testator is childless, but married, he must leave a minimum of one-half of his moveable estate to his spouse retaining full testamentary freedom over the other half estate. (See generally Marshall, *Introduction to Scots Law*, 2nd edn.)

As far as English law is concerned the ecclesiastical rules as to reserve shares in favour of spouse and family remained until the early fourteenth century, although they were not abolished in York and the City of London until 1704 and 1726 respectively.

The separate systems of ecclesiastical and common law courts survived the Reformation in England and their jurisdiction over personalty and realty respectively remained. The Statute of Wills 1540 did not affect the common law courts' grip on the disposition of realty, it merely brought recognition of the concept of a will of land in that court. This concept was developed by means of the common law court borrowing principles from the ecclesiastical courts, especially on the forms of a will. The Statute of Frauds 1677 laid down formal requirements for making a will which applied both to wills of realty and personalty. This applied except to wills of personalty involving less than £1 or where the testator was in extremis, that is, a soldier in actual military service or a seaman at sea. The Statute required the will to be in writing, signed by the testator and witnessed by three witnesses.

After the Reformation the power of the ecclesiastical courts diminished and in the seventeenth and eighteenth centuries the power of the court of equity grew. Equity began to give effective remedies to beneficiaries and next of kin who had lost money through maladministration or fraud by executors and administators, for example, by holding them liable to account as trustees. The construction of wills was also gradually transferred to the court of equity. In 1837 the Wills Act was passed setting out formalities for the making and revocation of wills, and some provisions on the operation of wills. In 1857 the Court of Probate Act was passed. This stripped the ecclesiastical courts of their remaining jurisdiction in testamentary matters which at that time was limited to pronouncing on the validity of wills and granting letters of administration. The newly constituted Court of Probate assumed this jurisdiction. In 1875 the Court of Probate became part of the Probate, Divorce and Admiralty Division of the High Court and in 1972 this division was reorganised and became the Family Division. The Family Division still grants probate and administration in non-contentious cases.

The legislation passed in 1925 assimilated the law of real and personal property and in doing so abolished the heir-at-law and old rules of inheritance. Thus in cases of intestacy, realty and personalty devolve according to the same rules. See the Administration of Estates Act 1925.

The question of the right of survivorship and joint tenancies should also be mentioned by way of background. Of course, the general principle is that the joint tenant inherits by right of survivorship upon the death of the other joint tenant.

The question of joint tenancy arose again in a recent case: *Renshaw* v *Bassetlaw District Council* [1991] EGCS 71. Graham and Freda Renshaw, the appellant's parents, were granted a joint tenancy by the respondent council of the premises located at 33 Ramsden Avenue, Worksop. The appellant's claim arose subsequent to the death of Freda Renshaw on 6 July 1989. Heald J in Worksop County Court dismissed the applicant's claim to succeed Freda as a secure tenant. This decision was the result of a 20 March 1989 transaction wherein Graham Renshaw terminated his part of the tenancy and on 1 May 1989 the council let the premises to Freda. The succession was barred after review of s88(1)(b) of the Housing Act 1985 which interpreted Freda Renshaw as a joint tenant who had become a sole tenant and thus a successor herself. The further succession to the appellant was not permitted.

Held: although Graham Renshaw's notice of termination was effective, s88(1)(b) of the 1985 Act did not apply. The section states: 'The tenant is himself a successor if ... he was a joint tenant and had become the sole tenant'. First, Parliament was considering only a single tenancy under ss87 and 88 of the 1985 Act. Second, paragraph (b) refers to a tenancy agreement where the joint tenant becomes a sole tenant under its terms. Freda Renshaw could not have been both a joint tenant and a single tenant of the same premises at the same time.

Another interesting point concerning tenancies and succession was discussed in *N & D (London) Ltd* v *Gadson* [1992] 2 EG 176. The respondent tenant succeeded to the tenancy of premises held previously by his father. The deceased had allowed the premises to fall into disrepair and the landlord sought a rent to take account of the need to redecorate and keep in good repair.

Held: a new interest was created with the respondent tenant's succession to the premises: the obligation of the predecessor did not affect the new interest. Accordingly, the state of disrepair was not the responsibility of the successor.

1.3 Nature of a will

The purpose of a will is to enable a person to dispose of his property as he wishes after his death. In English law a person has complete freedom to dispose of his assets as he chooses by will. However, as has already been pointed out, this was not always the position and even today the right to dispose of one's property on death in any manner chosen is curtailed by the Inheritance (Provision for Family and Dependants) Act 1975. This provision, it is said, does not interfere with testamentary freedom but it does at least curtail it by enabling the court to provide for the deceased's dependants should he fail to do so by his will.

Where a will is made disposing of all the property of the deceased then the property will be distributed according to the wishes expressed in the will. However, a person does not have to dispose of all his property by will in order for the will to be effective. A will may dispose of only some of his assets and to this extent effect will be given to his wishes, while as regards the remainder of his property he will be considered to have died 'partially intestate' and this property will be distributed in accordance with the intestacy rules. Some persons die without having made a will either because they had never given any consideration to the disposition of their assets after death, or because they had concluded a will was undesirable as it might lead to disputes among their relatives. In such circumstances the intestacy rules will apply; these set out a statutory order for the distribution of the estate and are to be found in the Administration of Estates Act 1925 (see below).

The main characteristic of a will is that it is a document which has no effect until the testator's death; until then it is only a declaration of intention as to how the testator's property is to be disposed of. See *A-G* v *Jones and Bartlett* (1817) 3 Price 368. For certain purposes, however, a provision in a will may be effective prior to death. This area is fully discussed in Chapter 3. For example, a will can revoke a prior will at the date of the revoking will's actual execution. This means that even though the second revocatory will is itself revoked prior to death the first will still remains a revoked document and is not revived. See *Re Hodgkinson* [1893] P 339.

Other characteristics of a will which are essentially dependent on this main characteristic are as follows.

1. The will can be altered or revoked by the testator at any time before his death. However, special methods for alterations and revocations as laid down in the Wills Act 1837 must be followed. See Chapters 4 and 5 below. If the will is expressed to be irrevocable this is irrelevant and the testator can always revoke it. See *Vynior's Case* (1609) 8 Co Rep 816.

2. The testator is free to dispose of the property referred to in the will in any manner he chooses during his lifetime. See *Bullock* v *Bennett* (1855) 7 De GM & G 283. In this respect the will is often said to be 'ambulatory' in character. Thus, for example, a testator who made a will in 1975 leaving his house Blackacre to X, is free to sell or give away the house at any time after the making of the will but before his death. The will only applies to the house if it still forms part of the estate at his death. Further, if the testator acquires more property after he made the will but before his death, this too may pass under the will provided the words used in it are wide enough to bring it within its dispositive clauses. See s24 of the Wills Act 1837 which concerns this point.

3. A beneficiary named in a will takes no interest in the property devised or bequeathed to him in the will until the death of the testator and even then, subject to limited exceptions, he will only be entitled to the interest given to him by the will if he is alive at the testator's death. See *Re Currie's Settlement* [1910] 1 Ch 329. A will should be compared with an *inter vivos* disposition which takes effect as soon as the property has been delivered or the appropriate formalities of transfer have been effected.

4. No particular form of wording is necessary for a will; it is sufficient if it is apparent that it is only to take effect on death and is executed in accordance with the statutory requirements laid down by s9 of the Wills Act 1837 (see Chapter 2). This is clear from the case of both *Milnes* v *Foden* (1890) 15 PD 105 and *Slinn* (1890) 15 PD 156. In both these cases the disponer executed deeds purporting to dispose of certain property. The deeds were not referred to as wills either expressly in the document or orally by the disponers. However, it was clear from the circumstances that these documents were intended to operate on the deaths of the disponers and therefore as they were validly executed in accordance with the statutory formalities of attestation and signature the deed were treated as the effective last wills of the disponers. A further case illustrating this point is the Scottish case of *Whyte* (1882) 2 App Cas 400, where the disponer executed some 'Notes on intended settlement'. Although the notes were not labelled as a will, the court treated these notes as a will because it found this to be the disponer's intention and the will was executed with sufficient formality. (In Scots law holograph wills need no attestation as was the case here.)

In *Re Berger* [1989] 2 WLR 147 the deceased was a devout orthodox Jew and it was assumed that he had died domiciled in England. Over the years he had executed parallel series of wills and zavah, handwritten documents in Hebrew. The judge found that the deceased had intended that his wishes expressed in the zavah should be obeyed and, if necessary, enforced by the rabbinical tribunal. The last zavah was executed on 6 August 1977, in accordance with the Wills Act 1837; the last will three days later, but its execution did not satisfy the requirements of the 1837 Act. Should the last zavah (with or without the incorporation of the invalid will) or the last valid will (executed on 15 July 1975) be admitted to probate? The judge decided in favour of the zavah, incorporating the invalid will: the beneficiaries under the 1975 will appealed.

The Court of Appeal dismissed the appeal. Sir Denys Buckley considered that 'the deceased intended to make certain dispositions of his property by the 1977 zavah.' He continued:

'... English law does not require a document which is intended to have testamentary effect to assume any particular form or to be couched in language technically appropriate to its testamentary character ... The 1977 zavah as translated contains the following passage: "Each of my sons ... should know that what I have written in this will is binding on you and additional to what was written in the English language will, and should any clarification be needed, the present will (in the Holy Tongue) [Hebrew] is the definitive one."

... I would therefore reject any argument to the effect that the 1977 zavah was intended only to have exhortatory or advisory effect but no legal effect under any system of law ... However many testamentary documents a testator may leave: "... it is the aggregate or the net result that constitutes his will, or, in other words, the expression of his testamentary wishes ... In this sense it is inaccurate to speak of a man leaving two wills; he does leave, and can leave, but one will."

... The judge's order pronounced in favour of the force and validity of the 1977 zavah incorporating therein the defectively executed English will dated 9 August 1977. In my opinion he was justified on the facts in treating the English will as incorporated in the zavah by virtue of the reference to the English will contained in the zavah. It is clear on the facts and from the language used in the zavah that the English will was a document which was in existence when the zavah was signed and so was capable of incorporation in the zavah.'

Some documents although drawn up in a well-settled form for a will may not be regarded as testamentary in nature especially if they are to operate before death. Thus, if the testator directed that the provisions of a document should operate ten years after its date the document would not be a will. See *Fletcher* v *Fletcher* (1844) 4 Hare 67. However, if a document contains provisions which are to operate on death as well as provisions which are to operate before death, the court may sever the document and permit the former provisions to operate as a will. See *Doe d Cross* v *Cross* (1846) 8 QB 714.

A testator who wishes to alter, amend, or add to his will in some way before his death does not necessarily have to rewrite the instrument incorporating the changes he desires. Instead, he can make a codicil to his will incorporating the changes. The codicil will have to be executed with the same formalities necessary for the will. It is in effect a supplement to the will and when the testator dies it will be admitted to probate with the will. If the will itself is for some reason refused probate, the codicil is capable of an independent existence and can therefore be admitted to probate itself. See *Falle* v *Godfrey* (1899) 14 App Cas 70.

Although the main function of the will is to dispose of property belonging to the testator it can also create interests and:

1. appoint executors to collect in, manage and distribute the estate and also charge a fee for so acting as executor;
2. appoint guardians of the testator's infant children after his death;
3. exercise any power of appointment exerciseable by the testator by will;
4. revoke or alter any previous will;
5. make directions as to the payment of taxes and duties which may be due on the assets passing under the will.

The general rule is that the testator may dispose of any property to which he is entitled by the will. This is subject to a number of limitations.

1. Where the testator was a joint tenant of property the property will pass to the surviving joint tenants automatically and therefore cannot be disposed of by will. This applies to both legal and equitable joint tenancies and a purely legal joint tenancy where the testator has no beneficial interest in the property. However, if the testator is a tenant in common in equity he can dispose of his interest by will. There are also provisions enabling a testator to sever a joint tenancy but this must be done prior to death by an instrument other than a will.
2. A person who has invested money or who has an interest in a friendly society can, if aged 16 or over, make a 'nomination' of his interest to a third party. In such circumstances the money etc will pass under the nomination and not under the will. See *Bennett* v *Slater* [1899] 1 QB 45. Nominations are dealt with in detail below.
3. Sometimes the moneys arising under an insurance policy affected on the testator's life may be payable to a third party named in the policy. Thus, in the case of a policy effected under s11 of the Married Woman's Property Act 1882, the policy will be taken out by the testator on his life for the benefit of his spouse and children and direct payment to the spouse and children is due outside the will. This has the advantage that the policy moneys are not subject to the claims of the testator's creditors. See *Re Flavell* (1883) 25 Ch D 89.
4. Company shares are normally capable of being disposed of by the will but sometimes the company's articles may restrict the disposition of shares by will by, for example, stipulating that the directors should have first chance to purchase them.
5. The testator can make directions in his will as to the disposal of his corpse, and his funeral, but he cannot make a binding disposition of his corpse so that the

executor's or administrator's power to dispose of the corpse has been removed. See *Williams* v *Williams* (1882) 20 Ch D 659. This is subject to some statutory exceptions.

In some instances it may be necessary to determine if a testator was making a will or an *inter vivos* disposition. This is because the former can only be effective if in accordance with the statutory formalities. In the Australian High Court decision in *Russell* v *Scott* (1936) 55 CLR 440 an elderly lady transferred money into a bank account in the joint names of herself and her nephew. The account was operated for the benefit of the elderly lady and was used for her purposes and benefit during her life and not her nephew's. However, she told her solicitor that any money left in the account was to be her nephew's. The High Court concluded that this was an *inter vivos* disposition, not a will. On this Starke J said:

'A testamentary disposition can only be made by will. But a disposition which does not require the death of the donor for its consummation is not testamentary ... A person who deposits money in a bank on a joint account vests the right to the debt or the chose in action in the persons in whose name it is deposited, and it carries with it the legal right to title by survivorship.'

There is particular difficulty in deciding whether non-statutory nominations of property designed to take effect at the death of the nominator are to be legally classified as wills and whether they need to comply with the formalities of the Wills Act 1837.

This problem was considered by Megarry J in *Re Danish Bacon* [1971] 1 WLR 248. It was held in this case that even if the nomination is non-statutory and is intended to take effect on the nominator's death, it is outside the scope of the Wills Act entirely. Presumably this approach can only be justified on the basis that the nomination is effective as an *inter vivos* trust which operates at the date of death as in *Fletcher* v *Fletcher*.

In certain circumstances rectification of a will is possible. This has been evidenced in the recent case of *Wordingham* v *Royal Exchange Trust Co Ltd and Another* [1992] 2 WLR 496. In 1975 the plaintiff's wife had made a will whereby, under clause 4, she exercised a power of appointment to appoint her interest in the income from her share of the residue under her father's will to the plaintiff for life if he should survive her. In 1979 she made another will, clause 4 of which contained the power of appointment.

In 1989 she decided to make a new will, and explained to her solicitor that she merely wished to alter her 1979 will, instead of making a completely new will, leaving those former provisions that did not require alteration as they were.

When the new will was drafted it did not contain a provision that corresponded to the former clause 4. It was engrossed and executed despite this omission. On this basis the plaintiff applied to the court for an order to rectify the will pursuant to s20(1)(a) of the Administration of Justice Act 1982 in order to include the clause that had been omitted due to a clerical error.

The solicitor acting for the plaintiff accepted that the omission of the power of appointment was an error on his part.

It was held that the judge was satisfied that the testatrix had intended that a clause in the terms of clause 4 in her earlier will should have been inserted in the new will, and that an error had occurred in the preparation of the later will. As a result the judge held that the error was a clerical one within s20(1)(a) of the 1982 Act, and that there should be an order for the rectification of the 1989 will.

1.4 Types of will

Before considering the various types of will that the testator may make, it is important to emphasise that the testator can leave only one will. It may well be that his testamentary wishes are embodied in several documents described as wills, codicils or the like. However, the sum total of these documents is his will as was stated in *Douglas-Menzies* v *Umphelby* [1908] AC 224:

'It is the aggregate or the net result that constitutes his will or, in other words, the expression of his testamentary wishes. The law, on a man's death, finds out what are the instruments which express his last will. If some extant writing be revoked, or is inconsistent with a later testamentary writing, it is discarded. But all that survive this scrutiny form part of the ultimate will or effective expression of his wishes about his estate. In this sense it is inaccurate to speak of a man leaving two wills; he does leave, and can leave, but one will.'

Conditional wills

A testator may make a will which is intended only to have effect on the happening of a specified event; such a will is a 'conditional will'. This was explained by Bigham P in *Re Vines* [1910] P 47:

'The rule appears to be that, when a will is made in terms subject to the happening of an event, that event must occur before it can become operative; whereas if the possibility of an event happening is stated merely as the reason for making the will, the will becomes operative, whether the event happens or not.'

Many cases have involved the question as to whether the will was or was not conditional. The following illustrate the point.

1. Cases where the will was held conditional:
    'If I should die at sea or abroad'. This phrase was used in the will of an English seaman and was held to render the will nugatory if the testator died in England. See *Lindsay* v *Lindsay* (1872) 27 LT 322.

    In a codicil to his will the testator stated: 'If I survive my wife ... and inherit under her will'. These words, it was held, indicated that the codicil was only to operate in the event of the wife's death. See *Re Thomas* [1939] 2 All ER 567.

2. Cases where the will was held not to be conditional.

The testator began his will: 'In case of any fatal accident happening to me, being about to travel by railway, I hereby leave'. The will was held unconditional as the testator was merely making a will because of the perils of a railway journey. See *In the goods of Dobson* (1866) LR 1 P & M 88.

The testator began his will: 'All men are mortal, and none knows how soon this life may be required of him. Lest I should die before the sun, I make this last will and testament'. The will was held to be unconditional. See *Burton* v *Collingwood* (1832) 4 Hagg 176.

In determining whether a will is conditional or not the court will have regard to the circumstances surrounding its being drawn up and executed. This is because such evidence may show that the testator could not have intended the will to be conditional if its wording would otherwise suggest that it is. Thus, in *In the Goods of Cawthorn* (1863) 3 Sw & Tr 417 the testator began his will: 'In the prospect of a long journey, I make this my last will.' Evidence showed that the testator wrote out the will before embarking on the long journey he referred to but did not execute it until after he returned. It was held that the will must be regarded as unconditional and admitted to probate.

Joint will

A joint will is a document which embodies the wishes of several testators and is treated as the will of each of them. Thus, for example, if four men executed a document in accordance with s9 of the Wills Act which provided: 'I hereby leave all my estate to my wife', this document would be a joint will. See *Re Duddell* [1932] 1 Ch 585.

Each testator who is a party to the joint will must execute it in accordance with s9 of the Wills Act. The will, once made, can be revoked by any of the parties to it in so far as it applies to him, even if some or all of the other parties to it are dead. See *Hobson* v *Blackburn* (1882) 1 Add 274.

On the death of any party to the joint will the document will be admitted to probate as his will. On the subsequent death of another party to the document the document will be admitted to probate as the will of that party also. See *Re Duddell*. There is little point in making a joint will today and they appear to have arisen only in cases where a power of appointment was given to two or more persons to be exercised jointly by them by will.

Mutual wills

A mutual will arises where several persons (but usually a husband and wife) wish to ensure that the survivor of them will enjoy their property and that, after the death of the survivor, the property will go to certain beneficiaries. Thus, for example, a husband and wife may enter into an agreement to make wills by which they leave all their property to the other as survivor of them and on the death of the survivor the property should go to a common third party. In such circumstances the agreement will cause no injustice to either of the parties to it should it be rescinded while they are both alive. However, should it be rescinded after the death of the first party this may cause injustice. Therefore, equity regards the agreement as irrevocable by the survivor and should he attempt to depart from it equity will give effect to it by the imposition of a trust.

The agreement

This is the essential element in a mutual will. There must be evidence that the parties to the arrangement agreed that their wills would not be revoked. A mere agreement to make wills in the same form is not sufficient. Evidence of this agreement may come from the wills themselves, for example, declarations, or be implied from the conduct of the parties, for example, circumstances in which the wills were executed. In *Dufour* v *Pereira* (1769) 1 Dick 419, Lord Camden said of a mutual will:

> 'It is a contract between the parties which cannot be rescinded but by the consent of both. The first that dies carries his part into execution. Will the court afterwards permit the other to break the contract? Certainly not.'

In *Gray* v *Perpetual Trustee Co Ltd* [1928] AC 391 the Privy Council considered the nature of the agreement and the evidence needed to establish it. Lord Haldane said:

> 'In *Dufour* v *Pereira* the conclusion reached was that if there was in point of fact an agreement come to that the wills should not be revoked after the death of one of the parties without mutual consent, they were binding. That they were mutual wills to the same effect was at least treated as a relevant circumstance, to be taken into account in determining whether there was such an agreement. But the mere simultaneity of the wills and similarity of their terms do not appear, taken by themselves, to have been looked on as more than some evidence of an agreement not to revoke. The agreement, which does not restrain the legal right to revoke, was the foundation of the right in equity which might emerge, although it was a fact which had in itself to be established by evidence, and in such cases the whole of the evidence must be looked at.'

Several reported cases illustrate the position as it stands today. In *Re Hagger* [1930] 2 Ch 190 a husband and wife made a joint will in which it was expressly stated that the parties had agreed to dispose of their property in the manner described therein and that there was to be no alteration or revocation of the document without agreement. It was held that there was a mutual will. In *Re Cleaver* [1981] 2 All ER 1018 a husband and wife made wills on the same day in the same terms but no agreement was mentioned in either of the wills. It was held that there was a mutual will because of various statements made by the wife who was the survivor of the parties. Nourse J emphasised that the mere simultaneity of wills and the similarity of their terms was not enough by itself to establish the necessary agreement but added that it was a relevant circumstance to be taken into account.

The more recent decision of the Court of Appeal in *Goodchild* v *Goodchild* [1997] 3 All ER 63 reinforces this approach. In this case a husband and wife made simultaneous wills in similar form in favour of their son after the death of the survivor of them. The wife died first and the husband remarried. The husband then made a new will leaving everything to his new wife. He died shortly after and his son brought an action contending that his parents had made mutual wills so that the new wife held his fathers' estate on trust for his benefit. The Court of Appeal held that there should be a clear contract between the parties that the wills would be irrevocable after the death of the first testator. The son argued that it was sufficient to show a common understanding between the testators at the time of execution of the wills. The argument was based on an analogy with secret trusts. The Court did not accept this argument, saying that a secret trust is only concerned with the property of a person in the position of the first testator, whereas in mutual wills the agreement was necessary to bind the property of the second testator. The evidence in this case did not prove a clear agreement not to revoke.

The trust

If the contract which lies behind the mutual will arrangement has been established then a trust will be imposed to ensure that the arrangement is carried through after the death of one of the parties to the arrangement. The reasons for the trust were explained by Lord Camden in *Dufour* v *Pereira* where he said:

> 'The parties by the mutual will do each of them devise, upon the engagement of the other, that he will likewise devise in manner therein mentioned. The instrument is the evidence of the agreement and he that dies first does by his death carry the agreement on his part into execution. If the other then refuses, he is guilty of fraud, can never unbind himself, and becomes a trustee of course. For no man shall deceive another to his prejudice. By engaging to do something that is in his power, he is made a trustee for the performance and transmits that trust to those who claim under him.'

Lord Camden's dicta indicate that the survivor of the parties to the agreement cannot, after the death of the first party, be allowed to depart from the arrangement and for this purpose a constructive trust is imposed. However, this should not be taken as indicating that the arrangement can never be set aside once made. Either party to the agreement can revoke it while they are both still alive by giving notice to the other: see *Dufour* v *Pereira*. This is because neither party will be deceived if the other changes his or her will. It has been held in *Stone* v *Hoskins* [1905] P 194 that the absence of notice is irrelevant if the first party to the arrangement dies having revoked his or her will, for the survivor is then free to depart from the agreement. This is supported by the decision in *Re Hobley (deceased)* (1997) The Times 16 June. In this case the court held that where one party to a mutual will alters the will, that would have the effect of releasing the survivor from the obligations of the mutual will. No trust would arise where the first testator to die does not do so carrying out the agreement, ie has unilaterally revoked the mutual will.

The authorities appear to indicate that the trust arises on the death of a party to the arrangement. This appears to be implicit in the decisions of *Dufour* v *Pereira* and *Stone* v *Hoskins* otherwise the arrangement might not be revocable during the lives of the parties. The decision in *Re Hagger* also supports this. In that case the ultimate beneficiary under the arrangement died after the first testator but before the second testator. The question arose whether his interest had lapsed or whether it passed to his estate under the terms of the trust. The court held the beneficiary took an interest in the remainder which was not subject to lapse.

The principles established in *Dufour* v *Pereira* were relevant to the very recent decision of *In re Estate of Monica Dale (deceased)* (1993) The Times 16 February. Here, a mother and father made identical wills, in accordance with a purported agreement, in favour of the plaintiff daughter and defendant son, bequeathing to them all their real and personal property in equal shares or the survivor of them. The father died without having altered or revoked his will and probate was granted to the plaintiff and defendant as executors.

After two years approximately the mother made a new will revoking all her former wills and appointed the defendant as executor and bequeathed to the plaintiff £300 and to the defendant the remainder of her property.

The plaintiff commenced proceedings against the defendant claiming that the defendant held the real and personal estate of the mother as trustee for them both in equal shares. A preliminary question arose as to whether it was necessary for the second testator to die to have obtained a personal and financial benefit under the will of the first to die in order for the doctrine of mutual wills to apply.

Held: the judge stated that the principles to be acted upon in imposing a trust to give effect to an agreement to make and not to revoke mutual wills would be found in the cases dealing with that topic and not those dealing with the availability of the remedy of specific performance. Accordingly, it was not necessary for the second testator to die to have obtained such a benefit under the will of the first to die for the doctrine of mutual wills to apply. The judge considered the case of *Dufour* v *Pereira* (1769) 1 Dick 419. In that case it has been held that there had to be a legally binding contract to make and not to revoke mutual wills and that the first testator had died having performed his part of the agreement. The aim of the principle was to prevent him from being defrauded. A fraud would include cases where the second testator benefited but there was no reason to confine the principle to just these cases. This was consistent with all authorities supported by some of them and in furtherance of equity's original jurisdiction to intervene in cases of fraud. It was ordered accordingly.

Scope of the trust

Assuming that the court has concluded that there is a mutual will, the next quesion is the extent of the trust. Does it cover all of the property of the party to die? To what property of the survivor does it apply? These matters may be dealt with by the wills themselves as in *Re Green* [1951] Ch 148 where a husband and wife each gave the residue of the estate to the other and stated that if the other died first the residue was to be divided into two moieties with one being treated as the testator's personal estate and the other as the benefit received from the other spouse. The wife died first and afterwards the husband made a new will. Vaisey J held that under the agreement the husband was entitled to dispose of the moiety regarded as his personal estate by a new will but that the other moiety passed under the mutual will.

In the majority of cases there will be little problem as regards the scope of the trust in relation to the property of the first testator. Normally, the trust will cover all of his or her property. However, the problem is the extent to which the trust applies to the survivor's property. Four possibilites arise.

1. The trust applies only to property held by the survivor at the death of the first party so that the survivor is free to dispose of property acquired thereafter. Quite apart from the difficulties involved in deciding what the survivor acquired after the death of the first party, it might be said that this possibility detracts from the arrangement in that the parties will normally have intended that all the property of both of them should devolve in a particular manner on the survivor's death.
2. The trust applies only to the property held by the survivor at his or her death. The main objection to this possibility is that it would permit the survivor to defeat the arrangement by disposing of the property by *inter vivos* disposition.
3. The trust applies to all capital assets of both parties whenever acquired so that the survivor is only entitled to deal with the income and not the capital. This would impose a trust on the survivor from the death of the first party regardless of circumstances with all the obligations and duties which are attached thereto. The survivor would be unnecessarily restricted in dealing with the property.
4. The survivor is to be treated as absolute owner of the property during his or her lifetime (subject to any stipulation to the contrary in the will) but when he or she dies the property must devolve in the manner agreed upon. This approach was referred to in the Australian decision of *Birmingham* v *Renfrew* (1937) 57 CLR 666 where Dixon J said:

> 'The purpose of an arrangement for corresponding wills must often be, as in this case, to enable the survivor during his life to deal as absolute owner with the property passing under the will of the first dying. That is to say, the object of the transaction is to put the survivor in a position to enjoy for his own benefit the full ownership so that, for instance, he may convert it and expend the proceeds if he chooses. But, when he dies he is to bequeath what is left in the manner agreed upon. It is only by the special doctrines of equity that such a floating obligation, suspended, so to speak, during the lifetime of the survivor can descend upon the assets at his death and crystallise into a trust. No doubt gifts and settlements, *inter vivos*, if calculated to defeat the intention of the compact, could not be made by the survivor and his right of disposition, *inter vivos*, therefore, not unqualified.'

1.5 Contracts to make a will

As stated above, a will is always revocable even if it is expressed to be irrevocable. However, a testator may make a contract to make certain provision for certain persons in his will. Thus, for example, the testator may promise to leave his girlfriend his house in his will should she marry him, or alternatively he may promise his son the residue of his estate should he come to live with him. Regardless of the nature of the contract it cannot affect the revocable nature of the will. Thus, should the testator make his will in the agreed form he is still free to revoke it at a later date. See *Robinson* v *Ommanney* (1883) 23 Ch D 285.

Although a testator is free to revoke his will even when he has agreed to leave property in a specified manner he may nevertheless be held liable for breach of contract for failing to honour the agreement. However, the contract would have to be legally binding as it is subject to the general principles of the law of contract. See *Re Fickus* [1900] 1 Ch 331. Thus, in *McPhail* v *Torrance* (1909) 25 TLR 810 an agreement to make 'ample provision' for a beneficiary was unenforceable as it was uncertain. Further, if the contract relates to land it will have to satisfy s40 of the Law of Property Act 1925, that is, evidenced in writing (see *National Provincial Bank* v *Moore* (1967) 111 Sol Jo 357) unless there has been part performance of the agreement. See *Wakeham* v *McKenzie* [1968] 1 WLR 1175.

Provided there is a legally binding contract the disappointed beneficiary will be able to sue for damages for breach of contract should the testator fail to honour his promise. See *Hammersley* v *De Biel* (1845) 12 Cl & Fin 45, that if the contract is to leave specified property by will the disappointed beneficiary can sue on the contract before the testator's death, if the testator has disposed of the property in a manner which puts it beyond his power to make the agreed provision. In that case the testator promised the plaintiff that he would leave her his house and land if she married him. After the marriage the testator conveyed the property to a third party. Damages were sought and obtained.

The court has also the power to order that specific property promised by the will be transferred to the promisee where this is possible. In *Synge* v *Synge* only damages were sought but Kay J made it clear that the court could compel the recipient of the property to convey it to the promisee. See also *Re Edwards* [1958] Ch 168. Thus, if T promised to leave Blackacre to X in his will if she married him, but instead left the property to Y, Y could be compelled to hand over the property to X. If Y has not received the property in due course of administration then the executors or administrators could be compelled likewise. However, these provisions would not be applicable if the property was sold to a *bona fide* purchaser for value without notice.

A contract to leave property by will is not broken merely because the will is subsequently revoked by operation of law. Thus, in *Re Marsland* [1939] Ch 820 there was no breach when the will was revoked by subsequent marriage of the testator. The same would probably apply where a disposition was revoked by divorce.

1.6 Nominations

Some organisations are given statutory power to make payments of moneys belonging to deceased persons without the need to require the production of a grant of representation provided the amount paid does not exceed a certain limit. Thus, for example, s25 of the Industrial and Provident Societies Act 1965 and s57 of the Friendly Societies Act 1896 authorise the committees of these organisations to distribute up to £5,000 (Administration of Estates (Small Payments) (Increase of Limit) Order 1984) belonging to the deceased among such persons who appear to them to be entitled by law to receive it. Similar provisions apply to deposits belonging to the deceased which are held in either the National Savings Bank or the Trustee Savings Bank.

A nomination is made when a depositor in an Industrial or Provident Society or a Friendly Society or the Trustee Savings Bank or National Savings Bank authorises payment of up to £5,000 in his deposit to be paid to a specified person or specified persons on his death. The nomination is only possible where it has been permitted by statute.

The formal requirements necessary to make a nomination will vary according to the statutory provisions applicable. However, as a general rule, the following are necessary:

1. it must be in writing;
2. it must be signed by the nominator in the presence of one witness;
3. it must be attested by the witness;
4. it must be sent by the nominator to the society or bank in his lifetime.

The main advantage of a nomination is that it can do away with the need for a will where a person's only assets are moneys in a Friendly Society. However, it does not dispense with the need for probate in other cases, no matter how small the estate might be. The nature of a nomination was explained by Lord Mersey in *Eccles Provident Industrial Co-operative Society Ltd* v *Griffiths* [1912] AC 483:

> 'The object ... is, in my view, to give the poorer members of society ... the power to make provision for the disposal, at their death, of this small sum without the expense being incurred of the making of a will or of administering this part of their estate ... Once made the nomination takes effect, not by creating any charge or trust in favour of the nominee as against the nominator, as was suggested during the argument (for the nominator can at any moment revoke the nomination) but by giving to the nominee a right as against the society, in the event of the death of the member without having revoked the nomination, to require the society to transfer the property in accordance with the nomination. Until death the property is the property of the member, and all benefits accruing in respect of it during his lifetime are his also.'

The main characteristics of a nomination are as follows.

1. It has no effect until the nominator's death and it is revocable until then. See per Lord Mersey in the *Eccles* case (above).
2. If the nominee predeceases the nominator the nomination lapses. See *Re Barnes* [1940] Ch 267.
3. A nomination can be made by a person who has attained the age of 16. This should be contrasted with the position in making a will, as s7 of the Wills Act

1837 provides that a person must be at least 18 in order to make a will (other than a privileged will).

4. A person can make both a nomination and a will and, provided they deal with different assets, they can operate side by side. See *Bennett* v *Slater* [1899] 1 QB 45.

5. If there is both a nomination and a will, then the property forming the subject matter of the nomination will not pass into the hands of the personal representatives under the will, but directly to the nominee. See *Bennett* v *Slater*.

6. Although nominations are regarded normally as arising by reason of a statutory provision, the case of *Re Danish Bacon* [1971] 1 WLR 248 decided that nominations can be non-statutory and yet have the same effects and consequences as statutory ones. In *Baird* v *Baird* [1990] 2 All ER 300 a non-statutory nomination was upheld and was not revoked by a subsequent marriage. It seems that such non-statutory nominations are a species of *inter vivos* trust but the precise legal principles governing their operation have never been fully worked out.

1.7 *Donatio mortis causa*

A donatio mortis causa is a gift given in anticipation of death (see also Chapter 17, section 17.2). Cases testing the scope of donatio mortis causa are rare, but a recent one posed an important interesting question which justifies mention and brief discussion here. Can a death-bed donation of a house take effect through the mere delivery of the title deeds to the potential donee?

In the case of *Sen* v *Headley* [1990] 2 WLR 620; [1990] 1 All ER 898 the facts were that an old man, aware that he was about to die from cancer, told the plaintiff that she could have the house after his death. The plaintiff was told that the property deeds were in a steel box on the premises, and that she should remove them as and when appropriate. There were no written documents of any type, formal or informal, involved. The old man died intestate. Did this gift succeed so that the plaintiff had the right to the house?

It was held by Mummery J in the Chancery Division that the donation failed, mainly because, in the absence of a deed or any other written document the donor had not effectively parted with his dominion over the land. In such circumstances *donatio mortis causa* had no application to informal gifts of land which did not comply with either the Law of Property Act 1925 or the Wills Act 1837.

Nevertheless the two questions, whether land was capable of passing by way of *donatio mortis causa* and whether the conditions were satisfied by the delivery of title deeds, were further debated in an appeal against Mummery J's decision. See *Sen* v *Headley* [1991] 2 All ER 636 (CA).

On an appeal against the decision that the gift failed, the appeal was allowed. Nourse LJ, delivering the court's judgment, said that the question whether the doctrine applied to a gift of land by delivery of the title deeds had not been directly decided in England. In *Duffield* v *Elwes* (1827) 1 Bli (NS) 497, at p538, Lord Eldon considered that it did not. Since then this view had generally been assumed to be correct. While the doctrine was agreed to be anomalous, this did not justify anomalous exceptions. If due account were taken of the present state of the law regarding mortgages and choses in action it was apparent that to make a distinction in the case of land would be anomalous. A *donatio mortis causa* was neither more nor less anomalous than any other. Every such gift was a circumvention of the requirements of the Wills Act. There was no reason why the additional statutory formalities for the creation and transfer of interests in land should be regarded as some greater obstacle. The only necessary step was the extension of the application of the implied or constructive trust arising on the death of the donor from the conditional to the absolute estate. While it was true that the House of Lords would not have taken this step in *Duffield*, the point was not decided in the 1827 case: had it been so they would have followed it. However, they could not in 1991 decide a case as the House of Lords would have decided it in 1827. They had to decide according to the law of the day. Accordingly, they held that land was capable of passing by way of *donatio mortis causa* subject to the three general requirements in all such cases. Nourse LJ (at 639) stated:

> 'First the gift must be made in contemplation, although not necessarily in expectation of impending death. Secondly, the gift must be made upon the condition that it is absolute and perfected only on the donor's death, being revocable until that event occurs and ineffective if it does not. Thirdly, there must be a delivery of the subject-matter of the gift, or the essential indicia of title thereto, which amounts to a parting with dominion and not mere physical possession over the subject matter of the gift.'

Brief mention should also be made of another case, which was decided just after the appeal hearing of *Sen* v *Headley*. See *Woodard* v *Woodard* (1991) The Times 15 March. The question arose whether a death-bed gift of a car by a father to his son was a *donatio mortis causa* (gift by reason of death). In the circumstances of this case the logbook and a second set of keys were not handed over to the donee. It was held that sufficient dominion over the car had been given to the donee to establish a *donatio mortis causa*. It was irrelevant that the son already had possession of the car and the set of keys since the words of gift could operate to change the nature of the donee's possession as bailee to possession of donee under an immediate gift or donatio mortis causa.

1.8 Living wills

Unlike an ordinary will which only takes effect on death, the living will or, as it is sometimes referred to, the 'advance directive', is designed to take effect at some given future date in the testator's life.

The legality of a living will has not as yet been tested in the English courts but it is more than likely that such a will would be enforceable in the courts in principle and would therefore be binding on medical practitioners. Indeed, many States in the USA have already adopted legislation giving living wills legal effect, while in Britain 'Exit' (the voluntary euthanasia society) is supporting a Private Members' Bill aimed at giving legal effect to such documents with the consequential protection for doctors who follow their terms.

The essential provisions of a living will would include:

1. the appointment of a 'healthcare proxy' who could be involved in decisions about the testator's medical treatment;
2. the type of treatment which they would wish for in the event of mental incapacity or permanent unconsciousness ('the persistent vegetative state');
3. a contact point as and when death is imminent.

There are, however, those who consider that existing common law rules suffice to give validity to such documents without the need for any further legislation. The Terrence Higgins Trust is of this opinion. Moreover, this view has been supported by a recent Court of Appeal decision involving the right of a hospital patient to refuse, on religious grounds, life-saving treatment (*Re T* [1992] 3 WLR 782). The facts in this case concerned a patient who signed a Form of Refusal to a blood transfusion. The question for the court was whether or not such a form of refusal was valid. Consideration had to be given to the long-established English legal principle that a person who is mentally competent has the absolute right to grant or withhold consent to medical treatment. Adults are presumed to be competent unless evidence is adduced to the contrary.

In the words of Lord Donaldson in *Re T*:

> 'This right of choice is not limited to decisions which others might regard as sensible. It exists notwithstanding that the reasons for making the choice are rational, irrational, unknown or even non-existent.'

The court held that four criteria must be fulfilled in order to grant legal validity to any refusal to consent to life saving treatment. These were:

1. the patient must have the capacity to make the decision, that is, they must not be influenced by drugs or be suffering from mental illness;
2. the patient should not be under the influence of a third party;
3. the nature and effect of the treatment which is being refused or consented to must be broadly understood by the patient;
4. the refusal by the patient must concern the actual circumstances in which the treatment is required.

In such a situation, therefore, these would amount to the test of mental competency. On the facts of the case the court held that T had not validly withheld consent to the administration of a blood transfusion in the circumstances because at the time of the signature of the form she was under the influence of drugs. T had also been subject to the undue influence of her mother who was a practising Jehovah's Witness.

In the context of living wills the decision of *Re T* is important insofar as it recognises the right of a patient to state in advance and in writing his or her objection to various types of treatment provided that the full criteria referred to above are fulfilled. Extending this argument, therefore, if provision can be made for the withholding of a blood transfusion in a life-threatening situation, in principle there seems to be no reason why the general refusal of treatment or particular types of treatment cannot also be allowed.

While the development of the living will form has been given impetus by the problems associated with Aids sufferers, presumably it can also be used by anyone concerned about the medical treatment that they may receive towards the end of their lives.

It should be noted that it is unlikely that a living will made at, for example, the age of 21 with the intention that it should take effect in the event of the possibility of suffering from senile dementia would remain valid if such illness occurred some 50 years later. Clearly the courts will require evidence of a continuing intention to have the wishes expressed in the will fulfilled during the intervening period.

In May 1992 the British Medical Association issued a statement on advance directives which acknowledges that there are 'significant benefits to advance directives within the framework of continuing doctor-patient dialogue'. The statement endorses the use of living wills and recommends that they should be drafted only after medical advice and counselling, and evidently accepts that doctors will normally comply with the contents. The statement also recognises, however, the right of doctors who have a conscientious objection to curtailing treatment to transfer the care of the patient to another medical practitioner. It advises a renewal of the document at least every five years, and that a copy should be filed with the patient's medical notes. In the circumstances it would appear that the use of living wills will become more and more of a reality.

Moreover, the House of Lords has now added its authority to the qualified recognition given to advance provision in a dictum in *Airedale NHS Trust* v *Bland* [1993] 2 WLR 316. Here Lord Goff acknowledged that in some circumstances the 'fundamental principle' of the sanctity of human life must give way to that of self-determination: 'a patient of sound mind, when properly informed' may request the withholding of particular medical procedures, even life sustaining ones. Lord Goff proceeded to include in the notion of self-determination the situation where:

> '... the patient's refusal to give his consent has been expressed at an earlier date, before he became unconscious or otherwise incapable of communicating it; though in such cases especial care may be necessary to ensure that the prior refusal of consent is still properly to be regarded as applicable in the circumstances which have subsequently occurred.' (p367)

Currently it is still an open question how far self-determination over medical care should be legally recognised and regulated by legislation, as well as the content of that legislation. The fact that proper scrutiny and debate should take place has been clearly expressed by Lord Mustill in *Bland* in relation to the 'moral, social and legal issues' raised by that case:

'The whole matter cries out for exploration in depth by Parliament and then for the establishment by legislation not only of a new set of ethically and intellectually consistent rules, distinct from the general criminal law, but also of a sound procedural framework within which the rules can be applied to individual cases.' (p392)

In December 1997, the Lord Chancellor's Department issued a consultation paper 'Who Decides' which proposes a number of legal reforms to give people clearer rights to say in advance what medical treatment they would accept if they became too ill to decide at the time. The proposals include the following.

1. A person through a 'living will' would be able to appoint a relative or other person with a continuing power of attorney to deal with their personal and healthcare matters. The person so appointed would be able to make decisions on a range of issues, eg the withdrawal of life prolonging treatment and the use of the mentally incapable person's money. However, the power to act on the mentally incapable person's behalf would not extend to decisions on marriage, divorce, sexual relations or voting.
2. There would be a new offence for a carer to ill-treat or wilfully neglect a person they had care of or whose property they controlled.
3. A new test whereby anything done for another who is incapacitated should be in that person's best interests, subject to safeguards.

The consultation paper is based on the recent Law Commission proposals on living wills/advance directives. The aim of the proposals would be to give better protection to people who are mentally incapable and to their carers.

Living wills is a controversial area of succession because it is part of the wider 'right to die' debate. Opponents of living wills see their promotion as nothing more than an attempt to introduce euthanasia by the back door. There are obvious dangers with living wills. For example, A might sign a living will when aged 30 requesting no medical treatment if he were later to suffer a specified illness: 30 years later, not having changed the 'will', A contracts the specified illness, and during the intervening 30 years a treatment has developed (even a possible cure) for the specified illness – if A was unconscious the doctors would be unable to provide that possibly life saving treatment because of the existence of the living will. Accordingly it is submitted that any legislation on this topic should require evidence of a continuing intention to have the wishes expressed in the will fulfilled during the intervening period. In this regard, it is interesting to note that in 1992 the British Medical Association in its statement on advance directives recommended a renewal of the document at least every five years.

Proponents of living wills counter the above argument – that an advance directive may become outdated and inappropriate because of developments in medical practice – by pointing out that a similar objection could be made to an ordinary testamentary will which may become unsuitable if family or financial circumstances change, and that is not a good reason for people not to make wills but emphasises the need for regular review.

The principle of living wills, that people should be given a say in what medical treatment should or should not be given to them when they are no longer capable of expressing their own wishes, must surely be correct.

2

The Formal Requirements for Making a Will

2.1 Introduction

It appears that wills were only capable of disposing of personalty in medieval times as the Statute of Wills 1540 was enacted to permit wills of real property. The only formal requirement laid down was that such wills should be in writing. The Statute of Frauds 1677 added to the formalities needed for a will of real property by requiring such wills not only to be in writing but also signed by the testator or by some person in his presence and by his direction and attested by at least three or four credible witnesses.

Prior to the Statute of Frauds 1677 there were no formal requirements imposed on the making of wills disposing only of personalty. The Statute of Frauds 1677 did not actually require wills of personalty to be in writing but it did impose other strict requirements as to the making of oral wills of personalty exceeding £30 in value so that thereafter it became standard to make such wills in writing.

The law remained unchanged until the passing of s9 of the Wills Act 1837 which followed the recommendations of the Real Property Commissioners in their fourth report in 1833. They recommended uniform requirements for all wills and justified the continuation of formal requirements for making a will 'on the ground that it is necessary to prevent the establishment of false wills, or to render titles certain and secure'. Section 9 of the Wills Act 1837 provided that:

> 'No will shall be valid unless it shall be in writing and executed in the manner hereinafter mentioned; (that is to say), it shall be signed at the foot or end thereof by the testator or by some other person in his presence and by his direction; and such signature shall be made or acknowledged by the testator in the presence of two or more witnesses present at the same time, and such witnesses shall attest and shall subscribe the will in the presence of the testator, but no form of attestation shall be necessary.'

The formalities laid down in s9 could be justified on four grounds.

1. As a ritual function ensuring that only those documents intended to have a dispositive effect were admitted to probate and to avoid loose statements or draft documents being considered as the will.
2. To provide evidence of the testator's wishes, the strict requirements of s9 ensured that there was strong and reliable evidence as to these wishes.
3. To protect the testator in making his will by cutting down the scope for undue influence or fraud on the testator and to ensure that he had knowledge and approval of the contents of the will. Thus, knowledge and approval of the will is not presumed in cases where the will is in the handwriting of another who benefits by that will, that is, suspicious circumstances or where the testator was blind or illiterate.
4. To ensure that the document drawn up was treated as a testamentary document and not as an inter vivos disposition of property.

The formal requirements enacted by s9 in 1837 have since been amended. In 1852 the Wills Act Amendment Act was passed so as to remove doubt as to what was or was not an acceptable place for the testator's signature on the will. Prior to 1852 the courts had shown a tendency to interpret the words 'at the foot or end thereof' in s9 in a very strict manner. The Wills Act Amendment Act together with s9 of the 1837 Act were repealed by the Administration of Justice Act 1982 and an amended s9 enacted by s17 of the Administration of Justice Act 1982 as a substitute for the s9 repealed. In this chapter the original s9 passed in 1837 will be referred to as the 'old s9' and the s9 passed in 1982 as the 'new s9.'

2.2 The 'new s9'

This provision came into operation on 1 January 1983 and applies to the will of a testator who dies after that date but the will of a testator who died before that date will be governed by the old s9. See s76(11) of the Administration of Justice Act 1982.

The new s9 provides:

'No will shall be valid unless –
(a) it is in writing, and signed by the testator, or by some other person in his presence and by his direction; and
(b) it appears that the testator intended by his signature to give effect to the will; and
(c) the signature is made or acknowledged by the testator in the presence of two or more witnesses present at the same time; and
(d) each witness either –
(i) attests and signs the will; or
(ii) acknowledges his signature, in the presence of the testator (but not necessarily in the presence of any other witness), but no form of attestation shall be necessary.'

2.3 Writing

The will must be in writing; this requirement was laid down in the old s9 and is still retained in the new s9. Writing provides strong evidence of the testator's wishes and reduces the scope for fraud after the testator's death when he is, of course, unable to give any evidence as to his wishes.

The term 'writing' has been given a broad interpretation. The will does not have to be in the testator's own handwriting, it can be in the hand of another, typewritten or even printed: see s5 and Sch 1 of the Interpretation Act 1978. The will may be written in either ink or pencil or a combination of both. However, if it is in both ink and pencil and there is a conflict between the writing in ink and that in pencil, the court will apply the presumption that the parts in pencil are merely deliberative and not intended to operate as the will and accordingly they will be excluded from probate. See *In b Adams* (1872) LR 2 P & D 367.

The will can be written in any language or code; it does not have to be in English. Thus in *Whiting v Turner* (1903) 89 LT 71 a will in French was admitted to probate, while in *Kell v Charmer* (1856) 23 Beav 195 a will containing bequests written in a jeweller's code was granted probate. Under s21(1)(a) of the Administration of Justice Act it is provided that 'meaningless parts' of a will may be explained by examining extrinsic evidence of the testator's intention. Accordingly it is now possible to interpret apparently meaningless codes and ciphers under this section and to admit this interpretation to probate. Prior to this enactment some cases, such as *Clayton v Lord Nugent* (1844) 153 ER 83, suggested that such meaningless codes could not be interpreted so as to reveal the testator's intention. No particular form is required either; the testator is free to express himself in whatever manner he considers appropriate. However, it is usually advisable to express the will in clear and simple terms so as to avoid difficulties as to the construction or meaning to be placed on the will or parts of it after the testator's death. Normally it is advisable to draw up the will with the assistance of a solicitor but there is no rule against home-made wills and a testator can acquire printed will forms from leading stationers for this purpose.

The will may be written on any material. Normally paper should be used and a direction from the Principal Registry of the Family Division in December 1974 stated that it is desirable that wills be prepared in a form which makes photographic reproduction easy, that is, A4 or foolscap paper in white with the will typed in black. Wills are, however, acceptable on materials other than paper, for example, in *Hodson* v *Barnes* (1926) 43 TLR 71 a will was written on an empty egg shell. Further in the case of *Murray* [1963] CLY 3621 a will written on a cigarette packet was admited to probate. There is no reason, apart from convenience, why a will should not be drawn up in stone or on wood or glass.

It is arguable that the requirement of writing has been overtaken by technological advances and ought to be relaxed. If a testator decided to make his will by speaking into a tape recorder or using television cameras so as to record it on a video tape, it would appear that such a will could not be admitted under s9 because it is not in writing, yet, in such cases, there is very little room to interfere with the testator's wishes. Such a will would not satisfy other requirements in s9, such as signing. Perhaps the time has come when provision should be made for the 'video' will, so as to avoid an unhappy distinction between a will recorded on video in a teletext form, which ought to be admissible, and a will recorded on video in spoken form.

2.4 Signature

The testator must either himself sign the will or direct another person to do it on his behalf in his presence. This requirement was in the old s9 and retained in the new s9.

The testator need not sign in his name or by his usual signature. The courts have interpreted this requirement in a broad fashion and any mark placed on the will by the testator which is intended to be his signature will suffice. Thus, in *In b Savory* (1851) 15 Jur 1042, the testator's initials were sufficient; in *In b Glover* (1847) 11 Jur 1022, an assumed name was held sufficient; in *In b Flinn* [1935] LJP 36, a thumb print passed as a signature and in *Jenkins* v *Gainsfort* (1863) 35 Sw & Tr 93, a stamped name was regarded as sufficient. A name need not be signed either. Thus in *Re Cook* [1960] 1 WLR 353, it was held that the words 'your loving mother' amounted to a good signature for the purposes of s9. However, the use of a seal will not do because a seal is not a signature. In *Grayson* v *Atkinson* (1752) 2 Vesy 459 Lord Hardwicke considered whether sealing was sufficient and he doubted this because the statute, in requiring the will to be signed, meant some evidence to arise from the handwriting and as many common seals were alike there was no certainty or guard that it was the act of the testator. *Quaere* whether the decision in *Jenkins* v *Gainsfort* is correct in respect of a stamped name. Where, however, the testator has affixed a seal to his will which is stamped with his initials then this will be an acceptable execution of the will under the case of *In the Goods of Emerson* (1882) 9 LR 1r 443.

The testator may be assisted by a third party in putting his signature to the will.

In *Fulton v Kee* [1961] NI 1 it was said to be permissible to guide the testator's hand in signing the will if he was very ill or blind. In such cases the court would obviously enquire as to whether the testator knew and approved of what he was signing. It is not permissible, however, to let the testator pass a dry pen over his or another signature already on the will because this is not an act of signing. See *Casement v Fulton* (1845) 55 Moo PCC 130.

In placing his signature on the will the testator must do all that he intended to do in signing. Thus, in the Irish case of *In b Kieran* [1933] IR 22 the testator was very ill in bed and tried to write his name but did not succeed in writing more than two indecipherable initials. His solicitor, who was present, asked whether he accepted what was written as his mark and the testator assented. The testator was held to have done all he intended to do by way of signing. This case was considered in and distinguished in the more difficult case of *Re Chalcraft* [1948] P 222 where the testator did not acknowledge her mark. In this case the testatrix signed the will while lying on her back in her death-bed. Because she was so ill and weak she only managed to sign 'E Chal' instead of 'E Chalcraft'. The will was admitted to probate. Willmer J summarised his reasons thus:

> 'I must ask myself the question whether on all the facts I can draw the inference that what she wrote was intended by her to be the best that she could do by way of writing her name. It seems to me that if I come to that conclusion, then I ought to accept this writing of "E. Chal" as being in law the signature of the deceased. Bearing in mind all the circumstances of the case – the weakness of the deceased, the difficulty in writing in that position – I come to the conclusion that this mark "E. Chal" on the document does amount in all the circumstances to a signature on the part of the deceased.'

It is clear that the testator need not sign the will himself but can, instead, direct another to sign it for him in his presence. A person who signs on behalf of the testator can sign either the testator's name or his own name. See *In b Clarke* (1839) 2 Curt 339. In *Smith v Harris* (1845) 1 Rob Ecc; 163 ER 1033 it was held that an attesting witness may sign on behalf of the testator.

2.5 Signature must be intended to give effect to the will

The new s9 brings in a major change as regards the effect of the signature. It must be appreciated that the new s9 only applies to the wills of testators who die after 31 December 1982. The date the will is actually executed is irrelevant for this purpose so that a will executed prior to 1983 will be governed by the new s9 if the testator dies after 1982. Under the old s9 it was necessary for the testator to sign his will 'at the foot or end thereof' and the main reasons for introducing this requirement in 1837 were that this was the usual place to sign documents and to prevent fraud. The strict requirement of the old s9 as to the position of the signature was also an attempt to avoid decisions such as that in *Lemaine v Stanley* (1681) 3 Lev 1 where a will commenced: 'I JOHN STANLEY, make this my last Will' and was held sufficiently signed by the testator's name appearing in the commencement. In such cases there was considerable scope for fraud by adding to the will after 'execution'.

The Law Reform Committee in its 22nd Report (Cmnd 7902) (*The Making and Revocation of Wills*), whose recommendations led to the passing of the new s9, considered that the reasons for the signature being 'at the foot or end' of the will no longer fulfilled their original purposes and therefore that the requirement should be abolished. One example cited was the now repealed Wills Act Amendment Act 1852 which widened the scope of the old s9 and said that a will cannot be challenged merely because there is a space between the end of it and the signature, thereby defeating the purpose of the old s9.

Under the new s9 the signature need not be at the 'foot or end' of the will, it can be on any part of the will so long as it appears that the testator intended to give effect to the will by it. Thus, it would appear that many cases where the will was refused probate under the old s9, would obtain probate under the new s9. It is submitted that the following case would be decided differently under the new s9.

In *Re Stalman* (1931) 145 LT 339 CA the testator wrote his will on a single page which was filled with writing to the bottom so that there was no room here for his signature. Therefore, he signed the will in the top right-hand corner. The Court of Appeal refused to admit the will to probate relying on the provisions of s1 of the Wills Act Amendment Act 1852. Lord Hanworth MR said:

> 'Though that section gives a wide geographical liberty to where a signature could be placed, the liberty does not go so far as to say that the signature could be placed at the beginning but in fact the last four lines provide that no signature should be operative to give effect to any disposition or direction which was underneath or which followed it. There is, therefore, an express prohibition that words following a signature cannot be operative.'

Such reasoning, and the 1852 Act, are now redundant and in a case such as *Re Stalman* the court would only be concerned with whether the signature, where it was placed, was intended to give effect to the will. However, it is important to note that the mere fact that the testator has signed the will is not of itself enough to allow the will to probate; the signature must show that he intended to give effect to it. Close examination of the facts of *Re Stalman* indicate that it is the sort of case where the new s9(b) would apply. See also *Re Harris* [1952] P 319.

In *Wood* v *Smith* [1992] 3 All ER 556 (CA) it was held that extrinsic evidence may be introduced to prove the intention to give effect to the will. The facts in this case were that a testator made a valid duly executed will, assisted by solicitors in 1978. Two days before his death in 1986 he made a holograph will which began with the words: 'My will by Percy Winterbone'. He did not sign his name at the foot of the will after writing the dispositions. When this was pointed out to him by the two attesting witnesses he replied that he had signed the will at the top, and that it could be signed anywhere.

The executors of the 1978 will sought probate of the earlier will on the basis that the document written by the testator just before his death was not a validly executed will as it did not comply with s9(b) of the Wills Act 1837 which required that 'the testator intended by his signature to give effect to the will'.

At first instance, it was held that probate should be granted to the 1978 will: the 1986 document, when signed by the testator, was not a will and could not by that signature be said to have intended to the dispositive provisions that followed. Only the 1978 will could be admitted to probate as a result.

It is interesting to note that although the judge accepted that the testator intended to authenticate what he was about to write, as well as to acknowledge this as his will, he could not hold the will to be valid. Despite, therefore, the amendment to s9 of the Wills Act 1837 by s17 of the Administration of Justice Act 1982, whereby a signature can occur otherwise than at the foot of the will, the document could not be regarded as valid because the testator should have made his will before signing it. As the testator had not made any dispositive provisions when he signed at the top of the will he could not give effect to the holograph to satisfy the legal requirements of s9(b) of the Wills Act by his signature. Further there was no signature that could be acknowledged by the testator under the Act. However, on appeal it was held that where the deceased set out the dispositive provisions as part of the same single operation after writing at the top of the document 'My will by Percy Winterbone', the provisions of s9 of the 1837 Act were satisfied. The Court of Appeal was satisfied that evidence of the testator's remarks to the witnesses was sufficient to prove his intention to give effect to the will. It is, however, unclear what 'one operation' means. It is worth noting that although the will in *Wood* v *Smith* was held to have complied with s9, it failed for lack of testamentary capacity.

There are several decisions based on the old s9 which, it is submitted, would be decided on different grounds today, although the same decision would in some instances be reached to admit the will to probate. In most of these cases the court was concerned to find a way around the strict requirement of the old s9 as as to admit the will to probate. They are as follows.

1. *In b Hornby* [1946] P 171. The deceased ruled an oblong box on the right-hand side, half way down a sheet of paper on which he wrote out his will filling the paper. The deceased then placed his signature in the box. Although the will and the signature were in different inks it was found as a fact that the oblong box was ruled out before the will was written. Wallington J considered the various possibilities as to the position of the signature permitted by the 1852 Act and relying on the words in the 1852 Act that the court must consider whether the signature, wherever it is, is so placed 'that it shall be apparent on the face of the will that the testator intended to give effect by such his signature to the writing signed as his will', he concluded:

   > 'In my opinion he so signed it (the will) with the intention of making it apparent on the face of the will that he intended to give effect by that signature to the writing signed as his will.'

The end of the will 'in the intention of the testator' was in the oblong box. This reasoning is no longer necessary under the new s9, but it is interesting to note the emphasis on the testator's intention that was possible because none of the prohibitions in the 1852 Act had been expressly contravened. It would be quite unnecessary for the court to consider anything other than the testator's intentions in a case like *In b Hornby* today.

2. *Palin* v *Ponting* [1930] P 185. The testatrix made her will on a printed form which was signed at the bottom of the first page. Above the signature were the words: 'See other side for completion' and on the other side of the page were the words 'Continuation from other side' with further dispositions of property beneath. The words on the first page were held to interpolate the words on the second page as above the signature on the first page so that they could be admitted to probate. The emphasis again was on the position of these words in relation to the signature but it is likely that in future only those parts of the decision which considered the testatrix's intention will be of use. In this case Bateson J said, after referring to dicta in *In b Birt* (1891) LR 2 P & D 214 which looked at the testator's intention:

> 'So here the words were clearly intended to join in the other clauses which were written on the back of the document.'

3. *In the estate of Long* [1936] P 166. The testatrix made a will contained on two sides of a sheet of paper. On one side was a list of bequests while on the other was the heading of the will, the appointment of executors and the testatrix's signature. The court read the will as beginning with the bequests and ending with the appointment of executors and the signature. Again, such re-arranging of the order of pages is no longer necessary as the court only has to be satisfied that the signature was intended to give effect to the whole document. See also *In b Mary Moorhouse Smith* [1931] P 225.

4. *Re Beadle* [1974] 1 WLR 417. The testatrix wrote her will on a single sheet of paper and signed it in the top right-hand corner; it was attested by one witness only. The will was put into an envelope and this too was signed by the testatrix with the signatures of the two executors beneath the words: 'We certify that the contents of this letter was written in the presence of ourselves'. The sheet of paper was obviously insufficient in itself as it was attested by only one witness but as the testatrix's signature was at the top it was ineffective in any event. See *Re Stalman* (above). The testatrix's signature on the envelope was only held to be for the purpose of identification as were the signatures of the witnesses. On the new s9(b) there is no doubt that the testatrix's signature on the sheet of paper would now be regarded as valid. However, it is still unlikely that the will would be admitted to probate under the new s9 because of the defect in the attestation by witnesses.

A number of decisions on the old s9 as to the position of the signature probably remain unaffected by the new s9. The decision in *In b Mann* [1942] P 146 should not be affected. In that case the court was concerned with the question whether the signature of the testatrix and two other persons on an envelope below the words 'Last Will and Testament of J I Mann' and containing an unsigned will were for the purposes of identification or in accordance with s9. The case is distinguishable from *Re Beadle* in that both the will and the envelope in the latter case contained the signatures of the testatrix. The will was therefore admitted to probate. Another decision which is not likely to be affected is *In the Estate of Little* [1960] 1 WLR 495 where the court was dealing with a will comprising several unattached pages. The issue here was whether the signature on the last page, which was on top of the other pages at the time of execution, was sufficient to make all the sheets a testamentary document. Sachs J applied a presumption that the will should, in such circumstances, be admitted to probate if it was in the room and under the control of the testator at the time of execution.

The decision in *Weatherhill* v *Pearce* [1995] 2 All ER 492 illustrates the way in which s9 is interpreted. Here the name of the testatrix was written by hand by her in the attestation clause. She took her will to the home of two elderly ladies who were retired civil servants in Truro. The will was headed 'The Will of ...' in Gothic printing and underneath in handwriting 'Mrs Doris Weatherhill' in capital letters. The word 'Dated' then appeared in printing and '10 June 1985'. The date was assumed to be correct and was not challenged. The will was written in the testatrix's own handwriting and the attestation clause read 'signed by the said testator, Doris Weatherhill, in the presence of us present at the same time who ... having subscribed our names as witnesses'. It was held that the appearance of DW's name in her own handwriting in the attestation clause was a signature for the purposes of s9 of the Wills Act 1837, as amended by s17 of the Administration of Justice Act 1982 and that this was clearly intended to give effect to the will.

Although this decision appears logical and unsurprising, it is helpful and enlightening in terms of understanding the formal requirements for making a will.

More recently in *Re Cynthia Chapman (deceased)* (1999) 29 January TELR July/August 1999 (Ch D) the deceased asked Barclays bank to help her to make a will. The bank prepared a draft which was signed by the testatrix and witnessed by two witnesses. The document was headed 'outline will provisions'. The provision left a large part of her estate to the National Trust. In September 1994 the deceased gave the bank new instructions excluding the National Trust and dividing the residue between the defendants, three charities. This new will was never executed. The testatrix died in April 1995. Had she died intestate, her entire estate would have passed to her sister who died after her leaving her estate to her husband. The husband executed a deed of variation to carry out the testatrix's intentions as expressed in the second will. The National Trust sought to prove the first will. Only one of the two witnesses to the first will was alive (and in his 80s) but had no recollection of witnessing the will. The court held that the first will fulfilled the formalities required by s9. They felt that it appeared from the face of the document that she intended for it to function as a will, even though it was headed 'outline will provisions'. The presumption of due execution allowed the court to treat the will as valid unless there was some evidence to rebut it. The fact that the on remaining witness could not remember the execution of the will was insufficient to rebut the presumption.

2.6 Signature by the testator in the presence of witnesses

There is no change by the new s9 of the requirement that the testator must make or acknowledge his signature in the presence of two or more witnesses present at the same time. The words of s9(c) are not dissimilar to those of the old s9. The Law Reform Committee recommended no change here because a rule requiring two witnesses provided a greater safeguard against forgery and undue influence than a rule which required only one or even none. The presence of two witnesses means that evidence can be obtained of the circumstances of execution of the will. This, however, is subject to the possibility that the witnesses may have died before the testator or be untraceable.

Under s9(c) the signature or acknowledgment thereof, must be made 'in the presence of' the witnesses. This means that both the witnesses must be aware of what was going on at the time. Thus, if a testator signed his will in a crowded room, bus, or train, the provision would not be satisfied because nobody would be aware of what he was doing.

This is illustrated by *Brown v Skirrow* [1902] P 3. The testatrix took her will to a local grocer's shop to execute it. There were two assistants in the shop behind counters at opposite ends of it. The testatrix signed in the presence of the first assistant while the second was serving a customer and unaware of what was going on. The first assistant attested the will and the testatrix then asked the second assistant to attest the will also.

Held: the will was not properly attested; it had not been signed in the presence of both witnesses while they were present at the same time. At the time of signing by the testatrix the second assistant was not aware of what was going on; it was insufficient that he was in the same room.

It is not necessary that the witnesses be informed that the document being signed is a will because they are attesting the testator's signature and not the will itself. See *Keigwin v Keigwin* (1843) 3 Curt 607. Further, if the testator signs the will in the presence of both witnesses, they need not actually see the signature. It is sufficient if they see him in the act of signing. Thus, in *Smith v Smith* (1866) LR 1 P & D 143 the testatrix signed her will while the witnesses stood at the other end of the room watching but unable to see the signature. When the witnesses were asked to subscribe the will the testatrix's signature was covered with a piece of paper as was the rest of the will. However, probate was granted to the document.

If the testator acknowledges his signature to the witnesses (as opposed to signing in their presence) then both the witnesses must be able to see the signature. In *Re Groffman* [1969] 1 WLR 733 Sir Jocelyn Simon P said:

> 'It seems to me that the authorities establish that the signature of the testator must be on the document at the time of acknowledgment ... and that the witnesses saw or had an opportunity of seeing the signature at that time, in other words, at the time of acknowledgment.'

It would appear that 'opportunity of seeing the signature' means 'physical opportunity' and that there can be no acknowledgment if the signature is concealed but the witnesses could see it if they asked the testator. The following two cases illustrate the position.

In *Blake* v *Blake* (1882) 7 PD 102 the testatrix had signed her will. Afterwards she asked two attesting witnesses to add their signatures to the document. At the time the witnesses signed, the testatrix's signature was covered with a piece of blotting paper, so they could not see it.

Held: the will was invalid. There had not been a proper acknowledgment of the testatrix's signature to the witnesses as they had no opportunity of seeing it.

(Contrast *Blake* v *Blake* with *Smith* v *Smith* above.)

In *Re Groffman* [1969] 1 WLR 733 the testator asked two friends to witness his will, on which he had already placed his signature, one evening when out visiting with his wife. The testator made a gesture in the presence of both witnesses to the effect that the will was in his pocket. He then took took each witness separately into a room and showed them his signature on the will. When the first witness signed he left the room and the other witness entered so that neither were present together when the testator showed his signature.

Held: the will had not been properly executed. There had not been an acknowledgment in the presence of both witnesses while present at the same time.

There has been considerable litigation on the point as to what constitutes a sufficient acknowledgment of signature by the testator. The most desirable thing is an express acknowledgment by the testator but it is clear that this is not essential. In *Daintree* v *Butcher* (1888) 13 PD 102 the testatrix said she had a document which needed two witnesses to sign it. This was held a sufficient acknowledgment and Cotton LJ said:

> 'When the paper bearing the signature of the testatrix was put before the persons who were asked by her or in her presence to sign as witnesses that was an acknowledgment of the signature by her. The signature being so placed that they could see it, whether they actually did see it or not, she was in fact asking them to attest that signature as hers.'

Gestures may be regarded as a sufficient acknowledgment if the testator is either dumb or unable to speak because of illness. See *In b Ouston* (1862) 10 WR 410.

If the testator asks someone to sign the will on his behalf the same rules apply here in relation to signing in the presence of two or more witnesses. It is possible that the testator may ask a third person to acknowledge his signature on the will. See *Inglesant* v *Inglesant* (1874) LR 3 P & D 172. However, it appears if the signature was put on the will by a third party in the presence of and at the direction of the testator, the testator must normally acknowledge this signature himself. See *In b Summers* (1850) 2 Rob Ecc 295.

2.7 Witnesses

Under s9(d) each of the witnesses must either (1) attest and sign the will or (2) acknowledge his signature in the presence of the testator. This provision retains the old law on witnessing the will with one important exception. Under the old s9 a witness could not acknowledge his signature on the will to the testator, if it was already there. Two reasons lay behind this. First, there was nothing in the old s9 to permit the witnesses to acknowledge their signatures to the testator. If the legislature had intended that they could do so it was strange that it was expressly provided that the testator could acknowledge his signature but that such express provision was absent in the case of witnesses. Second, the natural construction of the old s9 required that the testator sign the will first, or acknowledge his signature thereon, before either of the witnesses signed. The following case illustrates this.

In *Wyatt* v *Berry* [1893] P 5 the testator produced his will to a witness and acknowledged his signature thereon. The witness subscribed the will. It was then realised that two witnesses were needed so another witness was found. The testator then acknowledged his signature to both witnesses and the witness who had signed acknowledged his signature to the other witness who then signed.

Held: the will would be refused probate; there was no provision for a witness to acknowledge his signature. In any event the testator's signature or acknowledgment had to be made before the witness signed. Gorell Barnes J relied on the dicta of Sir H J Fust in *Moore* v *King* 3 Curt Ecc 242 who said:

> 'I am inclined to think the Act is not complied with unless both witnesses shall attest and subscribe after the testator's signature shall have been made and acknowledged to them when both are actually present at the same time. If the one witness has previously subscribed the paper and merely points out her signature when the testator acknowledges his signature in her presence and in that of the other witness, which latter witness alone then subscribes, that I hold not sufficient.'

The Law Reform Committee recommended a change to permit witnesses to acknowledge their signatures to the testator. This was largely to prevent a will being refused probate on purely technical grounds as happened in *Re Colling* [1972] 1 WLR 1440. Thus in *Wyatt* v *Berry* and *Re Colling* the wills would now obtain probate.

In *Re Colling* the testator, who was a patient in hospital, asked a nurse and another patient to witness his signature. While he was signing and before he had completed his signature the nurse was called away to attend to another patient. The testator nevertheless continued signing and the other witness then signed. When the nurse returned, the testator and the other witness both acknowledged their signatures and the nurse then added her signature.

Held: the will was invalid since both attesting witnesses had not subscribed the will after the operative signature or acknowledgment of the testator.

Under s9(d) the witnesses must sign or acknowledge their signature in the presence of the testator. This means both physical and mental presence. This can be seen in the cases of *Wright* v *Manifold* and *Norton* v *Bazzett*. In *Wright* v *Manifold* (1813) 1 M & S 294, the testator signed the will on his death-bed while the witnesses were in the adjoining room. Although the testator's bedroom was linked by a corridor to the witnesses' room there was no possibility that the testator could have seen them sign from the position where he lay in bed. Accordingly the execution of the will was invalid. Further in *Norton* v *Bazzett* (1856) 164 ER 569, where the facts were almost identical to those in *Wright*'s case, the execution of the will was likewise pronounced invalid. It must be appreciated that where the testator signs the will in a room without the presence of the witnesses s9 may still be complied with if the testator could have seen them sign. Thus, in *Casson* v *Dade* (1781) 1 Bro CC the witnesses were deemed to have signed in the testatrix's presence when the testatrix sat outside the solicitor's office where they were signing and could have seen the act of them signing through a window if she had wanted to. If the testator is very ill at the time of execution problems may arise in the case of witnesses signing when the testator becomes unconscious, for then he would not be physically present. See *In b Chalcraft* [1948] P 222. However, it is not necessary, as *Casson* v *Dade* illustrates, that the testator actually see the witnesses sign. It is sufficient if the testator knows they are signing, or could have seen them signing if he had wished. See *In b Trinnell* (1865) 11 Jur (NS) 248. If the testator is blind then this requirement will be satisfied if he could have seen the witness sign or had the opportunity of doing so if he had not been blind. See *In b Piercy* (1845) 1 Rob Ecc 278.

Section 9(d) also emphasises a point of law which remains unchanged from the old s9, namely that the witnesses need not sign in each other's presence. It is therefore permissible for either of the witnesses to leave the room while the other is signing the will. The Law Reform Committee considered the introduction of a requirement that witnesses should sign in each other's presence but decided against this because it would merely add a technical requirement in a place where the general practice was for the witnesses to sign in each other's presence. The law as laid down in *In b Webb* (1855) Dea & Sw 1 remains unchanged.

In *In b Webb* the testatrix made and signed her will on 18 March. On the following 13 May, she produced the will to two witnesses present at the same time and acknowledged her signatures on it to them. Immediately after the acknowledgment one witness left the room and in his absence the other signed the will. On return to the room the witness signed.

Held: the will was valid; the witnesses were not required by s9 to sign the will in the presence of each other.

The recent decision in *Couser* v *Couser* [1996] 2 All ER 256 should be noted. Where a testator acknowledged his signature to both witnesses and they attested to it separately but while all three were in the same room, the protestations of the first witness (that the will might not be valid as it had not been signed in the witnesses' presence) while the second witness was attesting served as an acknowledgement of her signature. If a testator could sign and later acknowledge his signature, so could a witness.

There is no requirement that the witnesses place their signature in any particular place on the will. This was the law under the old s9 and continues to be the law under the new s9. In *Roberts* v *Phillips* (1855) 4 E & B 450 Lord Campbell CJ considered this point and concluded:

> 'If the legislature in its wisdom should think that the signatures of the witnesses should be put on the same footing with the signature of the testator (ie "at the foot or end" under the old s9), they ought to use express language to indicate this intention. The mere requisition that the will shall be subscribed by the witnesses, we think, is complied with by the witnesses who saw it executed by the testator immediately signing their names on any part of it at his request, with the intention of attesting it.'

There is no required form for the witnesses' signatures either; normally they will sign in their usual name but any mark or initials intended as a signature will do. See *Phipps* v *Hale* (1874) LR 3 P & D 166. In *In b Sperling* (1863) 3 Sw & Tr 272 the words 'Servant to Mr Sperling' were held a sufficient signature by the witness. However, a witness cannot ask another to sign the will at his direction in the same way the testator can.

The Wills Act contains no requirements on the capacity of a person to be a witness. However, it is sensible to choose an adult of sound intelligence as the witness may be required to give evidence as to execution after the testator's death. In *Re Gibson* [1949] P 434, Pearce J held that a blind person could not act as a witness because:

> 'In the light of common sense and without authority, I should be inclined to hold that for the purposes of the Act, a 'witness' means in regards to things audible, one who has the faculty of hearing, and in regard to things visible, one who has the faculty of seeing. The signing of a will is a visible matter. Therefore, I think that a will is not signed in the presence of a blind person, nor is a blind person a witness for the purpose of the section.'

It is inadvisable to allow infants to witness the will, especially if they are very young and do not understand the nature and importance of the transaction. However, in *Smith* v *Thompson* (1931) 146 LT 14, a will was held to be effectively attested by an infant aged 16. It is also inadvisable to allow illiterates, mental patients or drunkards to act as witnesses. In the case of mental patients and drunkards it may be arguable that they are not mentally 'present' when the testator signs the will. In *Hudson* v *Parker* (1844) 1 Rob Ecc 14, it was said by Dr Lushington that:

> 'The witnesses should see and be conscious of the act done, and be able to prove it by their own evidence: if the witnesses are not to be mentally as well as bodily present they might as well be asleep, or intoxicated or of unsound mind.'

The effect of permitting a drunkard, mental patient or other person who is incapable of being a witness to attest the will is to invalidate the will; it will be refused probate. This is in spite of the provisions of s14 of the Wills Act which states:

> 'If any person who shall attest the execution of a will shall at any time of execution thereof or any time afterwards be incompetent to be admitted as a witness to prove the execution thereof, such a will shall not on that account, be invalid.'

This provision is of less importance today than it was when enacted in 1837; it is concerned with the competence of witnesses to give evidence as to the execution of the will in court and declared that merely because a witness was incompetent to give such evidence it did not affect the validity of the will. Thus, if one of the witnesses was an atheist at a time when such persons were incompetent to give evidence, this would not have affected the validity of the will. However, s14 does not have any bearing on cases where the person who was asked to act as a witness was incapable of doing so in the first place, as where the witness is blind or mentally unsound.

Special provisions are laid down in the Wills Act as to the attestation of the will by beneficiaries, creditors and executors.

Beneficiaries

A beneficiary or the spouse of a beneficiary under the will should never be asked to act as witness thereto because of the provisions of s15 which state:)

> 'If any person shall attest the execution of any will to whom or to whose wife or husband any beneficial devise, legacy, estate, interest, gift or appointment, of or affecting any real or personal estate (other than and except charges and directions for the payment of any debt or debts) shall be thereby given or made, such devise, legacy, estate, interest, gift or appointment shall, so far only as concerns such persons attesting the execution of such will, or the wife or husband of such person, or any person claiming under such person or wife or husband, be utterly null and void, and such person so attesting shall be admitted a witness to prove the execution of such will or to prove the validity or invalidity thereof, notwithstanding such devise, legacy, estate, interest, gift or appointment mentioned in such will.'

Under s15 if X is given a £10,000 legacy or other benefit under a will which either he or his spouse witnesses then the gift fails. X will receive nothing. In *In the Estate of Bravda* [1968] 1 WLR 479 Russell LJ said the rule was 'necessary to ensure reliable, unbiased witnesse of due execution'. Several exceptions exist to the rule in s15; these are dealt with in the chapter on devises and legacies below. If none of the exceptions is applicable a beneficiary who has lost his interest may well be able to recover his loss via a claim in negligence if the will was executed on professional advice as happened in the following cases.

In *Ross* v *Caunters* [1980] Ch 297 the testator instructed his solicitors to draw up his will on the terms he had given them and when ready for execution to post it to the plaintiff's home address where he was staying. The solicitors sent a covering letter with the will informing the testator how the will should be executed but failed to warn of the dangers of s15. As a result the plaintiff, who received benefits under the will, lost these because her husband was a witness thereto. The plaintiff sued the solicitors in negligence. The solicitors claimed that as a matter of public policy they should not be held liable.

Held: under the neighbour principle in *Donoghue* v *Stevenson* the solicitors owed a duty of care to the beneficiary and should have forseen that their omission might cause her injury. Having breached this duty they were liable for the resulting loss to her.

In *Clarke* v *Bruce Lance & Co* [1988] 1 All ER 364 the Court of Appeal held that a solicitor who had acted for a testator in preparing his will owed no duty of care to a beneficiary under that will when acting for the testator in a subsequent transaction which adversely affected the value of an asset which formed part of the beneficiary's potential interest under the will, because in the subsequent transaction there was no close degree of proximity between the plaintiff and the solicitors and the benefit of the plaintiff was not an object of the transaction. This case is important insofar as it deals with the extent of the duty of care. The Lord Justices made it clear in the course of their judgments that some limit had to be placed upon the extent of the liability.

Creditors

There is no restriction on creditors of the testator being made witness to his will. Section 16 of the Wills Act makes an express declaration to this effect. It states:

> 'In case by any will any real or personal estate shall be charged with any debt or debts, and any creditor, or the wife or husband of any creditor, whose debt is so charged, shall attest the execution of such will, such creditor notwithstanding such charge shall be admitted a witness to prove the execution of such will, or to prove the validity or invalidity thereof.'

Section 16 was passed to resolve doubts as to whether a creditor could be a witness. Under the Statute of Frauds 1677, this was in dispute. See Lord Camden's judgment in *Hindson* v *Kersey* (1765) and also *Wyndham* v *Chetwynd* (1758) Black Rep 95.

Executors

By s17 of the Wills Act it is made clear that an executor can witness the will of the testator. It states:

> 'No person shall, on account of his being an executor of a will, be incompetent to be admitted a witness to prove the execution of such will, or a witness to prove the validity or invalidity thereof.'

A danger lurks in this provision for solicitor-executors who would normally put in a charging clause in the will so as to obtain remuneration for their services. Section 17 does not affect such persons as witnesses merely because they are executors. But under s15 the charging clause would be ineffective by virtue of either the solicitor, executor or his spouse witnessing the will. See *Re Pooley* (1888) 40 Ch D 1.

2.8 Attestation

The old s9 provided that no form of attestation was necessary in the execution of the will. This continues to be the position under the new s9. However, an attestation clause in the will is advisable as it will avoid unnecessary delay in obtaining probate, because a presumption of due execution will be raised. See *Re Webb* [1964] 1 WLR 509. A typical attestation clause would read:

> 'Signed by the above named testator JOHN SMITH as his last will in the presence of us present at the same time who in his presence and in the presence of each other have hereunto subscribed our names as witnesses.'

If there is a proper attestation clause similar to that set out above then there is a presumption that the will was properly executed: see *Re Vere-Wardale* [1949] P 395; this presumption is rebuttable. If the will does not contain a revocation clause then the registrar must require an affidavit of due execution under r14 of the Non-Contentious Probate Rules 1987.

2.9 Negligence issues

The well established principle of English law is that, subject to a few exceptions, only a party to a contract is able to enforce it. This is the case even where a contract is clearly intended to benefit third parties. It is known as the Doctrine of Privity and has particular and often awkward consequences in respect of succession matters.

This doctrine means that intended beneficiaries have no direct means of securing the benefit; their only way forward is if an original party to the contract should choose to enforce it on their behalf.

This whole doctrine has come in for strong criticism and the Law Commission has provisionally recommended that it should be overturned by statute.

Several recent cases involving claims against solicitors for negligence emphasise the complex legal problems which may arise for lack of a simple right of recovery in the third party beneficiary. These cases concerned clients of solicitors who, having instructed their solicitors, died before these instructions were carried out. This arose, first, in *Lynne* v *Gordon Doctors and Walton*. The question for the court was whether anyone was in a position to sue the solicitors for negligence in failing to carry out their client's instructions.

In *Lynne* v *Gordon Doctors and Walton* (1991) 135 SJ 29 the circumstances involved a straightforward transaction of a mortgage loan supported by life assurance. A Mr Dryan raised a loan of £155,000 on the security of his home in

November 1987. It was a term of the mortgage offer that there should be in place a policy of assurance on Mr Dryan's life for a term of 13 years and for a sum of at least equal to the amount of the loan. When Mr Dryan died in October 1988 it was discovered that no such policy had been taken out. It was argued that the defendant's solicitors, who had acted for both Mr Dryan and the lending bank in respect of the mortgage, were at fault. When proceedings were commenced on behalf of Mr Dryan's estate, alleging breach of contract or tortious negligence, the defendants argued that the estate could enforce only such claims as it had inherited from Mr Dryan. Since he would have had no claim during his lifetime he had suffered no loss.

As a preliminary issue the point was taken before Phillips J.

Held: the failure by a professional adviser to ensure that a term policy is taken out on a client's life in fact means that the client is richer rather than poorer since he has no life assurance premium to pay. Further, the client could not be said to be deprived of the value which the policy would have had it been taken out; while the client still lives he can remedy the position by himself taking out a policy and, even if the premiums were then higher, this amount would be offset by those which had not been paid. As a result the deceased client could not be regarded as having suffered any loss as a result of the solicitor's negligence.

In *Smith* v *Claremont Haynes & Co* (1991) The Times 3 September a client wished to alter her will in favour of two specific relatives. She made her solicitor aware of her wishes. Despite knowing that the client was seriously ill the solicitor delayed several weeks before making an appointment to visit her, by which time the client was too ill to give instructions. The two intended beneficiaries commenced proceedings in a claim for negligence against the solicitor's firm.

Held: Deputy Judge Barnett followed, and indeed extended, the controversial case of *Ross* v *Caunters* [1980] Ch 297 whereby solicitors were held liable for positive negligence in the execution of a will which rendered a bequest invalid.

The question of the solicitor's negligence was dealt with again in the more recent cases, *Smith* v *Claremont Haynes & Co* (1991) The Times 3 September and *Layzell* v *Smith Morton & Long* [1992] 13 EG 118.

In *Layzell* v *Smith Morton & Long* [1992] 13 EG 118 the plaintiff's father had held an agricultural yearly tenancy of a farm with some 164 acres in Essex until the date of his death. The plaintiff and the deceased had managed the farm through a partnership but, because the farm required drainage, it was not a very profitable concern. In the absence of sufficient capital the plaintiff entered into an agreement with an uncle and a neighbour whereby contractual services were provided for the farm in return for certain financial payments. The deceased died on 17 August 1986, and on 26 September 1986 the landlord gave notice to quit the holding. The plaintiff's solicitors, the defendants, had failed to claim a right of succession for the plaintiff pursuant to s39 of the Agricultural Holdings Act 1986.

In this case the defendants acknowledged that this failure to claim rights of succession was negligent and constituted a breach of contract. The court therefore considered the following questions.

1. What were the prospects for the plaintiff succeeding his father as a tenant of the farm?
2. What compensation should he receive for the loss of those prospects?

The defendants argued that the plaintiff did not satisfy condition (a) in s36(3) of the 1986 Act. This provides for the eligible period throughout which an applicant must show that his only or principal source of livelihood was derived from agricultural work on the holding. In addition the plaintiff was not a suitable person.

Held: although the contractual services provided under the agreement with his uncle were at below market value, condition (a) in s36(3) of the Act was satisfied because the plaintiff's only or principal source of livelihood came from the farm during the material time.

There was no reason to suppose that there was a significant chance that the Agricultural Land Tribunal would have concluded that the plaintiff was not eligible to succeed. The evidence of unsuitability would have been regarded as trivial by the Agricultural Land Tribunal and there was no reason to suppose that there would have been a significant chance that the Tribunal would have concluded that the plaintiff was not suitable.

The fairest way to compensate the plaintiff for his loss and to put him in a position to retrieve his loss was through a sale and lease back approach to the assessment of damages. A calculation based on the initial capital required to acquire the freehold of a similar farm and the value to sell the freehold and then to enter a tenancy agreement similar to the one that he had lost were used as a measure of damages.

There has been another case recently that deals with succession rights to agricultural holdings and the income qualification for inheriting a tenancy under s36(3)(a) of the Agricultural Holdings Act 1986. This is *Welby and Another* v *Casswell* (1995) The Times 18 April, where it was held that this provision related to the right of an eligible person to apply for a new tenancy on the death of a tenant. It was for the court to decide whether the tenant qualified by deriving his principal source of livelihood from his agricultural work on the holding. To exercise the right to apply for a new tenancy on the death of the tenant of an agricultural holding, an otherwise eligible applicant had to derive his only and principal source of livelihood from his work on the holding and from no other source. It was immaterial that money from elsewhere might come into the farm account and be used for farming purposes. Although the landlord's argument to the contrary has been upheld in the Queen's Bench Division, the Court of Appeal agreed with the Lands Tribunal that a formal legalistic interpretation of s36(3)(a) was not required. In view of the frequency of cases in this area, the case is noteworthy.

In order to avoid any negligence problems the various elements required to fulfil this form of succession must be properly fulfilled by the applicant's adviser.

Professional negligence

The position as it stands in respect of the duty owed by a solicitor with regard to the drawing up or alteration of a will is that usually the breach of duty will only come to light after the testator has died, which means that it is too late to rectify the matter. Although the testator's cause of action will of course pass to the estate it will be a worthless cause of action both in contract and in tort. If action is taken against the negligent solicitor, only nominal damages will be awarded as the estate will be unable to show that it has suffered any loss. The real loss will be only suffered by intended beneficiaries who have not benefitted from the will either because of poor draftsmanship or because of lack of draftsmanship.

The case of *Ross* v *Caunters* [1980] Ch 297 had moved in the direction of enabling disappointed beneficiaries to sue the solicitor in certain circumstances. In that case the negligence arose because the solicitor allowed an intended beneficiary to witness a will, thereby debarring the beneficiary from taking his benefit. The Judge, Megarry V-C, held that the solicitor owed a duty of care to the intended beneficiary. That duty derived from and existed in parallel to the duty of care owed by the solicitor to his client. Unlike the case of *Hedley Byrne* v *Heller* [1964] AC 465 and its principle regarding negligent misstatements, there was no need to show an element of reliance on the solicitor by the intended beneficiary. Megarry V-C was thereby creating a new category of tortious liability for pure economic loss.

A more restricted approach towards the recognition of new categories of liability for pure economic loss has, however, occurred following the House of Lords' decisions in *Caparo Industries plc* v *Dickman* [1990] 2 AC 605 and *Murphy* v *Brentwood District Council* [1991] 1 AC 398. This approach is summed up in the famous dictum of Brennan J in the High Court of Australia in the case of *Sutherland* v *Heyman* (1985) 157 CLR 424.

> 'It is preferable, in my view, that the law should develop novel categories of negligence incrementally and by analogy with established categories rather than by a massive extension of a *prima facie* duty of care restrained only by indefinable "considerations" which ought to negative or reduce or limit the scope of the duty or the class of person to whom it is owed' (p481).

Whereas the decision in *Ross* v *Caunters* [1980] 1 Ch 297 would probably not be decided in that way today, it should be noted that the House of Lords in the *Caparo* case did not expressly overrule it and the Court of Appeal in *Punjab National Bank* v *De Boinville* [1992] 1 Lloyd's Rep 7 decided on the assumption that there was a recognised category of economic loss as a result of breach of this type of duty. Whether or not that would indeed be an extension of the *Ross* v *Caunters* principle in a case that was beyond its particular facts was what Judge Barnett QC had to look at in *Smith* v *Claremont Haynes & Co* (1991) The Times 3 September.

The topicality of these cases was demonstrated even more recently in *Kecskemeti* v *Rubens Rabin & Co* (1992) The Times 31 December. Mr Stanley Rubens of Rubens Rabin & Co, together with another solicitor from another firm, the latter never being the testator's legal adviser, were executors of the deceased's 1981 will. The beneficiaries were the testator's second wife Eva and his son by his first wife, the plaintiff. The argument centred around two properties and their proceeds of sale in relation to the estate.

Evidently it had been the intention of the testator that when the disputed properties were sold the plaintiff should receive half of the proceeds of the sale. Despite this intention, when the will was made these properties were held as joint tenancies by the testator and his second wife. Accordingly when the testator died the whole interest in both of the properties passed on to the second wife Eva by way of survivorship. The 1981 will had been made revoking an earlier will made in 1974.

The question was whether the law firm of Rubens Rabin & Co owed a duty of care to the plaintiff in respect of advice given to the testator when he made his new will.

Held: the judge, Macpherson J, said that the question was whether the defendants owed a duty of care to the plaintiff which could give rise to liability in negligence without there being any reliance by him upon the solicitor or his advice.

In the absence of any overruling or overtaking by other authorities, the law was that set out in the case of *Ross* v *Caunters* [1980] Ch 297. This decision had been criticised. His Lordship did not accept the broad assertion by the defendant that if there was a duty in this case, then such a duty must be owed generally to beneficiaries whatever the circumstances and however far in the future they may be identifiable. *Ross* v *Caunters* defined a limited area within which a solicitor might be liable to persons who were not his clients. Indeterminate classes of potential beneficiaries had to be individually considered.

Accordingly, in the circumstances of this case the defendants did owe a duty of care to the plaintiff when advising the testator in 1981.

Another case regarding professional negligence that should be noted is *White* v *Jones* [1995] 2 WLR 187, involving the duty of care, delay in carrying out instructions and whether the duty is owed to the beneficiary of the will. In this case, a testator ordered a firm of solicitors to draw up a new will in which his daughters were to be the main beneficiaries. However, the testator died before the execution of the will, due to negligent delay on the part of his solicitors. The intended beneficiaries sought to recover damages in negligence from the solicitors and the Court of Appeal ruled that they were entitled to such damages ([1993] 3 WLR 730). The solicitors appealed to the House of Lords.

Held: the appeal was dismissed (Lords Mustill and Keith dissenting). Although *Ross* v *Caunters* [1980] Ch 297 presented some conceptual difficulties in relation to the contractual nature of the relationship between solicitor and client and the fact that under general principle solicitors owed no duty of care to third parties, the interests of justice required that intended beneficiaries deprived of their legacy should have a remedy. The principle in *Hedley Byrne & Co Ltd* v *Heller & Partners Ltd* [1964] AC 465 should be extended so that a solicitor's assumption of responsibility towards his client extended also to intended beneficiaries.

A solicitor's responsibility to his client when instructed to draw up a will can be extended to an intended beneficiary under the proposed will.

The Lords, by a majority of three to two, confirmed the Court of Appeal's previous decision. It now seems, therefore, that if, due to unacceptable delay by a solicitor, a will is not drawn up, he or she is liable in negligence to potential third-party beneficiaries. However, most interestingly at the end of his judgment, Lord Goff added:

> 'Finally, there was the objection that if liability was recognised it would be impossible to place any sensible limits to cases in which recovery was allowed. There have to be boundaries to the availability of the remedy but they would have to be worked out in the future; as practical problems come to light before the courts.'

Evidently there will be some questions, in particular over 'what is a reasonable time in which a solicitor might be expected to prepare a will' and, indeed, as to extent of the liability itself.

This decision, as well as the decision in *Kecskemeti* v *Rubens Rabin & Co* (1992) The Times 31 December, obliges solicitors to take very full instructions before preparing a will – preferably by reference to a pre-prepared instructions list – and to be careful to act on instructions to prepare a will with due diligence. It remains to be seen, however, what will be decided by the courts in respect of the scope of liability in connection with the advice given to testators in as far as such advice may adversely affect potential beneficiaries. The principle established by the case of *Ross* v *Caunters* [1980] Ch 297, enabling disappointed beneficiaries to sue solicitors in certain circumstances, continues to develop.

However, in *Walker* v *Geo H Medlicott & Son* (1998) The Times 25 November the Court of Appeal said that a disappointed beneficiary should mitigate his loss by commencing rectification proceedings and should only commence a negligence action once that remedy had been exhausted. Clearly, this is only applicable where the beneficiary alleges that the solicitors had failed to give effect to the testator's intentions when drafting the will. *White* v *Jones* was distinguished as it was a case that was concerned with negligence in failing to draw up the will and an action in negligence was the only remedy available here.

The case of *Horsfall & Another* v *Haywards (A Firm)* [1999] 1 FLR 1182 (CA) provides an important qualification to the principle laid down in *Walker* v *Geo H Medlicott & Son*. The Court of Appeal made it clear that prospective beneficiaries under a negligently drafted will are not required to issue rectification proceedings to mitigate their loss and to exhaust that remedy before suing the solicitor in negligence if in fact there is no prospect of such proceedings resulting in any material recovery of the funds lost.

In *Worby and Others* v *Rosser* (1999) The Times 9 June (CA) the issue was whether a solicitor engaged in the preparation of *another will owed any duties to persons who had expectations under an earlier will*. This situation was quite distinct from that before the House of Lords in the landmark case of *White* v *Jones* (above) which established that delay by a solicitor in drawing up a will before a testator died could create a liability in negligence to disappointed beneficiaries. In that case the beneficiaries had suffered loss and had no remedy unless they could bring proceedings themselves (ie there was a gap in the law which required the court to fashion a remedy to enable the beneficiaries to recover their loss from the solicitor). However, in the instant case there was no such gap in the law. If a solicitor's breach of duty gave rise to expensive probate proceedings and unrecovered costs then prima facie those costs fell to be borne by the estate. The beneficiary's costs could be provided for out of the estate and its loss could be recovered directly from the solicitor (ie the remedy against the solicitor was the estate's remedy and there was no need to create an independent remedy for the beneficiary in the probate proceedings). Accordingly, the appeal would be dismissed.

The plaintiff's claim was certainly a novel one, 'perhaps startling' as Chadwick LJ put it. The litigation can be seen as yet another attempt to widen the liability of solicitors to disappointed beneficiaries when preparing wills which has followed the decision in *White* v *Jones* (see, for example, *Carr-Glyn* v *Frearsons (A Firm)* [1998] 4 All ER 225). The instant case was quite distinguishable from *White* v *Jones*. Here the allegation was that the defendant solicitor failed to ascertain whether the testator had capacity and whether he had not been unduly influenced. The Court concluded that there was no authority to suggest that in such circumstances a solicitor owed a duty to the testator and to the beneficiaries. Further, the practical consequences for solicitors if they were held to owe duties directly to beneficiaries under an earlier will was a pertinent factor in persuading the court to reject the plaintiff's claim.

Similar reasoning appears to have been applied in *Gibbons* v *Nelson* (2000) The Times 21 April where it was held that a solicitor could not be in breach of duty to a person of whom he was unaware.

The liability of a non-solicitor will writer was tested in the recent case of *Esterhuizen and Another* v *Allied Dunbar Assurance plc* (1998) The Times 10 June. In this case the beneficiaries to a will which only had one witness brought action against the defendants in respect of its will-making service. The court held that *White* v *Jones* should apply and the principles were not limited to solicitors but applied to a commercial will-writing organisation. This establishes that lay will writers are to be judged by the same standards applicable to solicitors and is a necessary and fair extension of the law.

3

Privileged Wills

3.1 Introduction

3.2 Soldier being in actual military service

3.3 Mariner or seaman being at sea

3.4 Section 2 of the Wills (Soldiers and Sailors) Act 1918

3.5 Extent of the privilege

3.1 Introduction

The formal requirements for making a will as laid down by s9 do not apply to privileged testators because s11 of the Wills Act states:

> 'Provided always, that any soldier being in actual military service, or any mariner or seaman being at sea, may dispose of his personal estate as he might have done before the making of this Act.'

The main reason for the privilege is that the persons to whom it is accorded, that is, soldiers and sailors, may when 'in actual military service' or 'at sea' be placed in danger and therefore be unable to obtain proper legal advice on making a will. But the court has not allowed this reason to restrict the operation of the rule. In *Re Wingham* [1949] P 187, Denning LJ said:

> 'It would be a great mistake, however, to argue therefrom that a soldier, who is not in danger, or who has legal advice at his elbow, cannot make a soldier's will.'

It will be noted that s11 is confined to the disposal of personal estate. Section 3(1) of the Wills (Soldiers and Sailors) Act 1918 expressly provides that testamentary dispositions of real property can be made by way of a privileged will.

3.2 Soldier being in actual military service

The term 'soldier' is given a broad interpretation and it includes all members of the army be they full-time professional soldiers, or part-time soldiers, such as members of the territorial army. The term 'soldier' also includes a member of the Air Force

48

under s5(1) of the Wills (Soldiers and Sailors) Act 1918 but it does not include civilian airmen.

Much difficulty has surrounded the interpretation of the words 'in actual military service' in the past. In *Drummond* v *Parish* (1843) 3 Curt 522, Sir H J Fust thought that because the idea of privileged wills for soldiers was derived from Roman law the test for deciding whether they were in actual military service was similar to the Roman test, that is, was the soldier so circumstanced that he would have been regarded as 'in expeditione'? This narrow test as to when a soldier was entitled to make a privileged will was decisively rejected by the Court of Appeal in *Re Wingham* [1949] P 187 where Denning LJ said:

> 'The rule is that a soldier "in actual military service" is privileged to make a will without any formalities. The plain meaning of the statutes is that any soldier, sailor or airman is entitled to the privilege, if he is actually serving with the Armed Forces in connection with military operations which are or have been taking place or are believed to be imminent. It does not, of course, include officers on half-pay or men on the reserve, or the territorials, when not called up for service. They are not actually serving. Nor does it include members of the forces serving in this country, or on routine garrison duty overseas, in time of peace, when military operations are not imminent. They are actually serving, but are not in actual "military" service, because no military operations are afoot. It does, however, include all our men serving – or called up for service – in the wars: and women too, for that matter. It includes not only those actively engaged with the enemy but all who are training to fight him. It also includes those members of the Forces, who, under stress of war, both work at their jobs and man the defences, such as the Home Guard. It includes not only the fighting men, but also those who serve in the Forces, doctors, nurses, chaplains, WRNS, ATS, and so forth. It includes them all, whether they are in the field or in the barracks in billets or sleeping at home. It includes them not only in time of war but also when war is imminent. After hostilities have ended, it may still include them, as, for instance, when they garrison the countries we occupy, or when they are engaged in military operations overseas. In all these cases they are plainly "in actual military service". Doubtful cases may arise in peacetime when a soldier is in, or is about to be involved, in military operations. As to these cases, all I say is that, in case of doubt, the serving soldier should be given the benefit of the privilege.'

The dicta of Denning LJ gives a clear statement of the meaning of 'actual military service'. In *Re Wingham* itself the issue was whether an airman in training in Canada during the Second World War was entitled to be treated as a privileged testator when he died in a crash during training. His will in the form of a letter to his relatives was admitted to probate as such.

Denning LJ referred to doubtful cases which may arise in peacetime as to whether the privilege ought to be accorded, for example, where a soldier is sent to a disturbed area. He concluded that soldiers should be given the benefit of the privilege in such circumstances.

One such doubtful case was in *Re Jones* [1981] 1 All ER 1. The deceased was a soldier serving in Northern Ireland in 1978. While on a military patrol intended to assist in the maintenance of law and order he was shot and wounded by an unknown gunman. On the way to hospital the deceased said to an officer and a warrant officer of his battalion, 'If I don't make it, make sure Ann gets all my stuff'. Ann was the fiancée of the deceased. The deceased died the next day. The deceased also left a written will by which he left all his property to his mother. The question arose whether the words spoken by the deceased amounted to a privileged will and this turned mainly on whether he was in 'actual military service' at the time.

Held: the deceased was on actual military service and his statement on the way to hospital was a privileged will. The fact that the enemy was an un-uniformed band of assassins and arsonists was irrelevant. The real test was not the state of the opponent or the character of the opponent's operations but the nature of the activities of the deceased and those with whom he was associated.

The decision in *Re Jones* recognises the changed nature of warfare. A similar issue arose in the Australian case *In the Will of Anderson* (1958) 75 WN (NSW) 334. Here the deceased was an Australian soldier sent to Malaya in 1955 to deal with terrorist activities. He was killed in action. The deceased had made a will after he received his orders to go to Malaya but it had only one witness. Myers J granted probate and on the issue whether the deceased was in actual military service, he said:

> 'In my opinion a state of war, in the sense of an international conflict, is not essential to a soldier being in actual military service ... In the present case there was no state of war and it is difficult to see how there could have been, for there was no nation or state with which a state of war could have been proclaimed to exist, but in all other respects there was no difference between the situation of a member of this force and that of a member of a military force in time of war. In my opinion the deceased was in actual military service and it would be unreasonable to hold otherwise.'

3.3 Mariner or seaman being at sea

The term 'mariner or seaman being at sea' is also given a wide interpretation and it includes both members of the Royal Navy and members of the merchant navy. Thus, in *In b Sarah Hale* (1915) 2 IR 362 it was said that the privilege extended to every person employed in any branch of the Royal Navy, from the highest to the lowest. Thus in that case it was held that a typist employed on board the *Lusitania* on a voyage from Liverpool to New York was entitled to the privilege while in *In b Knibbs* [1962] 1 WLR 852 it was held that a barman on a liner could make a privileged will.

There are a large number of cases as to what the term 'being at sea' means. All the decisions are at first instance and they appear to divide into two main categories: (1) where the voyage on ship has begun so that the mariner or seamen is considered to be 'at sea' and (2) where the mariner or seaman has orders to sail and for this reason considered to be 'at sea'.

Voyage begun
The cases on when a voyage has begun show no underlying principle and several would appear to be rather hard to support. In some cases the testator was considered

to be 'at sea' when he made the privileged will while moored or sailing on a river. Thus, in *In b Patterson* (1898) 79 LT 123, the deceased made his will on a gunboat in the Thames which was waiting to sail. The will was privileged in *In b Austen* (1853) 2 Prob Eccl 681 where the testator made his privileged will while engaged in naval operations on a river. Perhaps these cases can be supported by interpreting the words 'at sea' broadly so as to avoid technical distinctions as to what is nor is not 'at sea'. However, in *In b Lay* 2 Curt 375 the deceased was ashore in the middle of a voyage when he made a valid privileged will. In this case, 'at sea' would appear to have been interpreted as 'on a voyage'. *In b Lay* should be contrasted with *In b Corby* (1854) 1 Spink Ecc & Adm 292 where the deceased was ordered to join a ship at Melbourne, Australia, where he had been living for 12 months prior to sailing. Probate was refused to an alleged privileged will in that case because the deceased was joining the ship for the first time at the end of its outward journey from England solely for the purpose of returning to England and it was found that he made the alleged privilege will before he boarded the ship.

Orders to sail

In *In b Sarah Hale* (1915) 2 IR 362 the deceased only had orders to sail at the time she made the alleged privileged will in the form of a letter to a friend. The orders to sail were considered sufficient to entitle her to make a privileged will even though she was on dry land when she made it. A similar conclusion was adopted in *In b Newland* [1952] P 71 where the deceased wrote out a testamentary document while on leave in England at a time when he had orders to sail.

A seaman is not considered as 'being at sea' if his boat is laid up and he is ashore. This appears to be the conclusion in an Irish decision, *Barnard* v *Birch* (1912) 2 IR 404, where the court refused to admit an unattested document to probate as the privileged will of the captain of a ferry boat. At the time the document was drawn up the captain was ashore and his boat laid up for the winter months and he did not contemplate another voyage for several months. Commenting on this case in *In b Newland* [1952] P 71, Havers J said that the case was distinguishable from others in that the captain of the boat was, when sailing, at sea for a specified time every day and at home for the rest of the day. This would appear to indicate that seamen on short journeys, that is, cross channel ferries and the like, are not entitled to the privilege. It is worth comparing *Barnard* v *Birch* with the decision in *In b M'Murdo* (1868) LR 1 P & D 540 where it was held that a mate in the Royal Navy was entitled to the privilege at a time when he was serving on board a ship permanently stationed in Portsmouth harbour and there being no immediate intention to send her to sea. This decision appears to rest on the principle that the mate had joined a vessel on service and therefore commenced a voyage on it. However, on their facts, these decisions appear difficult to reconcile.

In some exceptional cases the deceased may be regarded as either a soldier on 'actual military service' or a sailor 'being at sea'. In *In the estate of Ada Stanley* [1916]

P 192 the deceased was a nurse employed under contract by the War Office on hospital ships. A letter she wrote giving directions as to the disposal of her property while on leave but with orders to sail was treated as a privileged will. The deceased could have been regarded as a sailor being at sea if *In b Sarah Hale* had been applied, but the court instead decided that by reason of the nature of her contract with the War Office she should be regarded as a soldier on actual military service.

Many of the decisions on the term 'mariner or seaman being at sea' were considered in *Re Rapley's Estate* [1983] 3 All ER 248 where the deceased purported to make a will while on leave in England at a time when he was apprenticed to a shipping company. The deceased was a minor at the time and the purported will was executed by one witness. The claim that the will was privileged failed because, although the deceased was a 'mariner or seaman' under s11 he was not 'at sea' at the relevant time because he was awaiting new orders to join a ship and these were only given to him some days after he made his purported will. Judge Finlay QC said the deceased might be regarded as 'in maritime service' (at sea?) if:

1. he is already in post as a ship's officer when he made the will: *Re M'Murdo's Goods*. See *In b Lay*;
2. he is already a member of a particular ship's company serving in that ship or on shore on leave or on shore on long leave. See *In b Patterson*; *In b Lay*; *In b Newland*;
3. he is employed by the owners of a fleet of ships having been discharged from one ship and already under orders to join another ship in that fleet. See *In b Sarah Hale*.

On the facts of the case, the deceased fell into none of these categories. The will also, of course, failed under ss7 and 9 of the Wills Act 1837.

3.4 Section 2 of the Wills (Soldiers and Sailors) Act 1918

This provision extended the meaning of s11 and states:

> 'Section 11 of the Wills Act 1837 shall extend to any member of His Majesty's naval or marine forces, not only when he is at sea but also when he is so circumstanced that if he were a soldier he would be in actual military service within the meaning of that section.'

The purpose of s2 was to avoid decisions such as that reached in *In the estate of William Edward Anderson* [1916] P 49, where the deceased, a member of the St John's Ambulance Association, was ordered to join a ship permanently stationed at Chatham. On the morning of his departure to join the ship, the deceased wrote out a document which purported to dispose of his property. The deceased was billeted at Chatham for several weeks and eventually he went to sea and was lost. The document he wrote could not be regarded as a privileged will because the deceased was not at sea when he made it, but in his father's house. Bargrave Deane J added:

'The language of s11 of the Wills Act is peculiar: the words are not identical with regard to soldiers and mariners. To come within the exceptions in that section, a soldier must be in actual military service, and if this deceased man had been a soldier, or if those words had applied to sailors or mariners, it might have been argued successfully that he came within the exception.'

Section 2 was applied in *In the estate of W C Yates* [1919] P 93, a case not dissimilar to *Anderson's* case. In that case the deceased, a member of the Royal Navy, was ordered to join his ship at Cape Town. He made an oral will at the railway station on the day of his departure and died in Cape Town. The provisions of s2 were applied and the issue whether he was 'at sea' was avoided.

It should be noted that s2 only applies to members of 'His Majesty's naval or marine forces'. It has no application to members of the merchant navy as Havers J pointed out in *In b Newland*.

3.5 Extent of the privilege

The main feature of a privileged will is that it does not have to comply with the provisions of s9 of the Wills Act. Thus the will may be oral as in *In the estate of W C Yates*, where the words were 'Remember that if anything happens to me everything I possess, or am likely to possess, is to go to your mother'. In many cases the privileged will takes the form of a letter, whether signed or unsigned. See *In b Sarah Hale*; *In b Ada Stanley*. But, whatever form it takes it must have been made *animo testandi*. Thus, in *In the estate of Knibbs* [1962] 1 WLR 852 the Court refused to treat the words spoken by a barman on a liner to a fellow barman in a casual conversation as a privileged will. Wrangham J said:

'I take two extreme cases to illustrate my meaning. A man who telephoned to his solicitor (under the conditions under which the privilege would be applicable) telling him what dispositions of property he intended to operate after his death, and asking him to do what was required, would clearly be performing a testamentary act because he would not only be stating what his intentions were, but stating them in circumstances which showed that he wished his intentions to be carried out as a result of what he was then saying. On the other hand, if a man said to a friend of his: "Well my intention is to cut out my wife and family altogether from my will and leave everything to my mistress but don't ever say a word to anybody about what I have told you", such a conversation could not possibly be a testamentary act, because although it reveals clearly the intentions of the deceased, it does so in such circumstances that the person hearing them could not be expected, and was, indeed, forbidden to take any step to see that they were put into effect.'

Although the words must be spoken or written *animo testandi*, the deceased need not be aware that he is making a will. Thus, in *Re Stable* [1919] P 7 the court held the words 'If I stop a bullet, everything of mine will be yours' to be a privileged will.

A privileged will may contain almost all directions and dispositions that could be comprised in a formal will. Thus, it can revoke any formal will made prior to the privileged occasion. In *In b Gossage* [1921] P 194 it was held revocation of a formal will could take place in an informal manner and there a letter from the deceased to his sister whilst he was serving in South Africa telling her to burn his will 'for I have aready cancelled it' was held sufficient. The privileged will may dispose of either personalty (see s11) or realty (see s3(1) Wills (Soldiers and Sailors) Act 1918), it may appoint guardians of the testator's children (see s4 of the 1918 Act, and a power of appointment either general or special may be exercised by a privileged will. See *Re Wernher* [1918] 2 Ch 82; *Re Chichester* [1946] Ch 289.

A minor may make a privileged will despite the general rule in s7 of the Wills Act. This was expressly provided for in s1 of the Wills (Soldiers and Sailors) Act 1918 in order to remove doubts raised by the decision in *Re Wernher* and it provides:

'... it is hereby declared and enacted that section eleven (of the Wills Act 1837) authorises and always has authorised any soldier being in actual military service, or any mariner or seaman being at sea, to dispose of his personal estate as he might have done before the passing of that Act, though under the age of eighteen years.'

See *In b Newland* where the deceased was only 16 years old when he made his privileged will. See also *Re Rapley's Estate* [1983] 3 All ER 248.

When the privileged occasion has passed so that a soldier is no longer on 'actual military service' or the seaman 'at sea' the privileged will nevertheless remains effective. Thus, in *Re Booth* [1926] P 118 a privileged will made in 1882 was admitted to probate on the testator's death in 1924. Once the privileged occasion has passed, revocation must be in one of the ways laid down by the Wills Act and, for example, subsequent marriage will revoke a privileged will under s18 of the Wills Act. See *Re Wardrop* [1917] P 54. In the case of a minor who has made a privileged will, it would appear that he can revoke this after the privileged occasion has passed but he cannot make a formal will afterwards, until he attains majority. See s3(3) of the Family Law Reform Act 1969.

The provisions of s15 of the Wills Act have no application to a privileged will. Thus in *Re Limond* [1915] 2 Ch 240 the testator's brother-in-law was a witness to the will and the residuary legatee. Sargent J held that s15 should be limited to cases where s9 applied.

Alterations to a privileged will, if it is in writing, are presumed to have been made during the privileged occasion and will be included in probate. See *In b Tweedale* (1874) LR 3 P & D 204. This should be contrasted with the presumption applied to formal wills, ie that alterations were made after execution and are therefore excluded. See *Cooper* v *Bockett* (1846) 4 Moo PC 419.

4

Incorporation by Reference

4.1 Introduction

A testator may, in the course of making his will, wish to refer to or include the terms of another document as part of his will. The most sensible course is to write out the terms of the document as part of the will. But this may be undesirable to the testator, because the document is too long, or inappropriate, where he is near death and the will must be executed quickly. In such cases the probate doctrine of incorporation by reference may be relied upon so as to allow the document to become part of his will without the need to write it out again. This doctrine is based entirely on case law and before it can be successfully applied three conditions must be satisfied. They are as follows.

4.2 Document must be in existence at the time the will is made

This requirement is to ensure that the testator does not reserve to himself the power to make future unwitnessed testamentary dispositions. Therefore it must be proved that the document which it is claimed is incorporated was actually in existence at the date the will was executed. The leading case is *Singleton* v *Tomlinson* (1878) 3 App Cas 404. The testator made a will in which he directed, *inter alia*, that his executors sell four landed estates named in his will. The landed estates were detailed in a

55

schedule attached to the will bearing the same date as the will and in the handwriting of the testator with his signature. The question arose whether the schedule could be referred to in order to identify the landed estates properly. The witnesses to the will could not remember seeing the schedule at the time of execution.

Held: it had not been clearly proved that the schedule was in existence at the time the will was executed and it could not be considered as incorporated into the will so as to be referred to as a matter of construction.

A document which was not in existence at the time the will was made may be incorporated into the will if it comes into existence before the will is republished either by re-execution or by a codicil. Thus, in *In b Lady Truro* (1866) LR 1 P & D 201 the testatrix made a will dated 15 September 1865 in which she bequeathed such articles 'as are contained in the inventory signed by me and deposited herewith'. The inventory was dated 21 September but subsequently the will was republished by a codicil dated 10 October. The inventory was incorporated because the will spoke of a document in existence on 10 October when republication had taken effect.

4.3 Document must be referred to as being in existence

The reference to the document in the will must be such that it can be considered to be in existence at the date the will was executed. If the will refers to the document to be drawn up at some future date there can be no incorporation. Thus, in *University College of North Wales* v *Taylor* [1908] P 140 the will referred to terms and conditions relating to a gift 'as one contained in any memorandum amongst my papers written or signed by me'. Although a memorandum was found which was dated prior to the will it could not be incorporated. In *In b Sutherland* (1866) LR 1 P & D 198 incorporation by reference was refused where the will referred to 'any existing or future memorandum signed by me'.

If the will refers to the document coming into existence in the future, republication of the will either by re-execution or a codicil will not bring about effective incorporation. In *In b Smart* [1902] P 238 Gorell Barnes said:

> 'Suppose that the will said: "I wish certain articles to be disposed of by my executors in accordance with a list which I shall hereafter write", and the testator then wrote a list such as was contemplated, and then, after that, a codicil was made confirming the will, one of the conditions at the date of the codicil which is necessary for incorporation would be fulfilled, namely the execution of a document, but the other condition would not be fulfilled, because the will, even speaking from the date of its so-called re-execution by that confirmation by the codicil, would still in terms refer to something which even then was future.'

In that case the testatrix made her will in 1895 and in it directed her trustees to give such of her friends as she might designate certain articles to be specified in a book or memorandum to be found with her will. A memorandum was made in 1898 and a codicil republished the will in 1900. Although the memorandum could be regarded as in existence at the date of the will, see *In b Lady Truro* (above), the will nevertheless after republication referred to the document to come into existence in the future.

4.4 Document must be clearly identified

The will must identify the document which it is claimed is incorporated into the will so that it cannot be mistaken for another. A vague reference will mean that there cannot be incorporation. Thus, in *In b Garnett* [1894] P 90 the testator referred to papers numbered 1 to 6 in his will as containing his testamentary wishes. The will and many papers were found in a drawer and it was impossible to identify the documents referred to precisely. Probate was refused to the papers because of the danger of mistake.

Parol evidence is admissible to identify a document claimed to be incorporated. In *Allen v Maddock* (1858) 11 Moo 427 the testatrix had asumed the name of Foote after separating from her husband, Allen. She made a will in 1851 referring to her as 'Anne Foote' and signed as such but it was not valid being attested by only one witness. A codicil was executed by the testatrix in 1856; it contained no reference to the will other than 'This is a codicil to my last will'. No testamentary papers other than this will and the codicil were found. It was sought to adduce parol evidence on this so as to identify the will and incorporate it into the codicil. On this the Privy Council held:

> '... the authorities seem clearly to establish that where there is a reference to any written document, describing as then existing, in such terms that it is capable of being ascertained, parol evidence is admissible to ascertain it, and the only question then is, whether the evidence is sufficient for the purpose ... The facts on which we rely are beyond all question admissible in evidence, namely that the paper in question was written by the testatrix, was found locked up in her possession at her death in a sealed envelope, on which there was an endorsement describing it as her will; and that after diligent search no other paper has been found answering the description'.

4.5 Effect of incorporation

Where there has been an effective incorporation, the incorporated document is admitted to probate as a part of the will; it will therefore be filed with the will in the probate registry. But if the incorporated document is very large filing it may be dispensed with. Thus, in *In b Balme* [1897] P 261 it was not necessary to file a large library catalogue incorporated into the will.

Incorporation may have the effect of saving an invalid will where a codicil has been executed to the will, which satisfies the requirements mentioned above. In such cases the difficulty will be to show that the codicil refers to the will as being in existence and that it is clearly identified. See *In b Heathcote* (1881) 6 PD 30. An earlier revoked will may also be incorporated by a later will or codicil. See *Re White* [1925] Ch 179.

Special provisions are applicable to the incorporation of *inter vivos* settlements into the will. The difficulty here is that the settlement may contain provisions which are inconsistent with the provisions of the Wills Act. Thus, if the settlement gave the settlor the power to vary or amend its terms, revoke it or give directions as to the payment of capital and income, these would conflict with the rule that a testator must not reserve to himself the power to make future unattested testamentary dispositions. It seems that in such cases, variations made in settlement after incorporation will be ineffective as part of the will.

In *Re Edwards* [1948] Ch 440 the testator directed in his will that his residuary estate should be held on the trusts of an existing settlement. This settlement provided, *inter alia*, that the capital and income were payable to such persons as the settlor should by memorandum direct and subject thereto for the settlor's wife and children. Two questions arose: (1) could the settlement be incorporated into the will, and, (2) if it was incorporated, how its provisions would take effect.

Held: the settlement could be incorporated into the will but provisions could take effect only to the extent that it could validly operate as part of a testamentary disposition. Therefore, the clauses permitting the settlor to make directions as to the destination of capital and income by a memorandum could not take effect as part of the will, so that the gift over took effect in favour of the settlor's wife his and children.

In exceptional circumstances the court may admit extrinsic evidence to decide whether incorporation by reference was intended by the testator. In *In the estate of Saxton* [1939] 2 All ER 418 the testator made a will which stated: 'I give devise and bequeath all my real and personal estate ... among the following persons and I hereby appoint executors to this my will.' The will was found in an envelope together with some lists containing beneficial dispositions. There were no dispositions in the will itself. Kenn Collins J considered the circumstances in which the testator made his will and the fact that the lists began 'I wish to leave the following amounts' as showing that there had been valid incorporation by reference.

4.6 Semi-secret trusts and incorporation by reference

The doctrine of semi-secret trusts is closely related to incorporation by reference. A study of this area is more appropriate to the law of trusts but it must not be overlooked that it is possible to give effect to an oral direction by the testator as to how the relevant gift in the will is to devolve. Although for fully-secret trusts this oral direction can be given by the testator at any time before he dies, the law on semi-secret trusts requires the testator to give the oral direction before or contemporaneously with the will's execution. This can be seen in the case of *Bateman's Will Trusts* [1970] 3 All ER 817.

4.7 Value and repercussions of the doctrine

The practical value of this doctrine is limited to those cases where complex points of detail arise, which are too bulky to be included in the will.

Since the incorporated document is treated as an ordinary part of the will and must be filed at the Probate Registry, incorporation is not an appropriate method of making sensitive testamentary gifts. Rather than allowing it to become a matter of public record, confidentiality can be better achieved by a secret trust.

It should be noted that this is a judicially created exception to the rule that a document that has not been executed in accordance with the provisions of the Wills Act 1837 will not be admitted to probate. Although the three conditions generally apply, exceptional cases have occurred, such as the very liberal decision in *Re Saxton's Estate*, which has been mentioned above. The general facts should be emphasised when considering the possible wider repercussions of the doctrine. There the testator in his will left all his property 'to the following persons' yet in the will there was no such list of persons. Instead, on his death lists of legacies were found, which were headed by the note by the testator that he intended the listed persons to benefit. It was held that the lists were incorporated and the persons could benefit.

While the decision has been criticised as being wrong in principle it is important to recognise that a properly drafted will should not refer to other documents unless the intention is that they should be incorporated.

The overlap between the operation of this doctrine and the revival of revoked wills is also noteworthy. While revival and republication of wills are dealt with in Chapter 8, the following points should be made here.

Reference in a later will

A revoked will may be incorporated by reference in a later will instead of itself being revived, such as in *Re White, Knight v Briggs* [1925] Ch 179. Here the testator directed by will that his trustees should hold property on certain trusts. He later revoked this will. He made a subsequent will in which he left property on the trusts declared by the previous will.

Held: the earlier will was incorporated in the later will.

No reference in a later will

In other cases and in the absence of reference in a later will, it should be remembered that there may be a possibility of a will being incorporated where it has not been revived or republished. The most important instance is where the earlier will is in itself defective and therefore has not taken effect. In circumstances of a basic deficiency in an earlier will republication is not effective. Nevertheless, provided the testator's intention is clear and is to the effect that the earlier will should be incorporated, there is no reason why incorporation should not be possible.

The recent case of *Re Berger* (1989) discussed at Chapter 1, section 1.3 should be recalled here as it indicates the more up to date trend of thought as regards incorporation and its repercussions.

4.8 Section 179 of the Law of Property Act 1925: statutory wills

Whereas it is preferable to have all of the provisions of a will in one document, in those cases where the will is likely to be extraordinarily long, statutory will forms may be used. These are forms published by the Lord Chancellor under the authority of s179 of the Law of Property Act 1925 which the testator may refer to in his will.

Where such forms are incorporated in this way they form part of the will in the usual manner.

5

Animus Testandi

5.1 Introduction

The maker of a will must satisfy the law as to the mental requirements for making a will in addition to satisfying the formal requirements laid down by s9 of the Wills Act. The mental requirement is generally referred to as *animus testandi*.

The written document which is the will is a series of directions by the testator as to his desires in respect of the disposal of his property after his death. As the testator may often make the will shortly before his death, there is a danger that the cause of death may have affected his mental faculties rendering him incapable of a will which embodies his true wishes. Further, illness may well give unscrupulous persons the opportunity to substitute a spurious will or insert clauses into a will without the knowledge and approval of the testator. To minimise these dangers, rules have been formulated to ensure that a will does represent the true wishes of the testator.

The general rule is that the onus of proof 'is in every case upon the general party propounding the will; and he must satisfy the conscience of the court that the instrument so propounded is the last will of a free and capable testator' per Parke B in *Barry* v *Butlin* (1838) 2 Moo PC 480. Normally, the personal representatives will have the duty of satisfying the court that the testator had the necessary mental capacity to make the will. However, if the will is rational on the face of it and duly executed there is a presumption that the testator had the necessary mental capacity and the will will be granted probate without difficulty. See *Barry* v *Butlin* (above). In these circumstances it will be necessary for any party who wishes to challenge the validity of the will on grounds that the testator lacked the requisite mental capacity to adduce evidence to rebut this presumption. If the presumption is successfully rebutted then the personal representatives or other parties propounding the will must produce evidence showing that the testator's ability to make a will was not in doubt.

In some cases a document may be duly executed as a will but never have been intended to operate as a will or only to operate in limited circumstances. Thus, if the will was executed merely for the purpose of demonstration or as an elaborate hoax it would not be granted probate.

This can be seen in the case of *Lister* v *Smith* (1863) 3 Sw & Tr 282. Here the testator purported to execute a will revoking an earlier will of his but he made the revocation with the sole object of inducing his mother-in-law to vacate certain property owned by him. It was held that as the testator's intentions in executing the document were not truly testamentary the document would therefore not be admitted to probate.

However, if it was designed to operate on a certain condition being fulfilled, it will be necessary to show that the condition is satisfied before probate could be granted, for example, a will which is only to take effect if the testator survives his wife. See *Nichols* v *Nichols* (1814) 2 Phill 180.

The validity of a conditional will was decided upon in *Corbett* v *Newey and Others* [1996] 3 WLR 729. The facts were that A, B's nephew, appealed against the upholding of B's will. B had intended for her will to take effect conditionally upon certain subsequent events. B asked her solicitor to draw up deeds of gift of land to her niece and nephew. B signed her will in September 1989 but asked her solicitor to insert the date of her signature after the transfers had been completed. However, the will made no reference to being conditional upon any such contingency occurring, and a question arose over the communications and correspondence between B and her solicitor as to whether B had made a valid conditional will which would take effect on completion of the two lifetime gifts.

Held: The appeal was allowed. The court held that the will was not valid as B did not possess the animus testandi required to execute a will (*Re Berger (deceased)* [1990] Ch 118 considered). B acted under the misapprehension that the dating of a will, not the signing thereof, constitutes execution. As a result, she lacked the necessary intention to make a valid will in the sense of a will intended to be immediately dispositive.

5.2 Mental incapacity

A testator may lack the necessary mental ability to make a will thereby rendering it ineffective. In order to decide if any particular matter deprives the testator of mental capacity the test in *Banks* v *Goodfellow* (1870) LR 5 QB 549 should be applied, where Cockburn CJ said:

> 'It is essential to the exercise of such a power [that is, making a will] that a testator shall understand the nature of the act and its effects; shall understand the extent of the property of which he is disposing; shall be able to comprehend and appreciate the claims to which he ought to give effect; and, with a view to the latter object, that no disorder of the mind shall poison his affections, pervert his sense of right, or prevent the exercise of his natural faculties; that no insane delusion shall influence his will in disposing of his property and bring about a disposal of it which, if the mind had been sound, would not have been made.'

The above test can be summarised as requiring three essentials, namely sound mind, sound memory and sound understanding.

Sound mind

By this is meant that the mind must be free from disease or defect which would otherwise affect the testator's ability to make a will. In *Banks* v *Goodfellow* Cockburn CJ dealt with the matter thus:

> 'If the human instincts and affections, or the moral sense, become perverted by mental disease, if insane suspicion, or aversion take the place of natural affection; if reason and judgment are lost and the mind becomes prey to insane delusions calculated to interfere with and disturb its functions, and to lead to a testamentary disposition, due only to their baneful influence – in such a case it is obvious that the condition of the testamentary power fails, and that a will made under such circumstances ought not to stand.'

It is really a question of fact whether a testator does or does not possess a sound mind. An idiot or natural fool would lack sound mind – described by Swinburne as 'so witless, that he cannot number to twenty, nor can tell what age he is of, nor know who is his father or mother, nor is able to answer any such easy question'. Mental patients or lunatics are not of sound mind while suffering from their mental disorder, provided it is a disorder which would affect their ability to make a will. Persons who are drunk at the time of making the will or under the influence of drugs do not have sound mind. On drunkards Swinburne said:

> 'He that is overcome with drink, during the time of his drunkenness, is compared to a madman; and therefore if he makes his testament at that time, it is void in law. Which is to be understood, when he is so excessively drunk, that he is utterly deprived of reason

and understanding; otherwise if he be not clean spent, albeit his misunderstanding be obscured, and his memory troubled, yet he may make his testament being in that case.'

See *Wheeler and Batsford* v *Alderson* 3 Hagg 602.

Presumably, drugs which affect the mind would be considered in the same way as drink whether they were administered to relieve illness or be taken by a drug addict. In *Barrett* v *Kasprzyk* LTL 4 July 2000 (unreported elsewhere) the deceased's son argued that the deceased did not have testamentary capacity when she signed the will due to the effect of the drugs she received whilst in hospital. Whilst in hospital the deceased gave instructions for her will to a legal executive from a firm of solicitors. The will left her entire estate to her brother and the claimant was appointed as sole executor. The court held that the administration of drugs for medical treatment could lead to the loss of testamentary capacity. However, in this case they were convinced by the evidence of the legal executive (who had taken instructions for the will) that the deceased had testamentary capacity. As such they found the deceased was aware of what she was doing and had the necessary testamentary capacity as required in *Banks* v *Goodfellow*. Senility, if at an advanced stage, may be such as to affect the capacity to make a will. See *Den* v *Vancleve* 2 South 660. Physical injury to the brain and physical illness which affects the brain may also affect the soundness of the mind. Thus, if the testator made his will after serious brain damage caused in a road traffic accident, its validity would be in doubt. In *Battan Singh* v *Amirchand* [1948] AC 161 a will was refused probate because it was made by a testator whilst in the last stages of consumption; he was so enfeebled by the disease as to be no longer of sound mind.

Sound memory

This requirement was fully explained in the American case of *Stevens* v *Vancleve* 4 Washington 267, where it was said of the testator:

'He must have memory; a man in whom the faculty is totally extinguished cannot be said to possess understanding to any degree whatever, or for any purpose. But his memory may be very imperfect; it may be greatly impaired by age or disease, he may not be able at all times to recollect the names, the persons or the families of those with whom he had been intimately acquainted; he may at times ask idle questions, and repeat those which had before been asked and answered, and yet his understanding may be sufficiently sound for many of the ordinary transactions of life. He may not have sufficient strength of memory and vigour of intellect to make and to digest all the parts of the contract and yet be competent to direct the distribution of his property by his will.'

The need is for a sound disposing memory and the question is not what degree of memory was possessed by the testator. He ought to be capable of recollecting the property he was about to bequeath; the manner of distributing it; and the objects of his bounty. However, it is not necessary that the testator be able to recollect these matters in detail, a broad idea of these is quite sufficient.

Sound understanding

By this is meant that the testator must understand the nature of the transaction in which he was engaged at the time he executed his will. Further, he must be able to understand the claims of his various relatives and friends on his bounty and the effect of the dispositions he is making. In deciding whether the testator had a sound understanding the court views the dispositions in broad terms rather than with the eye of a lawyer. Therefore, the fact that the testator has not left his wife or his children anything in his will does not raise the inference that he lacked testamentary capacity. In such circumstances the real issue is whether the testator knew, when he executed his will, that he was excluding his wife and children, was capable of recollecting who they were and their respective claims on his bounty, and deliberately formed an intelligent purpose of excluding them from any share of his property.

In *Harwood* v *Baker* (1840) 3 Moo PC 282 the testator executed his will on his death-bed leaving all his estate to his second wife, to the exclusion of the other members of his family. At the time of making the will, the testator was in a state of weakness from disease producing torpor of the brain, and rendering him incapable unless roused.

Held: the will was invalid as the testator was not capable of comprehending the nature of the claim of his other relatives, whom he had excluded. It was not sufficient to show that the testator knew he was giving all his property to his wife.

Degree of soundness

The requirements of sound mind, sound memory and sound understanding are not required in the highest degree from the testator. If this were so, many people of advanced years would be incapable of making a will. All that it is necessary to show is that the testator was able to discern and discreetly judge all those things and circumstances which enter into the making of a will. See *Banks* v *Goodfellow*. In this respect it is important to note that there is no sliding scale of soundness of mind such that a greater degree of soundness of mind is required to make a will than to do any other act. What is important is that the soundness of the testator's mind must be measured in relation to the facts and subject matter of each particular case. See *Broughton* v *Knight* (1873) LR 3 P & D 71 per Sir James Hannen. Thus, in a case where a testator had made a simple will of one sentence, he may be considered as being of sufficiently sound mind to satisfy the test in relation to this transaction. However, the same testator may not be considered as having sufficient soundness of mind to make a complex will.

This is indicated in *In the Estate of Park* [1954] P 112 (CA). The deceased made a will dated 1 March 1948. In May 1948 he suffered a stroke brought on by hardened arteries and although he recovered from the stroke he was thereafter at times eccentric. On 30 May 1949, the deceased married the plaintiff and on the same day he executed an elaborate will by which he left the plaintiff a modest part of his £120,000 estate. After the deceased's death his will was refused probate on the ground of lack of testamentary capacity. Consequently, the plaintiff sought a declaration that her marriage with the deceased was valid and thereby revoked the deceased's will dated 1 March 1948.

Held: the marriage was valid; it was a very simple contract which did not require a high degree of intelligence to comprehend. However, it could not be said in relation to the will that the testator had the ability to comprehend its complex arrangements.

Time for satisfying the test

The general rule is that the testator must have a sound mind, memory and understanding at the time he executed the will. This general rule may be affected by two presumptions.

1. There is a presumption that a person who lacked testamentary capacity at some time before the execution of the will continued to lack testamentary capacity at the date of execution. See *Banks* v *Goodfellow*. In such circumstances, the party propounding the will must adduce evidence of the testator's capacity to make a will. See *Banks* v *Goodfellow* and the more recent case of *Richards* v *Allan* LTL 18 December 2000.

   This case is a good illustration of the effect of the presumptions relating to testamentary capacity, knowledge and approval. The testatrix, aged 84, was admitted to hospital. Her medical notes indicated that she was very confused. Shortly after leaving the hospital, the defendant, A, whom she had known for more than 20 years, advised her to make a will. The testatrix gave instructions for a will appointing A to be her sole executrix and beneficiary. A relayed the instructions to her brother-in-law, a solicitor, and he drafted the will on the basis of the instructions relayed by A.

   On the day of the execution of the will, the testatrix appeared confused when visited by her doctor and a friend. A contended that the will was executed between the visits and that the testatrix was not confused at the time.

   The court held the will to be invalid. They applied the presumption that mental states continue. Further, as a beneficiary procured the execution of the will, there was no presumption of knowledge and approval of the contents of the will.

2. Where the testator had the requisite testamentary capacity before he executed his will, there is a presumption that he continued to have the ability to make a will until the contrary is proven. See *Chambers and Yatman* v *The Queen's Proctor* (1840) 2 Curt 514.

The general rule and the presumptions do not help in one particular case, namely, where the testator gives instructions for his will to his solicitor several days, or weeks, before it is presented to him for execution. In such cases it would appear that the appropriate time for satisfying the test of testamentary capacity is when the instructions were given. In *Parker* v *Felgate* (1883) 8 PD 171, Sir James Hannen P held that the testator need only be aware at the time of execution that he gave instructions for a will and that he believes the will he is executing is in accordance with those instructions. However, the dicta in *Parker* v *Felgate* can only be safely limited to instructions given to a solicitor directly by the testator. In *Battan Singh* v *Amirchand* [1948] AC 161 the Privy Council warned of the dangers in applying this to cases where the testator's instructions for a will were transmitted to the solicitor via a layman because of possible error, misunderstanding or deception by the intermediary layman.

In *Parker* v *Felgate* (1883) 8 PD 171 the testatrix gave instructions to her solicitor for her will after several interviews with him. Before a will could be prepared for execution the testatrix became very ill and a substitute was hurriedly drafted in accordance with her instructions for her to sign. The testatrix was falling into a coma at the time of execution. Her doctor aroused her and asked if her if she wished a lady friend to sign her will for her. She said 'Yes' and the will was signed and attested.

Held: the will was valid. Although the testatrix clearly lacked testamentary capacity to make a will at the time of execution, she believed that the will presented for execution was the one she gave instructions for and that it was in accordance with those instructions and this was sufficient.

Lucid intervals

A person who suffers from mental illness may have lucid intervals, depending very much on the nature of the illness, during which he may be considered as perfectly capable of making a will. However, even in such cases, the general presumption that the mental illness continues will operate. See *Banks* v *Goodfellow*. But against this presumption may be weighed the dicta in *Cartwright* v *Cartwright* (1795) 1 Phill 90, where it was said that if a testator makes a will after the onset of mental illness and that will is made in a rational way without assistance then it is strong proof of a lucid interval. Perhaps the matters referred to in *Cartwright* v *Cartwright* are a way of rebutting the presumption.

In *Cartwright* v *Cartwright* (1793) 1 Phill 100 the testatrix was insane from 1774 until 1794 when she died. She had made a will before the onset of insanity but had destroyed it. In November 1794 she called for pen, ink and paper and produced a perfect and well written will in which she preferred the nieces of her sister of the whole blood to the nieces of her two sisters of the half blood. She sealed the will and gave it to a friend.

Held: the will was valid. If a will was made by a person suffering from a mental disorder who had lucid intervals and it was unclear whether the will had been made in such an interval, then if the will is framed as to show no evidence of the mental disorder it will be valid.

The dicta in *Cartwright* v *Cartwright* may however be displaced if other circumstances suggest insanity. In *Clark* v *Lear and Scarwell* (cited in *Cartwright* v *Cartwright*) the deceased, a middle-aged man who was mentally disordered, escaped from his keeper and at a river he met and fell in love with a young lady. Afterwards he made a will leaving her a legacy of £1,000. The will was rational but was, nevertheless, considered invalid as being bottomed in insanity.

Insane delusions

Before the decision in *Banks* v *Goodfellow* the general rule was that any disorder of the mind rendered the testator incapable of making a will. No distinction was drawn between cases where the mental disease did affect the will and cases where it did not. This arbitrary rule was rejected in *Banks* v *Goodfellow* where Cockburn CJ said:

'It follows that a degree or form of unsoundness which neither disturbs the exercise of the faculties necessary for such an act, nor is capable of influencing the result, ought not to take away the power of making a will'.

Insane delusions are a classic example of a form of mental illness which may not affect the testator's ability to make a will. Much will depend on the nature of the delusion as the following cases illustrate.

In *Banks* v *Goodfellow* (1870) LR 5 QB 549 the testator had had delusions (since 1841) that he was being molested by a man who was long dead and that he was being pursued by evil spirits. He had been confined to an asylum on several occasions. In 1863 the testator made a will and he died in 1865 still afflicted by the delusions.

Held: the will was valid because the delusions could not have had any effect on the dispositions of property made by the testator or those whom he should consider when making those dispositions.

Contrast: *Dew* v *Clark* (1826) 3 Add 79. The testator left a will which excluded his only daughter from any benefit thereunder. Evidence showed that the testator had an irrational aversion for his daughter and had refused to see her during the first three years of her life.

Held: the will could not stand. The delusion had had a direct effect on the dispositions in the will.

In *Bull* v *Fulton* (1942) 66 CLR 295 the testatrix died aged 96 leaving a will in which she left nearly all her estate to a grand-nephew. The will was challenged by two nephews of the testatrix, both of whom were solicitors. They had for about 20 years looked after all the testatrix's legal affairs, but about 10 years before she died she developed unfounded beliefs that her nephews were forging her signature on share applications, transfers of land, etc. Consequently she excluded them from her will which had previously made them principal beneficiaries.

Held: the testatrix's unfounded beliefs of deceit and forgery amounted to insane delusions and, as they had affected the will, it was invalid.

In *Re Nightingale (No 2)* (1974) 119 Sol Jo 189 the testator made a will leaving the major part of his estate to his son. He then was admitted to hospital and became very ill. When his son visited him the testator formed the delusion that his son was trying to kill him. This was because the son tried to push back his father on to the pillows in order to help his breathing. Labouring under this delusion the testator made another will in which he revoked the previous gift to the son. The son claimed that the first will was still valid as the subsequent revoking will was executed under a delusion.

Held: the second testamentary document could not stand and was invalid on account of the father's unfounded belief that the beneficiary was attempting to shorten his life.

Testamentary capacity applies to parts of the will

The rule that the testator must have testamentary capacity applies to parts of the will as well as the whole. Thus a testator may have left a will and several codicils thereto at his death. If his testamentary capacity was impaired at the time of executing any of these documents, that document concerned would be refused probate. The nature of the testator's affliction may be such that it only affects certain dispositions in the will. In such circumstances the will will be admitted to probate minus the affected parts. Thus, for example, in *In the Estate of Bohrmann* [1938] 1 All ER 271 a testator left gifts to certain English charities. Subsequently the testator came under the delusion that London County Council were persecuting him as they were trying to buy his house from him for a hospital. The testator changed the gift to English charities to a gift to American charities. The will was admitted to probate without the gift to charity which was changed under the effect of the delusion.

Medical evidence to prove that the testator lacked testamentary capacity

Medical evidence should normally be called to prove any allegations that the testator lacked testamentary capacity. Further, even though many of the cases rely on long established principles in determining whether or not there was testamentary capacity, the court will take into account modern understanding and knowledge of mental illness and insanity. In the Australian High Court decision in *Timbury* v *Coffee* (1941) 66 CLR 277 it was alleged that a will was invalid because of the testator's alcoholism. Evidence showed he had developed suspicion, distrust and hostility towards his wife and took her social contacts with other men as signs of infidelity. The court referred to Stoddard on *Mind and its Disorders* and concluded the will was invalid as the testator displayed the signs of an alcoholic paranoiac.

5.3 Statutory wills

A person who clearly lacks the necessary mental capacity to make a will may nevertheless die testate even if he had not made a will before the onset of the mental disorder. Under s103 of the Mental Health Act 1983 the Court of Protection has power to order the execution of a will on behalf of an adult patient who is unable to make a will himself. Such a will is sometimes referred to as a 'statutory will'.

Section 103A of the 1983 Act lays down the formal requirements for the execution of a statutory will. They are:

1. that the will be expressed to be signed by the patient acting by the authorised person (the 'authorised person' means the person empowered by the Court of Protection to execute the will on behalf of the patient);
2. that the will be signed by the authorised person in the name of the patient, and with his own name, in the presence of two or more witnesses present at the same time;
3. that the will be attested and subscribed by those witnesses in the presence of the authorised person;
4. that the will be sealed with the official seal of the Court of Protection.

In the recent case of *Re Hughes (deceased)* (1999) The Times 8 January, Judge Weeks QC held that the formal requirements for the execution of a statutory will did not require the Court of Protection sealing the will during the lifetime of the patient. The purpose of sealing a statutory will is purely evidential: see r93 Court of Protection Rules 1994 (SI 1994/3046).

When a statutory will is made on behalf of a patient by order of the court, the effect is that the statutory will must be treated as if it were duly made by the patient and as if the patient were of testamentary capacity when he made it. See *Re Davey (deceased)* [1981] 1 WLR 164 per Fox J. In *Re D(J)* [1982] 2 All ER 37 Megarry V-C laid down five propositions which apply to the making of statutory wills.

1. It is to be assumed that the patient had a brief lucid interval at the time when the will is made.
2. During the lucid interval the patient has a full knowledge of the past, and a full realisation that as soon as the will is executed he or she will relapse into the actual mental state that previously existed, with the prognosis as it actually is.
3. It is the actual patient who has to be considered and not a hypothetical patient. The court must take the patient as he or she was before losing testamentary capacity and do for the patient in the will what the patient would fairly do for himself.
4. During the hypothetical lucid interval the patient is to be envisaged as being advised by competent solicitors.
5. In all normal cases the patient is to be envisaged as taking a broad brush to the claims on his bounty not an accountant's pen. Thus, the court will not make fine

measurements in disposing of gifts by will with reference only to the assets in the estate; other considerations will be taken into account also.

In *Re Davey (deceased)* [1981] 1 WLR 164, in September 1979, the deceased made a will leaving almost all of her estate worth £100,000 equally among 17 named relatives. This will was made three months after she moved into a nursing home. Between October and November 1979 the deceased was examined by two consultant psychiatrists who recommended that her affairs be placed in the hands of the Court of Protection. This was eventually done on 18 December 1979 and the Official Solicitor was appointed receiver. However, it came to the notice of the Official Solicitor that the deceased was married to a Mr Davey, a male nurse in the home she stayed in, on 14 December 1979, at a Fulham Register Office in secretive circumstances. Mr Davey was 48, the deceased was 92, at the date of the marriage. Since the marriage would have revoked the September will, the Official Solicitor applied to the Court of Protection to make a statutory will in the same terms as the September will on behalf of the deceased. The will was executed on 21 December 1979, the deceased died six days later. Mr Davey claimed that the will should be set aside as he had not been notified of the application to the Court of Protection.

Held: as a statutory will takes effect as the will of the patient duly made by her as if she were of testamentary capacity, it could not be set aside by the Court of Protection because the court's powers came to an end on the patient's death.

The powers of the Court of Protection in respect of a mental patient's disposal of an estate have been considered further in a recent case in which the patient was mentally disabled from birth.

In *Re C (a patient)* [1991] 3 All ER 866 (Ct of Protection) a mental patient, Miss C was born on 16 February 1916 suffering from severe mental problems. She lived at a hospital near London where she had been from the age of ten years: she was now 75 years old.

Miss C's mother died in 1918, and her father in 1953, leaving her property consisting of cash and investments valued at £1,600,000.

Miss C had little memory, understanding or capacity to communicate: she was completely blind and could not dress or undress herself, nor bathe herself. She was evidently incapable – and had always been incapable – of understanding the meaning or effect of a disposition of her property.

The current gross annual income of the fund was £57,000: from this sum £13,000 in income tax and £3,500 costs of administration had to be deducted. Under an earlier order of the Court of Protection Miss C made a covenanted payment of £3,000 to the hospital, leaving about £36,000 a year disposable income.

An application was made to the Court of Protection for an order making a will for her and for immediate gifts to be made out of her property.

Held: where a person who has been mentally handicapped since birth has inherited a substantial sum and would otherwise die intestate the court will make *inter vivos* dispositions and direct the execution of a will for the patient on the assumption that he or she would have been a normal decent person who would have acted in accordance with contemporary standards of morality. In doing so the court exercises its powers under s95(1)(c) of the Mental Health Act 1983 to make provision for other persons or purposes for whom or which the patient would or might be expected to provide if he or she were not mentally disordered.

5.4 Undue influence

Animus testandi or testamentary intention will not be present in cases where a testator has been forced or coerced into executing a document as his will. A will executed in such circumstances does not reflect the true wishes of the testator and on proof of the use of force or coercion it will be refused probate.

There are several definitions of undue influence in the reported cases. In *Wingrove* v *Wingrove* (1885) 11 PD 81 Sir James Hannen P said:

'To be undue influence in the eye of the law there must be – to sum it up in a word – coercion ... It is only when the will of the person who becomes a testator is coerced into doing that which he or she does not desire to do, that it is undue influence.'

In *Hall* v *Hall* (1868) 1 P & D 481 Lord Penzance said:

'In a word, a testator may be led but not driven, and his will must be the offspring of his own volition, and not the record of someone else's.'

Thus, if violence is threatened against the testator in order to extract a particular will from him, this amounts to undue influence. See *Hall* v *Hall*. The same applies if the testator is confined to a locked room, starved of food or fatigued by incessant talking to him when ill or weak. However, there will be no undue influence if persuasion or mere influence has been used. Thus, a wife or children who impress their moral claim upon the testator will not be guilty of having exerted undue influence. See *Hall* v *Hall*. Other examples were given by Sir James Hannen P in *Wingrove* v *Wingrove*:

'To give you some illustration of what I mean, a young man may be caught in the toils of a harlot, who makes use of her influence to induce him to make a will in her favour, to the exclusion of his relatives. It is unfortunately quite natural that a man so entangled should yield to that influence and confer large bounties on the person with whom he has been brought into such relation. A man may be the companion of another, and may encourage him on evil courses, and so obtain what is called undue influence over him, and the consequences may be a will in his favour. But that again, shocking as it is, perhaps even worse than the other, will not amount to undue influence.'

The burden of proof in allegations of undue influence rests with the party making the allegation. Therefore it is a claim which should not be made lightly and the party making the allegation ought to ensure that he has a full account of the facts. See *Craig* v *Lamoureux* [1920] AC 349 and *Biggins* v *Biggins* LTL 1 February 2000 (unreported elsewhere). In *Killick* v *Poutney and Another* (1999) The Times 30

April James Munby QC held that the defendant's inactivity and silence was not in itself sufficient ground for the court to draw adverse inferences against him. He further added that the role of the judge was to determine the deceased's true intention and allegations of undue influence had to be proved. Such evidence was in existence in this case and as such the will was declared invalid.

The probate doctrine of undue influence has no relation to the equitable doctrine of undue influence. The latter infers undue influence where a donee stands in a confidential relationship to a donor, for example, where the donee is a solicitor, doctor or priest. The distinction between the two doctrines was explained by Lord Penzance in *Parfitt* v *Lawless* (1872) LR 2 P & D 462 who said:

> 'In the first place, in those cases of gifts or contracts *inter vivos*, there is a transaction in which the person benefited at least takes part, whether he unduly urges his influence or not and in calling upon him to explain the part he took, and the circumstances that brought about the gift or obligation, the court is plainly requiring of him an explanation within his knowledge. But in the case of a legacy under a will, the legatee may have, and in point of fact generally has, no part in or even knowledge of the act; and to cast upon him, on the bare proof of the legacy and his relation to the testator, the burden of showing how the thing came about, and under what influence or with what motives the legacy was made, or what advice the testator had, professional or otherwise, would be to cast a duty on him which in many, if not most cases, he could not possibly discharge.'

Thus, in *Parfitt* v *Lawless* itself, it was held that an allegation of undue influence had to be proved by the party making it where the testatrix had left her substantial residuary estate to a Roman Catholic priest who had been her confessor.

One should note the important recent decision of *Simpson* v *Simpson* (1989) 19 Fam Law 20. This case also concerned the mental capacity of a testator and undue influence, and should be compared with *Parfitt* v *Lawless* discussed above. It is therefore noted in detail.

The plaintiffs in the case were the testator's children by a former marriage. The defendant was his third wife. By the provisions of his will the deceased's estate was to devolve on the defendant on trust, subject to the payment of the income and capital to the plaintiffs on the death of the defendant. The testator had developed a malignant brain tumour; as a result his mental processes had become impaired. The testator transferred substantial sums of money from bank and building society accounts into a joint account held with the defendant. By the time of his death, the testator had disposed of approximately 70 per cent of his estate in this way. The plaintiffs claimed that:

1. the testator did not have the mental capacity to make these dispositions in favour of the defendant; and
2. the defendant must be presumed to have exercised undue influence over the testator.

It was held in the Family Division by Mowitt J that:

1. the testator did not have the mental capacity to make the dispositions;

2. in the absence of any evidence to the contrary, there was a presumption of advancement in favour of the defendant. However, the presumption was in this case rebutted by evidence of intention. The evidence was that the transfer into the joint account made by the testator was only for convenience to facilitate the payment of bills and expenses by the defendant and was not an outright gift;

3. although the relationship existing between spouses did not itself give rise to a presumption of undue influence, it was possible in certain circumstances that such a presumption might arise. It did in these circumstances because of the illness and dependency of the testator.

5.5 Fraud

Animus testandi will not be present in cases where the testator has been prompted to make provision in his will, or exclude from his will, a beneficiary because of false statements made to him in relation to that beneficiary. Thus, in *Butterfield* v *Scawen* (1775) a will was refused probate on the ground of fraud because of a false representation made to the testator, that the woman who was the principal legatee had attempted to poison him, and that in consequence of this representation he had revoked the bequest in her favour.

Any form of deception practised on the testator which affects his will will amount to fraud. Thus, inserting clauses in a will before it is signed without the testator's knowledge will be sufficient, as will false representations by a beneficiary to the testator which become the motive behind a gift. Thus, in *Wilkinson* v *Joughin* (1866) LR 2 Eq 319 it was said that a gift in a will to a married woman who represented to the testator that she was free to marry him and did marry him would be omitted from probate for fraud. These particular examples also show that fraud may affect only part of the will as opposed to the whole will.

Fraud may arise from reading over a will to the testator by failing to convey to the mind of the testator the effect of his testamentary act or pretending that things which are being 'read' are in the will when they are not. See *Fulton* v *Andrew* (1875) LR 7 HL 448.

5.6 Knowledge and approval

The document which embodies the testator's wishes as to his property etc after his death must have his knowledge and approval if it is to be regarded as his will. The requirement of knowledge and approval is particularly important in cases where the will is drawn up on behalf of the testator by a third party, for example, where the testator dictates his instructions to his solicitor or his wife, because of the danger that the third party may deliberately vary the instructions in putting them to paper, or misunderstand them in this process. See *Parker* v *Felgate* (above).

In *Guardhouse* v *Blackburn* (1866) LR 1 P & D 109 Lord Penzance laid down the following propositions in relation to knowledge and approval of the will by the testator.

1. That before a will is entitled to probate, the court must be satisfied that the testator knew and approved of the contents at the time he signed it.
2. That except in certain cases where suspicion attaches to the document, the fact of the testator's execution is sufficient proof that he knew and approved the contents.
3. That although the testator knew and approved the contents the paper may be refused probate, if it be proved beyond all possibility of mistake that he did not intend the paper to operate as a will.
4. That although the testator did know and approve the contents the paper may be refused probate, if it is proved that any fraud has been purposely practised on the testator in obtaining his execution thereof.
5. Subject to the last preceding proposition, the fact that the will has been duly read over to a capable testator on the occasion of its execution, or that its contents have been brought to his notice in any other way, should when coupled with his execution thereof, be held conclusive evidence that he approved as well as knew the contents thereof.

   (NB This proposition is no longer considered to be good law. In *Re Morris* [1971] P 62 (below) Latey J said: 'It does not survive in any shape or form' and that reading over was only evidence that there may have been knowledge and approval. Much will depend on how the reading over took place; thus careful study of the will by the testator would be strong evidence of knowledge and approval while a glance over the will would be weak evidence.)
6. That the above rules apply equally to a portion of the will as to the whole.

The requirement of knowledge and approval will, as Lord Penzance's second proposition indicates, be presumed from the fact of execution by the testator. However, it is also clear from his propositions that there are certain cases where this presumption will not operate; in these cases the burden of proof is on the party propounding the will to show knowledge and approval. These are cases of suspicious circumstances, where there has been a mistake, and where the testator is dumb, blind or illiterate.

5.7 Suspicious circumstances

The classic definition of suspicious circumstances is contained in *Barry* v *Butlin* (1838) 2 Moo PC 480 where Parke B said:

> 'If a party writes or prepares a will, under which he takes a benefit, that is a circumstance that ought generally to excite the suspicion of the court, and calls upon it to be vigilant and jealous in examining the evidence in support of the instrument, in favour of which it

ought not to pronounce unless the suspicion is removed, and it is judicially satisfied that the paper propounded does express the true will of the deceased.'

The obvious danger which the doctrine of suspicious circumstances is intended to avoid is fraud by the party who wrote or prepared the will, on the testator. The doctrine is applicable in cases where the will leaves all the testator's estate or only part of the testator's estate to the party who prepared the will.

In *Fulton* v *Andrew* (1875) LR 7 HL 488 the testator made a will in 1870 which was in the handwriting of one of his executors, Wilson. The will contained a long list of legacies, including one of £100 to Wilson, and the residuary estate was bequeathed equally to Wilson and the other executor, Andrew. The testator's nephew challenged the will. Evidence showed that Wilson had left the will with the testator for a few days before execution and it also revealed discrepancies between the testator's instructions and the will. A jury found in favour of the will, except for the residuary gift. Probate was, however, granted to the whole of the will. On appeal:

Held: probate should not have been granted to the whole will. The executors had failed to alleviate the court's suspicion in relation to the residuary gift and it should have been excluded from probate.

Much will depend on the facts of each case in which suspicious circumstances arise as to what sort of evidence is required in order to remove the suspicion. This was dealt with in *Wintle* v *Nye* [1959] 1 WLR 284 by Viscount Simonds:

'The degree of suspicion will vary with the circumstances of the case. It may be slight and easily dispelled. It may, on the other hand, be so grave that it can hardly be removed. In the present case the circumstances were such as to impose on the respondent as heavy a burden as can well be imagined. Here was an elderly lady who might be called old, unversed in business, having no one upon whom to rely except the solicitor who acted for her and her family; a will made by him under which he takes the bulk of her large estate.'

The extreme case of *Wintle* v *Nye* should be compared with the example given in *Barry* v *Butlin* by Parke B:

'A man of acknowledged competence and habits of business, worth £100,000 leaves the bulk of his property to his family and a legacy of £50 to his confidential attorney, who prepared the will: would this fact throw the burden of proof of actual cognizance by the testator of the contents of the will, on the party propounding it, so that if such proof were not supplied, the will would be pronounced against? The answer is obvious, it would not. All that can be truly said is, that if a person, whether attorney or not, prepares a will with a legacy to himself, it is, at most a suspicious circumstance, of more or less weight, according to the facts of each particular case; in some of no weight at all, as in the case suggested, varying according to circumstances.'

In *Barry* v *Butlin* (1838) 2 Moo PC 480 the testator, an elderly man, made his will at the house of his attorney in the presence of two independent and respectable witnesses. By his will he left his attorney a quarter of his estate and left other legacies to friends. He left nothing to his only son. On the testator's death the son challenged the will on the grounds of lack of testamenary capacity, fraud and suspicious circumstances. The last allegation was based on the fact that the will was in the attorney's handwriting.

Held: although suspicion surrounded the gift to the attorney the court was satisfied that this was removed on evidence being adduced that the testator had excluded his son from his presence for criminal conduct and because the will was drawn up in the presence of independent witnesses.

Suspicious circumstances is not limited to cases where the party preparing the will takes a benefit for himself. It will also apply where the party preparing the will procures a benefit thereunder for a close relative or friend or any other circumstances which excites the suspicion of the court. In *Tyrrell* v *Painton* [1894] P 151 Lindley LJ said that the doctrine 'extends to all cases in which circumstances exist which excite the suspicion of the court'. The testatrix made wills in 1880 and in 1884 by which Painton was the main beneficiary. However, about 1890 the testatrix became disapproving of Painton's behaviour and on 7 November 1892 she made a new will leaving all her estate to Tyrrell. However, on 9 November 1892 Painton's son visited the testatrix with a friend and persuaded her to execute a will he had prepared, which left all her property to Painton. The testatrix died shortly afterwards. Probate was granted to the will but Tyrrell appealed.

Held: there were suspicious circumstances surrounding the execution of the will on 9 November and the evidence of Painton's son and his friend was not sufficient to remove this suspicion.

The dicta of Lindley LJ in *Tyrrell* v *Painton* have been applied in several other cases. These include *Thomas* v *Jones* [1928] P 162 where the testatrix's solicitor drafted the will leaving the bigger part of her estate to his daughter; *Brown* v *Fisher* (1890) 63 LT 465 where the testator was persuaded by his brother to travel a long distance to the office of a solicitor who normally did not act for him, and there made a will in favour of his brother; *Re Ticehurst* (1973) 123 NLJ 249 where the testatrix, aged 82, made a will in favour of a nephew and other relatives leaving them various houses which she left to the tenants thereof by a previous will. The later will was made on the basis of correspondence between the testatrix and her solicitor, with the nephew's wife conducting the correspondence on behalf of the testatrix.

The doctrine of suspicious circumstances only relates to the preparation or execution of the will and it cannot be applied beyond this. Thus, in *Davis* v *Mayhew* [1927] P 264 the only suspicious matter was the fact that the executrix, for many years after the testatrix's death, took no steps to obtain probate of the will which contained large bequests to the executrix's daughter. The Court of Appeal refused to consider this as a case of suspicious circumstances and the suspicion did not have 'a direct bearing on the question whether the testatrix knew and approved of its contents'. In *Re R (deceased)* [1951] P 10 allegations of drunkenness and of homosexuality by the deceased with a beneficiary were made. The latter did not amount to pleas of fraud or undue influence.

5.8 Mistake

Where a testator signs the wrong document as his will, as in *In the estate of Meyer* [1908] P 353, or signs a document as his will which contains words or the wrong words inserted without his knowledge or omits something without his knowledge, then a case of mistake arises.

Before s20 of the Administration of Justice Act 1982 came into operation there was very little that the court could do in order to correct a mistake in a will of which the testator did not know and approve. If there had been an omission of words from the will the court could not insert those words, even in clear cases of mistake, because there existed no power to rectify wills. See *Harter* v *Harter* (1873) LR 3 P & D 11. However, if words had been put into the will by mistake the court had a power to omit them. See *Re Phelan* [1972] Fam 33; *Collins* v *Elstone* [1893] P 1; *Re Morris* [1971] P 62.

In *Re Phelan* [1972] Fam 33 the testator executed a home made will in June 1968 under which his landlady and her husband were the main beneficiaries. In July 1968 the testator executed three further wills on printed will forms disposing of his investments in three unit trusts separately in each of the wills. All three wills were executed within a few minutes of each other and contained a printed clause revoking all previous wills. The executor sought a grant of probate to the three wills without the revocation clauses.

Held: the court would omit the revocation clauses in the printed wills since they had been included through either inadvertence or misunderstanding and therefore without the knowledge and approval of the testator.

Contrast: *Collins* v *Elstone* [1893] P 1. The testatrix left two wills and a codicil. The second will was on a printed form and disposed of a small life insurance policy which contained a printed revocation clause. When the second will was read to the testatrix she objected to the revocation clause but a misguided explanation of its effect quelled her objections. The question arose whether the clause could be excluded from probate.

Held: the testatrix knew of the presence of the revocation clause and decided to allow it to remain in her will. Therefore, it could not be omitted from probate. (This case has been strongly criticised since it is arguable that the testatrix did not know and approve the effect of the clause even if she knew and approved of its presence. However, to omit words which the testatrix knew were present in her will, could be regarded as 'venturing into' an area of uncertainty.)

In *Re Morris* [1971] P 62 the testatrix made a long and detailed will. Clause 7 contained 20 legacies. Sometime after executing the will the testatrix instructed her solicitor to draw up a codicil to revoke bequests contained in clauses 3 and 7(iv). However, the codicil was drawn up in terms: 'I revoke clauses 3 and 7 of my said will'. If the codicil were allowed to stand, some 19 other legacies in clause 7 would also be revoked.

Held: the court had no power to insert the Roman numeral (iv) in the codicil.

The only power was to omit words from the will or codicil. Since the manner in which the testatrix's intention could be most nearly effected, would be by omitting the reference to clause 7 in the codicil, this would be done.

The power to omit words could get rid of words of which the testator did not know and approve. In cases such as *Re Phelan* a satisfactory result was obtained in applying the power to omit the unintended revocation clauses. However, in *Re Morris* the result was not entirely satisfactory and the power was really being used in a manner which would get as near as possible to that which the testator clearly intended. An extreme example of the application of this power to get nearer to the testator's clear intentions was *Re Reynette-James* [1976] 1 WLR 161. In that case an important part of a trust of the residue was omitted from the will through a typing error thereby depriving the main residuary remainderman of his benefit but not those who were to take if he predeceased the life tenant. In order to ensure that the will accorded as nearly as possible with the testator's wishes, Templeman J excluded the whole of the residuary gift, save for the benefits given to the life tenants, from probate because this would mean that the intended remainderman at least obtained a benefit under the intestacy rules.

The problem with cases such as *Re Morris* and *Re Reynette-James* was that the power to omit words because of a mistake was being used as an inadequate substitute for rectification. Fortunately, such results are not likely to occur again because of the provisions of s20 of the Administration of Justice Act 1982 which came into force on 1 January 1983, and give the court the power to rectify wills in limited circumstances: subs (1) provides:

'If a court is satisfied that a will is so expressed that it fails to carry out the testator's intentions, in consequence –
(a) of a clerical error; or
(b) a failure to understand instructions,
it may order that the will shall be rectified so as to carry out his intentions.'

The effect of s20 is that in *Re Morris* the court could now insert the Roman numeral (iv) after the 7 in the codicil so as to give effect to the testatrix's intentions. In *Re Reynette-James* the missing portion of the residuary clause could be inserted. Other cases where rectification would now be available if similar facts arose again are: *Re Boehm* [1891] P 247, where the testator intended to give legacies of £10,000 to each of his daughters, Georgina and Florence. Unfortunately, both the relevant clauses in the will referred to Georgina. There was nothing the court could do to ensure that Florence obtained her benefit. But now s20 would permit the substitution of her name; and *In the Goods of Schott* [1901] P 190 the residuary clause in a will read 'to stand possessed of the net revenue', the word 'revenue' having been put in instead of 'residue'. In such a case rectification would now be available.

The power of rectification is not without its limitations. As with rectification generally it would appear that this power will not be resorted to unless there is no other way of resolving the difficulty. The court has always considered rectification as a last resort. Therefore, the power of the Court of Probate to omit words from a will for lack of knowledge and approval is by no means redundant. It will continue to be applicable in cases such as *Re Phelan* (above) where a power to rectify is wholly unnecessary. The power to rectify will, it seems, be wholly unnecessary in cases where the court has been able to correct an error on the face of the will as a matter of construction. In *Burchill* v *Clarke* (1876) 2 CPD 88 Amphlett LJ said:

> 'The courts of law and equity – for the rule was the same in both – where there is a manifest error in a document will put a sensible meaning on it by correcting or reading the error as corrected.'

Thus in cases similar to *Coles* v *Hume* (1828) 8 B & C 568 the court read in the word 'pounds' in a legacy where it was said to be a 'moral certainty'.

As s20 indicates the power to rectify is limited. The Law Reform Committee in its report pointed out that rectification would not be a remedy where:

1. the testator failed to appreciate the legal effect of the words used in his will. Thus it would appear that in cases similar to *Collins* v *Elstone* [1893] P 1, rectification is not available. In that case the testatrix asked a friend to execute a codicil to her will to dispose of the proceeds of a small insurance policy. The codicil was drawn up on a printed form with a revocation clause. The testatrix objected to the revocation clause but eventually allowed it to remain when told the whole will would be ineffective if it were omitted. The power to omit words could not be used as the testatrix knew and approved of the clause. Rectification would not be available either because this could only be effected by looking at the testatrix's purpose, and, as stated above, rectification has never been used for this purpose;
2. there was uncertainty as to the meaning of intended wording of the testator as this again would require the court to look at the testator's purpose. In such cases the problem is one for the court of construction;
3. the testator never had any intention relevant to the situation which actually occurred.

There is no definition of 'clerical error' in the 1982 Act but it is clearly intended to cover cases where there is a typing error or a slip of the pen or some other mistake in the process of committing the testator's intentions to the engrossed copy of the will. 'Failure to understand' the testator's instructions appears to contemplate cases where there has been a breakdown in communication between the testator and the draftsman as where the draftsman finds difficulty in understanding the testator's accent or where he fails to comprehend written instructions. The latter provision appears to follow a suggestion by Latey J in *Re Morris*.

In order to obtain rectification of a will the standard of evidence required, it appears, will be similar to that required for rectification in other cases. 'Convincing proof' as Russell LJ said in *Joscelyne* v *Nissen* [1970] 2 QB 86; 'strong irrefragable evidence' as Lord Thurlow said in *Countess of Shelburne* v *Earl of Inchiquin* (1784) 1

Bro CC 338; or evidence that would 'leave no fair and reasonable doubt upon the mind that the deed does not embody the final intention of the parties', per Lord Chelmsford in *Fowler* v *Fowler* (1859) 4 De G & J 250. Thus it will be necessary to produce draft copies of the will or written instructions of the testator or good oral evidence from reliable witnesses.

The remedy of rectification must be sought by those to whom it is available with reasonable speed. Under s20(2) an application for rectification can only be made with the permission of the court if more than six months have elapsed from the date on which the first grant of representation was made to the deceased's estate. This provision is to ensure that uncertainty is removed so that the personal representatives can safely distribute and that the beneficiaries can be reasonably sure of their benefit. If permission is sought for leave to bring an application outside the six months time limit it would appear that the court will follow the guidelines laid down in *Re Salmon* [1980] 3 All ER 532 and *Re Dennis* [1981] 2 All ER 140. These cases set out guidelines applicable to s4 of the Inheritance (Provision for Family and Dependants) Act 1975, a provision almost identical to s20(2). Section 20(4) states that a grant for the purposes of s20(2) does not include grants limited to settled land or to trust property or limited to personal estate alone or to real estate alone. Section 20(3) provides that personal representatives shall not be personally liable for having distributed the estate if they observe the provisions of s20(2).

5.9 Blind and illiterate testators

Testators who possess disabilities present special problems; there is a danger that unscrupulous third parties may take advantage of them. For this reason r13 of the Non-Contentious Probate Rules 1987 provides:

> 'Before admitting to proof a will which appears to have been signed by a blind or illiterate testator or by another person by direction of the testator, of which for any other reason gives rise to doubt as to the testator having knowledge of the contents of the will at the time of its execution, the registrar shall satisfy himself that the testator had no such knowledge.'

In *In the Goods of Geale* (1864) 3 Sw & Tr 431, Lord Penzance only granted probate to the will of a testator who was dumb, blind and illiterate when he was satisfied that the testator had, through various signs, shown that he knew and approved of the contents of the will. Again, in *Christian* v *Intsiful* [1954] 1 WLR 253, the testator was very old and his eyesight so defective that he was almost blind; the court was only prepared to conclude that he had knowledge and approval of his will after evidence to this effect had been adduced.

5.10 Drink and drugs: their effect on testamentary capacity

If a testator drinks excessively or takes drugs this fact will not *per se* destroy the testator's will making capacity. But if the drink or drug consumed severely affects the testator's ability to make a sound judgment, then any will so made while under the drink or drug influence will be invalid on the ground of lack of capacity. This was established in *Ayrey* v *Hill* (1824) 162 ER 269 (although here on the facts the intoxicated testator was held to have requisite testamentary capacity). In a case where lack of capacity is pleaded on this ground the alleged drinking or drug taking must attend the execution of the will. Thus in *Re R* [1951] P 10 the testator's will was challenged on inter alia the ground that he had been an habitual drunkard. However, it was not established that the drinking had actually affected the testator's judgment when he executed the will so this ground of challenge failed.

5.11 Methods of showing knowledge and approval

Where knowledge and approval are not presumed, that is, in cases of suspicious circumstances, mistake, and blind and illiterate testators, the party propounding the will must satisfy the court that there was knowledge and approval. This burden can be discharged in the following ways.

Evidence that the will was read over to the testator

As stated earlier, this is not conclusive evidence of knowledge and approval. In *Re Morris*, Latey J said it was evidence which must be given weight according to the circumstances. Thus, if the will was read slowly and explained, this evidence would be strong, while if it was read at a galloping rate to the testator, then knowledge and approval is unlikely to be gathered from this.

Evidence that the testator read the will himself

Again, much will depend on the circumstances of the case. If the testator merely casts an eye over the will, reading over will be of little probative value. However, if he studied the will carefully, the court will probably be satisfied as to knowledge and approval. Much will depend on the intellectual ability of the testator if he read the will over himself and a careful perusal of a will by a dim-witted testator who understood little of what he read would be of little probative value.

Comparing the testator's instructions with the will

If the testator sent written instructions to his solicitor for his will and the will was drawn up in accordance with these instructions, the instructions will be strong evidence of knowledge and approval if the will is in similar terms. If the testator dictated his instructions to his solicitor then the rough draft of these instructions may help to show knowledge and approval in cases of mistake or where the testator is blind or illiterate. However, instructions dictated to a solicitor would be of little help in removing suspicion if the solicitor obtained a large benefit under the will.

5.12 Infants

An infant cannot make a formal will in English law. It is obvious that a very young infant would have no idea of the nature and effect of a will while others may be subject to undue influence or have no knowledge and approval of their will. Therefore under s7 of the Wills Act, it is provided:

'No will made by any person under the age of eighteen years shall be valid.'

An infant will therefore always die intestate and his parents or brothers and sisters will in most cases take his estate, if any, under the intestacy rules. Two exceptions exist to s7, namely, an infant may make a privileged will (see Chapter 3), and an infant over the age of 16 years may make a nomination (see above).

A privileged infant testator may not be able to dispose of realty by privileged will. This is because an infant cannot own a legal estate in land and he may only hold an equitable interest in land.

By s51(3) of the Administration of Estates Act 1925 equitable interests in land belonging to unmarried infants must devolve as entailed interest.

6

Revocation of Wills

6.1 Introduction

6.2 Revocation by an express clause

6.3 Revocation by implication

6.4 Revocation by destruction

6.5 Revocation by marriage

6.6 Conditional revocation

6.1 Introduction

One of the characteristics of a will is that by its very nature it is revocable by the testator until his death. This arises through the ambulatory nature of wills. Further, a testator cannot make his will irrevocable and if the will does contain such a declaration it will not prevent the testator from subsequently revoking the will. See *Vynior's Case* (1609) 8 Co Rep 816. However, if the declaration was part of a binding contract the other party to the contract may have a claim in damages for breach of contract. See *Synge* v *Synge* [1894] 1 QB 466.

A testator is not at liberty to revoke his will in any manner he chooses. Section 20 of the Wills Act 1837 sets out methods by which a will may be revoked. Apart from these the only other methods of revocation are those contained in ss18 and 18A of the Wills Act and where there has been an obliteration under s21 of the Wills Act. An attempt to revoke the will by a method other than these will be ineffective.

6.2 Revocation by an express clause

Section 20 of the Wills Act 1837 provides:

> 'No will or codicil, or any part thereof, shall be revoked otherwise than as aforesaid ... or by some writing declaring an intention to revoke the same, and executed in the manner in which a will is hereinbefore required to be executed ...'

It is clear that under s20 an express clause in a will such as 'I hereby revoke all wills and codicils or other testamentary dispositions here to before made by me' will revoke all previous wills, provided the will in which the clause is contained is executed in accordance with the formalities laid down in s9.

It is irrelevant if the testator was misled as to the effect of the clause. In *Collins* v *Elstone* [1893] P 1 the court refused to strike out a revocation clause from a codicil which had the effect of revoking the testatrix's will and another codicil. The testatrix knew of the presence of the clause and had objected to it when it was read over to her by the draftsman of the will, but dropped her objections when the draftsman explained the effect of the clause in mistake terms, in that it only revoked insurance policies and not her will and codicil. The testatrix knew and approved of the clause and under the authority of *Morrell* v *Morrell* (1882) 7 PD 68 the court was bound to apply the principle that if the testator employs another to convey this meaning in technical language, and that other person makes a mistake in doing it, the mistake is the same as if the testator had employed the technical language himself. It is unlikely that a different decision would be reached on facts such as those in *Collins* v *Elstone* today. Rectification under s20 of the Administration of Justice Act would not be available here for the reasons given in Chapter 5, section 5.8.

A revocation clause will have no effect if the testator did not know and approve of its presence. Thus, in *Re Phelan* [1972] Fam 33 the testator executed a home-made will in favour of his landlady and later, under a mistaken belief as to the operation of wills, he executed three further wills on printed forms disposing of his holdings in three unit trusts. The printed revocation clause at the top of each printed will form was not deleted. All four wills were admitted to probate with the revocation clauses in the last three being omitted. See also *In b Oswald* (1874) LR 3 P & D 162.

A revocation clause may be limited in its ambit or conditional on certain events. Thus in *In the Estate of Wayland* [1951] 2 All ER 1041 a revocation clause in a will which declared that 'this will is intended to deal only with my estate in England', was construed as not affecting a previous will made by the testator to dispose of his property in Belgium. Conditions in a will relating to revocation may take many forms; it is not uncommon to find a will in which it is declared that it shall not take effect, if, for example, the testator's wife does not survive him. See *In the Estate of O'Connor* [1942] 1 All ER 546.

The document in which the revocation clause is contained need not be in the form of a will. It is sufficient if it is in a document which is executed with the necessary formalities. In *Re Spracklan's Estate* [1938] 2 All ER 345 the Court of Appeal had to consider the effect of a letter executed in accordance with s9 containing a direction 'will you please destroy the will already made out'. The court felt bound to follow the decision of Lord Penzance in *In b Durance* (1872) LR 2 P & D 406, where he said: 'If a man writes to another "Go and get my will and burn it", he shows a strong intention to revoke his will'. In the language of s20 of the Wills Act, the letter is a writing declaring an intention to revoke the will, and it is duly executed. However, Sir Wilfrid Greene MR stated that if the matter had been free from authority he would have come to a different conclusion because an intention to destroy is not neccesarily an intention to revoke.

In *Re Spracklan's Estate* [1938] 2 All ER 345 (CA) a month before her death the testatrix sent a letter to her bank manager, with whom her will was deposited, stating 'Will you please destroy the will already made out'. The letter was signed by the testatrix and two witnesses.

Held: the letter amounted to revocation of the will by a writing declaring an intention to revoke.

Note that s20 draws a distinction between a will, a codicil and some writing. In *In b Fraser* (1869) LR 2 P & D 40 Lord Penzance considered this distinction and concluded that a memorandum which did nothing more than revoke a will was merely a writing and did not need to be admitted to probate as it did not dispose of any property.

6.3 Revocation by implication

Section 20 of the Wills Act provides:

> 'No will or codicil, or any part thereof, shall be revoked otherwise than as aforesaid, or by another will or codicil executed in manner hereinbefore required'.

These words would appear to give the court authority to apply revocation by implication.

Revocation by implication is only relevant where there are several wills which do not contain revocation clauses or contain limited revocation clauses only. The question which arises in these circumstances is how different clauses should be construed if they deal with the same property or bequeath a legacy of the same amount. The fact that later wills do not contain revocation clauses will not necessarily prevent them from being treated as revocation of the earlier wills.

In *Dempsey* v *Lawson* (1877) 2 PD 98 the testatrix, who died in 1862, left a will dated 1860 which contained a detailed list of bequests and annuities and also set out detailed provisions as to the disposal of the residue. This will contained no revocation clause. An earlier will of the testatrix dated 1858 was propounded by the plaintiff; this also contained a detailed list of bequests and annuities and set out provisions as to the disposal of the residuary estate. However, there were significant differences between the two wills as to the beneficiaries of the residue; the 1858 will contained a gift of a share of residue to a Convent of the Sisters of Mercy at Bermondsey whilst the 1860 will did not. It was sought to have the 1858 will admitted to probate on the ground that it formed part of the testatrix's last will together with the 1860 will.

Held: the whole scheme of the 1860 will showed that it was intended to be a subsitute for the 1858 will which was revoked by it. Sir James Hannen P concluded:

'Even if the second instrument contains a general revocatory clause, that is not conclusive, and the court will, notwithstanding, consider whether it was the intention of the testator to revoke a bequest contained in a previous will ... On the other hand, though there be no express revocatory clause, the question is whether the intention of the testator, to be collected from the instrument, was that the dispositions of the earlier will should remain in whole or in part operative ... In the present case I am of the opinion that the intention of the testatrix, to be collected from the dispositions of the two wills, is that the second should stand alone, and be in complete substitution for the first ... and consequently that it does by implication revoke the 1858 will.'

The question whether there is, or is not, revocation by implication is one which is normally decided by construing the will and if necessary, admitting extrinsic evidence. See *Thorne* v *Rooke* (1841) 2 Curt 799; *In b Bryan* [1907] P 125. Thus, for example, if T made a will in 1970 leaving his farm Blackacre to X and in 1975 made another will leaving his farm Blackacre to Y, then if neither will contained an express revocation clause the later disposition, being wholly inconsistent with the earlier one, would prevail; Y would obtain Blackacre. In some cases it may be necessary to read the language of the will carefully to decide if there is revocation by implication. See *In b Bryan* or to resort to extrinsic evidence see *Methuen* v *Methuen*.

In *In b Bryan* [1907] P 125 the testatrix made a will in 1864 leaving, *inter alia*, a legacy to her niece and a sum of money on trust for her sister (the testatrix's sister) for life, remainder to her niece for life, remainder to the children of her niece. In 1867 the testatrix made a further will which, in substance, repeated the 1864 will but omitting the trusts in favour of the niece and her children, and cutting down the legacy to the niece. The 1867 will contained no gift of residue, unlike the 1864 will, and no revocation clause. The question arose whether the niece and her children were entitled to benefit under the trusts of the 1864 will on the ground that they had not been revoked by the 1867 will.

Held: on a true construction of the 1867 will it was clear that the testatrix intended it to supersede her 1864 will in all respects. The 1864 will was revoked.

In *Methuen* v *Methuen* (1816) 2 Phillin 416 the testator made a codicil to his will which conferred benefits on his wife and children. After the marriage of one of his daughters he made a further codicil to his will which after reciting that he had made provision for this daughter, proceeded to make dispositions in favour of the wife and the other daughters differing from those in the first codicil. There was nothing making it absolutely impossible that the testator meant their dispositions to be cumulative but if this were intended, the property of the deceased would not have been equal to the payment of all the legacies he had given.

Held: because of the doubt arising on the face of the instrument the court was entitled to look at extrinsic evidence relating to the facts known to the testator. On this evidence it was clear that the codicils were not meant to be cumulative.

6.4 Revocation by destruction

Section 20 of the Wills Act provides:

> 'No will or codicil, or any part thereof, shall be revoked otherwise than as aforesaid ... or by the burning, tearing or otherwise destroying the same by the testator, or by some person in his presence and by his direction, with the intention of revoking the same.'

It can be seen that under s20 revocation by destruction contains two elements: an act of destruction and an intention to revoke *(animus revocandi)*. See *Cheese* v *Lovejoy*.

The act of destruction must be one as specified in s20, that is, burning or tearing or *ejusdem generis* these. Thus, cutting the will up with a pair of scissors will do. See *Hobbs* v *Knight* (1836) 1 Curt 768. Or scratching the words of the will out with a knife will do. See *In b Morton* (1887) 12 PD 141.

If there is no appropriate act of destruction there can be no revocation by destruction as illustrated by *Cheese* v *Lovejoy* (1877) 2 PD 251 (CA). The testator crossed through his will with a pen and indorsed it 'all these are revoked'. He then crumpled it into a ball and kicked it into a corner of his sitting room. A housekeeper found the will and kept it in the kitchen until the testator's death. The question arose whether the will had been revoked.

Held: there must be an act of destruction as well as an intention to revoke; 'All the destroying in the world without the intention will not revoke a will, nor all the intention in the world without destroying: there must be the two.' The will was not revoked.

Destruction of the whole will is not necessary in order to have revocation by destruction. If a vital part of the will has been destroyed then the whole will is revoked. Vital parts means either the testator's signature or the witnesses' signatures. *Hobbs* v *Knight* (1838) 1 Curt 768; see *In b Morton* (1887) 12 PD 141. See also *In b Gullan* (1858) 1 Sw & Tr 23.

In *Hobbs* v *Knight* (1838) 1 Curt 768 the deceased made a will in 1835 and sometime after the Wills Act 1837 came into operation, he cut his signature from the will with a pair of scissors.

Held: the whole will had been revoked because the signature of the testator is necessary to the validity of the will; it is an essential part, without which the will cannot exist.

When considering whether a will has been 'otherwise destroyed' and therefore revoked, *Re Adams* [1990] 2 All ER 97 has emphasised the relevance of which parts of the will have been destroyed. In this case the testatrix made a will in 1976. In 1982 she telephoned her solicitor instructing him to destroy the will; he sent it to her saying that it would be better if she destroyed it. After her death in 1987, the will was found amongst her possessions: the typescript had been scribbled upon in many places with a blue-black ball point pen and the signatures of the testatrix and attesting witnesses had been scored out particularly heavily. The judge inferred that the testatrix had intended to revoke the will: had she succeeded in 'otherwise destroying' it within s20 of the Wills Act 1837?

Held: she had. As material parts of the will had been destroyed, the will as a whole had been revoked. It was wrong to draw a distinction between a case where the signature had been physically removed and a case where it was impossible to discern the signature by the normal senses by which a signature was normally discerned. On account of the heaviness of the scoring in the present case it was not apparent to the naked eye that the signatures were signatures or whose they were; that could only be inferred from other circumstances.

There can be revocation by destruction of a part of the will only, as opposed to the whole will. In such circumstances if the court is satisfied that the testator intended the remainder to be effective, it will be admitted to probate. Thus, in *Re Everest* [1975] Fam 44 the testator directed that his residuary estate should be held on trust but the parts of the will dealing with the trusts were found cut away at his death. The will was complete in all other respects. Probate was granted to the mutilated will on the basis that the trusts had been cut out but not such as to raise the inference that the whole will was intended to be revoked. See also *In b Nunn* (1936) 105 LJP 57 where part of the will was cut and remaining parts stitched together, it was held that there was partial revocation only. However, in some cases it may be impossible to come to any conclusion other than that the whole will was intended to be revoked, where the remainder of the will is unintelligible without the missing parts. In *Re Woodward* (1871) LR 2 P & D 206 the will presented to probate had some lines missing. As the remainder of the will still was intelligible the court granted probate of what was left of the will omitting the missing lines of handwriting. By contrast note the case of *Leonard* v *Leonard* [1902] P 243 where a testator made out his will on five sheets of paper. The will was kept at his bank but withdrawn frequently for amendments. At his death it was found that the original pages 1 and 2 had been destroyed and replaced by new pages. Pages 3, 4 and 5 were unintelligible without the original pages 1 and 2. Pages 3, 4 and 5 were considered revoked as were the substitute pages because they had not been properly executed.

Under s20 it is not necessary that the testator personally revokes the will by destruction; the section provides that the destruction may be done by some other person in the testator's presence and by his direction. See *In b Dadds* (1857) Dea & Sw 290. If the destruction takes place in a manner where the testator cannot see it, or see it if he desired, it is ineffective. See *In b Dadds*. The destruction must be at the direction of the testator; if there is an unauthorised destruction the will is not revoked as the necessary intention to revoke is not present. Thus, in *Gill* v *Gill* [1909] P 157 the testator's will was torn up by his wife in a fit of temper but was not revoked. If there is an unauthorised act of destruction there can be no subsequent ratification of this by the testator; it would appear that the destruction must be accompanied by the appropriate authority to revoke at the time it took place. See *Mills* v *Millward* (1890) 15 PD 20.

In *In b Dadds* (1857) Dea & Sw 290 the testatrix asked one of the executors of her will to take a codicil to the will and destroy it as she no longer wished it to have effect. The codicil was brought to the testatrix who was confined to bed. As there was no fire in the bedroom it was taken into another room and burned in the presence of the executor and several other persons but not in the presence of the testatrix.

Held: the codicil was not revoked and the executor and others who knew its contents were required to give evidence of these so that they could be admitted to probate.

In *Mills* v *Millward* (1890) 15 PD 20 the testatrix, who retained her will in her personal custody, showed it to her sister-in-law shortly before her death. The sister-in-law tore up the will in anger when she discovered that neither she nor her husband were to benefit under its terms. The sister-in-law apologised and urged the testatrix to make a new will. She refused, and died without a new will.

Held: the will was not revoked as the act of destruction had not taken place on the authority of the testatrix. The testatrix's refusal to make another will could not be construed as a ratification of the destruction and it was doubtful if this was possible in any event.

The act of destruction must be accompanied by an intention to revoke at the time of destruction (*animus revocandi*). If destruction takes place when the testator is drunk or under the influence of drugs, there is no revocation of the will. See *Brunt* v *Brunt* (1873) 3 P & D 37. The will is not revoked by destruction if it is torn up under the mistaken belief that it is ineffective. See *In the estate of Southerden* [1925] P 177. In such circumstances an intention to destroy the document is not the same as an intention to revoke the will.

In *Brunt* v *Brunt* (1873) 3 P & D 37 the testator, a publican, suffered from delirium tremens before his death but after he made his will. This condition rendered him liable to attacks in which he was in a state of automatism. While suffering from an attack at 2 am one morning, the testator took his will from an iron safe and tore it into bits. His wife retrieved the bits and locked them up.

Held: when the testator tore up the will he was not master of his actions and therefore the actual destruction had no effect. The bits of the will would be admitted to probate.

In *In the estate of Southerden* [1925] P 177 (CA) before going on a journey to America the testator made a will leaving all his property to his wife. On his return the testator destroyed his will by burning after saying to his wife: 'This is no good now. We have safely returned and it is all yours. We might as well burn it.' The testator mistakenly believed that his wife would receive all his property under the intestacy rules.

Held: when the testator burned the will he did so under a mistaken belief; as this belief was incorrect it could not be said that he had the necessary intention to revoke in the circumstances.

The testator must not only intend to revoke the will, he must also, where revocation is to take effect by way of destruction, do all he intended to do by way of destruction. In *Doe d Perkes* v *Perkes* (1820) 3 B & Ald 489 Bayley J said:

> 'If the testator had done all that he originally intended, it would have amounted to a cancellation of the will; and nothing that afterwards took place could set it up again. But if the jury were satisfied that he was stopped in medio, then the act not having been completed will not be sufficient to destroy the validity of the will.'

In *Doe d Perkes* v *Perkes* (1820) B & Ald 489 the testator had a quarrel with a devisee under his will and in anger took out his will and began to tear it with the intention of destroying it. He tore it into four pieces before he was restrained from tearing it further partly by a bystander and partly by apologies from the devisee. The testator calmed his temper and put it in his pocket. He later took it out again and said: 'It is a good job it is no worse'. The will was in four parts at the testator's death.

Held: not every tearing can be regarded as a cancellation of the will; the act of destruction intended must be completed. As the testator had intended to go further in his tearing of the will but for being restrained, he had not completed the destruction he intended and the will was not revoked.

In some cases the testator's will may be found at his death in a mutilated condition without any explanation or knowledge as to how this occurred. Under *Lambell* v *Lambell* (1831) 3 Hagg Ecc 568 there is a presumption that a will which has been kept in the testator's possession and is found torn or mutilated is assumed revoked. Like most presumptions it can be rebutted by evidence of contrary intention on the part of the testator. By contrast the later case of *Cowling* v *Cowling* [1924] P 113 suggests that a contrary presumption exists and a mutilated will is assumed to be still in force and unrevoked unless there is evidence of intent to revoke. While these two cases are not easy to reconcile the answer may lie in the extent to which the document is mutilated. Arguably a will with only slight mutilation will be subject to the presumption in *Cowling* while a will with extensive mutilation may fall under the presumption in *Lambell*.

Circumstances arise where the testator was known to have made a will but it cannot be found. In such circumstances if the will was known to be in the testator's possession the court presumes that it was destroyed by him with the intention of revoking it. In *Welch* v *Phillips* (1836) 1 Moo PCC 299 Lord Wensleydale said:

> '... if a will, traced to the possession of the deceased, and last seen there, is not forthcoming on his death, it is presumed to have been destroyed by himself, and that presumption must have effect, unless there is sufficient evidence to repel it. It is a presumption founded on good sense; for it is highly reasonable to suppose that an instrument of so much importance would be carefully preserved, by a person of ordinary caution, in some place of safety, and would not be either lost or stolen; and if, on the death of the maker, it is not found in his usual repositories, or else where he resides, it is in a high degree probable, that the deceased himself has purposely destroyed it. But, this presumption ... may be rebutted.'

The presumption was rebutted in *Sugden* v *Lord St Leonards* (1876) 1 PD 154 (CA).

Lord St Leonards kept his will and the codicils thereto in a black box to which he had the key. After his death the will but not the codicils were found to be missing from the box. It was possible for any one of a number of persons to have obtained the key to the box after Lord St Leonards' death. On discovering that the will was missing one of Lord St Leonards' daughters wrote out from memory the contents of the will and it was sought to admit her notes to probate as the will.

Held: all the evidence, including that in the codicils, indicated that Lord St Leonards believed he would die intestate; as the black box which contained the will could have been interfered with by persons other than the testator the presumption that the missing will had been revoked by the testator was rebutted. The note of the contents of the will would be admitted to probate as it was reliable.

Sugden v *Lord St Leonards* raises two important points: (1) that a will may be lost or destroyed in the testator's lifetime (without being revoked) or since his death; (2) that the loss of such a will is not necessarily fatal. In such cases the court is prepared to admit a draft of the contents of the will or a copy of the will to probate provided that it is established (1) that the will was duly executed and (2) what the contents of the will were by reliable evidence. See *Re Webb* [1964] 1 WLR 509.

In *Re Webb* [1964] 1 WLR 509 the testatrix's sister found a draft copy of the testatrix's will in a trunk shortly before the testatrix died. The testatrix at the time said: 'Don't throw that away; it's my will.' After her death the original will could not be found and a grant of probate was sought in respect of the draft copy. Evidence showed that the original will was probably destroyed by enemy action in 1940 and a witness, who was named as an attesting witness in the draft, remembered signing a document for the testatrix in the presence of the testatrix and a solicitor but did not know what this document was.

Held: the draft copy would be admitted to probate as secondary evidence of the contents of the will and the *maxim omnia praesumuntur rite essa acta* (all acts are presumed to have been done rightly and regularly) would have applied in the absence of evidence to the contrary, so as to conclude that the will had been duly executed.

6.5 Revocation by marriage

Under s18(1) of the Wills Act 1837 (as amended by s18 of the Administration of Justice Act 1982) it is provided that 'a will shall be revoked by the testator's marriage'. The purpose behind this general principle is to protect and benefit the testator's widow in case he should forget to change the will he made before his marriage. This general principle is subject to exceptions which are dealt with below. Under s73(6) of the Administration of Justice Act 1982 the amended provisions of s18(1) only apply to wills made after 31 December 1982. Thus if a testator died in 1983 leaving a will made before 1983, say 1981, then the amended s18(1) would not apply; the old s18 and s177 of the Law of Property Act 1925 would cover any issues on whether the will was made in contemplation of marriage.

For the purposes of s18 'marriage' includes a voidable marriage but not a void marriage. Thus, when the testator goes through a ceremony of marriage, whether it be valid or merely voidable, as a general rule, his will is revoked. Voidable marriages have given rise to difficulty in the application of s18 in the past. Under s12 of the Matrimonial Causes Act 1973, six grounds exist on which a marriage is voidable. They are:

1. marriage not consummated because of the incapacity of either party;
2. wilful refusal of the respondent to consummate the marriage;
3. either party did not consent to the marriage because of duress, mistake, unsoundness of mind, etc;
4. at the time of the marriage one of the parties was suffering from a mental disorder within the meaning of the Mental Health Act 1959 of such a kind or to such an extent as to be unfit for marriage;
5. at the time of the marriage the respondent was suffering from venereal disease in a communicable form;
6. at the time of the marriage the respondent was pregnant by some other person other than the petitioner. In these cases the marriage is recognised as effective in law until a petition is made by the appropriate party to have it set aside. Such a marriage revokes the will of a testator even if it is subsequently set aside, a point made clear in *Re Roberts* [1978] 1 WLR 653. The deceased made a will in 1973 when he was aged 60. In 1974 he married the plaintiff and he died in 1976. The plaintiff sought a grant of letters of administration to the deceased's estate. The defendant, a beneficiary under the 1973 will, alleged that the deceased suffered from senile dementia at the time of his marriage to the plaintiff and that the marriage was void and did not revoke his 1973 will.

Held: the marriage was only voidable under s12(c) of the Matrimonial Causes Act 1973 and it revoked the will under s18 of the Wills Act because the annulment of a voidable marriage was not retrospective so as to negate the effect of s18.

A void marriage will not bring s18 of the Wills Act into operation because as Lord Greene MR pointed out in *De Reneville* v *De Reneville* [1948] P 100 at 111:

'A void marriage is one that will be regarded in every court in any case in which the existence of the marriage is in issue as never having taken place and can be so treated by both parties to it without the necessity of any decree annulling it.'

The exceptions to the principle in s18(1) are as follows.

Wills made in the exercise of a power of appointment

Under s18(2) of the Wills Act it is provided:

'A disposition in a will in exercise of a power of appointment shall take effect notwithstanding the testator's subsequent marriage unless the property so appointed would in default of appointment pass to his personal representatives.'

This exception is similar to that which was contained in the old s18 of the Wills Act, which was replaced by the Administration of Justice Act 1982; only the language of the exception has been modified. The exception operates where the testator before marriage makes a will which, *inter alia*, exercises a power of appointment and where the instrument authorising the testator to exercise the power provides that in default of appointment the subject matter of the power shall devolve on persons other than the next of kin of the testator. See *In b Gilligan* [1950] P 32.

Example

Under a power of appointment T has power to dispose of £50,000 'to whomsoever he shall by will appoint and in default of appointment to his brother, X'. If T exercised the power to appoint all of the fund to Y, in a will made in 1979, and married in 1983 the exception in s18(2) would operate because if the power were revoked by the marriage it would only cause the gift in default to operate thereby giving the fund to X. T's next of kin, that is, his wife and any children he might have, could not in any circumstances benefit by the revocation of the exercise of such a power.

Contrast

Under a power of appointment T has power to appoint £50,000 'to whomsoever he shall by will appoint and in default of appointment to his wife and children, if any'. By a will made in 1979 T appoints the £50,000 to his brother X, and in 1983 T marries and subsequently has a family. The exception in s18(2) would not operate here because a revocation of the appointment in the 1979 will would confer benefits on T's next of kin, that is, his wife and children, because they take in default of appointment.

Wills made in contemplation of marriage

Under s18(3) of the Wills Act it is provided:

'Where it appears from a will that at the time it was made the testator was expecting to be married to a particular person and that he intended that the will should not be revoked by the marriage, the will shall not be revoked by his marriage to that person.'

It is sufficient if it appears from a will that at the time it was made the testator was expecting to be married to a particular person and that he intended that the will should not be revoked by his marriage. To ascertain the intentions of the testator in this respect it is permissible to hear extrinsic evidence, under the provisions of s21 of the Administration of Justice Act. However, the Law Reform Committee recommended that such extrinsic evidence should be limited to evidence under the armchair rule and not include mere evidence of intention because the latter would be a virtual invitation to litigation.

In order for s18(3) to operate the testator must contemplate marriage 'to a particular person'. A will in contemplation of any marriage the testator might enter into is insufficient. Thus, in *Re Hamilton* [1940] VLR 60 a will began 'Should I marry prior to my death'. These words would not satisfy the section. The same conclusion was reached in *Sallis* v *Jones* [1936] P 43 where the words at the end of the will were 'this will is made in contemplation of marriage'. The fact that the testator's chances of actually marrying the person contemplated as a wife are remote, are irrelevant. Should he never marry that person the provisions and exception to s18 will never operate. If he should marry someone other than the person to whom he contemplated marriage then the will will be revoked because the idea of the provision is to benefit his new wife.

Dispositions in a will intended to survive marriage

1. Under s18(4) it is provided:

    'Where it appears from a will that at the time it was made the testator was expecting to be married to a particular person and that he intended that a disposition in the will should not be revoked by his marriage to that person –
    (a) that disposition shall take effect notwithstanding the marriage; and
    (b) any other disposition in the will shall take effect also unless it appears from the will that the testator intended the disposition to be revoked by the marriage.'

2. The purpose of s18(4) is to overcome the difficulties of *Re Coleman* [1976] Ch 1 on the point that it was the whole will and not merely gifts in it which had to be in contemplation of marriage. In that case the testator left personal chattels, a stamp collection, £5,000 and a freehold house 'unto my fiancée, Mrs Muriel Jeffrey' and the residue of his estate to his brother and sister. It was held that the whole will was not in contemplation of marriage but only those dispositions made to the fiancée and therefore it was revoked by s18. It is clear that the gifts to the fiancée in *Re Coleman* would now survive marriage under s18(4)(b) and the dispositions to the brother and sister might also survive under s18(4)(b).

6.6 Conditional revocation (sometimes referred to as dependent relative revocation)

This arises where the revocation of the will is conditional on certain matters taking effect or coming to pass. If the condition is not fulfilled then the will remains unrevoked. Conditional revocation may arise in several different contexts.

A testator who has already made a will may decide to make a new one and before the new will is drawn up or executed he may revoke the old will by destruction. In such circumstances the question arises whether the revocation was absolute or unqualified, in which case it takes effect whatever happens; or conditional on a new will being made, in which case it does not take effect unless the condition is satisfied. See *Dixon* v *Treasury Solicitor* [1905] P 42; *Re Jones* [1976] Ch 200.

In *Dixon* v *Treasury Solicitor* [1905] P 42 (CA) a testator instructed his solicitor to draft a new will and at the time he gave the instructions he cut his signature of his old will being under the misapprehension that he could not make a new will until the old one had been revoked. He died before he could sign the new will.

Held: the old will had not been revoked because evidence showed the testator would, but for his mistaken belief, have allowed the old will to remain effective up until his new will was executed.

In *Re Jones* [1976] Ch 200 (CA) the testatrix made a will in 1965 leaving her small farm to the plaintiff and his sister. She kept the will in her custody. In 1970 she decided to change her will as the plaintiff and his sister did not visit her very often, and she made an appointment with her solicitor for this purpose. However, before she could keep this appointment she took seriously ill and died. Before her death the testatrix was asked if she had made a will and replied in the negative. After her death her will was found in a mutilated condition and several clauses were missing as well as the testatrix's and witnesses' signatures. The question arose whether there was conditional revocation.

Held: the revocation of the will was absolute and unqualified; there was nothing to show that the testator believed she had to destroy her old will in order to make a new one; it was impossible to conclude that she only intended conditional revocation from the manner in which she mutilated the will, her statement before death that she had no will, and her intention not to give her small farm to the plaintiff and his sister.

If a will is destroyed because of a mistaken belief by the testator as to the operation of the law or as to certain facts, this will not amount to revocation. In such circumstances the mistaken belief negatives an *animus revocandi*. Thus, in *In the estate of Southerden* [1925] P 177 a will by which the testator left all his property to his wife was destroyed in the mistaken belief that the wife would take everything on intestacy. The will was held not to be revoked. In *Campbell* v *French* (1797) 3 Ves 321 a will which was destroyed in the belief that two of the main legatees were dead was held not revoked; the condition on which revocation depended not being fulfilled.

Conditional revocation may arise in cases of revival. Under s22 of the Wills Act no will can be revived except by re-execution in accordance with s9. If a testator has made Will X in 1970 and made Will Y in 1980 he may, under a mistaken belief, revoke Will Y thinking that he is thereby reviving Will X. In such circumstances conditional revocation applies and the revocation of Will Y is ineffective. See *Powell* v *Powell* (1866) LR 1 P & D 209.

Conditional revocation may also apply to alterations. If a testator obliterates a legacy and substitutes a new legacy which is unattested or pastes a slip of paper over the legacy bearing a new figure, then the old legacy will remain effective if the court is satisfied that it was revoked only on the erroneous belief that the new legacy was effective. See *In b Horsford* (1874) LR 3 P & D 211.

Conditional revocation may operate where in normal circumstances there would be implied revocation. If T made a will in 1980 leaving Blackacre to X, and in 1981 made another will leaving Blackacre to Y, the gift to X is by implication revoked in the absence of an express revocation clause. However, the gift of Blackacre to Y may be conditional on it being effective, for example, it may be worded: 'Blackacre to Y if he shall survive me'. The question which arises in such circumstances is whether the gift to X is revoked in an absolute and unqualified manner or conditionally revoked. This is really a matter of construction in each case as is illustrated by the following case.

In *Re Robinson* [1930] 2 Ch 332 in her first will a testatrix left her estate upon trust to pay an annuity to her son, H, for life and on his death to be divided equally between her grandchildren who attained 21 years.

In her second will, the testatrix left all her estate to her son, H, absolutely. The absolute gift to H in the second will did not contain a revocation clause so the question arose whether the first will was still effective.

Held: apart from the different disposition in the second will there was nothing in it which indicated that the first will was revoked in an unqualified manner. In fact it appeared that the revocation was conditional on the absolute gift taking effect.

7

Alterations in Wills

7.1 Introduction

7.2 Section 21 of the Wills Act 1837

7.3 Conditional obliterations

7.4 Alterations before execution

7.5 Method of execution of s21 alteration

7.1 Introduction

A testator may, having drawn up his will, wish to make amendments to it, either before he executes it, or sometimes after it has been drawn up and executed. The wisest course in these circumstances is to draw up a codicil to the will making the amendment in clear terms. However, if circumstances do not permit the execution of a codicil or the testator does not desire to have one, the only alternative is to make the alteration on the face of the will itself.

7.2 Section 21 of the Wills Act 1837

If an alteration is to be made in a will after execution it must comply with the provisions of s21 in order to be effective. The section provides:

> 'No obligation, interlineation, or other alteration made in any will after the execution thereof shall be valid or have any effect, except so far as the words or effect of the will before such alteration shall not be apparent, unless such alteration shall be executed in like manner as hereinbefore is required for the execution of the will; but the will, with such alteration as part thereof, shall be deemed to be duly executed if the signature of the testator and the subscription of the witnesses be made in the margin or on some other part of the will opposite or near to such alteration, or at the foot or end of or opposite to a memorandum referring to such alteration, and written at the end or some other part of the will.'

As can be gathered from s21, alterations must be executed and attested in the manner required by s9 of the Wills Act but the requirements of s9 are satisfied if:

1. the testator signs and the witnesses attest the alteration in the margin or opposite or near the alteration;
2. there is a memorandum on some part of the will recording the nature of the alteration with the testator's signature and witnesses' subscription nearby.

It is not clear from the section whether the original witnesses to the will are required to sign the alteration. Presumably, new witnesses will suffice provided that the requirements of s9 are complied with. Under the authority of *Blewitt* (1880) 5 PD 116 the witnesses need only subscribe their initials to the alteration. (As this would be sufficient for the purposes of the witnessing of a complete will under s9 of the Wills Act.)

The section does, however, recognise the futility of trying to ignore obliterations in the will which have had the effect of making the words or effect of the will before the alteration 'not apparent'. Thus, if the testator scribbled over a clause in his will, pasted a strip of paper over it or scratched it out so that it was impossible to decipher afterwards, these acts would, if accompanied by *animus revocandi*, amount to effective obliterations and revocation of the parts of the will concerned. In *In the goods of Horsford* (1874) LR 3 P & D 211, Sir James Hannen said of this part of the section:

> 'I think it is impossible to read the words of the statute and not to say that it was the intention of the legislature that, if a testator shall take such pains to obliterate certain passages in his will, and shall so effectually accomplish his purpose that those passages cannot be made out on the face of the instrument itself, it shall be a revocation as good and as valid as if done according to the stricter forms mentioned in the Act.'

The test laid down in the cases to determine whether the words in a will are 'not apparent' is based on whether an expert can decipher them by natural means, that is, by inspecting the document in the condition it was left by the testator. See *In b Ibbetson* (1839) 2 Curt 337. It is permissible in the course of such inspection to hold the document up to the light and to use magnifying glasses but this is as far as the inspection can go. In *In the goods of Horsford* Sir James Hannen said:

> '... it has not been the practice to adopt any means of ascertaining what the words attempted to be obliterated were, other than mere inspection by the aid of glasses. Chemical agents have not been resorted to in order to remove any portion of the obscuring ink, and I do not think it would be proper to adopt such means.'

It is not even permissible to use such devices as infra-red photography to discover what is beneath the obliteration. In *In b Itter* [1950] P 130 the words beneath the obliteration were deciphered using such means but Ormerod J refused to admit them to probate for the reasons given by Sir H J Fust in *Townley* v *Watson* (1844) 3 Curt 761, who said 'apparent' must mean apparent on the face of the 'instrument itself'. Ormerod J then added:

> 'If the words of the document can be read by looking at the document itself, then I think that they are apparent within the meaning of the section, however elaborate may be the devices used to assist the eye and however skilled the eye which is being used, but if they

can only be read by creating a new document, as in this case by producing a photograph of the original writing on the codicil then I cannot find that the words are apparent. They may be discoverable ... but that is not the word used in the section .'

Obliterations must be accompanied by an intention to revoke the part concerned. If the obliteration was duly executed this would be presumed. However, cases may arise where it is clear that the obliteration was made accidentally as where the testator spills ink over his will. See *Townley* v *Watson* (1844) 3 Curt 761. In such circumstances it is permissible to use any means available in order to discover what the words were, for example, chemicals or infra-red photography. See *In b Itter*.

7.3 Conditional obliterations

Words in a will may only have been obliterated subject to certain conditions taking effect. If they do not occur then the obliteration will not operate as a revocation of that part of the will. Thus, if the testator pasted strips of paper over legacies in his will leaving the names of the legatees untouched, it may be possible to conclude that he had intended to revoke only on the substitution of new amounts. See *In b Horsford* ; *In b McCabe* (1873) 3 P & D 94.

In *In b Itter* [1950] P 130 the testatrix pasted strips of paper over the amounts of certain legacies in her will and wrote on them new amounts. The new amounts were signed by her but they were not attested. It was impossible to decipher the figures beneath the strips by natural means. The question arose whether it was possible to apply the doctrine of conditional revocation.

Held: because the testatrix had not pasted strips of paper over the names of the legatees, it was possible to infer that she had intended to revoke the original amounts only if the new amounts were effectively substituted.

Once it is clear that there was only conditional revocation it is permissible to use any means available to find out the words or figures obliterated. Thus, chemicals can be used to remove pasted strips. See *In b Gilbert* [1893] P 183.

7.4 Alterations before execution

The words of s21 refer to alterations made to the will after execution and therefore do not apply to alterations made before execution. However, there is a rebuttable presumption that all alterations were made after execution so as to bring them within s21. See *Cooper* v *Bockett* (1846) 4 Moo PC 419. The presumption therefore makes it highly advisable to attest all alterations, wherever made, so as to avoid difficulty. However, the presumption may be rebutted by evidence from the will itself, for example, where later parts of the will refer to the alteration, or extrinsic evidence. Thus, in *Keigwin* v *Keigwin* (1843) 3 Curt 607 evidence was heard from the draftsman of the will, while in *In the Estate of Oates* [1946] 2 All ER 735 the court referred to a draft of the will made before the will itself. The attesting witness can give evidence to rebut the presumption and under the Civil Evidence Act 1968, declarations by the testator that he made the alterations before executing the will are admissible.

If the alterations were made after the will was executed but before it was, for some reason re-executed, then the presumption just referred to applies. See *In b Shearn* (1880) 50 LJP 15. Sometimes an alteration will have been made after execution but before re-execution; in such circumstances it will be admitted to probate if the presumption is rebutted. See *In b Shearn*.

Where a codicil is made to a will it will have the effect of republishing it (as will re-execution) and confirming it at the time of the execution of the codicil. Thus, the will will for most purposes be brought forward and read as if made at the date of execution of the codicil. This can affect unattested alterations in the will and, if the normal principle on the effect of codicils were applied to unattested alterations made before the execution of the codicil, they would be valid. However, there is, again, a presumption that an unattested alteration in the will was made after the execution of the codicil. See *In b Sykes* (1873) LR 3 P & D 26. The presumption is rebuttable and in *In b Sykes* it was rebutted by evidence of a statement made by the testator. Further the authority of *Re Hay* [1904] 1 Ch 317 held that a codicil cannot give effect to an unattested alteration unless the codicil actually refers to that alteration. This follows a similar principle to the rules relevant to incorporation by reference.

7.5 Method of execution of s21 alteration

There is some disagreement over the method whereby alterations to a will are re-executed. The section seems to require that there be a full re-execution of the altered part of the will adding the testator's signature plus the signatures of the witnesses. Although the case of *Blewitt* seems to allow the initials of the executing parties to be used instead of full signatures, it is far from clear whether the parties can simply acknowledge their existing signatures on the document so as to give validity to the alteration. Under the case of *Re Dewell* (1853) 1 Ecc & Ad 103 an acknowledgement of existing signatures was accepted for the purposes of s21, but the later case of *Shearn* (1880) 50 LJP 15 did not accept the acknowledgements of existing signatures as valid. Now that a witness has the statutory power to acknowledge his existing signature under s9(d) of the Wills Act 1837 (as amended by the Administration of Justice Act 1982) the situation seems far from clear in relation to the interreaction between the new s9 and the existing s21 of the Wills Act.

As noted, alterations and codicils must comply with the Wills Act 1837, the purpose of which are to ensure that the genuine intentions of the testator be given proper effect and to exclude any possibilities of fraud, undue influence and the like. However, lack of these formalities themselves may interfere with what is obviously the testator's genuine intent. There have been occasions when the document in question is upheld by the court because of its obvious intent and with undoubtedly much effort on the part of the judge, despite the documents incorrect form. This benefit should, however, not be relied upon and never substitute for the necessarily meticulous drafting of wills and or codicils.

It was due to the lack of compliance with s21 of the Wills Act 1837 that the testator's amended will failed in the case of *In re White (deceased), Barker* v *Gribble and Another* [1991] Ch 1. The facts were stated in the judgment as follows. John G White validly executed a will on 2 January 1981 which provided that his executor (and first defendant in this case) Mr Gribble a 47 per cent share of the residue of his estate, 12 per cent to Mr Guy Williams (the second defendant), and 4.6 per cent to Mr Frederick Barker (the plaintiff). Mr White attempted to alter this will in December 1984 by reading the alterations to Mr Williams who wrote them on to the original will. Mr White checked it and then wrote at the bottom of the last page 'Alterations to Will dated 14.12.84 Witnesses'. It was then signed by Mr Williams and Mr Lancaster who was a beneficiary of a 0.6 per cent share. Mr White did not sign it again. The effect of these alterations would substantially increase the plaintiffs' share, reduce the share of the first defendant, and completely delete any share to the second defendant because of the rule (s15 of the Wills Act) that a beneficiary cannot also be an attesting witness.

There are two relevant provisions that allow alterations or amendments to become effective. Section 9 of the Wills Act 1837 (as substituted by s17 of the Administration of Justice Act 1982) applies if the amendments rise to the point of creating a new will, whereas s21 of the Wills Act of 1837 permits them as valid alterations alone. Section 21 requires alterations to be executed in a manner proper for the execution of a will, that is, all requirements of s9. Buckley J stated in *Re Hay* [1904] 1 Ch 317, 321: 'it is quite plain that an alteration in a duly executed will made after the execution thereof is not effective unless the alteration is executed in the manner required by the statute for the execution of the will'. Sections 9 and 21 alterations require that the will must be 'signed by the testator, or by some other person in his presence and by his direction'. Mr White or anyone on his behalf, did not sign the alterations and thus they are invalid as to s21.

As seen earlier s9 has four requirements all of which must be satisfied if the alterations are to be deemed a valid new will. First, s9(a) requires the will be in writing and signed by the testator. Mr White had signed his will in 1981; however, the will as altered in 1984 is now a completely different document. It was held that the 1981 signature did not meet the requirements of a signature for purposes of the '1984 will' because it was in no way part of the execution of the '1984 will'.

Although s17 of the Administration of Justice Act 1982 does not limit valid signatures to being located at the foot of the will, s9(b) of the Wills Act 1837 upholds the requirement that the actual time of the signing be subsequent to the drafting of the will. If there is not evidence to prove proper and timely execution, a will or codicil may fail to satisfy s9(b). However, see *Wood* v *Smith* [1992] 3 All ER 556 (CA).

Next, s9(b) states: 'no will shall be valid unless … it appears that the testator intended by his signature to give effect to the will'. It was not found that in 1981 Mr White had intended to give effect to the 1984 alterations either by the act of signing or by the presentation of his signature.

Section 9(d) states: 'No will shall be valid unless … each witness … attests and signs the will … in the presence of the testator'. The evidence in this case is inconclusive as to whether the 1984 witnesses were attesting the entire document or only the alterations. The court therefore looked to the document itself and found that the witnesses had attested only the alterations, not the entire will because the testator had written 'Alterations to Will', and not 'Altered Will'. It was held in *In the goods of Martin* (1849) 1 Rob Ecc Rep 712, 714 and *In the goods of Shearn* (1880) 29 WR 445, that when there is no conclusive evidence as to what the witnesses are attesting, that they are attesting alterations only.

Section 9(c) requires that the testator actually sign in the presence of the 1984 witnesses or acknowledge his signature in their presence. It cannot be determined whether Mr White acknowledged his signature to Mr Williams and Mr Lancaster and thus it is yet undetermined whether s9(c) has been satisfied.

Although Mr White's actions presented a logical and common sense presentation of his intent, the failings of three conditions of s9 of the Wills Act 1837 caused this altered will to be invalid and the original unamended will to be admitted to probate.

Another case that illustrates the issue of whether or not the court should pronounce in favour of a will in spite of the testator's failure to comply with the formal rules about execution is the case of *Re Finnemore* [1991] 1 WLR 793.

The testator had made three wills in succession. Each one contained substantial gifts, in identical form, to X. Also, each one contained a clause revoking previous wills. The first will had no problem, but the second and third wills were witnesses by X's husband. On the face of it X was deprived of any benefit: she could not claim under the last – the third – will since her husband had witnessed it as a result of s15 of the Wills Act 1837. Further she was concerned that she could not claim under the first will because it had been revoked.

Held: the revocation clauses in the second and third wills could be read distributively and, therefore, under the doctrine of dependent relative revocation, the gifts to X in the first will remained unrevoked.

8

Revival and Republication

8.1 Revival

8.2 Republication

8.1 Revival

A testator who has revoked his will either with or without making a new one, may wish to revive that will for some reason. One alteration is for him to write out the revoked will all over again and execute it in accordance with s9. However, this is cumbersome and unnecessary, especially if no changes are to be made in the document. The testator can instead take advantage of the provisions of s22 of the Wills Act 1837 which provides:

> 'No will or codicil or any part thereof, which shall be in any manner revoked, shall be revived otherwise than by the re-execution thereof, or by a codicil executed in manner hereinbefore required, and showing an intention to revive the same; and when any will or codicil shall be partly revoked, and afterwards wholly revoked, shall be revived, such revival shall not extend to so much thereof as shall have been revoked before the revocation of the whole thereof, unless an intention to the contrary shall be shown.'

Under s22 the testator is limited to reviving the revoked will by two methods only:

1. by re-executing the revoked will in accordance with the provisions of s9; or
2. by executing a codicil which shows an intention to revive the revoked will.

The cases make it clear that no other method of revival exists. Thus, in *Marsh* v *Marsh* (1860) 1 Sw & Tr 528 it was held that attaching a codicil to a revoked will by means of tape was no evidence in itself of an intention to revive the will. In *In b Hodgkinson* [1893] P 339 it was held that an earlier will could not be revived merely by the revocation of a later one. Thus, where the testator left all his property to one person by his first will and later made another will leaving all his property to a different person, the earlier will was revoked by implication by the later will and it was not revived by the mere revocation of the later will.

Where a codicil has been executed to revive a will, s22 requires that it should show an intention to revive the same. In *In b Steele* (1868) LR 1 P & D 575, Sir J P Wilde dealt with this particular requirement. He pointed out that prior to the Wills

Act 1837, if a codicil was executed it had two effects: (1) to affirm the existence of the will and, (2) to republish or affirm its validity. It was, therefore, before the Act, an inference which the law drew from the making of the codicil, that the testator intended to re-affirm his will and, if the will had been revoked by re-affirming it, to revive it. This theory could not hold good after the passing of s22 because:

> 'If the merely declaring that a particular paper was to be taken as a codicil to a particular will was all that the legislature required when it enacted that the codicil should "show an intention to revive" a revoked will, the words "showing an intention to revive the same" were quite needless, for every will so showed it. I therefore infer that the legislature meant that the intention of which it speaks should appear on the face of the codicil, either by express words referring to a will as revoked and importing an intention to revive the same, or by a disposition of the testator's property inconsistent with any other intention, or by some other expressions conveying to the mind of the court, with reasonable certainty, the existence of the intention in question.' (Per Sir J P Wilde)

The following decisions illustrate the approach to codicils which it is claimed 'show an intention to revive'.

In *In b Steele* (1868) LR 1 P & D 575 the testator made a will dated 16 January 1866. On 25 October 1866 he made a new will which revoked the earlier will. On 12 January 1868 the testator executed a codicil 'to his last will and testament which bears the date the 16th day of January last past', that is, 16 January 1867. The codicil also affirmed the testator's 'last will'.

Held: the codicil could not be taken as reviving the will dated 16 January 1866 for, although it contained latent ambiguity permitting the court to look at evidence of intention, this evidence did not show any intention to revoke the October will and revive the January will. The October will would be admitted to probate with the codicil.

In *Re Baker* [1929] 1 Ch 668 the testatrix made a will and a codicil in 1893. In 1907 she made another will revoking the former will and the codicil. In 1911 she made a codicil to the will of 1907. In 1921 she made another codicil which referred only to the will and the codicil of 1893, altered some of the provisions of that will, and otherwise confirmed the will and the codicil.

Held: the codicil of 1921 revoked the will of 1907 and the codicil of 1911 and republished the will and codicil of 1893; the dispositions contained in it were inconsistent with any other intention.

In *Re Dear* [1975] 2 NZLR 254 the testatrix made her first will in 1942 and then expressly revoked it by a later subsequent will in 1950. She then executed a codicil in 1962 which referred to the previously revoked will of 1942. Did this codicil therefore revive the 1942 will?

Held (by Wild CJ, Richmond J and Woodhouse J): the testatrix's reference in her codicil was insufficient to revive the earlier will of 1942 following *In b Steele*. The reference merely created an ambiguity but as there was no evidence to solve the ambiguity the court ruled in the circumstances that there was no revival.

Revival of a will by a codicil only applies where the document containing the former will is still in existence as may be the case where it was revoked by marriage, a revocation clause in a later will or by implication. It cannot be used where the will was revoked by destruction or where subsequent to revocation by the other means it is destroyed. This proposition is supported by dicta of Sir Cresswell Cresswell in *Rogers* v *Goodenough* (1862) 25 Sw & Tr 342, where he held that a codicil could not revive a will which had no existence. The reasons given were:

> 'When the instrument had been destroyed, it no longer existed either in law or in act; it did not exist as a will from the time the second will was executed; it no longer existed as a written instrument, as a paper writing, from the time it was burnt. Not being either a will or a writing, how could it again become a will? That question seems to be decided by the statute; the 9th section says "that no will shall be valid unless it be in writing, and executed in the manner hereinafter mentioned". It has been said that it could again become a will, because it was revived by the codicil; but it could not be revived in its original condition of a written instrument, and thus the very first thing required by the statute in order to make a will cannot be satisfied. It appears to me that the expression "no will shall be valid" applies equally to an original will and a revived will.'

A special provision is made in s22 for a will which is partly revoked and later wholly revoked. If such a will is revived then revival will only extend to such parts of the will as were effective before the whole was revoked. Thus, for example, if a testator made a will which originally left Blackacre to A, Whiteacre to B, and Greenacre to C but first revoked the gift to A and subsequently revoked the whole will, a revival would only breathe new life into the gifts to B and C. If the testator wished to revive the gift to A he would need to show a clear intention in this respect.

The main effect of revival is to bring the revoked will back into existence, but the effects go further. The revived will will be read as if it were made at the date of revival and not the date it was first drawn up. See s34 of the Wills Act 1837. This is dealt with in section 8.2. Unattested alterations in the received will may be effective through the fact of revival if the presumption that they were made after revival can be rebutted.

Often a will is revoked without the testator knowing of its revocation as where it is revoked by marriage. The question arises whether the testator can revive a will the revocation of which he is unaware of. The Malaysian authority of *Re Wan Kee Cheong* (1975) 2 MLJ 152 has held that a testator may revive a will previously revoked by his marriage even although he was unaware of the fact of revocation. There appears to be no English authority on the point.

8.2 Republication

Republication is a term which is, strictly, meaningless since the Wills Act 1837, since the process of publication of a will is no longer necessary. Section 13 of the Wills Act provides:

> 'Every will executed in manner hereinbefore required, shall be valid without any publication thereof.'

Publication was a declaration or other manifestation by the testator to the witnesses that the will was his. Republication arose where the testator reaffirmed his will in some way, for example, where he executed a codicil thereto. The use of the term republication has been subject to disapproval. In *Berkeley* v *Berkeley* [1946] AC 555 Lord Porte referred to it as 'an expression now meaningless, but still unhappily in use'. The term remains in use but it would appear to have taken on a different meaning, namely, to indicate a confirmation by the testator of his will.

Republication would appear to be only possible by the two methods laid down in s22 of the Wills Act, that is:

1. re-executing the will;
2. confirming the will by executing a codicil to this effect.

If either of these two methods are followed then republication will be implied if something can be found in the re-executed will or the codicil from which the inference can be drawn that, when making and re-executing or executing it, the testator considered the will as his will. This is illustrated by *Re Smith* (1890) 45 Ch D 632 in which a married woman made a will exercising a power of appointment under a marriage settlement in favour of her nephew, Richard. The will was of no effect at that time because it was made during her coverture, that is, marriage.

After her husband's death she executed a testamentary instrument disposing of shares in a gas company to her nephew, Oswald. This document made no reference whatever to the earlier will; if it had done so then the will could have been considered republished after the husband's death and effective. No inferences could be drawn upon which republication could be based. However, slight references will do, such as 'codicil to my will'. See *Skinner* v *Ogle* (1845) 1 Rob Ecc 363. Or where a codicil is executed describing itself as a codicil to a particular will. See *Re Harvey* [1947] Ch 285.

Republication has several important effects on the will. The most important of these is that the will is brought down to date of republication. In *Goonewardene* v *Goonewardene* [1931] AC 647 it was said of republication in relation to a codicil:

'The effect of confirming a will by codicil is to bring the will down to the date of the codicil, and to effect the same disposition of the testator's property as would have been effected if the testator had at the date of the codicil made a new will containing the same dispositions as in the original will but with the alterations introduced by the codicil.'

This statement of the law owes its origins to the provisions of s34 of the Wills Act which, *inter alia*, provides:

'... every will re-executed or republished or revived by any codicil shall for the purposes of this Act be deemed to have been made at the time at which the same shall be so re-executed, republished or revived'.

The other effects of republication flow from the fact that the will is deemed to have been made at the date of republication. They are as follows.

Construction

Republication may have the effect of making references in the will to persons or to property at the date of republication rather than at the date of the will. However, it must be emphasised that a reference to a married person in a will cannot be changed by republication. Thus, if a testator leaves Blackacre to X by his will and X predeceases the testator, the gift lapses. See *Re Wood's Will* (1861) 29 Beav 236. But if the reference is not to a named beneficiary, but instead refers to a relationship to the testator or some other person, republication may extend the operation of the will to persons not contemplated when the will was made as is illustrated by the following case.

In *Re Hardyman* [1925] 1 Ch 287 the testatrix made a will in 1893 by which she bequeathed, *inter alia*, a legacy of £5,000 'in trust for my cousin, his children and his wife'. The cousin of the testatrix was then married to his first wife, who died in January 1901. In November 1901, the testatrix, with the knowledge of the death of her cousin's first wife, made a codicil to her will. The codicil contained no reference to the bequest of £5,000. In 1903 the cousin of the testatrix remarried. The question arose whether the reference to the cousin's wife should be construed as to his first or to his second wife.

Held: the will and the codicil had to be read together and it appeared that after republication of the will the reference was to any lady whom the cousin might marry and not to the first wife. The second wife was therefore entitled to an interest.

References to property may also be altered by republication. This is particularly important in the case of specific legacies which would otherwise be considered to have adeemed because the testator has disposed of their subject matter before his death. Again, it must be emphasised that the general rule here is that the mere republication of a will does not revive a legacy adeemed in the interval. See *Cowper v Mantell (No 1)* (1856) 22 Beav 223. However, the provisions of s24 of the Wills Act provide:

> 'Every will shall be construed, with reference to the real estate and personal estate comprised in it, to speak and take effect as if it had been executed immediately before the death of the testator, unless a contrary intention shall appear.'

If s24 applies to a legacy, republication will have no effect on it. However, if the testator has referred to the subject matter of a legacy in a manner which makes it clear that he is referring to property he possesses at the date of making the will, the republication may effect the legacy and cause the republished will to attach to property other than that in existence at the date the will was made, as the following cases illustrate.

In *Re Champion* [1893] 1 Ch 101 the testator made his will in April 1873 by which he devised, *inter alia*, a freehold cottage and the land thereto belonging 'now in my occupation' to trustees upon trust for sale for his wife for life and then to his children in equal shares. In September 1873 he purchased two fields adjoining the cottage, and occupied them with the cottage until his death. In 1877 he executed a codicil to his will by which he appointed different executors and in all other respects confirmed his will. The question arose whether the fields purchased in September 1873 passed with the cottage.

Held: on reading the will as a whole, the testator showed that he used the word 'now' with reference to the date of the will. Since the will had been republished the reference to 'now' meant at the date of republication and the fields purchased in September 1893 passed together with the freehold cottage.

In *Re Reeves* [1928] Ch 351 the testator made his will in 1921 and by it he gave to his daughter 'all my interest in my present lease' of his house. At the date of the will the lease had an unexpired term of 3 years 6 months. After the lease expired the testator took a new lease on the house for 12 years and in 1925, after he had obtained the new lease, he executed a codicil confirming his will.

Held: the new lease passed to the daughter under the will. The codicil had republished the will and, therefore, on reading it as made in 1925, it referred to the new lease.

Alterations

Where an unattested alteration is made to a will after execution but before republication then the alteration will be admitted to probate on the presumption that it was made after the execution of the codicil being rebutted. See *In b Sykes* (1873) LR 3 P & D 26.

Incorporation by reference

Republication may have the effect of validly incorporating a document into the will where this has not been effectively done by the will itself. Thus, if the document comes into existence after the will, it may be incorporated by the codicil provided the codicil satisfies the other necessary conditions for incorporation. See *In b Hunt* (1853) 17 Jur 720. A will or codicil which is ineffective because it has not been properly executed may be incorporated into a codicil by reference and therefore become effective. Thus, in *In b Heathcote* (1881) 6 PD 30, the testatrix's will was in itself invalid but a codicil was executed which was described as 'a codicil to the last will and testament' of the testatrix. This was held to incorporate the will into the codicil on the court being satisfied that the testatrix had no other will.

Witnessing the will

A witness to a will, or the spouse of a witness are deprived of benefits thereunder by s15 of the Wills Act. However, if the will under which the witness or his spouse lost the benefit is republished and other persons act as witnesses for the purpose of republication then they will be able to obtain their benefits by virtue of the codicil effecting republication. See *Anderson* v *Anderson* (1872) LR 13 Eq 381.

Powers of appointment

A general power of appointment can be exercised by the donee of the power at any time, even before the power has been created. However, a special power cannot be exercised by the donee of the power until it has been granted to him. Therefore, the exercise of such a power prior to its being granted is ineffective. But if a testator given a special power exercises it before that time, any appointment may be saved by republication under a codicil. See *Re Blackburn* (1890) 43 Ch D 75.

Limitations of republication

There are limitations on the extent to which the court is prepared to apply republication and, in particular, the principle will not be applied in a manner which defeats the testator's intentions. In an Irish decision, *Re Moore* (1907) 1 IR 315, Barton J said:

> '... the courts have always treated the principle that republication makes the will speak as if it had been re-executed at the date of the codicil not as a rigid formula or technical rule, but as a useful flexible instrument for effectuating a testator's intentions'.

Thus, in *Re Moore*, the court refused to apply republication in a manner which would lead to a gift in the will itself being defeated by a codicil republishing the will. In *In b Rawlins* (1879) 48 LJP 64 the court also refused to apply republication in a manner which would cause a revocation clause in a will to defeat a codicil thereto. In that case the testator made a will containing a revocation clause revoking all previous testamentary provisions, and subsequently he executed a codicil. After both of these documents the testator decided to alter a clause in his will and he re-executed the will. Arguments to the effect that the revocation clause in the will as republished had revoked the earlier codicil were rejected. The re-execution was taken as a confirmation of the will and not a revocation of the will.

The limitations of republication were also considered in the Australian High Court decision in *Fairweather* v *Fairweather* (1944) 69 CLR 121. In this case the testator made a will in 1927 leaving his son a property known as 'Birnell Court' subject to a mortgage of £1,000 thereon. In 1928 the testator sold 'Birnell Court' to his son for £1,500. In 1929 he executed a codicil appointing a new executor and confirming the will and in 1936 he made another codicil making some alterations but not referring to Birnell Court and confirming the will again. The son argued that the effect of the codicils was to show that the testator intended him to have whatever interest he had in the property at his death, including the proceeds of sale. This was rejected and Latham CJ added:

> '... the true doctrine is that the confirmation of a will by a codicil republishes the will, but it only republishes so much of the will as still represents the will of the testator. If the words contained in the will have been deprived of their operation, either by an intermediate codicil, or by events which have occurred before the execution of the later codicil the effect of which is in question, then the confirmation of the will operates only to repeat so much of the will as was effective at the date of the later codicil'.

9

Legacies and Devises and Their Failure

9.1 Legacies and devises

The classification of legacies and devises is important because of the doctrines of ademption and abatement. Due to these doctrines a distinction is draw between specific, general and demonstrative legacies. The types of legacies were referred to by Viscount Haldane LC in *Walford* v *Walford* [1912] AC 658 in the following terms:

> 'Legacies are of three kinds: there is the specific legacy which is a specific res secured under the testator's will on his death; and, of course, it does not abate if the rest of the assets are insufficient for the payment of general legacies; but it has this disadvantage, that if the particular res which is the subject of the specific legacy disappears in the meantime, then the legatee gets nothing. The class of legacy at the other extreme is a general legacy which comes out of the residue and which abates if the residue is insufficient, but which, *prima facie*, under a rule of administration of the court, carries interest as from a year after the testator's death. There is an intermediate class of legacy, namely a demonstrative legacy, which is simply a general legacy, with the quality attached to it that it is directed to be paid out of a specific fund, and, if there is a shortage of assets and that fund remains, is paid out of that fund without abating. On the other hand if the fund does disappear, then it has this advantage over a specific legacy, that it is still payable, in virtue

111

of its quality of a general legacy, out of the testator's residue along with other general legacies'.

Specific legacies

1. A specific legacy is a gift by will of a particular part of the testator's personal estate: 'I give my Mini Metro Reg WYT 834Z to Y'. The particular thing given must be part of the testator's estate at his death and the gift must be described in such a way as to sever or distinguish it from the rest of the estate. The characteristics of a specific legacy were explained by Jessel MR in *Bothamley* v *Sherson* (1875) LR 20 Eq 304 in the following terms:

> 'In the first place it is a part of the testator's property. A general bequest may or may not be part of the testator's property ... In the next place, it must be a part emphatically, as distinguished from the whole. It must be what is sometimes called a severed or distinguished part. It must not be the whole, in the meaning of the totality of the testator's property, or the totality of the general residue of his property after having given legacies out of it.'

2. A gift of a particular thing, for instance, of shares of certain types, is not a specific legacy if there is nothing on the face of the will to indicate that the testator was referring to shares belonging to him, even though he may have in fact owned the shares mentioned. In *Re Willcocks* [1921] 2 Ch 237 the fact that the testator owned exactly the specific amount of shares as she had given, did not make the gift specific since there was nothing on the face of the will indicating that she intended to give those specific shares. See also *Re Gage* [1934] 1 Ch 536.

3. A gift of a part of a specified fund has been held to be specific. See *Ford* v *Fleming* (1728) 2 PW 469. Also a gift of money 'out of' specific money, or stock 'out of' specific stock, is specific. This must not be confused with a gift of money out of stock which is not specific, but demonstrative. See *Deane* v *Fest* (1803) 9 Ves 146.

4. A gift of the whole of the testator's personal estate may be specific. See *Roffe* v *Early* (1873) 42 LJ Ch 472. However, where a testator gave his personal estate to A, with certain exceptions, the gift was held not to be specific. See *Robertson* v *Broadbent* (1883) 8 App Cas 812. The same applies where the bequest is either preceded or followed by an enumeration of particular articles. See *Bothamley* v *Sherson* (1875) LR 20 Eq 304. However, where the enumeration of articles follows a gift of the residue the articles may be specific. See *Bethune* v *Kennedy* (1835) 1 M & Cr 114.

General legacies

1. A general legacy is a gift which is not a bequest of any specific part of the testator's estate. The gift is therefore to be provided out of the testator's general estate. The important thing about a general legacy is that it need not actually be

part of testator's estate. Thus a gift of a 'Mini Metro to X', need not be part of the estate. As Jessel MR said in *Bothamley* v *Sherson*, 'in which case the testator's executors must raise the money or stock' or, in our example, purchase the car. In other words, a general legacy does not refer to the actual state of the testator's property.

2. Because of the effect of the doctrine of ademption on specific legacies the court leans strongly in favour of general and not specific legacies. Thus, if there is some doubt as to which side of the line a legacy falls on it will usually be treated as a general legacy. In *Re O'Connor* [1948] 1 Ch 628 the testator bequeathed 10,000 £1 preference shares in his own company to his son and in a later clause in his will bequeathed a series of pecuniary legacies. At his death the testator had only 9,000 preference shares in the company, he was trustee of another 25,000 such shares under a family trust, and owned 85,000 ordinary shares. Roxburgh J concluded that the gift should be treated as a general legacy because (1) there was nothing in the words of the gift describing the shares as specific property of the testator, and (2) because on the evidence the testator never owned 10,000 such shares, either when he made the will or at his death.

Demonstrative legacies

1. A demonstrative legacy is 'in its nature a general legacy but there is a particular fund pointed out to satisfy it'. Per Lord Thurlow LC in *Ashburner* v *MacGuire* (1786) 2 Bro CC 108. Thus '£300 to John out of my account at the Nat West', is demonstrative.

   A demonstrative legacy has, therefore, two parts. The reason why its nature is general is that the payment of the legacy is of primary importance while the fund pointed to is only of secondary importance. This twofold property of a demonstrative legacy is important when considering the doctrines of ademption and abatement.

2. Sometimes questions of construction may arise as to whether a legacy payable out of a specified fund is a demonstrative legacy or is given only as a portion of the specified fund. This problem arose in *Paget* v *Huish* (1863) 1 H & M 663 where the testator specified five annuities to be paid out of the rents of his real estate. The question arose whether the amounts of the annuities could only be paid out of the rents or whether they could be treated as demonstrative legacies so that any deficiency could be made good from the general estate. Page-Wood VC concluded that on the wording of the will the gifts must be treated as demonstrative legacies.

Pecuniary legacies

A general legacy of money is usually called a pecuniary legacy. But s55(1)(ix) of the AEA 1925 gives an extended meaning to the term. This definition, however, seems to be only applicable for the purposes of the Act. *Re O'Connor* [1948] Ch 628 seems to bear this out, where a direction to pay pecuniary legacies out of the residue was held not to cover the payment of a general legacy of shares.

Devises

There are two types of devise. The essential nature of any devise is that it deals solely with the real estate of the testator.

Specific devises

A specific devise is a gift of real property under a will. The gift must be part of the testator's estate at his death and it must be described in such a way as to sever or distinguish it from the rest of the estate. Thus, 'My house, No 1 Fuller Street, London' or, 'My house in the county of Dyfed', are specific devises. Such a devise passes all benefits and burdens which the testator had in the property.

General or residuary devises

A general devise, or preferably a residuary devise, is a gift of real property by description. Thus, gifts of 'all my farms to X' or 'all my real property to Y' are residuary devises. Under s37 of the Wills Act 1837 a residuary devise includes any real estate over which the testator has a power of appointment, and such a devise shall operate as an execution of that power, unless there is a contrary intention on the face of the will.

Annuities

An annuity is, in general, a legacy and can be defined as a legacy of money payable by instalments. There are three basic types of annuities.

Specific annuities

A specific annuity is a gift of an already existing annuity which is in existence at the testator's death. Thus, 'I give to A the perpetual annuity to which I am entitled under X's will'. It must be noted that such an annuity can only be given if it continues after the testator's death; hence it must be perpetual or charged on land as a rent charge – but as to the latter see the Rent Charges Act 1976 for the restrictions on any subsequent creation of a rent charge.

General annuities

General annuities are annuities to be paid out of the testator's general estate. Thus 'I give to A during his life an annuity of £1,000 to begin from my death payable by equal quarterly instalments'.

Demonstrative annuities

These are annuities which are by their nature general annuities, but which are to be primarily out of a specific fund or 'specific part of the testator's property'. See *Paget v Huish* (1863) 1 H & M 663.

There are, however, two problems associated with annuities. First, is the annuity payable out of capital if the income is insufficient to meet it? Usually the capital can be resorted to if the income is insufficient, because the annuity is regarded as a charge on the whole fund as in the like case of a pecuniary legacy. See *Re Coller's Deed Trusts* [1939] Ch 277, 280. However, in the event of the annuity being charged on the capital as well as the income, and a deficiency has been made good out of the capital in any year, there is no right to recoup capital out of future income. See *Re Croxon* [1915] 2 Ch 290.

The second problem is how long will the annuity last? In the first instance this depends upon the true construction of the will. If it is simply 'to A' then it is for A's lifetime only. *Blewitt* v *Roberts* (1841) Cr & Ph 274. However, if the annuity is given to a corporation or an incorporated body capable of existing indefinitely then the annuity is *prima facie* perpetual. See *Re Jones* [1950] 2 All ER 239.

The rule that an annuitant is not entitled to the capitalised value has a number of exceptions.

1. Where the testator directs that an annuity be purchased for A for his life. See *Stokes* v *Cheek* (1860) 28 Beav 620. This is so because, it is argued, the annuitant could always sell his annuity once it had been purchased for him.
2. Where the trustees of an estate have the power to pay the purchase money of an annuity to A, A may take that money.
3. Where the estate is insufficient to pay pecuniary legacies in full and to secure the annuities, the annuitant is entitled to receive the capital sum calculated on the actuarial value of the annuity, with an abatement for the shortfall on the annuities and the legacies. See *Re Farmer* [1939] 1 All ER 319, 322.

This rule only applies where there are pecuniary legacies (or a pecuniary legacy) and not where there is a single annuity and no other legacy payable '*pari passu*' with it, and will also not apply where the will directs otherwise, either expressly or impliedly.

The date from which annuities are payable begins to run from the death of the testator. This is subject to any direction by the testator as to when the annuity should be paid, that is, 'to be paid monthly'.

There is no interest payable on arrears of an annuity (see *Re Earl of Berkeley* [1968] Ch 744) unless the non-payment of the annuity is the fault of those who hold the fund out of which it is to be paid.

9.2 The doctrine of ademption

A specific devise or a specific legacy or annuity fails by ademption if at the testator's death the subject-matter of the gifts has been destroyed or converted into something else by an act of the testator. A legacy of specific chattels is adeemed if they are sold during the testator's lifetime (*Ashburner* v *MacGuire* (1786) 2 Bro CC 108) or if they are lost or destroyed during or at the testator's death. As a general rule, even if the chattels are insured, the legatee has no right to the insurance monies. See *Durrant* v *Friend* (1851) 5 De G & S 343. The same applies to a specific devise of land which is afterwards sold, even though the proceeds may be impressed with a trust for re-investment in land. See *Re Bagot's Settlement* (1862) 31 LJ Ch 772.

As ademption is applicable whatever the testator's intention (*Re Slater* [1907] 1 Ch 665) it follows that a codicil republishing the will does not have the effect of passing to the legatee anything into which the gift may have been converted. See *Drinkwater* v *Falconer* (1755) 2 Ves Sen 623.

Specific legacies of stocks and shares

In the case of the testator selling the whole or part of the securities, the gift will adeem either wholly or 'pro tanto'. See *Ashburner* v *MacGuire*, above. Of course, the fact that the testator may subsequently purchase replacement securities will not revive the gift, since these will not be the specified gift. See *Re Gibson* (1866) LR 2 Eq 669.

Where there has been a change in name and form only which leaves the thing itself substantially the same, there is no ademption. Thus, in *Re Leeming* [1912] 1 Ch 828, where the testator had received 20 £5 preference shares and 20 £5 ordinary shares in the place of his original 10 £4 shares, it was held that the gift did not adeem, since there had been a change in name and form only. The same has been held in cases where the company has converted its shares into stock (*Oakes* v *Oakes* (1852) 9 Ha 666) and also where there has been a sub-division of the company shares as in *Re Clifford* [1912] 1 Ch 29. *Re Slater* (above) illustrates the reverse case, where a testator had bequeathed the interest arising from money invested in the Lambeth Waterworks Company. The company had been acquired by the Metropolitan Water Board under an Act of Parliament. This provided for compensation to be paid either in stock or money. The testator took the stock in the new company. It was held that the gift had adeemed. There was an absolute annihilation and destruction of the interest in the Lambeth Waterworks Company and therefore the new stock was substantially different from the old. These principles (from *Oakes* v *Oakes* and *Re Slater*) are general principles and have been applied in cases not concerning company takeovers and reorganisation. In *Re Dorman* [1994] 1 All ER 804 the testatrix granted X a power of attorney to manage her affairs. X closed a deposit account at Barclays Bank plc and opened another account at the same bank to benefit from a higher interest rate. The issue was whether the gift of money in the original deposit account was adeemed by changing the account.

The court held that the gift was not adeemed as the change was not substantial but only a change in name and form.

If the legacy is a general legacy of shares it is convenient to add here that it will fail if the shares have ceased to exist at the testator's death because it is impossible to obtain the shares or ascertain their value. See *Robinson* v *Addison* (1840) 2 Beav 515; *Re Plowright* [1971] VR 128.

Specific legacies of debts

Where a testator makes a specific bequest of a debt and it is either wholly or partially repaid during his lifetime, the gift will adeem in full or *pro tanto*. See *Humphrey* v *Humphrey* (1788) 2 Cox 185 where Lord Thurlow said:

'The only rule to be adhered to is to see whether the subject of the specific bequest remained in specie at the time of the testator's death, for if it did not, then there must be an end of the bequest'.

If the specific bequest is of a debt which is owed by the beneficiary, then even if it is repaid by him, it will not necessarily adeem since this may have been designed to secure it. See *Ashton* v *Ashton* (1735) 3 P Wms 386; *Re Wedmore* [1907] 2 Ch 277.

Specific legacies of chattels in a particular place

Where chattels in a particular place, such as in a house, are bequeathed, and are subsequently removed to another place, the question arises as to whether the place is a substantive part of the bequest or merely an additional description of the items. In *Land* v *Devaynes* (1793) 4 Bro CC 537, it was held that a bequest of certain items in a particular place passed the items, since the place was merely an additional description, and not therefore an essential part of the gift. See also *Lord Brooke* v *Earl of Warwick* (1803) 2 De G & Sm 425. If the removal of the items is only temporary as, for example, in *Re Johnson* (1884) 26 Ch D 538, where the property was removed for safe keeping, then the gift does not adeem. See also *Domville* v *Taylor* (1863) 32 B 604. Similarly, a gift of furniture in a house, for example, will pass any furniture to be placed there. See *Rawlinson* v *Rawlinson* (1876) 3 Ch D 302.

The problem which arises as to whether something is permanently or temporarily removed was discussed in *Re Zouche* [1919] 2 Ch 178. In that instance certain items had been placed at the bank for safe keeping and certain books had been sent to the British Museum. It was decided that the period of time that the items had been out of the house showed that they were no longer considered part of the contents of the house, and in consequence the gift adeemed.

Ademption by contract

A contract of sale entered into by the testator after the date of the will, though not completed until after the testator's death, will cause the gift to adeem. See *Re*

Edwards [1958] Ch 168. The legatee is, however, entitled to enjoy the property until the completion of the sale or until such time as the sale ought reasonably to have been completed. See *Townley* v *Bedwell* (1808) 14 Ves 591. If however, the testator makes a binding contract for sale, giving the property away, before making the will then the beneficiary is entitled to the proceeds of sale. See *Re Calow* [1928] Ch 710. The same result is achieved if the testator having made his will and then entered into a contract, confirms the will by codicil, after or contemporaneously with the contract. See *Re Pyle* [1895] 1 Ch 724.

In *Re Sweeting (deceased)* [1988] 1 All ER 1016, by a will dated 18 July 1978, the testator devised to specific devisees under two separate bequests a plot of land (the yard) which adjoined his house. Three weeks before his death the testator exchanged two contracts of sale, one for the sale of the house and the other for the sale of the yard for £57,000, but he died before either contract was completed. The question which arose for decision was whether the specific gifts of the yard in the will were adeemed by the contracts of sale so that the proceeds of sale fell into residue, having regard to:

1. the uncompleted and conditional nature of the sale contracts; and
2. the rule that a specific bequest of real property subject to an option was adeemed by the exercise of the option after the testator's death.

The specific devisees contended that the rule did not apply to a conditional contract as was present here.

However, Nicholls J in the Chancery Division held that the specific bequests of the yard were adeemed by the contract for the sale of the yard, for the following reasons: since the testator's wife had given her consent to the sale the testator could have compelled her to furnish the releases and the application for cancellation of the land charge which existed. Accordingly, the contract was specifically enforceable by or against the testator and it followed that the fact that the contract for the sale of the land was conditional at the time of the testator's death did not prevent the specific bequests of the yard from being adeemed by the contract.

Further, the rule converting real property into personal property at a date subsequent to the testator's death with the effect that a gift of the real property in the testator's will was thereby adeemed was not confined to options but extended to conditional contracts. Consequently, if a testator entered into a conditional contract for the sale of real property before his death the fulfilment of the condition after his death had the effect that the property was converted into personalty, and any gift of the property in the testator's will was adeemed either by the contract or by the completion of the contract. It followed on the facts of this case that completion of the yard contract had the effect of converting the yard into personal property, the specific gifts of the yard in the testator's will were adeemed and the proceeds of sale of the yard fell into the testator's residuary estate.

Ademption by exercise of an option to purchase

Where a beneficiary is entitled to a specific gift of property which is later impressed with an option to purchase granted by the testator to a third party, the beneficiary is entitled to nothing even if the third party does not exercise the option after the testator's death. However, the beneficiary is entitled to the use of the property until the option is exercised. This is known as the rule in *Lawes* v *Bennett* (1785) 1 Cox 167.

However, if the option is impressed upon the property before the making of the gift the beneficiary is entitled to the price payable under the option. See *Drant* v *Vause* (1842) 1 Y & CC 580; *Weeding* v *Weeding* (1859) 1 J & H 424.

The date from which the will speaks

Specific gifts which speak as from death (s24 of the Wills Act 1837) do not strictly adeem. Thus a gift to X of 'the car which I own at my death', does not fail by ademption even though the testator may have changed his car since the date of the will. The gift is to be ascertained at the testator's death not at the date of the will and can therefore only fail if there is no car owned by the testator at his death. See further Construction of Wills (below).

Demonstrative and general legacies, and annuities

These types of gift are not subject to ademption since they are to be provided out of the general estate. See *Bothamley* v *Sherson* (1875) LR 20 Eq 304. However, it is possible that the testator's intention concerning a demonstrative gift may be such as to indicate that the legacy is only to be paid out of the specified fund. If the fund is either no longer in existence or is insufficient the gift will adeem either wholly or 'pro tanto'. See *Paget* v *Huish* (1863).

9.3 The doctrine of lapse

A devise or legacy lapses if the beneficiary predeceases the testator. See *Elliott* v *Davenport* (1705) 1 P Wms 83; 2 Vern 521. Although this is the major example of the operation of lapse, testamentary gifts often lapse for other reasons such as the witnessing of a will by a beneficiary, for example, *Re Cotton* (1923) 19 Tas LR 57; or disclaimer of the gift by the beneficiary. The doctrine is a consequence of the ambulatory nature of a testamentary document, which has no effect until the death of the testator.

Gifts to tenants in common

Where a gift is to several named persons as tenants in common, should any of the beneficiaries predecease the testator, then his share will lapse. In *Page* v *Page* (1728)

2 P Wms 489 the testator devised his estate to six relations equally. One of the six died before him; the legacy to that relation was a lapsed legacy.

Gifts to joint tenants and class gifts

Where a testator makes a gift to several named persons as joint tenants the gift will not lapse unless all the beneficiaries predecease the testator. Thus, where a testator makes a gift to 'A, B and C jointly', and B predeceases the testator, that share will not lapse but will be taken by the surviving beneficiaries, A and C. See *Morley v Bird* (1798) 3 Ves 629. Also where one of a number of joint tenants witnesses the will and thereby loses his benefit due to s15 of the Wills Act, the surviving remaining joint tenants who have not witnessed the will take the share of the one who acted as witness. This is seen in *Young v Davies* (1863) 2 Drew & Sm 167.

Where the testator makes a class gift, where the members of the class are to be ascertained at the date of the will or, subsequently, the doctrine of lapse does not apply. This is so whether the gift is to tenants in common or joint tenants. For example, 'To all my children living at my death, equally'. If at the date of the will the testator had four children, should one predecease him, his share will not lapse. This is because the gift is only applicable to those who enter that class. Since the class is to be ascertained at the testator's death, any child not living at that date does not even enter the class, and is therefore never within the ambit of the gift.

Power of appointment

Where there is a power of appointment exercised by will, the appointee of the power must survive the donee of the power in order to take, otherwise the power lapses. See *Duke of Marlborough v Lord Godolphin* (1759) 2 Ves 611.

Effect of a declaration against lapse

The doctrine of lapse cannot be excluded by a declaration that the gift will not lapse, unless it is clear that the gift is to go to the estate of the legatee. See *Re Ladd* [1932] 2 Ch 219.

However, if there is a clear substitutional gift then the gift does not lapse. For example, a gift 'to X, but should he predecease me, then to his estate' or 'to X, but if he predeceases me to any of his children living at my death and if any be dead to their issue per stirpes'. See *Sibley v Cook* (1747) 3 Atk 572; *Gittings v McDermot* (1834) 2 M & K 69. A declaration that the gift should vest on the execution of the will will not save it from lapse. See *Browne v Hope* (1872) LR 14 Eq 343.

The effect of republication

The fact that the testator may make a codicil republishing his will, does not save a gift from lapse if the beneficiary has predeceased the testator. It makes no difference that the codicil is made after the death of the beneficiary and will not make it take effect as a gift to his estate. See *Hutcheson* v *Hammond* (1790) 3 Bro CC 127.

It can, however, alter the construction of the will. In *Re Hardyman* [1925] Ch 287 it was held that the republication of the will had altered the construction of the phrase 'in trust for my cousin, his children and his wife', to include any person whom the beneficiary might marry. Although it had initially referred to the wife who was living, the republication had altered that to include any wife. However, had the first wife been named, then the republication would have had no effect and the gift would have lapsed. See *Re Hardyman* [1925] Ch 287.

Statutory presumption of survivorship

Before 1926 if two people died making it uncertain as to who had died first, it was a matter of proving who died first. In *Underwood* v *Wing* (1855) 4 De GM & G 633 where a husband gave property to his wife and, if she predeceased him, to A, and the wife gave property to her husband and, if he predeceased her, to A, and they were both swept off a ship by the same wave and were never seen again, it was for A to prove who had died first. As A could not so prove who deceased who, he was not entitled to anything, under either of the wills.

By s184 of the LPA 1925 where:

'... two or more persons have died in circumstances rendering it uncertain which of them survived the other or others, such deaths shall (subject to any order of the court), for all purposes affecting the title to property, be presumed to have occurred in order of seniority, and accordingly the younger shall be deemed to have survived the elder.'

Section 184 applies in all cases of uncertainty as to the order of death and is not limited to multiple deaths or strict 'commorientes' events such as occurred in the leading case of *Hickman* v *Peacey* [1945] AC 304. It also applies, for instance, if A died at sea as a result of a shipwreck and B died as a result of an operation, and it was uncertain who died first. See *Hickman* v *Peacey* per Lord Simon 314–315. Lord Macmillan in *Hickman* v *Peacey* summarised the position:

'Can you say for certain which of these two dead persons died first? If you cannot say for certain, then you must presume the older to have died first. It is immaterial that the reason for your inability to say for certain which died first is either because you think they died simultaneously or because you think they died consecutively but you do not know in what sequence.'

Where two testators provide for the situation where their deaths may 'coincide' and their deaths occur in the same accident, but the order of death is uncertain, the statutory presumption applies. In *Re Rowland* [1963] Ch 1 a doctor and his wife made similar wills which directed that, 'in the event of the decease of my wife (husband) preceding or coinciding with my own' the residuary estate, in the case of the husband, was to be divided between his brother and nephew. It was held by

Harman and Russell LJJ with Lord Denning MR dissenting, that this clause amounted to covering the situation where the deaths were simultaneous in point of time, and as it was impossible to prove this in the event of a shipwreck, the statutory presumption applied and the wife was therefore presumed to survive the husband and everything went in the end to the nephew. See also *Re Pringle* [1946] Ch 124; *Re Whitrick* [1957] 1 WLR 884.

Exclusions of the statutory presumption

Under s46(3) of the AEA 1925 as amended by s1(4) of the Intestates' Estates Act (IEA) 1952, the general presumption that the younger survived the elder does not apply on intestacy if the older spouse is the intestate. Thus if a wife and a younger husband die in circumstances rendering it uncertain which died first, the wife will not take under the husband's intestacy, since the general presumption under s184 applies, and the husband will not take under the wife's intestacy since he is not presumed to have survived her under s1(4) of the IEA 1952. This rule is now virtually redundant as a result of the new s46(2A) of the Administration of Estates Act 1925 (as enacted by s1(1) of the Law Reform (Succession) Act 1995). This section provides that a person may only take on the intestacy of his or her spouse if they survive the spouse by 28 days.

It is possible to exclude the operation of s184 by including a so-called 'commorientes' clause, preventing the beneficiary from taking unless he should live for, say, a month after the testator.

9.4 Exceptions to the doctrine of lapse

Section 32 of the Wills Act 1837: estates tail

By the section there is no lapse of a devise in tail if at the testator's death there is any issue capable of inheriting under the entail. In the case of wills coming into operation after 1925, this also applies to entailed interests in personalty under s130(1) of the LPA 1925.

Section 33 of the Wills Act 1837: gifts to a testator's issue

This is the most important exception to the doctrine of lapse. However, all wills coming into operation after 1982 are now subject to the amendment under s19 of the AJA 1982. The new law will be examined after the old legal position has been discussed.

The 'old' s33 provides:

'... where any person being a child or other issue of the testator to whom any real or personal estate shall be devised or bequeathed for any estate or interest not determinable at or before the death of such person shall die in the lifetime of the testator leaving issue, and any such issue of such person shall be living at the time of death of the testator such devise or bequest shall not lapse, but shall take effect as if the death or such person had happened immediately after the death of the testator, unless a contrary intention shall appear by the will.'

What property is to be disposed of?

Section 33 is only applicable to devises and legacies which are not determinable at or before the death of the beneficiary. Thus s33 is not applicable to a gift of a life interest or to an interest in a joint tenancy. See *Re Butler* [1918] 1 IR 394. This section also does not apply to appointments under special powers. See *Holyland* v *Lewin* (1883) 26 Ch D 266. However, it does apply to general powers by virtue of s27 of the Wills Act 1837 which abolished the distinction between a general power over property and property itself. See *Re Jacob* [1907] 2 Ch 459.

Section 33 does not apply to class gifts where the class is to be ascertained at the testator's death or subsequently. In other words no person incapacitated from taking at the testator's death is even looked upon as being a member of the class. Thus the share of a member of the class incapacitated from taking because he witnessed the will (*Young* v *Davies* (1863) 2 Dr & Sm 167) or because he illegally killed the testator (*Re Peacock* [1957] Ch 310), does not lapse, but goes to the other members of the class. (See earlier on class gifts 2(b) and *Theobald on Wills*, 13th edn, para 2035–38). The section does not apply to contingent gifts, where the contingency is not fulfilled (*Re Wilson* [1939] Ch 780), nor does it apply to one of several joint tenants (*Re Butler* [1918] 1 IR 394).

The beneficiary and issue

The section requires that any issue of the beneficiary be living at the testator's death. This raises the question as to whether a child *en ventre sa mère* is living for the purposes of the Act. In *Elliot* v *Joicey* [1935] AC 209, disapproving *Re Griffith's Settlement* [1911] 1 Ch 246, the House of Lords held that a child *en ventre* was not 'living' for the purposes of the Act. (See below for change in this by the AJA 1982.)

Another question is whether the issue which the beneficiary leaves must be living at the testator's death or whether the gift is still saved if the beneficiary's issue leaves issue who is living at the testator's death, but is himself dead. It seems to be settled that this extension of the line of issue is within the section. See *Mower* v *Orr* (1849) 7 Hare 473.

In the case of the testator's death occurring after 1 January the Family Law Reform Act, by s16, extends the meaning of 'child' and 'issue' in s33 to include illegitimate children.

Under s39 of the Adoption Act 1976, an adopted child is treated as being the legitimate issue of the adopting parents and can thus presumably save a gift from lapse.

The statutory fiction of survival

The question of whether the effect of s33, assuming all the requirements have been met, merely passes the gift to the child's estate, or whether the child is deemed to have outlived the testator for all purposes, is an area of some difficulty. There are two possible interpretations. The so-called 'wide view' by which the child is deemed to survive the testator for all purposes, and the 'narrow view' which holds that the child is deemed to survive the testator only for the purpose of saving the gift. Upjohn J reviewing the case law in *Re Basioli* [1953] Ch 367 decided that on its true construction s33 only prolongs the life of the beneficiary for the purpose of saving the gift and for no other purpose. Thus the beneficiary will receive the gift and it will pass under his will or on his intestacy to those entitled at his *real* death.

One of the cases reviewed showed up a problem with this construction. In *Re Hensler* (1881) 19 Ch D 612, the testator devised a freehold house to his son. The son died during the testator's lifetime leaving issue living at the testator's death. In his will the son had devised all his property to his father. It was held that the property passed to the son by virtue of s33 but the devise to the father failed. The rather strange reasoning seems to be that the father was under some special disability and could not therefore take under his son's will.

Upjohn J argued that *Re Hensler* supported the narrow view but it is respectfully submitted that this is an erroneous analysis. The son took the gift by virtue of s33, that much is clear.

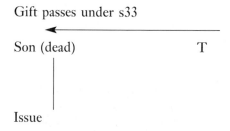

Gift passes under s33

Son (dead)   T

Issue

Under the 'narrow view' the estate of the son is distributed according to his will at the time of his real death. If that is so, then the gift does pass to the father as Hall V-C in *Re Hensler* seems to have realised. And since the gift to the father would have passed, the house should have gone to the trustees of the residuary real estate under the father's will. This did not happen.

The gift to the son was saved from lapse, but under his will the gift to the father failed, and therefore went on his intestacy. This, it is submitted, is a decision in favour of the 'wide view'. The reason is that if the 'fictitious' date of death is used, the gift to the father lapses, since the father has predeceased the son. The decision by Hall V-C is now clear and can be reasonably explained without recourse to ingenious but strange reasoning.

Whatever the rights and wrongs of Upjohn J's analysis, the decision in favour of the 'narrow view' is accepted.

Section 19 of the Administration of Justice Act 1982

Section 19 of the AJA now replaces s33 of the Wills Act 1837 and all deaths after 31 December 1982 are governed by it. This section provides:

'33(1) Where –
(a) a will contains a devise or bequest to a child or remoter descendant of the testator; and
(b) the intended beneficiary dies before the testator, leaving issue; and
(c) issue of the intended beneficiary are living at the testator's death,
then, unless a contrary intention appears by the will, the devise or bequest shall take effect as a devise or bequest to the issue living at the testator's death.
(2) Where –
(a) a will contains a devise or bequest to a class of persons consisting of children or remoter descendants of the testator; and
(b) a member of the class dies before the testator, leaving issue; and
(c) issue of that member are living at the testator's death,
then unless a contrary intention appears by the will, the devise or bequest shall take effect as if the class included the issue of its deceased member living at the testator's death.
(3) Issue shall take under this section through all degrees, according to their stock, in equal shares if more than one, any gift or share which their parent would have taken and so that no issue shall take whose parent is living at the testator's death and so capable of taking.
(4) For the purposes of this section –
(a) the illegitimacy of any person is to be disregarded; and
(b) a person conceived before the testator's death and born living thereafter is to be taken to have been living at the testator's death.'

Under the new s33(1) any gift which is saved from lapse will now pass the gift to the issue who saved it. In effect *Re Basioli* is now defunct and the problems with 'wide' and 'narrow' views are abolished. This clause is subject to any contrary intention by the will.

Section 33(2) covers gifts to members of a class who are children or remoter descendants of the testator. Where a member of the class predeceases the testator leaving issue living at the testator's death, the gift will take effect as if the gift included the issue in the class.

Section 33(3) makes it clear that all issue saving the gift shall take per stirpes through all degrees.

Section 33(4) expressly includes all illegitimate children under subs33(4)(a). Section 33(4)(b) overrules the decision in *Elliot* v *Joicey* (above). Therefore, under the new section, a child *en ventre sa mère* is taken to be living at the testator's death. In effect *Re Griffith's Settlement* is re-instated.

Gifts to discharge a moral obligation

A gift by a testator to X in discharge of a moral obligation, recognised in the testator's will, will not lapse if the beneficiary predeceases the testator since the court infers that the gift was intended to go to the beneficiary's estate. See Farwell J's judgment in *Stevens* v *King* [1904] 2 Ch 30, 33. The scope of this exception is uncertain and it is arguable that it only extends to the payment of debts, and no further.

9.5 Failure of gift through uncertainty

A gift may fail for uncertainty if, after considering any admissible evidence and any relevant rules of construction, either the subject matter or object of the gift are impossible to identify. See *Re Barlow* [1979] 1 WLR 278 'family and friends' and *Re Grant* [1980] 1 WLR 360 'Labour Party Property Committee'. Note the case of *Poulton's Will Trusts* (1987) 84 LS Gaz 981 where Warner J held that a remainder gift to 'relatives' of a named beneficiary was not void for uncertainty. Note also the case of *Re Tepper's Will Trusts* [1987] 2 WLR 729.

The courts will strive to construe the gift in some way so as to make it effective if at all possible. Thus in *Re Golay* [1965] 1 WLR 969 a direction that X could enjoy the use of a flat during her lifetime and 'receive a reasonable income from my other properties' was held valid, because what a 'reasonable' income was could be objectively assessed, and the court could undertake this assessment.

In *Anthony and Another* v *Donges and Others* (1998) The Times 22 July the testator in clause 4 of his will directed that his widow (D) should receive 'such minimal part of the [deceased's] estate as she might be entitled to under English law for maintenance purposes' provided that she survived the testator by at least 28 days. On the testator's death, his executors sought a determination as to whether clause 4 of the will was void for uncertainty or, alternatively, if the clause amounted to a gift, the amount of which was the sum D would have been entitled to on an application under the Inheritance (Provision for Family and Dependants) Act 1975. (D as the deceased's widow could have applied under s1(2)(a) of the 1975 Act.) The defendants were the widow and the three children of the deceased. The Court held that under English law the widow of a testator was not entitled as of right to a fixed percentage of her late husband's estate nor did the will confer upon the executors any discretionary power to determine the amount of maintenance under clause 4. Further, in consequence of *Re Hooker's Settlement* [1955] Ch 55, the court lacked the power to decide an entitlement under a will in a case like this. D, as the widow of the deceased, could apply to the court under s1(2)(a) of the 1975 Act for 'such financial provision as it would be reasonable in all circumstances of the case for a husband or wife to receive, whether or not that provision is required for his or her maintenance'. Clause 4 of the will did not prevent such an application. Accordingly, clause 4 was void for uncertainty and no deduction from the residuary estate had to be made for D's benefit.

This rule does not apply under the 'cy-près' doctrine. Thus a charitable bequest never fails for uncertainty even though the objects of the gift may not be indicated. See *Re White* [1893] 2 Ch 41, 53. However, the gift must be solely for a charitable purpose. Thus in *Chichester Diocesan Fund and Board of Finance* v *Simpson* [1944] AC 341 a gift for 'charitable and benevolent' purposes was held invalid on the grounds that the gift was not exclusively charitable.

9.6 Attesting witnesses and spouse

Under s15 of the Wills Act an attesting witness or his/her spouse cannot take under the will which he/she has attested. See *In the estate of Bravda* [1968] 1 WLR 479, 492.

There are a number of exceptions to the operation of this section. It does not apply in the following cases.

1. Where the will is a privileged will, which requires no attestation. See *Re Limond* [1915] 2 Ch 240.
2. Where a will which has been made has more than two witnesses, then in the case of deaths after 29 May 1968, the attestation of excess witnesses may be disregarded if the will would still be valid if the signature were removed. Section 1 of the Wills Act 1968 which is a response to *Re Bravda* (above).
3. Section 15 does not apply if the beneficiary signed the will, not in order to attest it, but for some other purpose, such as agreeing to the contents contained in it. See *In the goods of Sharman* (1869) LR 1 P & D 661; *In the goods of Smith* (1889) 15 PD 2.
4. Section 15 does not apply where the beneficiary was not the attesting witnesses' spouse at the time of attestation. See *Thorpe v Bestwick* (1881) 6 QBD 311.
5. Section 15 does not apply where the beneficiary/witness is a trustee of a gift under a will. See *Cresswell v Cresswell* (1868) LR 6 Eq 69.
6. It will not apply where the gift is later confirmed by a subsequent will or codicil not attested by the beneficiary/witness or spouse. See *Re Marcus* (1887) 57 LT 399.
7. And it does not apply where the beneficiary/witness or the spouse take under a secret trust. See *Re Young* [1951] Ch 185.

9.7 Forfeiture

Under a rule of public policy, frequently referred to as 'the forfeiture rule' a person who kills another cannot obtain any benefit or rights which result to him from the crime. In *Re Crippen* [1911] P 108 a husband murdered his wife and his estate could not inherit her money – he was hanged – because of the forfeiture rule. In that case Sir Samuel Evans P added:

> 'It is clear that the law is, that no person can obtain, or enforce, any rights resulting to him from his own crime; neither can his representative claiming under him obtain or enforce any such rights. The human mind revolts at the very idea that any other doctrine could be possible in our system of jurisprudence'.

The forfeiture rule prevents a killer or his estate benefiting if he murders a testator (see *Re Crippen*), or where he would benefit under the intestacy of the murdered victim. See *Re Sigsworthy* [1935] Ch 89. The rule also applies to cases of manslaughter. See *Re Hall* [1914] P 1. In cases of manslaughter it will apply if the manslaughter conviction was brought in on the ground of diminished responsibility, see *Re Giles* [1972] Ch 544 or in any case where the manslaughter resulted from 'deliberate, intentional and unlawful violence or threats of violence'. See *Gray v Barr* [1971] 2 QB 554 per Geoffrey Lane J; *Re K (deceased)* [1985] 1 All ER 403 per Vinelott J. Thus, it would appear from *Re K (deceased)* that the forfeiture rule may not apply to some cases of manslaughter, for example, an unintentional killing. The rule also seems to be inapplicable where the killer was insane at the time. See *Re Houghton* [1915] 2 Ch 173 but consider *Re Giles* on this point.

The decision in *Re H (deceased)* [1990] 1 FLR 441 (Gibson J) which concerned the case of a husband who was convicted of manslaughter is noteworthy. It involved the question of responsibility for actions where the plaintiff was the sole beneficiary under the deceased's will and whether he was precluded by the forfeiture rule on the basis of public policy in circumstances where he killed his wife as he was severely depressed and on anti-depressant drugs.

Reference should be made to the Forfeiture Act 1982. It should be recalled that the forfeiture rule as set out in the Forfeiture Act 1982 does not apply to every case of manslaughter, as noted above.

It was held that public policy did not require the application of the forfeiture rule in every case of manslaughter; the test was whether there had been deliberate, intentional and unlawful violence or threats of violence. In this case there was no such violence. Therefore the provisions of the Forfeiture Act 1982 would not apply. Even if the forfeiture rule had been applicable the court would have used its power under s2(1) of the Act to modify the application of the rule in the plaintiff's favour (*Gray v Barr* [1971] CLY 6012 applied).

There has been a more recent decision distinguishing *Re H (deceased)* and illustrating the forfeiture rule. This is the case of *Jones v Roberts* [1995] 2 FLR 422. In this case through his next friend, A sought to determine the question of whether his conviction for the manslaughter of his parents on grounds of diminished responsibility precluded him from inheriting his father's estate on intestacy. A argued that, according to *Gray v Barr* [1971] 2 QB 554, the court did not have to apply the forfeiture rule to every case of manslaughter, but instead it need only apply to those cases where the claimant was guilty of deliberate, intentional, and unlawful violence or threat of violence.

Held: the application failed on public policy grounds. The court held that it was not bound by *Re Royse* [1985] Fam 22 even though the facts in that case could not be distinguished from this case. However, the same conclusion would have been reached even if *Gray v Barr* could have been applied. The test in that case was met because A was criminally responsible for his actions and had used deliberate, intentional and unlawful violence.

The Forfeiture Act 1982 was passed in order to provide relief for certain persons guilty of unlawful killing, other than murder, from forfeiture of inheritance and other rights. Under s2(1) of the Act, it is provided:

'Where a court determines that the forfeiture rule has precluded a person ... who has unlawfully killed another from acquiring any interest in the property mentioned in subs(4) below, the court may make an order under this section modifying the effect of that rule'.

Under subs(4) the interests referred to are beneficial interests which the killer would have acquired (1) under the deceased's will or intestacy; (2) under any nomination; (3) by a *donatio mortis causa*; (4) under a special destination; (5) under the terms of a trust wherein the interest passed to the killer on the deceased's death.

The relief that may be given by the court under the 1982 Act is dealt with by s2(5) which provides that the court may make an order to modify the effect of the forfeiture rule in respect of any of the interests in property mentioned in subs(1) in either or both of the following ways: '(a) where there is more than one such interest, by excluding the application of the rule in respect of any (but not all) of those interests; and (b) in the case of any such interest in the property'. This provision was considered by Vinelott J in *Re K (deceased)* [1985] 1 All ER 403 who concluded that these words if read literally enabled the court to give some relief from forfeiture but not total relief. He refused to accept 'a result as bizarre as that'; there was a drafting error and, in his view, he could – and did – grant total relief. His decision on this was not appealed and the Court of Appeal confirmed his order. See [1985] 2 All ER 833.

In *Dunbar v Plant* (1997) The Times 13 August the Court of Appeal granted total relief against forfeiture. In this case the defendant was part of a suicide pact which ended in her fiancé's death, but despite all her efforts she survived. At first instance the deceased's father successfully contended that the commission of the offence of aiding and abetting a suicide brought the forfeiture rule into operation, thereby preventing her from benefiting from the proceeds of a life insurance policy taken out by the deceased for her benefit. The Court of Appeal held that the rule applied to aiding and abetting a suicide (Suicide Act 1961). However, the Forfeiture Act 1982 mitigated the harshness of the rule where public interest did not demand the imposition of any penal sanction. The decision makes it clear that in exercising discretion all the circumstances should be taken into account. The Court were also influenced by the fact that the assets in question were not derived from the deceased's family, but were the result of an insurance policy taken out by the deceased for his fiancée's benefit.

An application under the Forfeiture Act, as s2(1) indicates, cannot be made where the killer is guilty of murder; this is reinforced by s5 which states 'Nothing in this Act ... shall affect the application of the forfeiture rule in the case of a person who stands convicted of murder'. In other cases an application for relief from forfeiture must be brought within three months from the date of the conviction. See s2(3) and *Re Royse* [1984] 3 All ER 339.

The Forfeiture Act came into force on 13 October 1982; under s7(4) the court can make an order under the Act whether the unlawful killing occurred before or after the Act came into force. However, under s2(7) the court cannot make an order modifying the effect of the forfeiture rule in respect of an interest in property which, in consequence of the rule, was acquired by a person other than a killer or a person claiming through him before the Act came into force. These provisions were considered in *Re K (deceased)*, described further below, where the deceased was shot by his wife on 30 September 1982. She was convicted of manslaughter on 4 May 1983. As the killing took place two weeks before the Act came into force it was argued that the court had no jurisdiction under s2(7) to make an order in the widow's favour because the right of a person interested in the deceased's estate was a chose in action to see it was duly administered and to obtain his benefit in due course.

The position of joint tenants under the forfeiture rule and the Forfeiture Act 1982 was also considered in *Re K (deceased)* as the deceased and his widow were joint tenants of the matrimonial home worth £80,000. This had not been considered in English law before. Authorities in New Zealand and Canada held that in such cases the whole property should vest in the survivor of the joint tenants, that is, the killer, subject to a constructive trust on the deceased's share in favour of the next of kin other than the killer. See *Re Pechar* [1969] NZLR 574; *Schobelt v Barber* (1966) 60 DLR (2d) 519. Vinelott J did not adopt this approach; instead he treated the beneficial interest as vesting in the deceased and the killer as tenants in common. This point was not taken in the Court of Appeal.

In *Re K (deceased)* [1985] 2 All ER 833 (CA) the deceased and his wife were married in 1974; the deceased was then 63 and his wife 52. After two or three years of marriage the deceased became violent and made numerous physical attacks on his wife. The wife considered that these might be due to the onset of a brain tumour and remained loyal to him for this reason. In 1982 the deceased had a violent argument with his wife in the kitchen; during the course of this she picked up a 12 bore shotgun that was kept there for shooting rabbits, and pointed it at the deceased and released the safety catch. The deceased moved towards his wife and the gun went off killing him. The wife had no recollection of pulling the trigger. She was convicted of manslaughter and given a probation sentence. The deceased left a will under which all of his estate, valued at £412,000, was to go to the wife for life, remainder to certain relatives.

Held: the wife had been guilty of a deliberate threat of violence towards the deceased and, although the killing was unintended, the forfeiture rule applied. However, under the 1982 Act, which applied, relief from forfeiture would be granted. The wife had been loyal to and had suffered much violence at the hands of the deceased and, having regard to the fact that there were no other persons towards whom the deceased had a moral duty to provide, it would be wrong not to permit her to enjoy the benefits he had provided for her under his will.

Where forfeiture has an effect not just on the beneficiary's gift but also on any gift over, the Court of Appeal in the recent case of *Re Jones (deceased)*, *Jones v Midland Bank Trust Company and Others* (1997) The Times 29 April has indicated a reluctance to rewrite the will in favour of those entitled to the gift over. In this case,

Mrs Jones (the deceased) in her will dated May 1965 directed her estate to be held on trust for her son Robert and, in the event of his predeceasing her, 'for such of my nephews ... as shall be living at the date of my death.' In July 1991 Mrs Jones was killed by her son who was convicted of manslaughter and sentenced to three years' probation.

As a result of the forfeiture rule the son could not benefit under the will. The question was whether the gift over to the nephews would take effect or if the estate would devolve to her next of kin on intestacy.

The judge at first instance held in favour of the nephews by drawing an inference from the wording of the will that the testatrix would have intended for the nephews to succeed not only where her son had predeceased her but also if he had murdered her. The next of kin appealed this decision.

The Court of Appeal held that the judge at first instance was wrong to have drawn the inference he did as this involved a degree of speculation not permitted in the construction of wills. The event the testatrix had provided for (her son's death) was clear and had not occurred. Accordingly, the appeal was allowed and the residuary estate would devolve on the next of kin on intestacy.

The Court applied Slade LJ's reasoning in *Re Sinclair (deceased)* [1985] Ch 446 where he said at p455 that it was not 'open to the court to rewrite the will by adding other specific contingencies to those clearly expressed [in the will] on the basis of mere intelligent speculation as to what the testator might have intended if his marriage were to end in divorce.'

This decision was followed by the High Court in *TWGS v JMG and Others* [2000] 2 All ER 83. The court held that the forfeiture rule does not require the court to treat the murderer as having predeceased the victim for the purposes of s47(1)(i) of the Administration of Estates Act 1925. Under this provision the issue of the child of an intestate may take if that child had predeceased the intestate. In this case a son was convicted of murdering his parents, neither of whom left a will. The forfeiture rule applied and he was not entitled to benefit. A claim was brought by his son for entitlement under s47(1)(i) to the grandparent's estate. This claim failed. The court further held that where an earlier class of successor was in existence but disabled from taking, the next available class under s46(1)(v) of the 1925 was entitled to take.

The forfeiture rule may affect the rights of a defendant under the deceased's will or intestacy. If so, the question arises whether or not an application may be made under the Inheritance (Provision for Family and Dependants) Act 1975, specifically s1(1) of the Act. For further discussion, see Chapter 12, section 12.2, where the case of *Re Royse* [1984] 3 All ER 339 is considered.

9.8 Lapse by divorce

Prior to the Administration of Justice Act 1982 there was no concept of revocation by divorce in the law of succession. However, s18(2) of the Administration of Justice Act inserted a new s18A into the Wills Act 1837 (now substituted by s3 Law Reform (Succession) Act 1995, which applies to wills made by those dying on or after 1 January 1996, see below) and under this provision divorce causes the failure of certain gifts to a former spouse. The change followed recommendations of the Law Reform Committee in its 22nd Report on the making and revocation of wills. The Committee was divided on this matter and two views emerged:

1. that legislation be introduced to the effect that a divorced spouse be treated as predeceasing the testator so that only dispositions to that spouse would be revoked by the will;
2. that no change should be made in the law because divorce, unlike marriage, does not place new responsibilities on the testator.

The majority view was enacted as s18A(1) of the Wills Act and provided:

'Where, after the testator has made a will, a decree of a court dissolves or annuls his marriage or declares it void –
(a) the will shall take effect as if any appointment of the former spouse as an executor or as an executor and trustee of the will were omitted, and
(b) any devise or bequest to the former spouse shall lapse.
except in so far as a contrary intention appears by the will.'

Under both the new and the old versions of s18A(1) the whole will is not destroyed by divorce but only those parts under which the former spouse benefits or is appointed executor or executor and trustee. In many respects the provision recognises the powers of the court to settle property disputes between ex-spouses after divorce and the fact that a division of property between ex-spouses is normally intended to be a once and for all settlement. It is desirable to have provisions such as this which prevent ex-spouses receiving unintended windfalls because the testator has not reviewed his will after divorce.

Example

T married W in 1970. In 1975 he made a will leaving his house, Blackacre, a legacy of £25,000 and his motor car to W. In the same will T left £10,000 to each of his children A and B and the residue of his estate to his brother X and sister Y. In 1980 T divorced W and settled any financial claims she had against him. In 1983 T died. Under s18A(1) the devises and bequests to W would lapse but all other dispositions in the will would remain effective.

The provisions of the former s18A(1)(b) (which still applies to the wills of those who died before 1 January 1996) provided that the effect of divorce is that any devise or bequest to the former spouse shall 'lapse'. The use of the term 'lapse' in this context was considered in *Re Cherrington* [1984] 1 WLR 772 where Butler-Sloss J interpreted the term as referring to the former spouse predeceasing the testator. Such interpretation would have the effect of allowing gifts over to third parties which were only to operate if the spouse died before the testator came into operation. In that case the issue concerned the appointment of executors because the testator made a will in 1966 appointing his wife sole executrix in clause 2 and leaving her all his estate in clause 3. Clause 3 contained a proviso that if the wife should predecease the testator then by clause 4 a son and his solicitor should be executors and by clause 6 his estate should be divided between his two sons. The testator divorced his wife in January 1983 and died in March 1983. The effect of interpreting 'lapse' as referring to the former spouse predeceasing the testator was to enable the appointment of the executors to take effect. However, this interpretation of 'lapse' was not accepted by the Court of Appeal in *Re Sinclair (deceased)* [1985] 1 All ER 1066; 'lapse' simply meant 'fail' in this context without qualification and irrespective of the consequences. *Re Cherrington* was, thus, overruled.

In *Re Sinclair* the testator was married in 1953 and made his will in 1958. By clause 3 the will devised and bequeathed all of the testator's estate to his wife 'provided she survives me for a period of one month'. Clause 4 of the will stated 'If my said wife shall predecease me or fail to survive me for the period aforesaid' then the estate was to go to the Imperial Cancer Research Fund. The testator and his wife were divorced in 1962 and the testator died in October 1983. The former spouse survived the period of one month referred to and there was no dispute that s18A had caused the gifts to her to fail. However, doubts arose whether the combined effect of the will and s18A was to cause the testator's estate to devolve on the fund or to devolve to the next of kin on intestacy.

Held: the word 'lapse' should be interpreted as 'fail' on s18A(1)(b) and the provision should not be treated as a deeming provision so that it should be read 'any devise or bequest to the former spouse shall fail with the same consequences as if the former spouse had died in the testator's lifetime'. Accordingly, s18A was of no assistance in determining if the gift over to the fund took effect. It merely prevented the former spouse from benefitting. The provisions of clause 4 only could help the fund to benefit under the will and as not all of the contingencies referred to had taken effect the gift would pass to the next of kin.

In arriving at this conclusion Slade LJ added that he had more than 'a sneaking suspicion' that if the testator had addressed his mind to the contingency of divorce, he would have wished the estate to go to the fund. However, the court declined to rewrite the will and neither s20 nor s21 of the Administration of Justice Act were invoked in the argument.

This decision has been referred to as the '*Re Sinclair* trap'. The effect of *Re Sinclair* was that legal advisers had to draft gifts over to take effect on a gift to a spouse failing for any reason. Since home-made wills were unlikely to do this, there was a danger of unintended intestacies. Section 3 Law Reform (Succession) Act 1995 amends s18A Wills Act 1837 so that it now states that after divorce or annulment a spouse is to be treated as having died on the date of the divorce or annulment. Section 3(2) Law Reform (Succession) Act 1995 provides that subs (1) 'has effect as respects a will made by a person dying on or after 1 January 1996 (regardless of the date of the will and the date of the dissolution or annulment)'. However, there is no need to amend existing wills, as the conventional clause will continue to be perfectly satisfactory.

Under s18A(3) cases where an ex-spouse is given a life interest under the testator's will are dealt with. In such circumstances the life interest will lapse under s18A(1) and the remainder will take effect immediately on the testator's death. Further, if the remainder was contingent on the termination of the life interest it shall be treated as if it were not so contingent as the contingency will be disregarded.

Example

X leaves all his estate to his wife Y for life, remainder to his children in equal shares. After the date of the will, X's marriage with his wife Y is terminated by a decree of divorce. The life interest will be ignored if X dies leaving his will unchanged and his children will take the remainder immediately on his death.

Section 18A(2) takes into account those cases where an ex-spouse is deprived of benefits under the testator's will by s18(1) but did not obtain a financial settlement after divorce before the testator's death. To avoid any doubt s18A(2) expressly declares that the rights of a former spouse to apply for financial provision under the Inheritance (Provision for Family and Dependants) Act 1975 are not affected.

It should be noted that s18A only applies to cases where a marriage has been dissolved or annulled by a decree of the court. This would not cover void marriages because no decree of the court is necessary here. However, it is surprising that no provision is made to cover cases where there is a bigamous marriage which one of the parties believes to be genuine and in reliance on that belief makes a will in favour of the other party. Perhaps this is because of the provisions of the Inheritance (Provisions for Family and Dependants) Act 1975.

Under s73(6) of the Administration of Justice Act 1982 the provisions of s18A will apply to the will of a testator who dies after 31 December 1982. As seen, the *new* s18A applies to the wills of testators dying on or after 1 January 1996.

Law Reform (Succession) Act 1995

Section 3 Law Reform (Succession) Act 1995 substitutes a new s18A into the Wills Act 1837, altering the effect on a will of a testator's divorce or the annulment of his marriage. For testators dying on or after 1 January 1996, provisions of the will appointing the former spouse as executor or trustee, or conferring a power of appointment on the former spouse, will take effect as if the former spouse had died on the date of divorce or annulment. The same applies to any devises or bequests to the former spouse.

9.9 Disclaimer

A person may disclaim his interest under either a will or intestacy and if no-one has altered their position in pursuance of the disclaimer, he may retract it at any time. In *Re Cranstoun's Will Trusts* [1949] Ch 523 Romer J said:

> 'What, then, is the position of a person who renounces a legacy and then thinks better of it on the hypothesis that no one has taken any steps to alter his position in consequence of that renunciation? In the absence of any authority I should have thought that it was open to anyone at any time to change his mind, when no one has acted to his hurt on the faith of the renunciation.'

9.10 The effect of failure

Legacies and devises fall into the residue or go on intestacy. Residuary devises which fail are treated the same as residuary bequests under s25 of the Wills Act 1837 for the purpose of devolution of the estate. Residuary bequests go on intestacy. This can be excluded if there is a contrary intention. Thus, a residuary gift to A and B as tenants in common, where the gift to A fails for some reason, would normally go on intestacy. However, should the testator indicate that any failed share should pass to the other or others then the gift will not lapse.

The doctrine of acceleration

Under this doctrine the testator is ordinarily presumed to have intended an acceleration of subsequent interests where a prior interest fails in consequence of the donee being prevented from taking. See *Re Kebty-Fletcher's Will Trusts* [1969] 1 Ch 339. Thus a devise to a person for life with remainder in fee, where the life tenant cannot take, is valid and the remainder is accelerated. The will can expressly exclude the operation of this doctrine.

Where a life tenant disclaims his life interest which has no retrospective effect, there is a clear case for acceleration. In *Re Harker's Will Trusts* [1969] 1 WLR 1124, where the life tenant released and surrendered his life interest to trustees so that it merged and was extinguished in the reversionary interest, there was acceleration and the life interest was destroyed.

However, there can be no acceleration if there are no persons in existence who could take, as for instance, where there is a gift to A for life, and then to her children and A has no children. See *Re Townsend's Estate* (1886) 34 Ch D 357.

Double acceleration

Where a preceding life interest fails so that a class interest is accelerated the question arises as to whether the date for closing the class is also accelerated. If it is, then certain persons may be excluded from the gift which they might otherwise have taken.

Where the life interest is either void *ab initio* (*Re Johnson* (1893) 68 LT 20) or is ended prematurely (*Re Crowther's Trusts* [1915] 1 IR 53), it has been held that the closing of the class is also accelerated.

The main area of contention is whether a life tenant can by voluntarily disclaiming his interest affect the membership of a class by causing the date of closure to accelerate. In *Re Davis* [1957] 1 WLR 922 it was held that such a voluntary action would accelerate both the gift and the date of closure of the class. This case has been heavily criticised and was not followed in *Re Harker's Will Trusts* [1969] 1 WLR 1124 where there was a gift to A for life with the remainder to her children who attained 21 years. In this case Goff J held that the release of the life interest by A destroyed that interest and accelerated the gift. It did not, however, accelerate the closing of the class which remained open until the death of A. No distinction is to be drawn between a release and a disclaimer for these purposes.

Partial intestacy

This is dealt with in Chapter 11.

10

Construction of Wills

The construction of wills is mainly concerned with ascertaining what the words used in a will mean in the context of the property of persons they refer to. Difficulties may arise with the words of the will in two ways. (1) Because the words used are in themselves ambiguous or unclear. The court's task here is to decide what the testator actually meant. See *Perrin* v *Morgan* [1943] AC 399; *Re Bailey* [1945] Ch 191. (2) Because the words used when applied to the circumstances they refer to do not make sense. See *Charter* v *Charter* (1874) 7 HL 364; *Re Jackson* [1933] Ch 237. The law relating to the construction of wills was amended by the provisions of ss20, 21 and 22 of the Administration of Justice Act 1982. The rules which applied prior to these provisions coming into force on 1 January 1983 will be considered first; the new provisions are considered in section 10.9 below.

10.1 General principles of construction

The court's duty when constructing a will is to ascertain the expressed intention of the testator. Therefore, the court is concerned with determining the meaning of the words used in the will.

In effect this rule of construction excludes conjecture as to what the testator might have meant. The best explanation of this is by Cotton LJ in *Ralph* v *Carrick* (1879) 11 Ch D 873:

'Even very intelligent persons whose minds are not so trained are accustomed to jump at a conclusion as to what a person means by considering what they, under similar circumstances, think they would have done. That is conjecture only, and conjecture on an imperfect knowledge ... because the facts known to the testator may not be all before them, and the testator's mind ... may not have been constituted as their minds are constituted so that it cannot be concluded that he would have acted in the same way.'

One should note the case of *Henley* v *Wardell* (1988) The Times 29 January. The key issue in this decision was the drafting of a will. The facts show how important proper drafting is, and it is therefore noteworthy here.

This case, which was decided in 1988 but received little publicity, has significant implications for the way in which a will should be drafted in cases where the will draftsman seeks to vary the provision of s32 of the Trustee Act 1925. The case was concerned with the exclusion of certain limitations on the advancement of capital imposed by s32 of that Act.

The testator's will gave a life interest to W and the remainder to the children when 21 years old. By clause 10 of the will the trustees were given the power to advance capital from the fund created by the will. Clause 10 sought to vary s32 by the inclusion of the words: 'to the intent that the powers given to the trustees by s32 Trustee Act 1925 shall be enlarged so as to permit my trustees in their absolute and uncontrolled discretion to advance at any time the whole of any expectant or presumptive share to any of my children'.

It was held by Mr John Mowbray QC (sitting as a Deputy High Court Judge of the Chancery Division) that:

1. this clause merely increased the amount that could be advanced to a beneficiary under the provisions of the statute, namely one-half. It was not effective to remove the requirement that the life-tenant must consent to the advance under s32(1)(c);
2. the court indicated that if will draftsmen sought to exclude the necessity of obtaining the life-tenant's consent, they must say so expressly, for example, by such words as 'and s32(1)(c) of the Trustee Act 1925 shall not apply (to this will)'.

The second general principle states that when words and expressions that are used are unambiguous and their application to the circumstances of the will does not lead to any difficulty of construction, then they are to be given their ordinary meaning. As Lord Wensleydale said in *Abbott* v *Middleton* (1858) 7 HLC 68:

'It is now, I believe, universally admitted, that in construing a will, the rule is to read it in the ordinary and grammatical sense of the words, unless some obvious absurdity, or some repugnance or inconsistency with the declared intentions of the writer, to be extracted from the whole instrument, should follow from so reading it.'

This could, of course, lead to some rather eccentric dispositions taking effect, but since a testator may dispose of his property as he chooses, this does not provide a sufficient and necessary condition for construing the words in another sense.

This principle does not apply if the word or expression has more than one meaning. In *Perrin* v *Morgan* [1943] AC 399, reversing [1942] Ch 345 sub nom *Re Morgan*, the testatrix in a home-made will made some specific devises and gave 'all moneys of which I die possessed' among 14 named nephews and nieces. Farwell J and the Court of Appeal with obvious reluctance held that the gift comprised money in the strict sense to the value of £840, but not stocks and shares to the value of £33,000. The House of Lords unanimously reversed this decision and held that the whole personal estate passed. Lord Simon stated the general principles. Words which have not got one natural meaning, but several meanings, each of which, in appropriate circumstances, may be regarded as natural; it follows that there is no fixed legal meaning which the courts must adopt in preference to the popular meaning and that the duty of the court is to ascertain without prejudice as between various usual meanings which is the correct interpretation of the particular will. In the circumstances the testatrix was using the term 'money' in its popular rather than its legal sense.

The case of *Gammon* (1986) The Times 27 February also involved a construction of the word 'money' and it was held following *Perrin* v *Morgan* that money should be construed in a wide popular sense.

Technical words or expressions must be taken as having been used in their technical sense. In *Doe d Winter* v *Peratt* (1843) 6 M & G 314 House of Lords, Parke B laid down this general principle:

'It is a rule in the judicial exposition of wills, that technical words, or words of known legal import, are to be considered as having been used in their technical sense, or, according to their strict acceptance, unless the context contains a plain indication to the contrary.'

The essential nature of this principle is that there is a presumption that such words have been used in their technical sense, but that presumption can be rebutted by clear evidence to the contrary. In *Re Bailey* [1945] Ch 191 a testatrix concluded her will with the words 'I leave Y as my residuary legatee'. Her estate consisted largely of realty. In this case the court held that there was sufficient context to constitute a 'plain indication to the contrary' that the words were not used in their technical sense. The court therefore held that the sense of these words was actually 'residuary beneficiary'. However, compare the case of *Re Cook* [1948] Ch 212.

The testator's intention, collected from the entire will, must be given effect, even if this leads to the literal sense of the words being overturn, or extended beyond their usual meaning. The intention of the will can affect the interpretation of the words in a will in several ways. It can fix the meaning of ambiguous words, control the sense of clear words and generally alter the meaning of words in ambiguous or difficult circumstances. See *Re Haygarth* [1913] 2 Ch 9. For example, in *Key* v *Key* (1853) 4 De GM & G 73, the testator devised his 'estate' to A for life, charged with annuities. He continued: 'But in case the aforesaid annuitants, or any of them, shall survive the said A, I then give the aforesaid estate unto B, charged with the aforesaid annuities.' From the literal meaning of these words, B's interest was conditional on one or more of the annuitants surviving A. The court held, that given the general intention of the will as a whole, B was to take in any event on A's death, and the words supposedly setting up the condition were to be read as merely making the property liable for the annuities until all the annuitants had died.

It is also possible for the court to supply words where there is an omission by implication, if the nature of the omission is clear. The crucial point here is that there must be no room for doubt as to the nature of the omission. For instance in *Re Whitrick* [1957] 1 WLR 884 (CA) the testatrix made a will giving everything to her husband but added; 'in the event of my husband and myself both dying at the same time' then the estate to be held on trust for three named people. It was held that the gift over was intended to take effect in the event of her husband predeceasing her as well as dying at the same time. As Jenkins LJ stated:

> 'The reading of words into a will as a matter of necessary implication is a measure which a court of construction should apply with the greatest caution. Many wills contain slips and omissions and fail to provide for contingencies which any testator would obviously wish to provide. The court cannot rewrite the testamenary provisions in wills which come before it for construction. This type of treatment of an imperfect will is only legitimate where the court can collect from the four corners of the document that something has been omitted and, further, collect with sufficient precision the nature of the omission.'

When construing codicils the central principle is to interfere as little as possible with the dispositions of the will. In particular, where a codicil purports to revoke a clear gift under the will, the revocation must be unambiguous. If there is any doubt then the person claiming under the will must succeed. In *Doe d Hearle v Hicks* (1832) 1 Cl & F 20 Tindal CJ laid down the rule of construction in the following manner:

> 'If such a devise in the will is clear, it is incumbent on those who contend it is not to take effect by reason of a revocation in the codicil to show that the intention to revoke is equally clear and free from doubt as the original intention to devise; for if there is only reasonable doubt whether a clause of revocation was intended to include the particular devise, then such devise ought undoubtedly to stand.'

See *Re Lawrence's Will Trusts* [1972] Ch 418 for a recent case on this point.

In *Re Stoodley* [1915] 2 Ch 295 the testator's codicil clearly conflicted with his earlier will as the residue was disposed of to different beneficiaries in each document. As this was a case of clear contradiction the codicil being the later document prevailed.

It now appears that in construing a will, the court can take into account the manner in which the words of the will were written. Thus a court of construction has, in some cases, looked at the original will to ascertain the punctuation, the effect of a blank, the introduction of capital letters. For example, in *Child v Elsworth* (1852) 2 De GM & G 679, a testator listed several legacies, the last of which was followed by the words, 'to be paid twelve months after the decease of A'. The question arose as to whether this statement applied to all the legacies or merely to the last of them. In coming to the decision that it applied to all the legacies, the fact that the gifts and the clause were in one single sentence closed by a full stop, with no other punctuation, was considered to be an important indication of the testator's intention. *Gauntlett* v *Carter* (1853) 17 Beav 586 is another authority for this principle. In that case the testator devised his estate 'Bullen Court, Strand and Maiden Lane'. The property, 'Bullen Court', was off the Strand, so the question arose as to whether the word 'Strand' was part of the description of 'Bullen Court' or actually indicated another property owned by the testator in the Strand. In holding the latter construction, the court took note of the fact that there was a comma before and after the word 'Strand', thereby indicating that it was a separate description of a different property. As already mentioned blanks may be taken into account when construing a will (*Re Stevens* [1952] Ch 323) as well as erasures made before the will was executed. See *Manning* v *Purcell* (1855) De GM & G 55.

Two further cases should be noted: *Howell* v *Howell* [1992] IR 290 and *Berkeley Leisure Group* v *Scott and The Spastic Society* (1992) 29 October (ex rel Paul Ashwell, Barrister).

Howell involved the construction of a will and whether a gift to the other residuary beneficiary succeeded.

By his will a testator left certain property to one brother J and 'all my stocks and any other assets I may have' to another brother, D. J predeceased the testator. Another brother, P, would benefit if the failed gift was distributed as an intestacy. P brought proceedings to determine whether the bequest to D should be regarded as residuary. Carroll LJ held that the bequest to D was not residuary. The reference in the will to 'any other assets' meant any assets other than those already mentioned. The testator's intention had been to divide his estate between two of his brothers and the expression 'any other assets' was used in the context of distinguishing what the division was to be rather than in the context of a residuary gift.

The *Berkeley* case involved whether a pitch agreement also passed in an estate including a mobile home bequeathed to charity. The testator had bequeathed his entire estate to The Spastic Society, a registered charity. Among the assets was a mobile home with the benefit of a pitch agreement subject to s3 of the Mobile Homes Act 1983. A preliminary point referred to whether or not the agreement came to an end on the death of the testator. It was held by Baker J that The Spastic Society was a person entitled to the mobile home by virtue of the deceased's will. The agreement endured for the benefit of the charity under s3(3)(b) of the Act.

Mention should also be made of the most recent relevant decision. This is the case of *Re Dorman (deceased)* [1994] 1 WLR 282. Here it was held that where the transfer of moneys, in ignorance of the terms of a will, to a second bank account was a change in form only, the moneys passed as a specific legacy rather than to the residuary legatees.

By clause 2 of her will made on 29 September 1987, the testatrix stipulated that the balance of a numbered deposit account was to be added to the capital of a trust fund from which she received income. Prior to her death, and in ignorance of the terms of the will, on 16 July 1990 the account was closed and a new account was opened to take advantage of better interest rates. The entire moneys in the first account were transferred. After her death on 27 January 1991, the court was asked to decide whether the moneys in the second account passed to the specific legatees named in clause 2, or to charities named as residuary legatees.

The court found that on a true construction of the will the moneys passed as a specific bequest under clause 2 rather than into the residuary estate. The arrangements under the new account were in effect identical to the old account. It was to be inferred that the change to the second account was a change in name and form only.

10.2 Admissibility of evidence

Surrounding circumstances

Evidence as to the surrounding circumstances at the date when the will was made is admissible to explain or elucidate the meaning of particular words used in the will. This is sometimes known as the 'armchair' principle. Blackburn J in *Allgood* v *Blake* (1873) LR 8 Ex 160, laid down the general rule that:

> 'In construing a will, the court is entitled to put itself in the position of the testator, and to consider all material facts and circumstances known to the testator with reference to which he is taken to have used words in the will, and then to declare what is the intention evidenced by the words used with reference to those facts and circumstances which were (or ought to have been) in the mind of the testator when he used those words.'

The point here is that the meaning of the words or expressions used in the will may only become apparent in the light of surrounding circumstances, rather than from the context of the will itself. It is then open to the court to 'look into the extrinsic circumstances of the case to see whether the meaning of the words be sensible in any popular or secondary sense in which with reference to those circumstances they are capable'. See *Re Glassington* [1906] 2 Ch 305 per Joyce J quoting Wigram, *Extrinsic Evidence*. This principle is almost always going to concern the identity of either objects or the subject matter of gifts in a will. However, it has to be noted that this principle is to no avail if the word or expression has and can only be used to ascertain which of two or more proper meanings a word might have; it can never fix a totally unusual meaning on a word. It is only the context of the will which can achieve that. See *Higgins* v *Dawson* [1902] AC 1. As Lord Shand said:

> 'In the class of cases in which you cannot tell exactly what is given or to whom it is given because of obscure or doubtful expressions of the testator's will in regard to the particular conditions of his property, you must have recourse to extrinsic evidence to ascertain his meaning.'

See *Higgins* v *Dawson*, above.

The principle can be put in these terms. Where the identity or extent of the subject matter is in question, extrinsic evidence (including surrounding circumstances, treatment, habits of speech, but not declarations of intention) can be given to show what was intended. Not merely that a person or thing exists to which the document might refer, but also that such a person or thing was in fact intended. For example, in *McKeown* v *Ardagh* (1847) Ir R10 Eq 445, the testator left a legacy to the 'Patagonian, Chilean and Peruvian Missionary Society'. Evidence was adduced that there was no such society but that there was a 'South American Society' which did have missions in those places, and the testator knew and subscribed to it. The legacy was given in that society. See also *Re Ofner* [1909] 1 Ch 60 (CA) and *Wray* v *Wray* [1905] 2 Ch 349.

The rule also applies where there are several subjects or objects in competition. For example, in the case of *Charter* v *Charter* (1874) 7 HL 364. The testator appointed by his will his 'son Forster Charter' as executor. His son, Forster Charter, had actually died some years previously, but the testator did have two sons who were living, William Forster Charter and Charles Charter. In the Court of Appeal Lord Penzance decided in favour of Charles and therefore the previous grant to William was revoked. On appeal to the House of Lords, the decision was upheld in Charles' favour. The court, however, made the following observation as to the admissibility of evidence. As Lord Cairns LC said in his judgment:

> '... this is not a case in which any parol evidence of statements of the testator, as to whom he intended to benefit, or supposed he had benefited, by his will, can be received ... The only case in which evidence of this kind can be received is where the description of the legatee or of the thing bequeathed is equally applicable in all its parts to two persons, or to two things.'

Evidence was admissible that Charles lived at home, therefore the statement, 'so long as they reside together in the same house' was more appropriate to him than to William. Circumstantial evidence of what the intended meaning of the testator was, is inadmissible in cases of uncertainty. For example, in the case of *Doe d Hiscocks* v *Hiscocks* (1839) 5 M & W 363, the testator devised land to 'John Hiscocks, the eldest son of (my son) John Hiscocks'. The testator had two sons; Simon, his elder son and John, his second son, who was however, the eldest son by a second marriage. It was held that although the circumstances of the family might be adduced to show which son was intended, as there was only a misdescription of the object, and not an equivocation, declarations by the testator as to who was the intended beneficiary were inadmissible.

A well-known example is to be found in *National Society for the Prevention of Cruelty to Children* v *Scottish National Society for Prevention of Cruelty to Children* [1915] AC 207. The testator left a legacy to the 'National Society for the Prevention of Cruelty to Children'. This was the exact name of the English Society in London. The Scottish Society claimed the gift, and it was clear that the testator had paid no attention at all to the English Society. It was held, however, that there was no equivocation, as only one society answered the description completely. Therefore, declarations by the testator as to which society he meant, were inadmissible. It was therefore decided that the society which precisely fitted the name should take. This case was treated not as one of equivocation, but of correct and less correct description. It must always be borne in mind that the court did not decide that further inquiry into the facts and circumstances were excluded merely where someone or thing is correctly described. See *Grant* v *Grant* (1870) LR5 CP 727 (Ex Ch). The recent case of *Funnel* v *Stewart* (1995) The Times 9 December in which a testatrix instructed that her residuary estate should be used for spiritual work conducted by a certain group is also relevant. The group was described and its objectives were charitable. Accordingly, no further evidence as to whether the work was effective was required. In this case it was held that the private religious meetings were not charitable as they were confined to a closed group. Nevertheless that element was subsidiary to the faith healing activities for the community, which had now become a recognised public benefit. In the alternative, the religious services contained a sufficient element of public health so as not to invalidate the charitable purpose of the gift. In the circumstances of this case it was unnecessary to consider whether evidence that the faith healing was actually effective was required. This is a useful decision when considering evidence of intention in the construction of wills.

Evidence of intention

In general, evidence as to the actual declared intentions of the testator is inadmissible. There is, however, an exception in cases where an equivocation arises. Formerly prior to the enactment of s21 of the Administration of Justice Act 1982 evidence of the intention was inadmissible to aid the construction of wills save in the case of equivocation caused by latent ambiguity. Where there was patent ambiguity on the face of the will extrinsic evidence not admissible to establish the meaning of the terms of the will. However, in respect of testators who die after 1982 extrinsic evidence of intention is readily admissible (see section 10.9, below). The recent decision in *Watson* v *National Children's Home* (1995) The Times 31 October illustrates this. The decision confirms that where the will is ambiguous s21 enables extrinsic evidence of the deceased's intention to be admitted. In this case the testator made a will in 1974 leaving one half of his estate to the National Children's Home and the remaining half to the National Canine Defence League, conditional on the latter caring for any of his domestic pets. If the National Canine Defence League did not agree to this then the residue would pass to the National Children's Home. At the time he made his will the testator owned one dog which predeceased him and was never replaced. The National Children's Home, relying on the authority in *Re Brown's Will* (1881) 18 Ch D 61, claimed that the National Canine Defence League could not fulfil the Testator's condition and therefore could not take the gift. Accordingly they claimed that the National Children's Home would be entitled to the entire estate.

Held: the condition imposed by the testator's will was impossible to fulfil and should be deemed as spent. As such the National Canine Defence League were entitled to their share of the gift absolutely. Clause 3 of the will must be construed as requiring the National Canine Defence League to care for the testator's pets but if the testator had no pets the gift should still pass. If construed in this manner, it would be deemed ambiguous and s21 Administration of Justice Act 1982 would apply, allowing extrinsic evidence of the testator's intention to be admitted. The testator had clearly stated his intention and only if his request that any animals be looked after by the National Canine Defence League was refused would the gift fail and the residue pass to the National Children's Home. In the circumstances of the case the National Canine Defence League had not refused, they merely could not fulfil the request. Therefore the estate would be divided equally between the two charities.

What is an equivocation? There are three types. First, the same name or description fits two persons or things exactly. Second, the same name or description fits one accurately and the other in a popular sense but less accurately. An example of this second type is to be found in *Bennett* v *Marshall*. In this case the testator devised some property to, 'William Marshall, my second cousin'. The testator had no second cousins of that name. He did, however, have two first cousins once removed, one of whom was called William Marshall, the other William J R B Marshall. It was held that since there was an equivocation, declarations of intention were admissible, to remove the doubt as to which cousin was to take.

The third type of equivocation arises where the same name or description fits two objects equally but subject to an inaccuracy common to both. Provided it be a mere blank or applicable to no other thing or person, the court may then reject the inaccuracy as demonstrably false, and the residue will then form the equivocation. In *Re Hubbuck* [1905] P 129 the testatrix appointed as her executrix, 'my grand-daughter'. At the date of her will the testatrix had three grand-daughters. It was held that in cases where there occurred only a partial blank and not a complete blank, extrinsic evidence, including that of the testator's intentions, was admissible in order to ascertain which grand-daughter was intended. See also *Phelan* v *Slattery* (1887) 19 LR 177.

Evidence of the testator's intention is not excluded merely because it appears from other parts of the will that there are two persons equally answering the description. The case of *Doe d Gord* v *Needs* (1836) 2 M & W 129 illustrates this point. Here the testator devised one house to 'George Gord, the son of George Gord', another house to 'George Gord, the son of John Gord', and a third to 'George Gord, the son of Gord'. It was held that evidence of the testator's intention was admissible to show that by the third devisee he, in fact, intended George Gord son of George Gord.

There is no equivocation if the description is equally applicable to two persons or things, but upon the true construction of the will it is decisively shown which of the two was meant by the testator. But if there are slight and inconclusive indications of the testator's intentions, this is not sufficient to exclude the definition from being treated as equivocal. Thus a gift to Morgan Morgan, followed by a gift to Morgan Morgan of Mottvey where there were two Morgan Morgans, one of whom came from Mottvey, is not enough to show that the first Morgan Morgan was not the one who came from Mottvey. See *Doe d Morgan* v *Morgan* (1832) 1 Cr & M 235. On the other hand, where the testator made a devise to 'Matthew Westlake, my brother and to Simon Westlake, my brother's son, my house called S, jointly and severally', it being proved that he had three brothers, Thomas, Richard and Matthew, each of whom had a son called Simon, it was held that where it was clear on the construction of the will that it was Matthew Westlake's son that was meant, there was no equivocation and therefore evidence of the testator's intention was inadmissible. See *Doe d Westlake* v *Westlake* (1820) 4 B & Ald 57. See also *Douglas* v *Fellows* (1853) Kay 114.

A rule of construction may resolve an equivocation. A good example is *Re Jackson* [1933] Ch 237. In this case the testatrix left her entire estate on trust for sale for her two brothers and two sisters 'and my nephew Arthur Murphy'. The testatrix had two legitimate nephews and an illegitimate nephew. All three nephews were called Arthur Murphy. It was held that in the circumstances before the court it was entitled to look at evidence of the testatrix's family, and if such evidence showed that the illegitimate nephew was intended this could not be disregarded. There was such evidence. If the testatrix had had only one legitimate nephew and one illegitimate nephew, the reference would not have been equivocal since it is presumed that such references refer to legitimate relations, therefore no evidence of the testator's intention would have been admissible. Again, if there had been only two legitimate nephews the statement would have been equivocal but the gift would have failed since it would have been impossible to resolve the ambiguity.

When evidence of intention is admissible, declarations made by the testator before and after, as well as declarations contemporaneous with, the will are admissible. See *Langham* v *Sanford* (1816) 19 Ves 641, 649.

Extrinsic evidence: s21 Administration of Justice Act 1982

Under s21 extrinsic evidence, including evidence of the testator's intention, may be admitted to assist in the interpretation of wills in three cases. This means that it will no longer be the case that direct evidence can only be admitted where there is an equivocation. The wording of the section is not, however, particularly clear and it seems likely that a possible approach may be to try and bring each will under the section as a whole and not to spend too much time drawing distinctions between the three classes of case to which the section refers.

By s21(1)(a) the court now has power to admit evidence, including evidence of intention, in all cases where any part of the will is 'meaningless'. The word 'meaningless' in this context may mean that it applies where part of the will fails to make any grammatical sense or where the words used in the particular context have no meaning.

For example, where the testator had given 'to my son William the sum of i.x.x. To my son Robert Charles the sum of o.x.x.' the reference to i.x.x. and o.x.x. would be 'meaningless'. It would therefore appear that the court could now admit evidence of the testator's intention. See *Kell* v *Charmer* (1856) 23 Beav 195. This paragraph does not appear relevant in cases where their literal meaning is clear enough, but the words have no meaning when they are read in the light of surrounding circumstances.

Under s21(1)(b) the court may now admit evidence, including that of the testator's intention, where 'the language used in any part of it is ambiguous on the face of it (the will)'. Thus, where the testator uses a word such as 'money' or 'issue' which is capable of bearing more than one meaning depending upon the circumstances of its use this will be applicable. The paragraph refers to the language of a part of the will being ambiguous. A possible problem may arise since it is not clear whether it means 'ambiguous' when that part of the will is read on its own, or 'ambiguous' when the will is read as a whole. The latter construction appears to be correct, thus where the language loses its ambiguity once the whole will has been construed, the section would not apply. Section 21(1)(b) is applicable, therefore, where a word or phrase used is capable of bearing more than one meaning and the particular meaning which the testator intended cannot be ascertained from the will as a whole. Thus in the case of *Baylis* v *Att-Gen* (1741) 2 Atk 239 a beneficiary's actual name was left blank in the will. This was a patent ambiguity and extrinsic evidence could not be brought in to solve it (but see *Doe d Gord* v *Needs* (1836) 2 M & W 129). The new s21(1)(b) would now solve the problem presented by a case such as *Baylis*.

The provision was considered in *Re Williams* [1985] 1 All ER 964 where a testatrix left a home-made will which set out a list of 25 names divided into three groups. The groups were of unequal size and contained no common theme as each contained next of kin, close relatives and organisations. The will contained no indication as to the purpose of the list and groupings and there were no words of gift used. However, the testatrix wrote a letter to her solicitors the day before her death asking them to give various legacies to the members of the groups she wanted in her will. The question arose whether the letter could be admitted under s21(2). Nicholls J held that the will was ambiguous on its face and admitted the letter under s21(1)(b). However, he found it of no assistance when construing the will. He added that extrinsic evidence could be admitted under s21(1)(b) and s21(2) to show which of two or more possible meanings the testator had attached to a particular word or phrase, as long as that meaning was one which the word or phrase as read in its context was capable of bearing. However, if the meaning was one which the word or phrase cannot bear then the court cannot apply the provisions.

Section 21(1)(c) deals with cases where the language of any part of the will is 'ambiguous in the light of surrounding circumstances', and evidence, other than that of testator's intention, has failed to resolve the ambiguity. For example, this paragraph may apply to cases like *National Society for the Prevention of Cruelty to*

Children v *Scottish National Society for the Prevention of Cruelty to Children* [1915] AC 207. The testator left a legacy to the NSPCC, the exact name of the English society. However, the testator lived in Scotland and had shown interest in the Scottish society. The court refused to admit this evidence to show that the Scottish society was intended and applied the money to the English society which was correctly described. It would appear that this paragraph would be applicable and evidence of the testator's intention would be admissible. As noted above, the recent case of *Watson* v *National Children's Home* (1995) The Times 31 October confirms the position in the case of deaths since 1982.

Sections 20 to 21 overlap to some extent. The Law Reform Committee recognised this and considered that the proper approach was to decide the correctness of the words in the will in the first instance, that is, whether they are in the will by mistake, or omitted by mistake, and then to interpret the will.

10.3 Equitable presumptions

Extrinsic evidence of the testator's intention is admissible to rebut three equitable presumptions, or to support such presumptions if there is evidence to rebut them.

The ground for admission of evidence is not in the first instance to show the intention of the document but to decide whether the presumption is raised or not. See *Kirk* v *Eddowes* (1844) 3 Ha 509. If no presumption is raised, or if there is no proof offered to rebut it, then evidence to create or strengthen it is inadmissible. When the meaning of the document is clearly ascertained by construction, no evidence of intention can be given by both sides, but if the presumption of intent is raised then it is always rebuttable and therefore supporting evidence is allowed.

Satisfaction of portions

The rule only applies to portions given by a father or someone *in loco parentis*. See *Fowkes* v *Pascoe* (1875) 10 Ch App. It does not apply to a mother, unless proof is given that the duty of providing for the child has been assumed by her or has fallen on her.

A gift only constitutes a portion if it has been made for the purpose of establishing the child or of making permanent provision for him. (Where there is no evidence as to the purpose of the gift then if the sum is substantial in itself, this will raise the presumption). See *Re Hayward* [1957] Ch 528. Thus, if the testator (father or person *in loco parentis*) has covenanted to provide for a child, for instance on her/his marriage, and afterwards in his will makes a substantially similar provision, equity, presuming against double portions, holds that the latter is in satisfaction of the former, unless otherwise expressed. Evidence may be admitted to rebut the presumption.

For example, in *Re Tussaud* (1878) 9 Ch D 363, a testator made a settlement upon his daughter at her marriage of £2,000 to be paid six months after his death. He paid the trustees of the settlement £1,000 in part satisfaction of the sum. In his will he subsequently left her a legacy of £2,800. In order to rebut the presumption against double portions, evidence that the testator had declared that he intended the legacy to be in addition to the settlement, and not in satisfaction of it, was held admissible.

Satisfaction of debts

A presumption of satisfaction is raised where a legacy is left to a creditor of equal or greater amount than the debt. Evidence is admissible to support or rebut the presumption. In *Plunkett* v *Lewis* (1844) 3 Ha 316, A, a father, owed his daughter a debt. He settled property on her at her marriage far in excess of the debt. The settlement was expressed to be 'in consideration of natural love and affection'. It was held that a presumption that the debt was satisfied had been raised. Therefore evidence in support or rebuttal was admissible.

Contrary to the rule as to portions, equity leans against the satisfaction of debts. There are three requirements which equity makes before the presumption is raised. First, the testator must owe the debt to the creditor before he makes the will or codicil. This is because there can be no intention to satisfy a debt before it is incurred. Second, the testator must give a pecuniary legacy which is equal to or greater than the debt. A sum less than the debt does not give rise to the presumption. See *Eastwood* v *Vinke* (1731) 2 P Wms 613. It must be a pecuniary legacy, so a devise of land or a residuary legacy or a current account will not raise the presumption. See *Horlock* v *Wiggins* (1889) 39 Ch D 142; see also *Re Huish* (1890) 43 Ch D 260. Third, the pecuniary legacy must be as advantageous to the creditor as the debt. For example, in *Clark* v *Sewell* (1744) 3 Atk 96, a legacy which was to be paid one month after the testator's death was treated as less beneficial than the debt. However, the presumption will probably arise if the testator gives an immediate legacy, with no fixed time for payment, since, although it is only payable at the end of the executor's year, it carries interest.

Extrinsic evidence of the testator's intention is admissible in such cases to rebut the presumption. The presumption can also be excluded by a contrary intention. In *Chancey's Case* (1725) it was held that where there was a direction to pay debts and legacies this constituted an expressed contrary intention, therefore the creditor was entitled to both the debt and the legacy. Again a direction to pay debts also constitutes a contrary intention. See *Re Manners* [1949] Ch 613.

Ademption and repetition of legacies

Ademption

Where a father or person *in loco parentis* leaves a legacy to a child and afterwards makes an advancement, the legacy is presumed to be adeemed *pro tanto*. Thus in *Re Pollock* (1885) 28 Ch D 552, A, by a will in 1874, bequeathed to B, her husband's niece, '£500 according to the wish of my late husband'. In 1881 A paid B £300, making an entry in her diary, 'A legacy from B's uncle'. It was held that the presumption was raised, therefore evidence that A, a year before payment, had told her friends that she had asked B whether she wanted £300 now or £500 by will, and that B had written saying she preferred the former, was admissible. This evidence was not as proof that the conversation had taken place, but as showing A's intention at the time of the conversation. This case is by way of exception to the rule that the person giving the gift must be father or *in loco parentis* since it occurs where both the legacy and a later gift are expressly given for a particular purpose. For example, in *Re Corbett* [1903] 2 Ch 326, the equitable presumption was raised where the testator left a legacy to a hospital's endowment fund and subsequently made an *inter vivos* gift for the same purpose.

Repetition, legacies cumulative or substitutional

Legacies whether identical in amount or not, given to a stranger legatee by different instruments are cumulative unless otherwise expressed. This is a rule of construction, therefore, evidence 'contra' is inadmissible.

Legacies, given by different instrument, but identical both in 'amount' and motive, are substitutional; this being a legal presumption it is rebuttable by evidence. The court will only raise this presumption where there is the double coincidence of the same amount and the same motive in each instrument. In *Hurst* v *Beach* (1823) 5 Madd 351 a testator left a legacy to B, for a certain amount and expressed to be for a certain motive. Later the testator left a legacy of the same amount and for the same motive to B, in a codicil. Declarations by the testator that he intended the legacies to be cumulative were admissible to rebut the presumption of substitution.

However, there must be an expressed motive and not merely a descriptive reference. See *Roch* v *Callen* (1848) 6 Ha 531. Legacies given by the same instrument are cumulative if they are of different amounts, unless otherwise stated. See *Brennan* v *Moran* (1855) 6 ICLR 126. If the amount is the same then there is a presumption that they are substitutional. See *Burkinshaw* v *Hodge* (1874) 22 WR 484. In that case there was a gift to trustees, and the legacies were introduced by the words 'upon trust to pay', and 'upon further trust to pay'. Here there was an intention to give both. Probably in both cases these presumptions are rules of construction and therefore not rebuttable by evidence.

The presumptions of satisfaction and ademption do not apply in favour of strangers

The presumptions are only applied against a child in favour of other children and not in favour of a widow or stranger or grandchild. See *Meinertzagen* v *Walters* (1872) LR 7 Ch 670; *Re Heather* [1906] 2 Ch 230. Thus, if the testator divides his residue between his sons A and B and a stranger C and after making his will gives A a portion of £3,000, and his distributable residue is £15,000, the doctrine will not apply in favour of C, who will receive £5,000, but it will be applied in favour of B, with the result that B will receive £6,500 and A, having already received £3,000 as a portion, will get from the executors £3,500 only. See *Re Vaux* [1938] Ch 581, 590.

10.4 Section 24 of the Wills Act 1837

In construing a gift in a will, it is important to determine whether the testator was referring to subject matter falling within the terms of the gift which he possessed at the date of executing the will or whether he was referring to subject matter he might have which fell within the terms of the gift at the time of his death. Thus, for example, if T devises 'the house I live in' to X in a will dated 1980 and he lived in Whiteacre then but later sold Whiteacre and purchased Blackacre in which he lived at his death in 1966, the question arises whether Blackacre passes under the gift. If the gift is construed as referring to the house T lived in when he made the will then the sale of Whiteacre would have caused the gift to adeem. See *Re Sikes* [1927] 1 Ch 364. But if it is construed as referring to the house T lived in when he died then Blackacre passes to X. See *Re Willis* [1911] 2 Ch 563. The provisions of s24 of the Wills Act are important in determining the date at which the will is to be construed with reference to the subject matter of gifts. It provides:

> 'Every will shall be construed, with reference to the real estate and personal estate comprised in it, to speak and take effect as if it had been executed immediately before the death of the testator, unless a contrary intention shall appear by the will.'

The effect of this provision would appear to be that, *prima facie*, gifts must be construed with reference to the subject matter in the estate immediately before the testator's death. This *prima facie* rule may be rebutted by evidence to the contrary. The clearest case of evidence to the contrary is where the gift is, in its terms, clearly a specific gift. But, even here, the gift may be specific *vis-à-vis* property in the estate at death.

Section 24 applies to specific gifts, general gifts and residuary gifts. It is important to note that the section is concerned only with the construction of gifts; it does not say that a will is to be construed as if it were made on the day of the testator's death. See *Re Portal and Lamb* (1885) 30 Ch D 50 per Lindley LJ.

As regards specific gifts, it is here that s24 assumes considerable importance. In the majority of cases a specific gift will be referring to property comprised in the testator's estate at the date he made his will. However, it can also include a reference to property in the estate at the testator's death, for example, 'the house I live in at my death to X'. This is because the definition of a specific gift only requires that it be part of the testator's estate; it does not require it to be part of the estate at any particular time. See *Bothamley* v *Sherson* (1875) LR 20 Eq 304. If the specific gift expressly or by implication refers to property in the testator's estate at the date of his will then s24 will be excluded; there is a 'contrary intention' appearing by the will. The importance of this is that if the gift is specific and construed as showing a contrary intention to s24 and the subject matter is replaced between the date of the will and the date of death, then the gift will have adeemed and, consequently, the beneficiary will receive nothing. Thus, in *Re Sikes* [1927] 1 Ch 364 a testatrix made a specific bequest of 'my piano'; she sold it after making the will and replaced it with another piano. It was held that the legacy failed by ademption. In *Re Gibson* (1866) LR Eq 669 a bequest of 'my one hundred North British Railway preference shares' was held to refer to those shares the testator possessed at the date he made the will. Thus, as these shares had been sold after the date of the will and replaced, the gift adeemed. In this case Wood V-C added:

> 'When there is a clearly indicated intention upon the face of the will, to give a single specific thing and nothing else, it would be a very narrow construction of s24 of the Wills Act to hold that you must sweep in everything to which the words might be held to apply, without the slightest reference to the state of things existing at the date of the will.'

Thus in many, but not all, cases where the word 'my' is used, the gift will be considered as referring to the state of things at the date of the will and excluding s24.

In some decided cases a specific gift has included the word 'now' and the question has arisen whether the inclusion of this word shows a contrary intention under s24 of the Wills Act. Thus, for sample, if T devised 'the house I now live in' to X, the reference to now might be construed as referring to the house he lived in when he made the will. Whether the gift will be so construed depends upon whether the use of the word 'now' is to be regarded as an essential part of the description of the gift, in which case there is a contrary intention under s24, or whether it is to be regarded as mere addition to the description and not part of it. In *Re Champion* [1893] 1 Ch 101 the testator devised a freehold cottage and its adjoining lands 'now in my occupation'. After he made the will he acquired more lands adjoining the cottage. If there was a contrary intention under s24 these lands would not pass under the devise; if there was no such contrary intention then the gift would be construed immediately before death and to include the newly acquired lands. The former view was adopted because the will showed that the word 'now' was used as an essential part of the description of the property. Contrast *Re Willis* [1911] 2 Ch 563 where a testator devised 'all my freehold house and premises situate at Oakleigh Park, Whetstone ... and known as "Ankerwyke" and in which I now reside'. The word 'now' was not considered as an essential part of the description of the devise but merely additional words to identify the property being referred to.

The effect of s24 on ademption has already been referred to but, as *Re Champion* illustrates, it may also be important in determining if new interests acquired by the testator after he made his will can come within the gift. If the gift is specific and to be construed as at the date of the will in respect of references to property it will not include later-acquired interests. But there appears to be one exception to this, namely where the testator enlarges his estate in realty between the date of the will and his death. In *Re Fleming's Will Trusts* [1974] 1 WLR 1552 the testator made a gift of 'my leasehold house, 54 Narcissus Road'. Before his death the testator acquired the freehold interest in the property. Templeman J held that the freehold passed under the gift; he said:

'A gift of property discloses an intention to give the estate and interest of the testator in that property at his death; a mere reference in the will to the estate and interest held by the testator at the date of the will is not sufficient to disclose a contrary intention.'

Perhaps the conclusion is that the reference to the leasehold was merely additional description and not an essential part of the description.

Whether s24 applies or has been excluded by a contrary intention may be important in determining if the subject matter of a gift has been cut down by subsequent acts of the testator. This is illustrated by *Re Evans* [1909] 1 Ch 784 where the testator devised his 'house and effects known as Cross Villa, situate in Templeton'. At the date of the will the house had extensive grounds but afterwards the testator divided the grounds and created two new plots on which he erected two semi-detached houses. Joyce J held that the precision of description in the will showed a contrary intention so that all the property passed. However, if s24 had not been excluded the extent of the property would have been reduced as the argument in that case clearly shows.

Problems may arise in applying s24 in cases where the will contains a bequest of shares and these shares have been sub-divided or otherwise altered after the date of the will. This arose in *Re Clifford* [1912] 1 Ch 29 where the bequest was of 'twenty-three of the shares belonging to me in the London and County Banking Company Limited'. The testator had 104 £80 shares at the date of the will. Afterwards the shares were sub-divided, each £80 share being sub-divided into four £20 shares. The testator never dealt with his shares after making his will. On his death it was argued that the bequest only passed 23 £20 shares. Swinfen Eady J rejected this because there was a contrary intention under s24 so the testator was taken as referring to £80 shares before sub-division. Accordingly 92 £20 shares passed under the bequest. Note there was no ademption here as there was a change in name and form only, not in substance. See *Re Slater* [1907] 1 Ch 665.

Section 24 only affects the subject-matter of gifts; it does not affect the construction of the will as regards the objects of a gift. In the latter case the object referred to in the will will be taken to be the object at the date the will was made. Thus, for example, a bequest to 'John Smith of Blackacre' will refer to the John Smith of Blackacre at the date of the will. Two exceptions exist to this rule, namely (1) that the will may make it clear that the object is to be construed as at the date of death, or (2) where the gift is to the holder of a title or office for the time being. Thus, in *Re Whorwood* (1887) 34 Ch D 446 a gift of an heirloom to 'Lord S' was construed as a gift to the holder of the title at the date of the will in the absence of indications to the contrary. But, in *Re Daniels* (1918) 87 LJ Ch 661 a gift to the Lord Mayor of London was held to be a gift to the holder of that office for the time being.

10.5 Section 27 of the Wills Act 1837

Section 27 of the Wills Act provides that any general gift of real or personal estate shall be construed so as to cover such property over which the testator has a general power of appointment and shall operate as an execution of that power unless there is a contrary intention. The effect of s27 is to put property over which the testator has a general power of appointment on the same footing as his own property.

Classification of powers under s27

The terms of s27 are applicable only to general powers of appointment; thus it is necessary to determine what is a general power for the purposes of the section.

1. A power to appoint generally except for certain specified people is not a general power within s27. See *Re Byron's Settlement* [1891] 3 Ch 474. However, should the excepted person die before the power is exercised it then becomes a general power. See *Re Byron's Settlement* (1891). Again, a power limited to those living at the appointor's death is not within the section. See *Re Jones* [1945] Ch 105.
2. A power to appoint only by a will which expressly refers to the power is outside the section, being incompatible with the condition that the appointment be in 'any manner he may think proper'. See *Re Phillips* (1889) 41 Ch D 417.
3. A gift of all property 'over which I shall have any power of disposition by will' is a sufficient reference to exercise a general power of appointment by will expressly referring to the power. A devise by a testator of leaseholds upon such trusts as his wife might have declared or should thereafter declare with respect to the disposition of her residuary estate by her will gives the wife a general power. See *Bristow* v *Skirrow* (1859) 27 B 585. Where a testator gives a beneficiary power to direct that a given sum may be raised and paid to such persons as the donee thinks fit, this gives a general power of appointment within s27. See *Re Jones* (1886) 34 Ch D 65; *Re Wilkinson* [1910] 2 Ch 216.

Where the testator makes a gift of 'such part of my personal estate as shall consist of money or securities for money' or 'all stocks, shares and securities which I possess or to which I am entitled', this is construed as a bequest of personal property described in a general manner, and will exercise the general power so far as it extends to property of the kind described. See *Turner* v *Turner* (1852) 21 LJ Ch 843; *Re Jacob* [1907] 1 Ch 445; *Re Doherty-Waterhouse* [1918] 2 Ch 269. General pecuniary legacies are also within s27 because they constitute a 'bequest of personal property described in a general manner'. See *Hawthorn* v *Shedden* (1856) 3 Sm & G 293.

Section 27 does not operate if there is a contrary intention. A contrary intention can be defined as the conscious non-exercise of the power. See *Scriven* v *Sandom* (1862) 2 J & H 743. However, the mere fact that a power is contained in a settlement made before the will, does not, of itself, raise the presumption that there is a contrary intention. Again, should the testator attempt to exercise the power but for some reason it proves ineffectual, this will not prevent a residuary gift from passing the property subject to the power. See *Re Spooner's Trust* (1851) 2 Sim (NS) 129; *Re Box's Settlement* (1945) 172 LT 312. The fact that the exercise fails by lapse or revocation is irrelevant. See *Re Jarrett* [1919] 1 Ch 366. No contrary intention is shown if the testator gives a life interest to a person, and if that person survives the testator the power is gone. And, interestingly, no contrary intention is shown by the appointment of a life interest under a special power to a person who also takes a life interest by virtue of a general power, if the property under the power is disposed of in default of its use. See *Moss* v *Harter* (1854) 2 Sm & G 458. (See *Theobald*, 13th edn, p294 on power to bar entails under s176 of the LPA 1925.)

10.6 Whether gift is absolute or for life

Under s28 of the Wills Act 1837 a devise to a person without words of limitation is to be construed as passing the fee simple or other whole interest over which the testator had power to dispose of by will, unless there is a contrary intention. The rule does not apply where an annuity is given to a person without limitation. The question arises as to whether it was intended to be for life or perpetual. In such a case the interest being ready created will not be affected by the section. See *Nicholls* v *Hawkes* (1853) 10 Ha 342.

Sometimes a testator will give a legatee 'what remains' of certain property which has been 'given' to some other person. The question arises as to whether the testator intended an absolute and then a gift over of what remains – in which case the absolute gift remains but the attempted gift over is void – or does the testator intend to cut the absolute interest down to a life interest? In some cases it is impossible to decide from the language of the will, in which case the first gift is construed as being absolute; therefore the gift over fails either for repugnancy or because the subject matter of trust is uncertain. See *Perry* v *Merrit* (1874) LR 18 Eq 152; *Pushman* v *Filliter* (1795) 3 Ves 7.

Thus in *Re Minchell's Will Trusts* [1964] 2 All ER 47, a testator in a home-made will gave his wife everything he possessed or had to leave to his wife 'for her lifetime and after her death if anything should be left over I would like it to be divided as follows'. The court held the words 'for her lifetime' did not constitute words of limitation as there was no mention of a trust of income, and therefore this weighed in favour of an absolute gift. Also considered was the fact that the testator appeared to envisage that all, nothing or something might be left over; this was, of course, contrary to a life interest in which the whole property would be in existence at the death of the life tenant. Thus the widow took the estate absolutely. The court was clearly influenced by the fact that this was a home-made will and that 'one man's nonsense is no guide to another man's nonsense'.

If the proper construction of a gift shows that the testator intended merely a life interest, then the use of a phrase like 'whatever remains' will not stop that intention from being fulfilled. These words could be construed as merely referring to the residue remaining after allowing for normal wear and tear or consumption during the lifetime of the life tenant. See *Re Cameron* (1967) 62 DLR (2d).

In *Hancock* v *Watson* [1902] AC 14, Lord Davey stated:

> 'If you find an absolute gift to a legatee in the first instance and trusts are engrafted or imposed on that absolute interest which fail either from lapse or invalidity or any other reason, then the absolute gift takes effect so far as the trusts have failed, to the exclusion of the residuary legatee or next of kin as the case may be.'

The rule applies where there are apparently two inconsistent provisions in a will, a gift to a person absolutely and later a provision that the gift be subject to certain trusts, say to the children. If that person dies childless, the trusts fail, and under the rule he takes the gift absolutely. Thus the testator is presumed, under the rule, to have only intended to modify the absolute gift so far as to give effect to the trusts. See *Fyffe* v *Irwin* [1939] 2 All ER 271, 282.

The main problem in all these cases is in determining whether there is an absolute gift in the first instance. For the rule to apply, the court must be satisfied that the testator had separated the gift from the rest of his estate, and that behind the engrafted trusts there remains an interest vested in the legatee which will spring up and take effect so far as the engrafted trusts do not exhaust the subject matter of the gift. See *Re Goold's Will Trusts* [1967] 3 All ER 652.

An example is where there is an absolute gift followed by a proviso cutting it down in certain respects. However, although there may be a gift to a legatee, it may be in one continuous sentence together with the restrictions so that an absolute interest cannot be spelt out of the will. See *Lassence* v *Tierney* (1849) 1 Mac & G 551. Thus, if the gift runs straight into a whole series of limitations, the gift is obviously limited. See *Re Payne* [1927] 2 Ch 1.

10.7 Rules for ascertaining classes

To ascertain the class to take under a gift of a fund the court has adopted certain rules of convenience, the principle being that the class is to be ascertained as soon as possible in order that beneficiaries may know what their shares are and the executor may begin to distribute the fund. The rules are known generally as the class closing rules. See *Andrews* v *Partington* (1791) 3 Bro CC 401.

The class closing rules have been criticised from time to time. The main criticism has been that their application frequently runs counter to the intentions of the testator, in the sense that the testator intends all the members to participate in a fund. The rule in *Andrews* v *Partington* provides that the class shall close at the date at which the first member of the class is to take. As stated, this is a rule of convenience designed to assist early vesting. The rule may be excluded by a contrary intention shown by the testator in his will. See *Scott* v *Earl of Scarborough* (1838) 1 Beav 154.

Individual gift to each member of a class

Where there is a gift of a particular sum to each member of a class, the class is fixed at the testator's death. Thus, if a testator leaves £100 to each of the children of A, only those children living at the testator's death are included in the class. This is so also if the gift is contingent upon some event. See *Ringrose* v *Bramham* (1794) 2 Cox Eq 384. Thus if a testator makes the gift contingent on each member of the class attaining 21 years it is only those children alive at the testator's death who can take, provided they fulfil the contingency. If there are no children alive at the testator's death, the gift fails. See *Re Belville* [1941] Ch 414; *Rogers* v *Mutch* (1878) 10 Ch D 25. If the rule were otherwise, the executors would be unable to distribute the residue until the parent had died.

There is, however, a modification to the rule if there is a postponement such as an intervening life interest. Thus, where a testator gives his estate to X for life and after his death to pay £100 to each of the children of A, the class will remain open until the death of the life tenant. Therefore, children born after the testator's death but before the life tenant's death are included in the class. See *Att-Gen* v *Crispin* (1784) 1 Bro CC 386.

The rule can be excluded, so as to allow children born after the testator's death to take, if there is no inconvenience caused or it is expressly envisaged. Thus where a testator set aside a fund to pay the legacies there is no inconvenience and the rule is excluded. In this case, however, the gift was demonstrative not specific. *Evans* v *Harris* (1842) 5 B 45. The second exception occurred where the testator expressly included those children born after his death. See *Defflis* v *Goldschmidt* (1816) 19 Ves 566.

Immediate class gifts without any age requirement

Under a gift to a class without any provisions as to the time of vesting, the class closes at the testator's death, if any members of the class are alive at that time to the exclusion of after-born members. See *Viner* v *Francis* (1789) 2 Cox 190. The same rule applies where the gift is vested but the time for payment is postponed until the youngest member of the class attains a specified age. See *Re Manners* [1955] 1 WLR 1096. Again the class is not enlarged if there is a gift over in the event of all or any of the class not attaining 21 years, nor by a gift over in default of children. See *Davidson* v *Dallas* (1808) 14 Ves 576.

Where there are no children alive at the testator's death then the class remains open indefinitely and all the children are entitled whenever born. See *Weld* v *Bradbury* (1715) 2 Vern 705.

Class gift following life interest

An example of such a gift is 'to X for life, and after X's death to the children of A'. The class, in this instance, closes on X's death, in other words when the postponement ends. See *Re Emmet's Estate* (1880) 13 Ch D 484. If however, there are no children of A in existence at X's death, the class will remain open indefinitely. *Chapman* v *Blissett* (1735) Cas t Talb 145. Since in a gift in this category the class will normally remain open until the life tenant's death, all those born before the life tenant's death are included as well as all those born before the testator's death. See *Re Knapp's Settlement* [1895] 1 Ch 91. However, should any child die after the testator's death but before the life tenant's death then his share will not lapse but will pass to his personal representatives as an asset of his estate. See *Devisme* v *Mello* (1782) 1 Bro CC 527.

If no children are born before the death of the tenant for life all after-born children are included. See *Wyndham* v *Wyndham* (1790) 3 Bro CC 58. However, this rule does not apply if there is a clear intention that distribution is to be made once for all when the fund falls into possession. See *Godfrey* v *Davis* (1801) 6 Ves 43.

The release or disclaimer by a life tenant of his life interest does not necessarily have the effect of altering the membership of the class of remaindermen to take. Thus, where there is a gift to A for life, remainder to the children of A, all the children of A, who must be ascertained at A's death, are members of the class. If A had released his life interest *inter-vivos* this would not have excluded after-born children of A. Thus the prior release or disclaimer of a life tenancy does not affect the composition of the class, unless the construction of the will demands it. See *Re Harker's Will Trusts* [1969] 1 WLR 1124; *Re Kebty-Fletcher's Will Trusts* [1969] 1 Ch 339.

Class gift where contingency is imposed on each member

Where there is contingent class gift which is immediate, the class closes on the testator's death if any member of the class has satisfied the contingency at that time. See *Picken* v *Matthews* (1878) 10 Ch D 264. For example, if a testator makes a gift of '£5,000 to the children of A who attain 21 years', the class will close at the testator's death if any of the class have attained 21 years at that time. If there are no children of A who have satisfied the contingency at the testator's death, the class will close when the first member attains 21 years. In this type of case the class-closing rule is known as the rule in *Andrews* v *Partington*.

In *Re Drummond's Settlement* [1988] 1 All ER 449 under a 1924 settlement the settlor declared that certain funds were to be held on trust for himself during his lifetime and thereafter for such of his three daughters as were living at his death and attained the age of 21 or married under that age and for the issue of any daughter who predeceased him, such issue to take their parents' share equally among themselves on their attaining the age of 21 or marrying under that age. The beneficial interests created or intended to be created by the settlement were set out in a single continuous and unpunctuated clause.

The clause provided that 'after the decease of each of the daughters' her share of the trust fund was to be held on trust for such of her children or other issue as she directed in her will and in default of such direction then in equal shares for each of her children as attained 21 or if female married under that age. The clause provided, finally, that if a daughter died without any child living to take a vested interest in her share, that share was to be divided equally 'amongst such of the daughters as shall then be living and the issue of any of them who may be then dead'.

All three daughters survived the settlor and in 1984 one of the daughters, E, died without issue. The trustees of the settlement sought the determination of the court on the question whether E's share was to be held on trust for the surviving two daughters or whether the trust relating to E's share infringed the rule against perpetuities because potential beneficiaries would have included the issue of either of the other daughters if they had predeceased E.

At first instance it was held that the limitation was void for remoteness and that there was a resulting trust in favour of the settlor's estate.

The Court of Appeal held that the point of time to which the words 'shall then be living' in the final part of the clause referred was the death of each of the daughters, with the result that there could be no perpetuity because the daughters were all lives in being at the date of the settlement and the interests in each share had to vest within 21 years from the death of the last surviving daughter. E's share accordingly fell to be divided in equal shares between the surviving daughters.

When the class closes in either of the above examples, all those children in being at the testator's death are included in the class, but to become entitled to their share they must all satisfy the contingency. In the case where there are no children at the testator's death, the class probably closes when the first child attains 21 years, and children born after that are excluded. See *Pearce* v *Cotton* (1839) 1 B 352; *Re Bleckly* [1951] Ch 740.

Contingent class gift following a life interest

In the case of a gift to A for life, then to A's children who attain 21 years, the class closes at the life tenant's death, or when the eldest attains 21, which ever is last. See *Clarke* v *Clarke* (1836) 8 Sim 59; *Re Emmet's Estate* (1880) 13 Ch D 484. If the life interest is determinable by some event, for instance if the life tenant marries, the class will close at the determination or when the first child attains 21 years. See *Re Bleckley*, above.

If there is no child alive at the life tenant's death or when the life interest determines, the class closes when the first child reaches 21 years, to the exclusion of all those born afterwards. See *Re Bleckley*, above.

The prior release or disclaimer of the life tenancy will not affect the composition of the class unless the construction of the will demands it. See *Re Harker's Will Trusts* [1969] 1 WLR 1124.

Gift of income to a class

The class closing rules do not apply where a testator makes a gift of income to a class. For example, if there is a gift of the income of a fund of £250,000 equally between the children of A, then all A's children regardless of when born are entitled. This is so even where there is a contingency imposed on the members of the class.

Although none of the children is excluded from the class, they may be excluded from receiving the income on a particular instalment. For instance, if at the testator's death there is only one child alive, that child will receive the whole of the first instalment. When another child is born thereafter the income from the subsequent instalments is divided equally between the two children. See *Re Ward* [1965] Ch 856.

10.8 Statutory rules of construction

Adopted children: Adoption Act 1976

An adopted child is treated as the legitimate child of the adoptive parents and not as the child of the natural parents. This applies to the construction of wills where the testator dies after 31 December 1975 irrespective of the date of the adoption order, but this is subject to a contrary intention. Where there is a gift in a will which depends upon the date of birth of a child the disposition is to be construed as if:

1. the adopted child had been born on the date of the adoption;
2. two or more children adopted on the same date had been born on that date in the order of their actual births.

These rules do not affect any reference to the age of a child. For instance, a testator makes a gift by will to A's children 'living at my death or born afterwards'. The testator dies in 1976; after his death A adopts a child, born in 1974. The child can take the gift as he is treated as being born (under (1) above), after the testator's death even though he is not a child living at the testator's death. Further, a gift to the children of A 'living at my death or born afterwards before any one of such children for the time being in existence attains a vested interest and who attains the age of 21 years': A's adopted child (born in 1974) can take if he is adopted before any other child obtains a vested interest and if that adopted child satisfies the contingency. That 21 years is measured from the *real* date of birth, that is, 1974. Thus if a gift is to 'the eldest son of B' and B has a natural son (born 1974) and an adopted son (born 1973 and adopted 1975), if eldest refers to the age of the child the adopted son takes, but if not the natural son takes on the basis of rule (1) above. See ss39 and 42 of the Adoption Act 1976.

Legitimated children: s5 of the Legitimacy Act 1976

A legitimated child is entitled to take under a will any interest where the testator dies after 31 December 1975 as if they were born legitimate. This is, however, subject to a contrary intention.

Where there is a disposition which depends on the date of a child's birth the rules are the same as those which apply to adopted children.

Illegitimate children: Family Law Reform Acts 1969 and 1987

The 1969 Act applies to wills executed after 31 December 1969 and the 1987 Act to wills executed after 3 April 1988. In both cases if a will is executed before the relevant date but confirmed by codicil after the relevant date it will not be treated as made after the relevant date. The common law governs wills executed before 31 December 1969.

At common law, a gift by will to a group of relations is construed, *prima facie*, as a gift to legitimate members of that group only. This presumption could be rebutted by evidence of a contrary intent. In some cases it might be clear from the wording of the will that illegitimate relations were to be included or there might be only illegitimate relations of the description.

This common law rule of construction was reversed by the Family Law Reform Act 1969. When this Act applies, a gift by will to persons related in some manner to some other person is to be construed as including any illegitimate persons of that class. This rule applies unless a contrary intent appears so that a testator could exclude it by, for example, making a gift to 'the legitimate children of X'.

The Act did not apply to the construction of the word 'heir', to any expression used to create an entailed interest, or to the devolution of property which would devolve with a title of honour.

These rules were slightly changed by the 1987 Act. The general principle of the Act is that references to any relationship between two persons are to be construed without regard to whether the father and mother of either of them, or the father and mother of any person through whom the relationship is deduced, were married to each other at any time. Again this rule of construction applies 'unless the contrary intention appears'.

The Act does apply to the construction of the word 'heir' and to expressions used to create an entailed interest, but not to the devolution of property which would devolve with a title of honour.

10.9 The Administration of Justice Act 1982

Rectification: s20

The court now has a limited power to rectify wills. 'If a court is satisfied that a will is so expressed that it fails to carry out the testator's intentions, in consequence (1) of a clerical error; or (2) of a failure to understand his instruction; it may order that the will shall be rectified so as to carry out his intentions' (s20(1)).

The courts have equitable power to rectify a deed which by mistake does not express correctly the common intention of the parties to it and statutory powers to do so on application by a party affected. The correction concerns generally an error, such as a clerical error, which is made by mutual mistake, and is allowed at the court's discretion on applicaiton by an affected party. See the recent case of *Wordingham* v *Royal Exchange Trust Co Ltd and Another* [1992] 2 WLR 496. In 1979 the testatrix made her will. Under clause 4 of the will she exercised the power of appointment in order to appoint her interest in the income from her share of the residue under her father's will to the plaintiff for life if he should survive her. The plaintiff indeed outlived the testatrix. In 1989 the testatrix, wishing to make a new will, explained to her solicitor that she intended to alter the 1979 will instead of re-drafting a brand new will, leaving the earlier provisions to stand where it was not necessary to alter them.

A new will was drafted and executed. However, the new will did not contain the clause that corresponded to clause 4 of the 1979 will.

Held: the words 'clerical error' used in s20 were to be construed as meaning an error made in the process of recording the intended words of the testator in the drafting or transcription of his will. This meaning was to be distinguished from an error made in carrying out his intentions through the choice of words of the draftsman, and contrasted with the mistaken choice of words because of a failure to understand the testator's intention. These cases were covered by sub-clause (b) of s20 of the Administration of Justice Act.

On the facts the failure to include in the draft new will a paragraph following the provisions of clause 4 of the 1979 will, was an error made in the process of recording the intended words of the testatrix which constituted a clerical error within s20(1)(a). It was therefore found that the order rectifying the 1989 will was justified. The more recent decision in *Re Segelman (deceased)* [1995] 3 All ER 676 should be noted regarding the testator's intention in circumstances where the will contained a proviso restricting the class of beneficiaries. Since the failure to delete the proviso was considered to be a clerical error rectification was ordered.

The court previously had a power to correct errors but it was severely restricted. This was a power to omit words from probate where it was clear that the testator did not know and approve of them. For example, in *Re Morris* [1971] P 62, a testatrix made a will where clause 7 contained 20 legacies; later she instructed her solicitor to revoke clause 3 and clause 7(iv). However, the solicitor prepared a codicil which actually revoked the whole of clause 7. The testatrix executed the codicil without noticing the mistake. The nearest that the court could get to giving effect to the testatrix's intention was to omit the number 7. This type of case would now come under s20(1)(a) since this was a clerical error. The court could therefore have inserted the roman numeral '(iv)'. See also *Re Reynette-James* [1976] 1 WLR 161 and *In the goods of Schott* [1901] P 190, where the court was unable to substitute the word 'residue' for 'revenue'.

Under s20(1)(b) it will still be necessary to distinguish between situations where the draftsman had understood his instructions but failed to use the correct legal language to carry them out and situations where he has simply failed to understand his instructions. In the former case, the court has no power under this section to rectify the will. In *Collins* v *Elstone* [1893] P 1, the testatrix knew and approved of a revocation clause in a codicil and so the court could not omit the clause because this would have involved an inquiry into the testatrix's intentions. Thus, the court will still have to consider whether the testator knew and approved of the contents of the will and adopted any mistakes made; to go beyond mistakes would be to move into the realm of the testator's purpose. The Law Reform Committee in its 19th Report argued that any wider power of rectification would infringe this principle and stated that it did not:

> '... consider that rectification is an appropriate remedy where it cannot be shown that the words of the will are not those which the testator meant to use or intended to be used on his behalf. To go beyond this is to pass into the wider realms of the testator's purpose.'

The duty of the court has always been to ascertain the meaning of the words used by the testator, not to guess what the testator might or might not have meant. See Cotton LJ's statement in *Ralph* v *Carrick* (1879) 11 Ch D, above. Evidence must be adduced to show the form and nature of the mistake alleged. The most important evidence will be the instructions given to the draftsman of the will together with any available drafts of the will. Other contemporaneous statements of the testator are admissible, but oral statements by beneficiaries are unlikely to be of great value, although they too will be admissible.

Section 20(2) provides for a six month time limit on applications for rectification. The six month period runs from the date on which the first grant of representation is taken out, which means that it is possible to rectify a will after probate has been granted. The six month period is not absolute and the court may grant permission to make an application out of time. There are as yet no guidelines as to what the court will take into account on an application under s20 out of time, but it seems likely that the considerations applicable will be similar to those applied for out of time applications under the Inheritance (Provision for Family and Dependants) Act 1975. See Chapter 16, section 16.3, below.

Section 20(3) protects those personal representatives who distribute estates after the six month period for application under this section has passed. Distribution within the six months is not covered by this sub-section and it is doubtful whether it would protect personal representatives who have notice of an application for leave to apply out of time.

Whether gift is absolute or for life: s22

Section 22 provides that:

> 'Except where a contrary intention is shown it shall be presumed that if a testator devises

or bequeathes property to his spouse in terms which in themselves would give an absolute interest to the spouse, but by the same instrument purports to give his issue an interest in the same property, the gift to the spouse is absolute notwithstanding the purported gift to the issue.'

This section applies where a testator appears to give his spouse an absolute gift by will but follows it up with a direction that on her death what remains of the gift should go to his children. This section does not apply where either the initial gift is to a person other than the spouse of the testator or the alleged interests in remainder vest in any persons other than the testator's issue. In such a case the section does not apply and the usual rules of construction apply.

The operation of this section is subject to a contrary intention being shown. It might be thought that such a contrary intention must appear from the will itself, otherwise the position wuld be virtually the same as where problems arise in respect of gifts to persons not within the section, that is, the language could be said to be ambiguous and therefore evidence of intention would be admissible under s21. However, the alternative view that a contrary intention can appear other than on the face of the will is certainly arguable and probably correct. On this view the presumption that the testator intends to give his or her spouse an absolute interest will only arise when there is no evidence of the testator's intention.

11

Intestate Succession

11.1 Introduction

A person is said to die 'intestate' when he does not leave a will. In such circumstances statutory rules of intestate succession will apply to his estate and provide directions as to how it should be distributed. These statutory rules are contained in the Administration of Estates Act 1925 and subsequent amending legislation.

Cases where a person has died without leaving a will are often referred to as cases of 'total intestacy'. Such cases may arise for a variety of reasons:

1. the deceased forgot to make a will;
2. the deceased was young and had not directed his mind to making a will;
3. the deceased was an infant and unable to make a will because of s7 of the Wills Act 1837;
4. the deceased deliberately chose not to make a will because it would have been troublesome and expensive;
5. the deceased made a will but it was revoked by a subsequent marriage under s18 of the Wills Act 1837;
6. the deceased's will is held to have been wholly revoked in a manner recognised by the law of succession.
7. the deceased lacked the requisite testamentary capacity to make a will.

Cases also arise where a person has made a will which does not dispose of his entire estate. Thus, for example, a testator may have left his dwelling house and a legacy of £30,000 to his wife but failed to mention how other assets in his estate should be dealt with, such as his business. To the extent that the will does not deal with the estate, the intestacy rules will be tagged on to the will so as to determine how property undisposed of by the will should be distributed. Cases such as this are often referred to as 'partial intestacy'. There are a variety of reasons why partial intestacy may arise:

1. the deceased has been careless in making his will in that he did not make a gift of residue by the will;
2. the will contained a gift of residue but the residuary legatee predeceased the testator causing the gift to fail;
3. the residuary gift failed for uncertainty, perpetuity, illegality or because the legatee witnessed the will etc;
4. the residuary gift has been revoked;
5. the residuary gift lapsed under s18A of the Wills Act;
6. the residuary gift was subject to forfeiture.

There has been an interesting recent decision illustrating the problems of intestacy. In *Edwards* v *Strong* (1994) The Times 9 November the issues concerned succession in title in the case of intestacy and the effect of a notice served on beneficiaries of the estate.

In this case it was held that the phrase 'successor in title' refers to the person/s in whom property is vested and who are in a position to convey the property. Pending the grant of letters of administration the successor in title was the President of the Family Division. On the facts the plaintiffs had done nothing to give B reason to suppose that they accepted the notice and they were not successors in title for the purpose of the exercise of the option. Neither were they agents of the President of the Family Division. The option had not been exercised validly and the notice was ineffective.

As a result of s14 Law of Property (Miscellaneous Provisions) Act 1994 the powers formerly vested in the President of the Family Division now vest in the Public Trustee. Property already vested in the President vests instead in the Public Trustee, as does the estate of any testator who died earlier and to whose estate the statute will now apply. Certain procedural changes in s17, which affect notices in the case of all deaths, can be referred to in Chapter 17, section 17.3.

11.2 History

Before 1926 realty and personalty devolved differently under the rules of intestate succession. The realty vested in the heir on the intestate's death and the personalty in the personal representatives for the benefit of the next of kin.

11.3 The trust with power to sell

Before 1996, s33(1) of the Administration of Estates Act 1925 provided that the personal representatives would hold the estate of an intestate on trust for sale. Under s33 the personal representatives had a general power to postpone sale, coupled with a duty not to sell the personal chattels and reversionary interests unless required for administration or for some other special reason. The Trusts of Land and Appointment of Trustees Act 1996 has amended this provision so that the personal representatives now hold the property:

> 'On the death of a person intestate as to any real or personal estate, that estate shall be held on trust by his personal representatives with the power to sell it': see Sch 2, para 5(2).

This amended section appears to provide a greater degree of flexibility to the personal representatives, as there is no duty to sell but only a power to sell.

The purpose behind s33(1) is to enable the personal representatives to deal with the administration of the estate. Under the amended s33(2) they are directed to pay out of the ready money of the deceased and any net money arising out of the disposal of any other part of the estate 'all such funeral, testamentary and administration expenses, debts and other liabilities as are properly payable thereout' in the first instance, and then divide the residue among those entitled to it.

Under s33(3) the personal representatives have the power to invest the residuary estate either in full or in part during the minority of any beneficiary. The investments must however be authorised investments. Section 6(1) of the 1996 Act gives the personal representatives the powers of an absolute owner when dealing with any trust of property which includes land.

11.4 Distribution on total intestacy

Section 45 of the Administration of Estates Act abolished descent to heir, curtesy, dower and escheat, and s46 set out a new order for the distribution of the residuary estate of an intestate, that is, the property left in his estate after the payment of debts, expenses etc. Section 46 also places widows and widowers on an equal footing.

The rights of the surviving spouse

Under the table set out in s46(1) distribution to the surviving spouse depends upon the spouse 'surviving' the deceased. Section 1(1) LR(S)A 1995 provides that an intestate's spouse cannot take a share on intestacy unless he or she survives the intestate by 28 days. Where the spouse does not so survive, the intestate's property will be dealt with as if there had been no spouse.

The personal chattels

In all circumstances where there is a surviving spouse he/she is entitled to the personal chattels of the deceased absolutely. For these purposes 'personal chattels' are defined by s55(1)(x) of the Administration of Estates Act 1925 as meaning:

> '... carriages, horses, stable furniture and effects (not used for business purposes), motor cars and accessories (not used for business purposes), garden effects, domestic animals, plate, plated articles, linen, china, glass, books, pictures, prints, furniture, jewellery, articles of household or personal use or ornament, musical and scientific instruments and apparatus, wines, liquors and consumable stores, but do not include any chattels used at the death of the intestate for business purposes nor money or securities for money.'

The above definition includes almost all items which might be found in the home of the average citizen. However, it should be noted that chattels which were used by the deceased for business purposes are excluded from the definition. It appears that partial usage for business purposes is sufficient to exlude a chattel from s55. Money and securites for money are also excluded. Money for these purposes does not include notes or coins kept as a collection but rather circulating banknotes, coins and cheques. See *Re Collin's Will Trusts* [1971] 1 WLR 37 (Ch D).

The value of an item is immaterial in deciding whether it comes within s55. In *Re Crispin's Will Trusts* [1975] Ch 245 (CA), a collection of clocks and watches valued at £50,000 was held to be personal chattels. Nor does it appear relevant that the deceased collected certain items as an investment. In *Re Reynolds* [1966] 1 WLR 19 (Ch D), Stamp J was not impressed by the argument that as the deceased kept a stamp collection valued at £1,848 as an investment it could not be a personal chattel.

In some instances the court appears to have taken the view that certain assets can only be regarded as business assets and therefore outside the definition of s55. In *Re Ogilby* [1942] Ch 288 (Ch D) it was argued that a herd of shorthorn cattle were kept by the deceased on his farm not for profit but rather for personal interest and should be regarded as personal chattels. On reviewing the number of cattle involved and the acreage of the farm, Simmonds J considered it was impossible to regard the farm as anything other than a business. However, his dicta indicate that the keeping of one pet pig, lamb or cow could bring the animal within the definition of 'personal chattel'.

There have been decisions on the exact meaning of one or two items mentioned in s55. In *Re Hutchinson* [1955] Ch 255 the words 'carriages, horses, stable furniture and effects' came up for review. It was argued that these words should be read together rather than individually so limiting the meaning of horses to domestic horses. This was rejected and it was held that 12 racehorses kept by the deceased for recreational purposes were within s55. In *Re Whitby* [1944] Ch 210 (CA) it was argued that 'jewellery' for the purposes of s55 was limited to articles of adornment such as a brooch and did not include uncut diamonds. The Court of Appeal refused to accept such a limited definiton. In *Re Crispin* (above), it was argued that if clocks were kept in a repository, on loan to a museum or locked up in a room they could not be treated as 'furniture' for the purposes of s55. Russell LJ considered this to be irrelevant. The words 'articles of ... personal use', appear to have a wide meaning for the purposes of s55 and are not restricted to items like clothes or umbrellas but can also cover articles used as part of a hobby. Thus, in *Re Chaplin* [1950] Ch 507 (Ch D), a motor yacht used by the deceased for pleasure was held to be within these words.

Particular problems arise where the chattel has a mixed use and is used for business as well as pleasure purposes. This point arose in *Re MacCulloch* (1981) 44 NSR (2d) 666 where a yacht was used partly to produce an income by way of hire and partly as the owner's personal holiday retreat. It was held here that the dominant use of the chattel will determine whether it is a personal chattel for the purpose of intestacy. On the facts of this case as the dominant use was a business one the yacht did not constitute a personal chattel.

The statutory legacy and interest in residue

The other benefits which the surviving spouse receives depends very much on whether the deceased left issue or parents or brothers and sisters of the whole blood. According to s46(1) distribution will be as follows:

Surviving spouse but no issue, or parents or brothers and sisters of the whole blood or their issue – in this case the surviving spouse will take all of the deceased's property.

Surviving spouse and issue – in this case the surviving spouse receives:

1. personal chattels as defined by s55;
2. a statutory legacy of £125,000;
3. interest on the statutory legacy from the date of death until the date of payment;
4. one-half of the residuary estate to be held on trust for the surviving spouse for life and subject thereto on trust for the issue of the deceased. The other half of the residue is held on trust for the issue in equal shares absolutely contingent on attaining the age of 18 or marrying. This is dealt with below.

Surviving spouse and either parents or brothers and sisters of the whole blood of the deceased or their issue – in this case the surviving spouse receives:

1. personal chattels as defined by s55;
2. a statutory legacy of £200,000;
3. interest on the statutory legacy from the date of death until the date of payment;
4. one-half of the residuary estate to be held on trust for the surviving spouse absolutely. (The other half of the residue will go to the parents of the deceased in equal shares absolutely or to the survivor of them. If the deceased had no surviving parents then to his brothers and sisters of the whole blood in equal shares.)

Problems may arise as to the right of a surviving spouse to the statutory legacy under s46 when the deceased died intestate leaving assets, both moveable and immoveable, in England and abroad. If the deceased was domiciled in England then

s46 will apply to his moveables, wherever situated, and his immoveables in England. The section will not apply to immoveables abroad so the benefits the spouse gets from these under foreign intestacy law will not be taken into consideration in assessing her entitlements under s46. This point arose in *Re Collens* [1986] 1 All ER 611 where the deceased died intestate domiciled in Trinidad and Tobago, leaving both moveables and immoveables in that jurisdiction and leaving immoveables in England. The widow's claims in Trinidad on intestacy were settled for $1 million. It was held that she could claim under s46 for a share in the deceased's immoveables in England without bringing into account the benefits she obtained in Trinidad. The deceased's moveables were governed by the law of his domicile and his immoveables were governed by the law of the place where they were situated. Note also the case of *Osoba* [1979] 2 All ER 903.

Section 18 of the Family Law Reform Act 1987 states that references to any relationship between two persons are to be construed without regard to whether the father and mother of either of them (or of any person through whom the relationship is deduced) were married to each other at any time. The consequence of this provision is to remove the distinction between legitimate and illegitimate relations for the purposes of intestate succession. An illegitimate person is able to succeed on the intestacy of his brother, sister, grandparent, uncle and aunt and correspondingly they can succeed on his death intestate.

Redemption of life interests

In the above subsection, it was pointed out that where there is a surviving spouse and issue the surviving spouse is entitled to a life interest in half of the residue. Under the provisions of s47A(1) of the Administration of Estates Act 1925, the surviving spouse has a right to redeem the life interest if he/she chooses. The life interest will be valued and the capital value thereof paid to him/her. The purpose of the provision is to avoid trusts where the capital sum involved is small. The income in such cases would be eaten up by administrative costs or of little real benefit to the surviving spouse.

Rights in respect of the matrimonial home

The surviving spouse is entitled to require the personal representatives to appropriate any dwelling-house in which he/she was resident at the death of the deceased in or towards satisfaction of any absolute interest of the surviving spouse in the real or personal estate of the deceased. This right was given by s5 and Schedule 2 of the Intestates' Estates Act 1952.

The purpose of this provision is to enable a spouse to continue to enjoy occupation of a matrimonial home which had been the property of the deceased. Although s41 of the Administration of Estates Act 1925 gives the personal representatives a power to appropriate property, such as the home, in satisfaction of

legacy, it is only exercisable at the discretion of the personal representatives. It was this shortcoming which led to the surviving spouse being granted the specific right to acquire the matrimonial home.

The provisions are mainly applicable to freehold dwelling houses rather than those which are rented. A surviving spouse's right to occupy a rented property will normally be dealt with by the Rent Act 1977.

In four cases set out in Schedule 2 para 2 of the Act, the right of appropriation is only exercisable with the consent of the court if it is satisfied that such an appropriation is not likely to diminish the value of assets in the residuary estate or make them more difficult to dispose of. These cases are where the dwelling-house forms part of business assets. They are:

1. where the dwelling house forms part of a building and interest in the whole of the building is comprised in the residuary estate; or
2. the dwelling-house is held with agricultural land and an interest in the agricultural land is held in the residuary estate; or
3. the whole or part of the dwelling-house was at the time of the intestate's death used as a hotel or a lodging house; or
4. a part of the dwelling-house was at the time of the intestate's death used for purposes other than domestic purposes.

If the surviving spouse wishes to exercise the power of appropriation in respect of the matrimonial home, the following matters laid down in Schedule 2 must be observed:

1. the power must be exercised within 12 months of the first grant of representation being taken out of the deceased's estate;
2. by giving notice in writing to the personal representatives.

The personal representatives are directed by Schedule 2 para 4 not to sell the house within the 12 month period referred to above without first obtaining the written consent of the spouse unless it is needed to pay off debts of the estate.

The right of appropriation is exercisable notwithstanding that the surviving spouse is one of the personal representatives of the deceased's estate and a trustee thereof. See Schedule 2 para 5(1). If the surviving spouse is of unsound mind consent may be given on his/her behalf by a receiver etc. See Schedule 2 para 6(1), and if the surviving spouse is an infant, the power is exercisable as if he/she were an adult. See Schedule 2 para 6(2).

When the surviving spouse gives notice to the personal representatives to appropriate a dwelling house to his/her share of the estate a valuation must be made of the house to decide the extent of set-off against the surviving spouse's other entitlements. The relevant date for the valuation for these purposes is the date of appropriation. See *Re Collins* [1975] 1 WLR 309 (Ch D).

A part appropriation, part sale transaction is permitted under the provisions of Schedule 2 para 1(1) of the 1952 Act. See *Re Phelps* [1979] 3 All ER 373 (CA).

In *Re Phelps* [1979] 3 All ER 373 (CA) when a husband died intestate in February 1971 his widow was then entitled to interests valued in total at £8,750 under the intestacy provisions. The estate contained a house which the widow occupied at her husband's death and in June 1972 she exercised the right to appropriate that house to her share of the estate. Due to rises in house prices the value of the house at June 1972 exceeded the widow's entitlement. The widow was willing to pay the difference between these two sums out of her own personal funds. The question arose whether she could do so.

Held: the provisions in Schedule 2 para 1 should be given a broad interpretation and read in the light of the provision of Schedule 2 para 5(2) which interpreted 'appropriation' in a wide manner and which was wide enough to include part appropriation, part sale transactions.

It should be noted that the mere fact that the surviving spouse is given a power of appropriation in respect of the matrimonial home does not create any equitable rights in the house. See *Lall* v *Lall* (1965) 1 WLR 1249 (Ch D).

The right of the issue

If the deceased leaves no surviving spouse then all of the residuary estate is held on trusts for the issue. If the deceased left a surviving spouse then after the surviving spouse has received the personal chattels and statutory legacy, the residue is divided into two parts; one is held on trust for the surviving spouse for life, remainder to the issue, and the other half is held on trust for the issue.

Section 1(2) Law Reform (Succession) Act (LR(S)A) 1995 (which applies to deaths on or after 1 January 1996) provides that children will not have to bring lifetime advances into account against their entitlement on intestacy from now on, and that on a partial intestacy a surviving spouse and issue will not have to bring gifts by will into account against such entitlements, thus abolishing the old hotchpot rules.

Example

Mr White dies on 2 January 1996 survived by his wife Mary and two children, Paula and Richard. He gave Paula £30,000 two years before his death to assist with the purchase of a flat. In his will Mr White gave £50,000 worth of shares to Richard, and the matrimonial home worth £300,000 and personal chattels of £5,000 to Mary. The remainder of his estate is undisposed of, and it amounts to £525,000.

Now none of the gifts made by Mr White need to be brought into account and they are irrelevant when distributing his undisposed-of property. As a result, under the intestacy rules Mary has a statutory legacy of £125,000 and a life interest in one half of the balance (ie in £200,000). The rest of the estate is held equally for Paula and Richard on the statutory trusts.

The statutory trusts

The share of the deceased's estate to which the issue are entitled is held on statutory trusts. Under s47(1)(i) of the Administration of Estates Act 1925 the share of the issue is divisible between the children of the deceased who are living at the death of the deceased subject to them fulfilling the contingency of attaining 18 years or marrying. If a child of the deceased has predeceased him then that child's issue (if any) will take their parents' share in equal shares per stirpes. If a child of the deceased has predeceased him leaving no issue then that child is ignored in distribution. However, it should be noted that no issue can take whose parent is living at the death of the deceased and so capable of taking.

Examples

1. X dies intestate leaving £90,000 which is to be divided between his issue. X had four children, A, B, C and D. A and B died before X, A left no issue, B left three children E, F and G. C is still alive and has two children H and J and D died two days after X leaving one child K. Under s47(1)(i) distribution will be as follows:

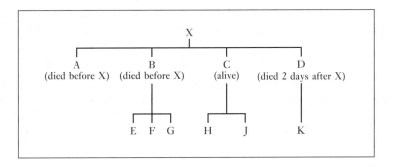

A will be ignored in distributing the £90,000 as he died before X without issue. Although B also died before X he left children and they will take B's share (one-third of £30,000) per stirpes and it will be divided between them equally, that is, £10,000 each. C is alive; he will receive a one-third share or £30,000 and his children will take nothing because he is alive. D died two days after X, but as he survived X, his share will not go to his child K, but instead will pass in accordance with D's will or on his intestacy.

2. Z, a young man, dies leaving four children, A, B, C and D. A is 20, B is 19, C is 17 and D is 13. Thus:

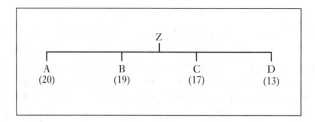

A and B will take their shares immediately as they have fulfilled the contingency of reaching 18. The shares of C and D will be held on trust for them until they attain 18. If either or both of them do not attain that age they, and any issue they may have, will be ignored in distribution and their shares divided among those who do attain 18. Thus, if only D did not attain 18, his share would be divided equally between A, B and C.

Hotchpot

Section 1(2) of the Law Reform (Succession) Act 1995 abolishes hotchpot in cases where the intestate dies on or after 1 January 1996. Cases where death occurs before this date may still arise so it is important to consider the position before the 1995 Act.

Under s47(1)(iii) of the Administration of Estates Act it is provided:

'Where the property held on the statutory trusts for the issue is divisible into shares, then any money or property which, by way of advancement or on the marriage of a child of the intestate, has been paid to such child by the intestate or settled by the intestate for the benefit of such child (including any life or less interest and including any property covenated to be paid or settled) shall, subject to any contrary intention expressed or appearing from the circumstances of the case, be taken as being so paid or settled in or towards satisfaction of the share of such child or the share which such child would have taken if living at the death of the intestate, and shall be brought into account, at a valuation (the value to be reckoned as at the death of the intestate), in accordance with the requirements of the personal representatives.'

Section 47(1)(iii) only applies where the property held on the statutory trusts is to be divided among two or more children of the deceased. It has no application if the deceased left only one child. This is because its main purpose is to attain equality between the children of the deceased. See *Re Ashton* (1934) 78 Sol Jo 803.

As the purpose of the provision is to attain equality between the children it cannot be used to increase the share of the surviving spouse. Thus, if the residue is £20,000 after the surviving spouse has received other benefits, £10,000 should be held on trust for the surviving spouse and £10,000 for the issue. If the deceased left only one child who received an advancement of £10,000 this £10,000 would not be taken into account as part of the total residuary sum, for this would increase the residue to £30,000 and benefit the surviving spouse by another £5,000.

'Advancement' is construed widely for the purposes of s47(1)(iii). However, the section indicates that the money or property must have been paid or settled for the benefit of the child. Thus, it would appear that if the deceased gave money to a child (X) of his, to help X to buy a house as a gift on the marriage of X's son Y, this might not have to be taken into account.

Advancements are only to be taken into account if the deceased has shown no contrary intention. Normally such contrary intention will be inferred from the circumstances surrounding the advancement. This matter was considered in *Hardy* v *Shaw* [1976] Ch 82 (Ch D). A father, who owned a family company, gave each of his three chilren 600 shares in the company. One daughter (X) subsequently married a man of whom the father strongly disapproved. On his death, the father left the whole of his estate to his wife, including his remaining shareholding in the company. The widow gave all the remaining shares in the company to the other two children in her lifetime and eventually died intestate. X claimed that these *inter vivos* gifts of shares to the other children should be taken into account as advancements. It was argued against this that as the mother and father had disapproved of X's marriage and regretted that she had obtained shares in the company, such shares received *inter vivos* should not be taken into account as advancements under s47(1)(iii) as there was a contrary intention.

Held: the test whether there was a contrary intention for the purposes of s47(1)(iii) was subjective and concerned whether the inference could be drawn that the donor's intention was that the gift should not be brought into hotchpot. The widow had shown an intention not to give X any further shares but it could not be concluded from that that she also intended to exclude X from her inheritance altogether, in that she had not directed her mind as to what should happen to her property on her death. Therefore the *inter vivos* gifts of shares had to be brought into hotchpot.

When an advancement has to be brought into hotchpot it must be brought into account at a valuation to be reckoned at the deceased's death. Thus, if the deceased bought a house for his son on his marriage which cost £15,000 and which on the deceased's death was worth £30,000 the house would be brought into hotchpot at a value of £30,000.

The hotchpot provision contained in s47(1)(iii) is applicable only to the children of the deceased and not to remoter issue.

Example
X died intestate leaving four children A, B, C and D, but no spouse. X's net estate is £50,000 and he made *inter vivos* gifts of £15,000 to A, £10,000 to B and £5,000 to C. For the purposes of determining the presumptive share of each child the advancements will be added to the £50,000 net estate. This totals £80,000 divided by 4 = £20,000 for each child. For deaths prior to 1 January 1996 – but not deaths since then following the recent amendment – on distribution of the £50,000 net estate the receipts would be:

A gets	£5,000
B gets	£10,000
C gets	£15,000
D gets	£20,000
Total	£50,000

The share of each is £20,000 minus what he/she has already received.

The rights of other relatives

Under s46 of the Administration of Estates Act other relatives of the deceased will obtain no benefits on intestacy if there is a surviving spouse and/or issue. As noted above, if there is a surviving spouse but no issue and the deceased left parents or brothers and sisters surviving him, the parents or brothes and sisters will take a half share of the residue. Where there is no surviving spouse or issue then the deceased's residuary estate will be held on the statutory trusts for the following:

1. to the father and mother of the deceased in equal shares absolutely (s46(1)(iii)) or the survivor of the father and mother of the deceased (s46(1)(iv));
2. if there is no father or mother, for the brothers and sisters of the whole blood, in equal shares per stirpes;
3. if there are no brothers and sisters of the whole blood, then among brothers and sisters of the half blood in equal shares per stirpes;
4. if there are no brothers and sisters of the half blood, then among the intestate's grandparents in equal shares;
5. if no grandparents, then among the uncles and aunts of the whole blood in equal shares per stirpes;
6. if no uncles and aunts of the whole blood, then among the uncles and aunts of the half blood, in equal shares per stirpes;
7. if no uncles and aunts of the half blood, then to the Crown, the Duchy of Lancaster or the Duke of Cornwall, as the case may be, as *bona vacantia*.

Where there are relatives who fall within one of the classes above they will take to the exclusion of any relatives in a lower class. Thus, if the deceased was unmarried and childless and his closest living relative was his brother, that brother would take all the estate to the exclusion of other relatives, even half brothers and sisters in the next class. The per stirpes rule applies to some of the class of remoter relatives listed above. Thus, if the deceased's closest living reative was a cousin, that cousin would take the estate per stirpes through the deceased's aunt or uncle.

11.5 Legitimacy, legitimation, illegitimacy and adoption

The provisions of the Administration of Estates Act 1925 originally applied to legitimate children of the deceased and their issue. Modifications have been made to this by subsequent statutory provisions so as to give rights to legitimated, illegitimate and adopted children on intestacy.

Legitimate children

This will obviously include children whose parents were married at the time of conception or at the time of birth. However, problems can arise where a child is the offspring of a voidable or void marriage. The position in such cases is as follows.

1. *Voidable marriage.* Where a voidable marriage is dissolved by a decree of nullity granted after 31 July 1971 this only annuls the marriage from the date the decree is granted. Therefore the marriage is treated as if it existed up until that time and any children conceived or born before the date on which the marriage was annulled will be treated as legitimate. See s16 Matrimonial Causes Act 1973.
2. *Void marriage.* Normally a child of a void marriage is treated as illegitimate. But under s1(1) of the Legitimacy Act 1976 a child of a void marriage will be treated as being legitimate if at the time of sexual intercourse or at the time of marriage, if later, both or either parties to the marriage, reasonably believed that the marriage was valid.

The following case should be considered here because it has relevance not only for the discussion of void marriage but for this section as a whole.

In *Spence, Re, Spence* v *Dennis* [1989] 3 WLR 834 Addy Pidwell ('the mother') married Frederick Love in 1895: in 1911 she gave birth to twins, one of whom is the first defendant. Shortly thereafter she went to live with Thomas Spence, taking the first defendant with her. She gave birth to the intestate in 1912 and to the plaintiff in 1916. In 1934 she 'married' Thomas Spence he, it was assumed, reasonably believing that the marriage was valid: in fact the mother's marriage to Frederick Love was never dissolved. The mother died in 1949, Frederick Love in 1953 and Thomas Spence in 1957. Following the death of the intestate in 1985, in that year the first defendant obtained a grant of letters of administration claiming to be a sister of the whole blood. In 1988 the plaintiff issued a writ claiming to be a legitimate brother of the whole blood of the intestate and the only person entitled to his estate. The Treasury Solicitor, the second defendant, contended that neither the plaintiff nor the first defendant was a legitimate brother or sister of the whole or half blood and accordingly that the intestate's estate devolved on the Crown as *bona vacantia*.

The question was whether a person could be treated as legitimate under s1(1) of the Legitimacy Act 1976 notwithstanding that he was born before his parents entered into a void marriage?

Held: this question would be answered in the negative. In the words of Morritt J:

'... the structure and context of the 1976 Act as a whole, which differentiates between a child to whom s1(1) applies and a legitimated person as defined and the words used in s1(1) all point to the conclusion that s1(1) only applies to a child born after the void marriage. Such a child when born is treated as the legitimate child of his parents. To hold otherwise would involve a change of status during his life which the Act does not recognise and for which it makes no provision.'

It should be recalled that s1(1) of the Legitimacy Act 1976 provides that:

'The child of a void marriage, whenever born, shall ... be treated as the legitimate child of his parents if at the time of the act of the insemination resulting in the birth or, where there was no such insemination, the child's conception (or at the time of the celebration of the marriage if later) both or either of the parties reasonably believed that the marriage was valid.'

In *Re Spence*, the judge at first instance held that the section did not legitimate the brothers because the aim of the section is to treat a child born *after* a void marriage, in the given circumstances, as his parents' legitimate child. The provision does not alter the status of a child born *before* a void marriage. The opening words of the subsection, that is 'the child of a void marriage', require that there should have been a ceremony of marriage before the birth, and the word 'whenever born' cannot enlarge the meaning of that expression.

In the appeal *Re Spence (deceased), Spence v Dennis and Another* [1990] 2 WLR 1430; [1990] 2 All ER 827, the Court of Appeal (Sir Nicholas Browne-Wilkinson V-C and Nourse and McCowan LJJ) upheld the decision of Morritt J. The appellant's most cogent argument was that the words 'whenever born' in s1 apparently indicated that it was irrelevant whether the child was born before or after the ceremony. However, the court was satisfied that, since the 1976 Act was a consolidating statute, those words should have the same meaning as the equivalent words in the Legitimacy Act 1959, namely 'whether born before or after the commencement of this Act'. Beyond that in their view it was clear that the purpose of the section and of the following sections of the Legitimacy Act was to regulate the status of children born *after* the void 'marriage'.

It should be remembered, however, that the relevant death in this case took place before the coming into force of the Family Law Reform Act 1987 on 4 April 1988. Under that Act, when identifying relationships for the purpose of the intestacy rules, no distinction is made between people whose parents are or were married to each other and people whose parents are or were not.

Legitimated children

Where the parents of a child who is illegitimate at birth subsequently marry each other, the child will be legitimated from the date of marriage under s5(4) of the Legitimacy Act 1976. A child who has been legitimated is entitled to succeed on intestacy in the same manner as a legitimate child and if a legitimated child dies intestate, his estate will be distributed among those who would have received his estate if he had been born legitimate.

Illegitimate children

At common law illegitimate children and their issue had no rights of succession on the intestacy of their parents, grandparents or other relatives and on the death of the illegitimate child intestate, his relatives had no rights of succession either. However, an illegitimate child's spouse and his legitimate issue could succeed on his intestacy. Some improvement was made on the illegitimate child's position under s9 of the Legitimacy Act 1926 by which an illegitimate child was permitted to succeed on his mother's intestacy in very limited circumstances.

The position of illegitimate children was radically altered by the Family Law Reform Act 1969 which implemented the recommendations of the Committee on the Law of Succession in relation to Illegitimate Persons (1966) Cmnd 3051. Section 14(1) of the 1969 Act provides:

> 'Where either parent of an illegitimate child dies intestate as respects all or any of his or her real or personal property, the illegitimate child, or if he is dead, his issue, shall be entitled to take any interest therein to which he or such issue would have been entitled if he had been born legitimate.'

By s14(3) it is provided that the provisions of Part IV of the Administration of Estates Act 1925 (which deals with the distribution of the estate of an intestate) shall have effect as if:

1. any reference to the issue of the intestate included a reference to any illegitimate children of his and to the issue of any such children; and
2. any reference to the child or children of the intestate included a reference to any illegitimate child or children of his.

It is clear that by s14(1), an illegitimate child is put on equal footing with legitimate children as regards rights of succession on intestacy. Section 14(2) goes on to state that the parents of an illegitimate child have the same rights of succession in relation to his estate as they would have in the case of a legitimate child. However, these provisions do have shortcomings and they do not place illegitimate children in the same position overall as legitimate children.

1. The Act only permits an illegitimate child to take on the intestacy of his parents. It does not apply to the intestacy of any other relative, such as a grandparent or other children of the illegitimate child's parents. Thus, if X died intestate and he had one child, A, who predeceased him, leaving an illegitimate child, B, in such circumstances B would not take anything from X's estate. He is not covered by s14(1). However, B would have been able to succeed to property in A's estate if A had died intestate, as that case is covered by s14(1). Likewise, if X died intestate and his next of kin were his brothers and sisters, A, B and C, if C was illegitimate he could not take anything on X's intestacy. A and B would take everything. Note that the provisions of the amended s33 of the Wills Act (see

Chapter 9, section 9.3 above) would alter the position in the former case mentioned here so that B could benefit by reason of these provisions.

2. The legitimate children or issue of an illegitimate child can succeed on the death of a grandparent intestate but illegitimate children cannot, as the following example illustrates:

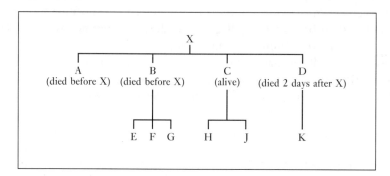

If A, B and C were all alive at the intestate's death, then, as his children they would take a one-third share of each of his estate, (assuming there is no surviving spouse). As seen above C takes his share by virtue of s14(1). However, if C had predeceased the intestate, the question would arise as to how his one-third share should be dealt with under the per stirpes rule. Under s14(1) it is clear that D would be entitled to succeed on the intestacy of his grandparent, even though C, his father, was illegitimate. However, there is nothing in s14 to permit E to share on the intestacy of his grandparents. Accordingly, D would take all of C's one-third share per stirpes under s14. But under the amended s33 of the Wills Act, D and E would share equally.

A recent case was heard before the European Court of Human Rights on the issue of inheritance by an illegitimate child. In spite of the case being a complaint against The Netherlands, it is interesting to consider how the issue of human rights can have an effect on matters of succession.

In *Camp* v *Netherlands* [2000] 3 FCR 307 a father died intestate before he could marry the complainant's (S) mother and before the complainant's birth. S was granted letters of registration (as per the law in The Netherlands). The Dutch courts held that the letters of legitimation could not apply retrospectively so according to Dutch law S could not inherit under his father's estate. The ECHR held that the difference in S's treatment in comparison to a child born to married parents or recognised by its unmarried father, meant that S had been discriminated against.

Clearly the position in England and Wales is as discussed above. However, this case is a good example of the current climate on human rights and its impact on all areas of law.

Adopted children

Under the Children Act 1975 an adopted child is to be treated in law:

1. as a child of the marriage, where the adoptors are a married couple;
2. as a child born in wedlock to the adoptors, in any other case.

These provisions appear to give adopted children the same rights of intestacy as legitimate children of the adoptors. For the purposes of deciding whether an adopted child was living at the death of the deceased, so as to enable him to succeed on intestacy, s42(2) of the Adoption Act provides that an adopted child is to be treated as born on the date of adoption. This ensures that an adopted child born before the deceased's death but adopted afterwards cannot participate in that intestacy.

Children of parents who were unmarried at the time of birth

It has been noted that in general in the case of deaths occurring before the entry into force of the Family Law Reform Act 1987 an illegitimate relationship was not recognised for the purposes of distribution of property on intestacy. This general rule was eased slightly by s9 of the Legitimacy Act 1926 and then made subject to two limited exceptions in s14 of the Family Law Reform Act 1969. (See also section 11.5 'Illegitimate children', above.)

This legislation meant that sometimes an illegitimate child could succeed on his mother's intestacy and, as regards deaths occurring on or after 1 January 1970, an illegitimate child (and his legitimate issue) could take on his parents' intestacy as if he had been born legitimate. Further, his parents could take on the child's intestacy on the same basis. However, no other relationships were recognised. For instance, an illegitimate child could not benefit on the intestacy of brothers and sisters or grandparents; nor could such relatives benefit in the event of the intestacy of the illegitimate child.

Section 18 of the 1987 Act has made sweeping changes in respect of deaths occurring after 4 April 1988. As noted, the distribution of the assets on intestacy (and otherwise) is to be determined irrespective of whether or not the parents of a particular person were married to each other.

The legislation also affects the protection for personal representatives in the case of intestate succession. Section 20 of the 1987 Act removes the protection which previously existed for personal representatives who distributed the assets in the estate unaware of illegitimate claimants. The current position apparently is, therefore, that personal representatives should carry out an investigation to find out whether or not there are living relatives of the deceased who exist and whose parents were not married.

Despite s20, however, it seems that the general protection in respect of claimants of the estate that are available to personal representatives under s27 of the Trustee Act 1925 and the Benjamin Order procedure (see Chapter 19, section 19.2 and

Chapter 20, section 20.4, below) is relevant as regards the claims of persons whose parents were not married.

Further, the effect of s18(2) of the Family Law Reform Act 1987 is important. This makes special provision for the administration of an intestate's estate. It provides that where the parents of a child who die intestate were not married to each other at the time of that child's birth there is an assumption that the child has not been survived by his father or by any person related to him only through his father. Accordingly, in the absence of evidence to the contrary the personal representatives can proceed to distribute the estate on the basis that no such persons are alive.

It is helpful to clarify the position by illustrations.

Example 1

A, whose parents never married, dies intestate. He has no wife or children. He is known to be survived by his mother but nothing is known of his father or of his father's relatives.

As the personal representatives are entitled to presume that the father and his relatives have predeceased A, A's mother will benefit from the whole of the estate.

Example 2

Here again A, whose parents never married, has died intestate leaving no wife or children. The difference is that A's mother is dead and the only relative on his mother's side still living is her brother of the whole blood, that is, A's maternal uncle. There is no information regarding A's father or of any of the father's relatives except that the father's brother of the whole blood is known to be alive, that is, A's paternal uncle.

In this instance, A's estate will be divided between the two uncles. The personal representatives of A's estate are entitled to presume that the father and father's relatives other than the known brother have predeceased A.

11.6 Partial intestacy

Introduction

This arises where a testator has died leaving a will which disposes of only some of his property. This may occur for several reasons such as that the will was incomplete or did not contain a gift of residue; a residuary legatee predeceased the testator; or the residuary gift was for some reasons declared ineffective, for example, uncertainty, lack of knowledge and approval by the testator, irregularities in executing the will or some manner of revocation.

Where there is a partial intestacy, the provisions in the will must be applied first; it is only after this that the intestacy rules are applied so as to complete the distribution of the estate. This matter is clear from the words of s49 of the Administration of Estates Act which states:

'Where any person dies leaving a will effectively disposing of part of his property, this part of the Act shall have effect as respects the part of his property not so disposed of subject to the provisions contained in the will'.

When s49(1) speaks of 'the provisions contained in the will', this is construed as referring only to operative provisions. Thus, if a provision in the will fails, this provision will be ignored and the intestacy rules applied regardless of it. But, if a provision is still effective or operating it will prevail over anything in the intestacy rules.

Distribution on partial intestacy

Under s49(1) of the Administration of Estates Act, set out above, Part IV of the Act is to apply to the distribution of the property undisposed of by will. In effect this means that the intestacy rules are tagged on at the end of the will. Thus, for example, if T died leaving a will which did not deal with his residuary estate, then such property as would have fallen into such a gift will pass to T's next of kin as defined by s46 of the Administration of Estates Act. If T had a wife and children then they would obtain the property undisposed of by the will.

Where there is a surviving spouse, problems may arise in applying the intestacy rules to the property undisposed of by the will. In *Re Bowen-Buscarlet's Will Trusts* [1972] Ch 463 (Ch D) a testator left the residue of his estate on trust for his wife for life but failed to direct what was to happen thereafter. When the testator died in 1967 his wife and a married daughter survived him. The question arose as to how the undisposed of remainder should be distributed. Under the intestacy rules the wife was entitled to the personal chattels, a statutory legacy plus interest thereon and a life interest in half the residue. Should the wife be able to take a statutory legacy out of a fund in which she already had a life interest? Should she be entitled to a life interest in a fund under the intestacy rules in which she already had a life interest under the will? Goff J held that the widow was entitled to take a statutory legacy out of the undisposed of remainder as her life interest and the statutory legacy merged. Thus, for example, if the residue was valued at £100,000 and the widow was entitled to take a statutory legacy of £30,000 then her life interest would merge with that part of the residue which goes to meet this legacy. However, Goff J held that the widow could not take a life interest in the residue on intestacy because she could not enjoy this life interest until the life interest under the will came to an end. As such it is impossible for her to enjoy this life interest. Thus, in the example above, once the widow takes her statutory legacy of £30,000 she will have a life interest in the remaining £70,000 under the terms of the will. If she was given the right to take a further life interest in half of the £70,000 under the intestacy rules this would be meaningless as it would not increase the interest in that fund which she already has under the will. The only way in which this benefit could be obtained is through the life interest under the will coming to an end. As this life interest is normally terminated by death, it is then too late to bring the life interest under the intestacy rules into operation. However, it is doubtful if *Re Bowen-Buscarlet* applies to cases where the widow disclaims the life interest under the will or where it terminates on the occurrence of a contingency. It is noteworthy that the principle in *Bowen-Buscarlet* has been adopted in the commonwealth authority of Wade (1980) Qd R 70.

Under s49(1) of the Administration of Estates Act two special hotchpot rules are applied in cases of partial intestacy for deaths before 1 January 1996. These are designed to ensure fair distribution of the intestate's estate among his next of kin.

The surviving spouse. Under s49(1)(aa) the surviving spouse of the intestate is required to bring into hotchpot beneficial interests acquired under the will, other than personal chattels specifically bequeathed, against the statutory legacy payable to her under the intestacy rules. This hotchpot rule does not affect the personal chattels or any life interest given to the surviving spouse under the intestacy rules.

Example

X died leaving a will in which he left his wife a legacy of £10,000, his motor car (worth £3,000) and a life interest in a fund of £50,000. The value of property undisposed of by the will is £70,000. S had two children A and B.

Under s49(1)(aa) X's widow will have to bring the legacy of £10,000 into hotchpot and also the value of her interest in the fund of £50,000. In the latter an actuarial valuation will be necessary. However, the motor car, being a personal chattel under s55(1)(x) of the Administration of Estates Act, is not brought into hotchpot. As X left children, the widow's statutory legacy would normally be £40,000, but because of s49(1)(aa) the legacy will be reduced by the amount of the benefits to be brought into hotchpot. So if the life interest was valued at £8,000, the widow would be deemed to have had benefits totalling £18,000 under the will and the statutory legacy would be reduced to £22,000, that is, £40,000 minus £18,000.

The issue. Under s49(1)(a) beneficial interests acquired by any issue of the deceased under his will must be brought into hotchpot on partial intestacy. The section is poorly drafted and must be set out in full:

> 'The requirements (of section forty-seven of this Act) as to bringing property into account, shall apply to any beneficial interests acquired by any issue of the deceased under the will of the deceased, but not to beneficial interests so acquired by any other persons.'

Because this provision refers to s47(1)(iii) (the provision requiring children of the intestate to bring into hotchpot advancements received from the deceased during his lifetime) it is arguable that s49(1)(a) should be limited to benefits received by the children of the deceased under the will and not benefits received by his remoter issue under the will. However, such a construction would be inconsistent with the use of the word 'issue' in s49(1)(a). Not suprisingly two views exist as to the proper construction of s49(1)(a).

The stirpital construction. This appears to have gained acceptance as the most appropriate construction of s49(1)(a) and has been applied by the court in three classes, namely, *Re Young* [1951] Ch 185, *Re Morton* [1956] Ch 644 and *Re Grover's Will Trusts* [1971] Ch 168. In *Re Young*, Harman J held that s49(1)(a) was 'meant to produce, as it were, a stirpital division, in equality so far as possible, and that is why the word 'issue' is used here, although the word 'children' is used in s47. Any member of the family belonging to a certain branch must bring in everything that has been taken or acquired under the will by that branch'.

Example

X leaves a will by which he leaves £5,000 each to his children A and B. He also leaves A's two children C and D £1,000 each, but leaves nothing to B's only child E. X's will did not dispose of all his estate, and £20,000 is to be distributed among his children A and B on partial intestacy.

Under s49(1)(a), A and B will have to bring into hotchpot the legacies of £5,000 they each received. In addition, under the authority of *Re Young* the legacies of £1,000 which C and D received will have to be brought into hotchpot. The total sum available when legacies are added in is £20,000 + £5,000 + £5,000 + £1,000 + £1,000 = £32,000. Each branch of the family is entitled to £16,000. As A's branch has already received £7,000, A will therefore receive £9,000 out of the £20,000 available on intestacy. B received £5,000 by the will, so he will receive a further £11,000.

In *Re Young* [1951] Ch 185 Ch D a testator gave his wife a life interest in his residuary estate and directed that on her death the residue should be divided into one-seventh shares for his children with six children receiving one-seventh shares absolutely and one child receiving a life interest in a one-seventh share with remainder to his children. A child who was given a one-seventh share absolutely pre-deceased the testator. The question arose whether the child who had been given a life interest only was required to bring only the value of his life interest into hotchpot or the whole value of the one-seventh share his branch of the family received on distribution on partial intestacy.

Held: the whole one-seventh share had to be brought into hotchpot.

The distributive construction. This construction of s49(1)(a) was suggested by Pennycuick J in *Re Grover* and it would tend to support the arguments put forward in *Re Young* that only the value of the life interest should be brought into hotchpot. Under this construction:

> '... any descendant of the testator who acquires a beneficial interest under his will brings that interest, and nothing more, into account against his share under the partial intestacy. So, for instance, a child of the testator would bring into account any beneficial interest acquired by that child under the will, but nothing more, and similarly a grandchild of the testator would bring into account any beneficial interest taken by that grandchild.'

12

Family Provision

12.1 Introduction

This subject is concerned with legislation which permits the dependants of a deceased person to apply to the court in order that reasonable financial provision can be made for them out of his estate where the deceased's will or intestacy or the combination of both have not made such provision for them.

One of the reasons for the introduction of legislation giving the court power to provide for dependants of the deceased lies in the fact that at present the owner of property has, in English law, complete freedom in disposing of that property on death. Thus, for example, if X has a wife and two small children, he has no legal obligation to leave them anything in his will and could if he so desired leave all his property to a non-member of his family.

It was not until 1938 that legislation was first introduced to give the court power to order that reasonable provision be made out of the deceased's estate for the maintenance of a dependant; this was the Inheritance (Family Provision) Act 1938. This legislation was designed to permit the court to make provision for the maintenance of the deceased's wife and children out of his estate, if this had not already been done. For the purposes of the 1938 Act maintenance was given a restrictive interpretation and applicants had to show some need for support.

The 1938 Act was considered by the Law Commission in its report on family property and it proposed amendments so as to enable a spouse to obtain financial provision from the deceased's estate which went beyond mere maintenance but rather was based on similar lines to those applied in divorce proceedings. Proposals were also made to extend the court's powers to award maintenance beyond the categories of surviving spouse and children. These proposals are now embodied, along with other changes which are mentioned below, in the Inheritance (Provision for Family and Dependants) Act 1975. This Act came into force on 1 April 1976.

Recently there have been some changes to the limits of jurisdiction of the county courts under the Inheritance (Provision for Family and Dependants) Act 1985. Whereas prior to 1 July 1991 the county courts only had jurisdiction if an estate were under £30,000, county courts now have unlimited jurisdiction as a result of the High Court and County Courts' Jurisdiction Order 1991, Article 2 and the amended s25 of the County Courts Act 1984. The High Court is no longer considered the appropriate court of trial if the applicant expects to recover less than £25,000, provided that the case is not exceptionally complex and does not raise questions of importance to persons who are not parties. In any case where the applicant expects to recover less than £50,000 a county court should be really considered as the court of trial.

Changes have also occurred as a result of the Law Reform (Succession) Act 1995 so that the Inheritance (Provision for Family and Dependants) Act 1975 now permits a person who was living with the deceased as husband or wife – although not actually married to them – to make a claim under the 1975 Act where death occurs on or after January 1996. This is as a result of s2 of the Law Reform (Succession) Act 1995. The court may take into account the co-habitee's age, the length of the relationship and the contribution made by the co-habitee to the welfare of the deceased family. The co-habitee has to show that the financial provision is required for his or her maintenance. Therefore, although the position of co-habitees has been improved, the surviving spouse is still the only claimant who is not required to show this.

Rule changes consequent upon the implementation of the Act are contained in the Family Proceedings (Amendment) Rules 1996 (SI 96/816 (L1)).

12.2 Who can apply under the 1975 Act?

Before any person can apply to the court for an order for reasonable financial provision under the 1975 Act, as amended by the Law Reform (Succession) Act 1995, is essential that it be shown that the deceased domiciled in England and Wales (see s1(1)). It is clear that if the deceased died domiciled in another jurisidiction then his dependants should seek their remedy in that jurisidiction.

The right to bring an application under s1(1) is a right which is personal to the applicant and it does not survive for the benefit of the applicant's estate after his or her death under s1(1) of the Law Reform (Miscellaneous Provisions) Act 1934. This point arose in *Whytte* v *Ticehurst* [1986] 2 All ER 158 where a husband died in February 1984 and in July 1984 his widow made a claim under the 1975 Act but she died in December 1984 before her claim was heard. The widow's personal representatives were refused leave to carry on the claim on behalf of her estate under s1(1) of the 1934 Act. Although the judgment of Booth J in this case is confined to the position between a married couple, it is submitted that the same principle applies to other categories of applicant under s1(1) of the 1975 Act. The principle in *Whytte* v *Ticehurst* has been confirmed in the subsequent case of *Re R (deceased)* [1986] Fam Law 58.

Finally, the recent decision in *Re Bramwell* should be considered in respect of the validity of the right to bring an application.

In *Bramwell, Re, Campbell* v *Tobin* [1988] 2 FLR 263, in 1975 a widow aged 65 married a widower of 71; they parted company in 1979; the husband died in 1986, his wife six months later. Between the two deaths, the wife instructed solicitors to make a claim under the Inheritance (Provision for Family and Dependants) Act 1975. After the wife's death, the plaintiff sought to pursue such a claim; the defendants (the husband's executors) applied to have the proceedings struck out.

Held: the defendants' application would be successful as the plaintiff had no *locus standi*. Sheldon J stated that:

> '... in my judgment, a claim under the Inheritance (Provision for Family and Dependants) Act 1975 – as with a claim for financial provision under the Matrimonial Causes Act 1973 – neither gives rise to nor becomes a "cause of action" within s1(1) of the Law Reform (Miscellaneous Provisions) Act 1934 unless an order has been made in respect of it before the death of the surviving spouse or other potential claimant; until then it remains no more than a hope or contingency of no surviving value to a deceased's claimant's estate.'

Under s1(1) of the 1975 Act those persons who are entitled to bring an application are listed; they fall into five classes.

Section 1(1)(a) 'the wife or husband of the deceased'

For an applicant to fall within this category a marriage which was subsisting at the deceased's death must be proved. See *Re Watkins* [1953] 1 WLR 1323. A judicially separated spouse also comes within this category; this can be inferred from s1(2)(a) of the Act which, in defining what 'reasonable financial provision' is for a spouse, differentiates between judicially separated and other spouses. Any person who in good faith enters into a void marriage with the deceased will come under s1(1)(a) according to s25(4) unless either:

1. the marriage of the deceased and that person was dissolved or annulled during the lifetime of the deceased and the dissolution or annulment is recognised by the law of England and Wales; or
2. that person has during the lifetime of the deceased entered into a later marriage.

In *Re Sehota (deceased)* [1978] 3 All ER 385 it was held that an application by 'the wife of the deceased' included, for the purposes of s1(1)(a), a wife of the deceased under a polygamous marriage. In that case the deceased had lawfully married two wives in India before 1948; an application by the second wife was permitted even though polygamous marriages are not permissible in English law.

Section 1(1)(b) 'a former wife or former husband of the deceased who has not yet remarried'

Under s25(1) 'former wife' or 'former husband' is defined as:

> 'A person whose marriage with the deceased was during the deceased's lifetime dissolved or annulled by a decree of divorce or of nullity of marriage made under the Matrimonial Causes Act 1973.'

Under this definition it is clear that there can be no application by a person whose marriage was dissolved outside England and Wales, or under earlier divorce legislation.

The term 'remarriage' is dealt with by s25(5) of the Act which provides:

> 'Any reference in this Act to remarriage or to a person who has remarried includes a reference to a marriage which is by law void or voidable or to a person who has entered into such a marriage, as the case may be, and a marriage shall be treated for the purposes of this Act as a remarriage, in relation to any party thereto, notwithstanding that the previous marriage of that party was void or voidable.'

In simple terms s25(5) states that 'remarriage' includes cases where a former spouse enters a void or voidable marriage and that there is considered to be a remarriage even though the applicant's first marriage was void or voidable and set aside.

Section 1(1)(ba) 'any person not being a person included in paragraph (a) or (b) above to whom subsection (1A) applies'
Subsection (1A)

> '... applies to a person if the deceased died on or after 1st January 1996 and, during the whole of the period of two years ending immediately before the date when the deceased died, the person was living –
> (a) in the same household as the deceased, and
> (b) as the husband or wife of the deceased.'

This new category of claimant was introduced by s2 Law Reform (Succession) Act 1995. As a result, any person who meets the criteria can now make a claim for a share of the deceased's estate.

Cohabitees are only entitled to bring a claim if they have lived for a period of two years ending with the death of the deceased 'as the husband or wife of the deceased' which of course excludes same-sex couples. This is an area which may find itself subject to challenge in the light of the Human Rights Act 1998.

When deciding whether or not to make an order in favour of an applicant. the court always has to consider the common guidelines set out in s3 I(PFD)A 1975 and, in addition, special guidelines set out there for each category of applicant. A special guideline is introduced for the court to consider in relation to an application by a cohabitee. The court must have regard to:

1. the age of the applicant and the length of the period during which the applicant lived as the husband or wife of the deceased and in the same household as the deceased; and
2. the contribution made by the applicant to the welfare of the family of the deceased, including any contribution made by looking after the home or caring for the family.

Prior to this amendment, of course, many cohabitees were able to apply under s1(1)(e) (below) as 'persons maintained by the deceased'. However, they had to show that they had been maintained by the deceased immediately before his death. The new category removes the need for a cohabitee to show financial dependence.

Despite recent amendments referred to above it should be noted that cohabitees are still treated less generously than surviving spouses. A cohabitee can only receive such financial provision as it would be reasonable for them to receive for maintenance. By comparison, a surviving spouse is entitled to receive such financial provision as it would be reasonable to receive, whether or not the provision is required for maintenance.

Section 1(1)(c) 'a child of the deceased'
Under s25(1) 'child' includes an illegitimate child and a child *en ventre sa mere* at the death of the deceased. A stepchild is not within s25(1); such an applicant must bring an application under s1(1)(d). See *Re Leach* [1985] 2 All ER 754. It should be noted

that there is no age limit placed on children of the deceased so as to confine applications to young children only. In *Re Callaghan* [1984] 3 All ER 790, Booth J pointed out that the reference to 'child' in s1(1)(c) related to the relationship between the deceased and the applicant and was not to be construed as limited to a minor or dependent child. Oliver J in *Re Coventry* [1979] 2 All ER 408 stated that 'an application for maintenance for a male child of full age who is able to earn his own living should be entertained only in the most exceptional circumstances'.

Williams v *Johns* [1988] 2 FLR 475 is a fairly recent decision concerning a claim by an adopted child. This case involved an application by an adopted son. The deceased had left the whole of her estate to her natural son. Before her death she had stated that she had considered that she had made sufficient provision for the applicant in her lifetime and felt no moral obligation to the applicant. The adopted son claimed under the Inheritance (Provisions for Family and Dependants) Act 1975.

The applicant's claim under the 1975 Act was on the basis that he was impecunious, as well as because the deceased had shown him considerable affection during her lifetime. Furthermore, at the time of the application the applicant was 43 years old and unemployed.

It was heard by the county court judge, Micklem J who dismissed the application, holding that two stages must be given adequate consideration.

1. The *reasonableness* of the provision, if any, made by the will had to be considered. When assessing this, it was for the plaintiff to establish an obligation that he should be maintained out of the estate beyond the mere fact of an adoptive relationship.
2. The test was *objective*. On the facts of this case the plaintiff had failed to prove such an obligation. The fact of his own poor financial circumstances and the deceased's affection for him were not sufficient. Since he was physically fit and capable of taking employment to maintain himself, the test was not satisfied.

One should also note the recent case of *Re Collins (deceased)* [1990] 2 WLR 161 Hollings J, regarding inheritance under the 1975 Act, in which a mother died intestate. The issues were again a family provision and adoption (one of children being adopted) and whether they were entitled to apply for provision.

Reference was again made to the provisions and evolved principles relating to s3 of the Inheritance (Provision for Family Dependants) Act 1975; and ss39(2) and 42(4) of the Adoption Act 1976.

As was noted in the case of *Williams* v *Johns* the right to apply for provision under the 1975 Act is not preserved on adoption. The facts were that A was the mother of two children, a girl born in 1970 and a boy in 1979. She died intestate in 1980, survived by her husband and leaving an estate worth about £35,000. The boy was adopted in March 1987. In June 1987, both children applied for provision out of the estate under the 1975 Act.

In the circumstances, it was held that the application of the boy would fail as the right to apply for provision under the 1975 Act is not preserved on adoption, but the girl would be awarded £5,000 (*Whytte* v *Ticehurst* [1986] CLY 3548 considered; *Re E (deceased)* [1966] CLY 12596 applied). There have been two recent decisions that are noted below: *Re Jennings (deceased)* [1994] 3 WLR 67 and *Goodchild* v *Goodchild* [1997] 3 All ER 63. In the former the application did not suceed, while the latter application did. The key to success appears to be the presence of a moral obligation, as is seen in the discussion of *Re Coventry* below. In *Re Jennings (deceased)* A was the only child of B and his wife. The parents separated and A was brought up by his mother and stepfather. B made no financial provision for A's upbringing and died with an estate of £300,000 leaving the substantial residue to three charities but making no provision for A. A was married with a house and mortgage and owned two companies, the income from which provided A and his family with a comfortable standard of living. A applied for reasonable financial provision to be made for him out of B's estate. The judge found that there had been no good reason for B's failure to have made provision to support A in his childhood and that it had been unreasonable for B to have made no provision for A's maintenance. A was awarded £30,000 from the estate. The residuary legatees appealed.

Held: the residuary legatees' appeal was allowed. It was held that on an application for financial provision the court had to ask whether it would be reasonable for the applicant to receive a sum for his maintenance. Where the applicant was an adult capable of earning his own living, some special circumstances, such as a moral obligation of the deceased towards the applicant, had to be established before such provision would be made. Such special circumstances were limited to matters that were still operative at the date of the deceased's death. They did not include a moral failure to support the applicant during childhood which in the circumstances of the case had no lasting effect on the applicant. (*Re Coventry (deceased)*, *Coventry* v *Coventry* [1979] 2 All ER 408 applied.)

This ruling confirms that a failure by a parent to provide for an infant during the infant's childhood could not be used to found a claim for provision from the deceased father's estate when the infant had become an adult, in the absence of any moral obligation.

On the other hand in *Goodchild* v *Goodchild* the child's application succeeded. In this case, in 1988, A and B made similar wills in favour of their son, C, whereby they left their estate to him after the death of the survivor. B died in 1991 and in 1992 A remarried. In November 1992 A made a new will leaving everything to his second wife, D, and in 1993 he died. C sought a declaration that D held A's estate on trust to give effect to the mutual wills of A and B. C also brought a claim under the Inheritance (Provision for Family and Dependants) Act 1975 as a child of the deceased.

Held: in circumstances where there was a clear mutual agreement, the law would give effect to the intention of the parties by means of a floating trust. Such a trust would not be invalidated by the second testator's remarriage. On the facts of the case it could not be established that the wills, although simultaneous and in the same form, were mutually binding in law. Nevertheless, in view of the fact that B clearly intended that A would give effect to what she believed were their mutual intentions, there arose a moral obligation to make some provision to C. The case was an exceptional one in this respect. The parties were urged to try to come to some financial arrangement as regards the part of the estate attributable to B's assets in order to make some provision for C.

The findings of the court support the fact that in an exceptional case, particularly where there is a moral obligation, the child of the deceased can make a successful application under the 1975 Act.

The approach taken by Oliver J in *Re Coventry* has not been followed in more recent decisions. In *Snapes* v *Aram and Others* (1998) The Times 8 May the Court of Appeal held that it was not necessary for an adult child to prove a moral claim or some other special circumstances to succeed in a claim under the 1975 Act. In this case an application for provision was brought by the testator's daughter, aged 58. At first instance she was awarded maintenance of £3,000 a year. The defendants appealed on the basis that an adult child must always show a moral obligation or some other special circumstance to be able to claim under s1(1)(c) of the 1975 Act. The Court of Appeal dismissed the appeal. A crucial factor in the decision appears to be the fact that the father was clearly favourably disposed towards his daughter and had recognised that some provision should be made for her if his estate was large enough. Furthermore, the Court was entitled to take into account all relevant matters at the date of the trial. In this case the Court felt that it was appropriate to take into account the fact that the estate had enjoyed a substantial windfall as the result of the sale of property.

In the more recent case of *Espinosa* v *Bourke* [1999] 1 FLR 747 (CA) it was held that a 'moral obligation' was not a threshold requirement. Instead, moral obligations should be taken into account where relevant and in addition to any legal obligations. In this case the deceased and his grandson moved to live with his adult daughter on the basis that she would look after them. She gave up her job and ran the house while the deceased paid the bills, the mortgage and for some improvements to the home. In the last year of the deceased's life the daughter spent most of her time in Spain, leaving the deceased, aged 87, to be cared for by the grandson and the cleaner. The deceased left his entire estate to his grandson indicating in his will that he had made no provision for his daughter as she had been adequately provided for in his lifetime. The daughter's claim for provision out of the estate was made on the basis that the deceased had promised his wife to leave her portfolio of shares (which he inherited) to their daughter.

The Court of Appeal allowed the daughter's appeal on the basis that the trial judge had placed too much emphasis upon the need for an adult child to demonstrate a moral obligation and failed to balance other considerations, such as the promise made to his wife and the fact that her earning capacity was doubtful.

These two most recent decisions of the Court of Appeal indicate a more liberal approach to applications from able-bodied adult children. The *Coventry* approach to these applicants does not now appear to be relevant.

Section 1(1)(d) 'any person (not being a child of the deceased) who, in the case of any marriage to which the deceased was at any time a party, was treated by the deceased as a child of the family in relation to that marriage'

This was a new category of applicant introduced by the 1975 Act, prior to which only the deceased's own children or adopted children could apply. It would now appear that if the deceased married a woman who had children of a previous marriage or otherwise, and those children were treated as children of that marriage by the deceased, then they are eligible to apply. The category also appears to include children who do not belong to either the deceased or his spouse but who were treated as children of the deceased's family, such as an orphaned nephew.

The meaning and effect of s1(1)(d) was considered in *Re Callaghan* [1984] 3 All ER 790 and *Re Leach* [1985] 2 All ER 754. In the former case Booth J held that 'child of the family' should be construed as referring to the relationship between the deceased and the applicant and not confined to a claim by a minor or dependent child. In the latter case Slade LJ pointed out that s1(1)(d) refers to 'a child of the family in relation to that marriage' not 'during the subsistence of that marriage'. Thus, the treatment of an applicant by a surviving spouse after the death of her other spouse could be a relevant factor in deciding if the applicant came within s1(1)(d). As to what treatment would qualify under s1(1)(d) Slade LJ considered that the mere display of affection or kindness of hospitality by a stepparent towards a stepchild would not be sufficient. In the case of a minor there would have to be some treatment of the stepchild as 'an unfledged person' while in the case of a mature stepchild he approved the dicta of Booth J in *Re Callaghan* who said:

> 'The acknowledgment by the deceased of his own role of grandfather to the plaintiff's children, the confidences as to his property and financial affairs which he placed in the plaintiff and his dependence on the plaintiff to care for him in his last illness are examples of the deceased's treatment of the plaintiff as a child, albeit an adult child, of the family. All these things are part of the privileges and duties of two persons who in regard to each other stand in the relationship of parent and child.'

In *Re Callaghan* [1984] 3 All ER 790 the plaintiff was born in 1937; he was an only child and his father died in 1943. The plaintiff thereafter lived in a house owned by his mother. In 1950 the deceased came to live in the house as a lodger and some time later the deceased and the mother began living together as man and wife with the deceased treating the plaintiff as his son. The plaintiff married in 1960 and in 1972 the deceased and the mother married. The mother died in 1980 and the deceased shortly thereafter. During the deceased's last illness the plaintiff and his wife looked after the deceased. The deceased died intestate, and his three sisters were entitled to his estate worth £31,000 under the intestacy rules. The plaintiff made a claim under s1(1)(d).

Held: the plaintiff was not barred from applying under s1(1)(d) because he was an adult. The deceased had on the facts treated the plaintiff as his own child and he could apply under s1(1)(d). Considering the obligations the deceased had undertaken in this respect and his lack of any obligations to his sisters a lump sum of £15,000 was awarded to the plaintiff.

In *Re Leach* [1985] 2 All ER 754 (CA) the plaintiff's father married her stepmother (the deceased) in 1960 when the plaintiff was aged 32 and no longer living in the family home. The plaintiff's father died in 1974 leaving all his estate to the deceased apart from some small bequests. The deceased died intestate in 1981. The plaintiff who had never lived in the same house as the deceased or been maintained by her made this application under the 1975 Act against the deceased's estate.

Held: the plaintiff was entitled to bring an application under s1(1)(d) even though she was 55. This was because the deceased had assumed the responsibilities and privileges of a parent towards the plaintiff both before and after the father's death. In the circumstances reasonable provision was an award of half of the deceased's estate.

Section 1(1)(e) 'any person (not being a person included in the foregoing paragraphs of this subsection) who immediately before the death of the deceased was being maintained, either wholly or partly, by the deceased'
This category was introduced by the 1975 Act. It allows mistresses and what are often described as 'common law wives' to bring applications. Recognition is therefore given to the fact that many couples cohabit as man and wife and undertake towards one another all the duties and obligations of a married couple, but without the formality of marriage. Distant relatives will also come within this category. Thus, in *Re Wilkinson* [1978] 1 All ER 221, a claim was made under this category by an applicant who was the sister of the deceased.

It should be noted that an applicant under s1(1)(e) must not fall within any of the other paragraphs in s1(1). This, it appears, is to avoid applicants under one of the other heads basing their claim on s1(1)(e) as well where different considerations may be applied.

For an applicant to fall within s1(1)(e), it must be shown by that applicant that he/she 'immediately before the death of the deceased was being maintained either wholly or partly by the deceased'. 'Immediately before' for the purpose of s1(1)(e) does not mean that one has to examine the *de facto* state or balance of maintenance at the moment before the death of the deceased. In *Re Beaumont* [1980] 1 All ER 266, Megarry V-C held that one had to look at the settled basis or arrangement between the parties as regards maintenance and that the court was confined to looking at this matter at the moment before death to see if such arrangement was substantially maintaining. 'Maintained' for the purposes of s(1)(e) is further defined in s1(3) of the Act which provides:

'A person, shall be treated as being maintained by the deceased, either wholly or partly, as the case may be, if the deceased, otherwise than for full valuable consideration, was making a substantial contribution in money or money's worth towards the reasonable needs of that person.'

In *Re Wilkinson* [1978] 1 All ER 221 Arnold J held that an applicant had the onus of knowing he/she was being 'maintained' in order to come within s1(1)(e) and to prove (1) that the deceased was making a substantial contribution in money or money's worth towards the needs of the applicant and (2) that the deceased was doing so other than for full valuable consideration. The relevant time for deciding in (2) whether there was full valuable consideration given by the applicant is at the time the deceased was making the relevant contribution. In *Re Beaumont* (above), Megarry V-C followed *Re Wilkinson* with approval and added that the matter was one of weighing up the value of the services rendered by the applicant to the deceased, to see if they were full valuable consideration for the maintenance which the applicant says the deceased provided.

In *Re Wilkinson* [1978] 1 All ER 221 the applicant went to live with her sister in 1969 when she was 61. The applicant's sister was a childless widow who was at that time suffering from progressively worsening arthritis. The applicant was provided with free board and lodging and had all her household expenses paid for by her sister. In return, the applicant acted as a companion to her sister in the years before the sister's death; she helped her to dress and shared light housework and cooking. The heavy housework was done by a home help. In the period before the sister's death, the applicant had to sit up with her at night. The sister died in 1976 and the applicant claimed under s1(1)(e) of the 1975 Act.

Held: the applicant was being maintained by her sister before the sister died. The value of the services provided by the applicant did not constitute full valuable consideration for the free board and lodging and expenses provided by the sister.

From the facts of *Re Wilkinson*, it is clear that the question of maintenance is determined by looking at what the applicant received as against what the applicant gave. Thus if the applicant had been asked to pay all her own expenses and for the board and lodging in *Re Wilkinson* she could not have been said to be a dependant. If she had only received free board and lodging in return for her services, she would not have been regarded as being maintained. The case was very much a borderline one and its facts should also be contrasted with the situation where the applicant is not expected to do anything in return for free board and lodging etc. Clearly, there would be maintenance in such a case.

In *Re Beaumont* [1980] 1 All ER 266 (Ch D) the deceased and the applicant lived together from 1940 until the deceased's death in 1976 in a bungalow belonging to the deceased. When they retired each received a state pension and the deceased also received a civil service pension.

The applicant paid the deceased for his accommodation and contributed to the weekly shopping bill. The deceased paid all the outgoings on the bungalow and did all housework and cooking.

The applicant owned and maintained a car for their joint use, and he also did gardening and decorating work round the bungalow for which he was reimbursed by the deceased. Before her death, the deceased gave the applicant £550 of premium bonds and by her will left her bungalow to her three sisters. The applicant claimed under the 1975 Act. One question which arose was whether the applicant was being 'maintained' for the purposes of s1(1)(e) and s1(3).

Held: the applicant was one of two people of independent means who had chosen to pool their individual resources to enable them to live together without either undertaking any responsibility for maintaining the other. His claim therefore failed.

It is clear from *Re Beaumont* that there is no maintenance where two parties make contributions of equal value towards providing a home and food and drink for themselves jointly. The position in that case is no different from that of a few students or other flat sharers who live together because it is cheaper to do so than to live separately.

In the event of intestacy and provision for dependants and whether a person is 'being maintained', additional guidelines are emerging in the recent case law when the court is considering the 1975 Act and, in particular, s1(1)(e) of the Inheritance (Provision for Family and Dependants) Act 1975. From the decision in *Bishop* v *Plumley* [1991] 1 WLR 582, it emerges that the question of whether a person is 'being maintained' for the purpose of s1(1)(e) and (3) of the Inheritance (Provision for Family and Dependants) Act 1975 should be looked at in the round applying a commonsense approach and avoiding fine balancing computations.

In the case of the surviving spouse the 1975 Act provides a higher standard of provision for the widow or widower 'whether or not that provision is required for his or her maintenance' (s1(2)(a)). The practical effect of this higher standard of provision was discussed in *Moody* v *Stevenson* [1992] Ch 486 (CA) (see section 12.7), which considered the specific reference to the fiction of the divorce and what the applicant spouse would have received in such circumstances under s3(2) of the Act. In *Moody*, the estate comprised only the former matrimonial home, the applicant was a second spouse and the deceased had moved to a nursing home prior to her death. The court regarded the divorce fiction as a logical starting point, awarding the deceased a life interest in the former matrimonial home by carrying out an appraisal of the position upon divorce and applying the provisions of the Matrimonial Causes Act 1973. In fact, the wording of s3 does not indicate that this is required. As noted in the judgment of Oliver LJ in the Court of Appeal decision in *Re Besterman (deceased)* [1984] Ch 458 (at p469), which is described more fully in section 12.7:

> 'The figure resulting from the section 25 exercise is merely one of the factors to which the Court is to have regard and the overriding consideration is what is "reasonable".'

It has been argued that the divorce fiction may be useful in establishing a minimum entitlement but should not dictate a rigid maximum award.

The forfeiture rule (see Chapter 9, section 9.7) may affect the rights of a dependant under the deceased's will or intestacy and, if so, the question arises whether that dependant can make an application under s1(1) of the 1975 Act. This matter was considered by the Court of Appeal in *Re Royse* [1984] 3 All ER 339. In this case the plaintiff applied under the 1975 Act after finding that she had been deprived of her rights as sole beneficiary under her husband's will because she had been convicted of his manslaughter. The plaintiff's conviction occurred before the Forfeiture Act 1982 came into force. Apart from the 1982 Act the court held she could not seek financial provision under the 1975 Act because it could not be said that the absence of reasonable financial provision was attributable to the provisions of the husband's will or his intestacy, but rather to the operation of the forfeiture rule. Consequently, the plaintiff could not meet the basic requirements of s2 of the 1975 Act. This point would not have affected the plaintiff if her conviction occurred after the Forfeiture Act came into force since by s3(1) it provides that:

> 'The forfeiture rule shall not be taken to preclude any person from making an application under [*inter alia*, any provision of the 1975 Act]'.

12.3 Time for making applications

Under s4 of the Act it is provided:

> 'An application for an order under section 2 of this Act shall not, except with the permission of the court, be made after the end of the period of six months from the date on which representation with respect to the estate of the deceased is first taken out.'

Applicants must be vigilant in bringing their claims under the Act as claims can only be brought after the end of the period of six months from the date of the grant of representation with the permission of the court. The purpose of this limitation is to enable the personal representatives to safely distribute the estate to the beneficiaries under the deceased's will or intestacy after the six month period has expired. However, if there is any reasonable prospect of a claim being brought under the Act, the personal representatives should not distribute the estate within the six month period. If they do so, they may incur personal liability to meet orders made under the Act. However, no such personal liability will exist after the end of the six month period for distribution of the estate. According to s20(1) the personal representative is not personally liable in such circumstances even if he ought to have realised that:

1. the court might grant leave to bring an application at the end of the six month period; or
2. the court would vary an order already made so as to increase or decrease the amount the applicant would receive.

If a successful application is brought under the Act outside the time limits prescribed and the estate has been distributed the applicant's only remedy is to recover what he/she can from those to whom it has been distributed. See s20(1).

Under s4 it is provided that the time for making an application runs from the date on which a grant of representation is first taken out. This refers to the first effective or valid grant of representation so that a grant made to a will which is later found to be invalid will not be taken into account. This was considered in the following case.

In *Re Freeman* [1984] 3 All ER 906 the deceased died in 1978 leaving a will making provision for the plaintiff, with whom he had been living for over 10 years, and for his parents. The executor proved the will in 1979. In 1981 the deceased's mother took proceedings claiming the will was invalid for improper execution. In 1983 the grant of probate to the will was revoked and the mother granted letters of administration. Under the intestacy rules the mother was entitled to the deceased's estate. The plaintiff brought proceedings under s4 of the 1975 Act in April 1984, eight months after the mother was granted letters of administration and three and a half years after probate had been granted to the revoked will.

Held: under s4 time began to run from the date when the first effective grant had been made, ie the grant to the mother.

For the purposes of determining when a grant was first taken out to the deceased's estate, it is provided by s23 that grants limited to settled land or trust property or to personal estate shall be left out of account unless a grant to the remainder of the estate has been previously made or made at the same time.

As s4 states, leave to bring applications out of time must be obtained from the court. Guidelines have been laid down as to what should be considered in deciding to grant such leave. In *Re Salmon* [1980] 3 All ER 532, Megarry V-C identified the following guidelines.

1. The court's discretion under s4 is unfettered. This discretion will therefore be exercised judicially in accordance with what is just and proper.
2. The onus of proof is on the applicant to make out a substantial case for its being just and proper for the court to exercise its statutory discretion to extend time.
3. It must be considered how promptly and in what circumstances the applicant has sought the permission of the court after the time limit has expired. This is not a matter of looking at the length of time which has elapsed but, instead, at the reasons for the delay and whether any warning was given to the defendants of the proposed application before the time limit expired.
4. It must be considered whether any negotiations were commenced within the time limit and time has run out while they were proceeding. If there were negotiations commenced out of time this would also be relevant especially if no objection had been made that time had expired.
5. It must be considered whether or not the estate has been distributed before a claim under the Act had been notified. From the point of view of beneficiaries there is a real difference between an expectation of money and the actual receipt of money. In the latter case the beneficiary may change their position by making purchases and gifts they would otherwise not have made. The hardship which may arise from this must be considered.

6. It must be considered whether a refusal to extend time would leave the applicant without redress against anybody. Thus, if the applicant's claim was not made in time because of faulty advice from her solicitor, possible remedies in negligence against the solicitor will be borne in mind. In *Re Dennis* [1981] 2 All ER 140 a seventh factor was added.

7. It must be considered whether the applicant was able to satisfy the court that he had an arguable case that he was entitled to reasonable financial provision out of the estate. The criterion applied here would be similar to those applied in deciding whether a defendant should have leave to defend in proceedings for summary judgment.

In *Re Salmon* [1980] 3 All ER 532 Ch D the applicant and the deceased were married in 1932 but parted company in 1944 after an unhappy marriage and never saw each other again. There was no divorce. The deceased died in 1978 leaving an estate of £75,000. A grant of administration was made to his estate in December 1978 so the six month time limit for applications expired in June 1979. In February 1979 the applicant wrote to the administrators asking for an ex gratia payment in lieu of proceedings under the 1975 Act. This was refused so she obtained legal aid and counsel's opinion etc, and did not issue proceedings until November 1979. By that time most of the estate had been distributed. The applicant sought leave to bring her application out of time.

Held: leave to apply out of time would be refused because: (1) the delay was the fault of the applicant's side; (2) there were no negotiations of her claim or any warning to the other side that an extension of time would be sought; (3) almost all of the estate had been distributed; (4) the applicant probably had a claim in negligence against her solicitors.

In *Re Dennis* [1981] 2 All ER 140 (Ch D) the deceased was a millionaire who had during his lifetime given his spendthrift son £90,000 and other sums of money which were dissipated. By his will the deceased left the son a £10,000 legacy duty free and £30,000 duty free to be held under protective trusts but made no other provision for him. The deceased died in November 1977 and probate of his will was granted in January 1978. In February 1980 the son issued a summons seeking permission to make an application out of time under s4. At that time the son was aged 38, had no resources or capital, was unemployed and owed about £50,000 in capital transfer tax on the gifts he received from the deceased. His claim was limited to the amount of capital transfer tax he had to pay.

Held: the son did not have an arguable case under the Act as a claim for maintenance thereunder was one to enable an applicant to discharge recurring living expenses rather than to discharge obligations to his creditors. The application would be dismissed.

In contrast is the recent decision of the court in *Stock v Brown* [1994] 1 FLR 840 in which an applicant successfully discharged the burden following the *Salmon* guidelines. This case demonstrated that in exceptional circumstances the long expiry of the statutory time limit – six years on the facts – would not prevent an application where there is no prejudice to other beneficiaries.

There have been further decisions on this point, such as *Re C (deceased) (leave to apply for provision)* [1995] 2 FLR 24, which concerned the late application by a child against the father's estate. The late application was allowed, particularly as the claim did not prejudice other beneficiaries. See also *Re W (a minor) (claim from deceased's estate)* [1995] 2 FCR 689.

The question has been raised whether an application can be brought before steps have been taken to obtain a grant of representation to the deceased's estate. Whereas s19(3) indicates that there should be a grant before an Order is made under the Act, s4 of the 1975 Act does not appear to inhibit an application being made before the grant. This matter came to be considered in a recent case, *Re McBroom (deceased)* [1992] 2 FLR 49. Here appeal was made against an Order striking out an application made before a grant. The question was whether such an application was indeed valid. Eastham J dismissed the appeal. He applied *obiter dictum* in *Re Bidie* [1949] Ch 121 although this was stated in a totally different context, and did not consider *Re Searle* [1949] Ch 73 where it was expressly decided that an application could be made before grant.

Whereas *Re Bidie* and *Re Searle* were decided under the legislation prior to s4 of the 1975 Act, in fact the wording of s4 is more favourable to applicants who wish to expedite their litigation. Although the Judge may have been wrong in coming to his conclusion in *Re McBroom (deceased)*, this case is not going to the Court of Appeal. Unless and until *McBroom* is overruled, applicants should apply for a discretionary grant to be made to a nominee under s16 of the Supreme Court Act 1981 before issuing proceedings.

Once the claim is issued the claim form must be served within four months of the date of issue (see CPR 7.5). In *Barker* v *Casserly* LTL 24 October 2000 the applicant was applying under s1(1)(e) as a person maintained. He issued his claim form one day before the end of the six months from date of grant. The applicant sent the relevant documents to the first defendant's last known address and to her solicitors.

The first defendant had moved abroad. The third defendant was temporarily abroad and his solicitors acknowledged service. The district judge extended the validity of the claim form in case it had not been served within four months of issue. The third defendant argued that the district judge had no power to do so. Rimer J rejected this argument and said that the district judge had acted in accordance with the overriding objective of the CPRs to achieve justice. He commented that it would have been contrary to the claimant's rights under ECHR for the court not to have such powers.

This case is a good example of the impact of human rights on probate.

12.4 Consideration of an application by the court

The wording of s1(1) and s3(1) of the Act make it clear that the consideration of an application is a two-stage process. First, the court must look to see if the will or intestacy or the combination of both was such as not to make reasonable financial provision for the applicant. If it is concluded that reasonable financial provision was made, the case is finished. But should the court consider that reasonable financial provision was not made for the applicant, it must go on to determine what would be reasonable financial provision for the applicant.

In determining the matters mentioned in the previous paragraph, the court must have regard to the meaning of 'reasonable financial provision' and, in addition, the various factors laid down in s3 of the Act which must be borne in mind.

12.5 What is reasonable financial provision?

This term is defined in s1(2) of the Act and a different standard is applied in the case of applicants under s1(1)(a), that is, husband or wife of the deceased, to that which is applied in other cases.

The 'surviving spouse' standard under s1(2)(a) is:

> 'Such financial provision as it would be reasonable in all the circumstances of the case for a husband or wife to receive, whether or not that provision is required for his or her maintenance.'

This provision brings into force the recommendation of the Law Commission that the claim of a surviving spouse under the Act should be treated on the same footing as one claiming financial provision on a divorce. This standard does not apply to cases where the deceased and the applicant were judicially separated at the date of death; here the applicant is, *prima facie*, only entitled to have his or her case considered on the basis of the lower standard in s1(2)(b). However, under s14 of the Act the court has a discretion to apply the surviving spouse standard to judicially separated spouses and also to some applicants under s1(1)(b), that is, a former spouse who has not remarried, if:

1. the deceased died within 12 months of the decree of the divorce or nullity of marriage being made absolute or of the decree of judicial separation being granted; and
2. no application has been made for financial provision in the matrimonial proceedings, of if made, had not been determined at the time of death.

The purpose of s14 is to ensure that a former spouse is not deprived of rights to financial provison which would have been made in the matrimonial proceedings if there had not been a death.

The standard applied in other cases under s1(2)(b) is:

'Such financial provision as it would be reasonable in all circumstances of the case for the applicant to receive for his maintenance.'

No definition of 'maintenance' has yet been put forward in the cases. In *Re Christie* [1979] 1 All ER 546, the judge treated maintenance as being equivalent to providing for the well-being or benefit of the applicant. This was disapproved of by Oliver J at first instance and by Goff LJ in the Court of Appeal in *Re Coventry*. In *Re Coventry*, Oliver J considered that 'maintenance' should be construed in the same way as under the previous legislation. Therefore, the statement in *Re Borthwick* [1949] Ch 395 is still relevant where it was said:

'Maintenance does not only mean the food [the applicant] puts in her mouth, it means the clothes on her back, the house in which she lives, and the money which she has to have in her pocket, all of which vary according to the means of [the deceased] ... Maintenance cannot mean mere subsistence.'

In *Re Dennis*, Browne–Wilkinson J was of the view that 'maintenance':

'Connotes only payments which, directly or indirectly, enable the applicant in the future to discharge the cost of his daily living at whatever standard is appropriate to him. The provision that is to be made is to meet recurring expenses, being expenses of living of an income nature. This does not mean that provision need be by way of income payments. The provision can be by way of lump sum, for example, to buy a house in which the applicant can be housed, thereby relieving him pro tanto of income expenditure.'

No precise definition has been put upon the word 'maintenance' because as Goff LJ said in *Re Coventry*:

'What is proper maintenance must in all cases depend on all the facts and circumstances of the particular case being considered at the time, but I think it is clear on the one hand that one must not put too limited a meaning on it; it does not mean just enough to enable a person to get by; on the other hand, it does not mean anything which may be regarded as reasonably desirable for his general benefit or welfare.'

'Maintenance' was again considered in *Re Leach* [1985] 2 All ER 754 where the judge at first instance applied a test from a Canadian authority, *Re Duranceau* (1952) 3 DLR 714, namely:

'Is the provision sufficient to enable the dependant to live neither luxuriously nor miserably but decently and comfortably according to his or her station in life?'

The dicta in the cases above indicate that the purpose of the Act is to provide for the applicant if the deceased has not done so and should have done so. In *Re Coventry* Oliver J warned against misinterpretation of this purpose and said:

'It is not the purpose of the Act to provide legacies or rewards for meritorious conduct. Subject to the court's power under the 1975 Act and to fiscal demands, an Englishman still remains at liberty at his death to dispose of his own property in whatever way he pleases or, if he chooses to do so, to leave that disposition to be regulated by the laws of intestate succession.'

In *Re Coventry* [1979] 2 All ER 408 (Ch D) the deceased was married in 1927 and acquired a house at that time jointly with his wife. In 1931 the deceased's only child, a son, was born. Up until 1957 the son was in the navy but he returned home then to live with the deceased when the deceased's wife left home. The son lived rent-free in the house but he did some domestic work and paid for food, and for a time gas and electricity, in return. In 1961 the son got married and until this marriage ended in 1971 the son's wife lived in the house rent-free also but doing some domestic duties in return. The deceased died in 1976 leaving an estate of £7,000 all of which would pass to his widow on intestacy. At that time the son was aged 46, and earning £52 a week out of which he paid his wife £12 a week maintenance. He had no savings and if required to move, would have to find alternative accommodation.

Held: the court would not interfere with the dispositions by the deceased merely because it considered that he had acted unreasonably, but only if the deceased had not made adequate provision for the applicant. In order to succeed, the applicant would have to show a moral claim over and above the claim of a blood relationship to be maintained by the deceased. This was not discharged merely because the applicant found himself in necessitous circumstances. The claim failed.

A recent decision following this judgment should be noted. In *Cameron* v *Treasury Solicitor* [1996] 2 FLR 716 A (the Treasury Solicitor) appealed against a decision awarding the net estate of a deceased ex-husband, C, to his ex-wife, B, under the I(PFD)A 1975. B was married to C until the couple were divorced in 1971, and a clean break order was made by consent in 1981. There were no children of the marriage, neither party remarried, and C died intestate with his estate devolving upon the Crown as bona vacantia. B claimed that C had not made reasonable financial provision for her. Due to the fact that the estate was small (the estate amounted to £7,677) it was agreed that if B was successful she should be awarded the entire estate. A argued that the judge was not entitled in law to find that the estate had not made reasonable financial provision for B when he had not found that C owed any legal or moral obligation to B. B relied on her continuing friendship with C after their divorce, her financial circumstances, her worsening ill health and the fact that there were no other beneficiaries apart from the Crown.

Held: the appeal was upheld. The court held that the fact that the Crown was the only beneficiary was not relevant to B's claim and that her claim had to be considered on its own merits. The court went on to say that there were no special circumstances to demonstrate that the lack of provision was unreasonable. Similarly, there could be no moral claim merely because of the financial difficulties of the claimant or her ill health (*Re Coventry (deceased)* [1980] Ch 461 (CA) followed).

When considering the objectives of the 1975 Act, it is also helpful to review the recent case of *Kusminow* v *Barclays Bank Trust Co Ltd* [1989] Fam Law 66. The plaintiff, aged 78, had married in 1958; she was Polish in origin, her husband was Russian, but they had spent their married life in England. The plaintiff left her husband in 1984 and he died the following year. By his will, made in 1968, he divided his estate between his nephew and niece who lived in the Soviet Union. The plaintiff made a claim under s2 of the Inheritance (Provision for Family and Dependants) Act 1975 and, for the purposes of the hearing, it was agreed that the value of the deceased's estate was about £100,000. The plaintiff, an arthritis sufferer, lived in a rented flat; she had savings of about £20,000 and a retirement pension. The nephew and niece lived in conditions of some poverty.

Held: taking into account the respective needs of all the parties, the plaintiff would be awarded a lump sum of £45,000.

Sir Stephen Brown P explained that when making an order under s2 of the 1975 Act the court had to have regard to the matters set out in s3. They included a provision that in the case of an application by the wife of the deceased the court should have regard to the provision which the applicant might reasonably have expected to receive if, on the day on which the deceased died, the marriage instead of being terminated by death, had been terminated by divorce. This was a case where a final disposition should be made. The plaintiff would have to ensure that she had sufficient money to provide not only income but also accommodation of a satisfactory kind. Regard must be had too to the fact that there was need on the part of the beneficiaries who should each receive a substantial capital sum.

The case of *Davis* v *Davis* [1993] 1 FLR 54 should be mentioned in the discussion of family provision and whether life interest in the majority of the estate was reasonable financial provision. Just prior to his death the testator gave £15,000 to his second wife and executed a will bequeathing two pieces of furniture to his son from his first marriage and the remainder of his chattels to his wife, the residue of his estate to the trustees, with a life interest to the wife. The trustees bought a house for the wife.

At the time of the appeal the assets in the trust consisted of £12,000 in cash, a share in a farm worth £75,000 to be realised in two years, £20,000 due from the estate of the testator's uncle, as well as the expectation of a share from the estate of the deceased's father when the life tenant died. The widow claimed that the will had failed to make reasonable financial provision insofar as no capital payment had been made. She claimed that the freehold of the house should be transferred to her. The judge dismissed her application.

Held: the Court of Appeal dismissed her application. The widow had been accommodated and proper and adequate provision had been made for her maintenance. The judge at first instance had taken into account all relevant considerations, therefore there was no reason for the appellate court to interfere.

12.6 The common guidelines

Under s3(1) of the Act seven guidelines are set out which must be considered in all applications under the Act, first, to decide if reasonable provision has been made, and second, if necessary, to decide what provision should be made. In deciding these matters s3(5) provides that the court must have regard to the facts known at the date of the hearing. This permits the court to look at events which occurred after the deceased's death and which affect the applicant's position. So, for example, if the applicant won on the pools or suffered a great misfortune after the deceased died, these would be taken into account. Further, under s21 the court can take into account statements made by the deceased, whether made orally or in a document or otherwise, as to his reasons for not making any or any greater provision for the applicant. The guidelines in s3(1) are as follows.

First, the financial resources and financial needs which the applicant has or is likely to have in the foreseeable future.

Second, the financial resources and financial needs which any other applicant for an order under s2 of the Act has or is likely to have in the forseeable future. Under this guideline the court will look at the applicant's present and projected income, the effect of the applicant's marital status upon this, and how near the applicant is to retirement. It will also consider the applicant's financial commitments, for example, mortgages, hire-purchase arrangements and bank overdrafts. See *Re Leach* [1985] 2 All ER 754.

Third, the financial resources and financial needs which any beneficiary of the estate of the deceased has or is likely to have in the foreseeable future. Under s3(6) it is stated that 'financial resources' includes earning capacity and that in assessing 'financial needs', the court shall take into account financial obligations and responsibilities. In dealing with these matters it is clear that the court has to perform a balancing act between several parties, that is, the applicant, other applicants and the beneficiaries. This is especially important if the estate is quite small. As an example, the deceased left his estate worth £40,000 to his 18-year-old son and left his wife and a mistress unprovided for. In an application by the wife, her financial resources would be considered under s3(1)(a) but it would also be important to consider the position of the mistress under s3(1)(b) so that one applicant is not given preferential treatment over the other. Further, under s3(1)(c), the position of beneficiaries has to be considered to avoid the problem of an order being made under s2 which takes away a large part of the estate from a beneficiary who would, if left little or nothing, have a potential claim under the Act.

Fourth, any obligation and responsibilities which the deceased had towards any applicant for an order under the said s2 or towards any beneficiary of the estate of the deceased. The purpose of this guideline is to ensure that emphasis is placed on the obligations and responsibilities of the deceased towards the applicant and not upon preserving the interests of beneficiaries under the estate. Thus, in *Re Besterman (deceased)* [1984] 2 All ER 656, the court took into account the obligations and responsibilities the deceased had towards his wife of 18 years standing, until his death. She had been a good wife who had enjoyed an extremely high standard of living during the marriage and had few capital resources of her own. The deceased's obligation was viewed as one to enable his wife to enjoy, as far as possible, the standards she had enjoyed during the marriage. In *Re Callaghan* [1984] 3 All ER 790

Booth J considered that the obligations that arise from a blood relationship and of the deceased having shared his life in the past with his blood relatives were in themselves of little weight.

Fifth, the size and nature of the net estate of the deceased. The size of the estate is often an important factor in determining whether any order should be made, especially if the estate is small. In such circumstances, it may not be possible to satisfy the claims of all the applicants. Thus, for example, if the deceased had a wife and a mistress and his estate was worth only £5,000 it would be impossible to make any satisfactory award. Under the 1938 Act Ungoed-Thomas J said that the smallness of an estate was an important factor in three respects.

1. In considering the availability of state aid. There is no point in making an order if the effect is only going to be to relieve social security funds *pro tanto*. In fact an order in such a case may well be a disservice to the applicant in so far as claiming social security is concerned. Of course, if the estate is large these matters will be irrelevant.
2. In considering the extent to which the estate can effectively contribute to the applicant's maintenance.
3. In relation to the costs of an application which, if they are paid out of the estate, may leave little or nothing for the applicant or the beneficiaries. Costs are normally awarded out of the estate and if the action is heard in the High Court they may be substantial. This problem is alleviated to some extent as claims in relation to smaller estates can now be brought in the county court.

The origin of the estate is relevant here. If the surviving spouse helped to earn the property, this will be a strong factor in his/her application.

Sixth, any physical or mental disability of any applicant for an order under s2 or any beneficiary of the deceased. If the deceased had a disabled child whom she/he supported, this would entitle the child to a claim that the support be continued. However, in dealing with such a case, state aid must be taken into account. Thus, in *Re Watkins* [1949] 1 All ER 695, it was held reasonable for the deceased to leave nothing to his mentally ill daughter from his £23,000 estate since she was detained in a private mental hospital, had no hope of recovery and would be transferred to a state hospital.

Note by way of contrast the case of *Re Wood* (1981) (Lexis Transcript) where a mentally handicapped adult daughter was successful in applying for reasonable provision under the Act.

More recently the case of *Re Debenham (deceased)* [1986] FLR 101 establishes that the court will treat favourably the claim of a disabled adult child. Here the claimant was an adult daughter aged 58 who had only been left the sum of £200 by her mother out of an estate of £172,000. The claimant was physically disabled and suffered from epilepsy. The claimant was awarded the sum of £3,000 by way of immediate legacy plus an annuity of £4,500 per annum until further order.

Seventh, any other matter including the conduct of the applicant or any other person, which in the circumstances of the case the court may consider relevant. This guideline allows the court to consider any other factor it regards relevant in the circumstances of the particular case. Emphasis is put upon conduct. In *Wachtel* v *Wachtel* [1973] Fam 72 Lord Denning in dealing with an application for financial provision in a divorce case said conduct was relevant where it was 'both obvious and gross, so much so that to order one party to support another whose conduct falls into this category is repugnant to anyone's sense of justice'. Thus if the deceased's wife had left him to live with another man, or had murdered him, the court may regard these as grounds for declining to give financial provision or reducing such provision substantially. Conduct does, however, go beyond moral conduct. In *Re Cook* (1956) 106 LJ 466 the fact that the deceased's daughter had devoted her life to looking after him was taken into account. The court, under this guideline, can consider anything else which is appropriate to the case. Thus, for example, in *Re Leach* [1985] 2 All ER 754, it was considered appropriate to take account of encouragement by the deceased to the applicant to enter financial commitments to buy a house on the basis that the applicant would receive a substantial sum of money on the deceased's death.

12.7 The particular guidelines

In subs(2), (3) and (4) of s3 special guidelines are set out which must be taken into account by the court in the particular applications to which they are relevant.

Spouses and former spouses

Under s3(2) the court must in applications under s1(1)(a) or s1(1)(b) have regard to:

1. the age of the applicant and the duration of the marriage. The age is important in that the claim of a young spouse will be much weaker than that of an old one, as a young spouse could still go out to work. The duration of the marriage will be a factor in the strength of a claim. Thus if the marriage broke down in a short time the spouse's claim would be weak in contrast to that of a spouse who was married to the deceased for 20 years or more;
2. the contribution made by the applicant to the welfare of the family of the deceased, including any contributions made by looking after the home or caring for the family. A wife who has devoted all her time to the deceased's home and family will have a strong claim, in contrast to one who left the deceased to live on her own many years before his death. In applying these factors much will depend on the circumstances of each case.

In addition to the above factors, the court must also, in the case of applicants under s1(1)(a), have regard to the provision which the applicant might reasonably have expected to receive if on the day on which the deceased died, the marriage, instead of being terminated by death, had been terminated by a decree of divorce. The purpose of this guideline is to remove the discrepancy which formerly existed between spouses who obtained provision in divorce proceedings and spouses who obtained provision under an application at the deceased's death. In future it is clear that spouses applying under the 1975 Act will be treated in much the same way as spouses seeking provision on divorce. The guideline in (c) does not apply to a spouse who was judicially separated from the deceased at his death because such a spouse could take the opportunity to apply for financial provision under the Matrimonial Causes Act 1973.

The guideline in (c) was considered by the Court of Appeal in *Re Besterman* [1984] 2 All ER 656. Oliver LJ considered that it brought into the calculation of what the spouse should receive under the 1975 Act the provisions of s25 of the Matrimonial Causes Act 1973. Under s25 the court is to have regard to the financial needs, obligations and responsibilities which each of the parties to the marriage has or is likely to have in the foreseeable future and, having regard to their conduct, the financial position in which they would have been if the marriage had not broken down and each had properly discharged his or her financial obligations and responsibilities towards the other. However, it was stressed that the s25 provisions are only one factor in deciding what is reasonable financial provision for a spouse under s1(2)(a) of the 1975 Act. Thus, it seems that a figure which the court might have awarded the applicant spouse on divorce under s25 must be considered under s1(2)(a) to see if it is a reasonable figure in all the circumstances to award; in some cases it might be too low. In *Re Besterman* the trial judge's award was increased because it only took into account the spouse's financial needs and the amounts required for her maintenance and took no account of possible future contingencies. It was held that reasonable provision should not be confined to maintenance of the spouse but, in the circumstances, should include a sufficient sum so as to relieve the spouse of any anxiety for the future. See also *Re Bunning* [1984] 3 All ER 1.

In *Re Besterman* (*deceased*) [1984] 2 All ER 656 (CA) the plaintiff, who was aged 66 at the time of the application, married the deceased in 1958 when she was 42 and he was 54. The marriage was amicable and lasted until the deceased's death in 1976. The deceased was a very wealthy man and the plaintiff enjoyed an extremely high standard of living up until his death. The deceased left an estate of over £1.5 million and by his will he left the plaintiff an annuity of about £3,500 and some personal chattels but bequeathed the remainder of his estate to charity. The trial judge awarded the plaintiff a lump sum of £259,000. The plaintiff appealed because the award was less than she might have expected to receive on divorce under s25 of the Matrimonial Causes Act 1973, that is, about £350,000 and also because the judge misdirected himself by adopting maintenance as the criterion of reasonable financial provision.

Held: 'maintenance' was only one of the matters to be taken into consideration in considering the position under s25. Further the award was too low to satisfy the criterion of reasonable provision and the award would be increased to £378,000 in the circumstances.

In *Re Bunning* [1984] 3 All ER 1 (Ch D) the deceased and the plaintiff married in 1963 when they were aged 56 and 34 respectively. There were no children and the plaintiff helped the deceased to run his business and keep the matrimonial home. The deceased gave the plaintiff gifts of money and shares during the marriage. In 1978 the plaintiff left the deceased and she never returned. The deceased died in 1982 leaving a will making no provision for the plaintiff. The deceased's estate was worth £237,000 and the plaintiff had assets worth £98,000 which represented what the deceased gave her. The plaintiff applied under the 1975 Act contending that under s25 of the Matrimonial Causes Act 1973 she would have been entitled to a lump sum of about £90,000.

Held: an award of £60,000 would be made as this when added to the £98,000 already received would give her half of their total assets after deducting the costs of her application. It would enable the plaintiff to maintain a reasonable lifestyle and take into account the total of their joint assets, the fact that the matrimonial home had been sold and the fact that the plaintiff was comparatively young and needed a reasonable degree of financial security for what was most likely to be a long widowhood.

In *Moody* v *Stevenson* [1992] Ch 486 (CA) the applicant was the widower of the deceased: they had married in 1971 when he was aged 61 and she was aged 66.

The testatrix had lived with the applicant until 1984 when she moved into a nursing home. When she died in 1988 the testatrix left her modest estate by will to her step-daughter. This included the house.

The applicant sought an order for 'reasonable financial provision' under ss1, 2 and 3 of the Inheritance (Provisions for Family and Dependants) Act 1975. In the county court his claim had been dismissed: the legatee had been granted an order for possession of the house. The applicant appealed.

Held: the appeal was allowed. Mustill LJ said that the 1975 Act placed a claim by a surviving spouse on a new footing as a claim for 'reasonable financial provision'. Following s3(2) the court was to have regard to the provisions a spouse might reasonably have expected to receive if on the day of death the marriage had been terminated by divorce. The county court judge should have decided the case by asking: 'What would a family judge have ordered for the couple if divorce instead of death had divided them?' Had the judge applied this test – the proper test – he would have made an order permitting the applicant to remain in the house as long as he wished.

This case should be contrasted with the decision in *Jessop* v *Jessop* [1992] 1 FLR 591. The applicant was a widow who made her application under the 1975 Act against a woman with whom the deceased intestate had been living. Apparently the deceased had been married and had maintained two families.

Originally the house in which the deceased lived with his second family had been owned by the respondent, with the financial assistance of her mother. In order to repay her mother she had subsequently borrowed from a building society. The house was then put into the joint names of the deceased and the respondent to enable the respondent to take through the right of survivorship when the deceased died.

By virtue of the intestacy provisions the applicant became entitled to a small amount of cash on the death of the deceased.

At first instance the judge had ordered that £10,000 should be paid to the widow by the respondent in respect of the deceased's severable share in the property.

Held: the Court of Appeal overruled the first instance decision. It held that on an objective basis the judge had to decide whether reasonable provision had been made by will or intestacy. In contrast to matrimonial proceedings, there were no broad powers under the 1975 Act proceedings, to make equitable distribution of any available assets.

Insofar as this case implied that, in the absence of reasonable provision under a will or intestacy, no further order can be made the decision provides an interesting comparison with that discussed above in *Moody* v *Stevenson*.

One issue that has been raised in the cases is whether the divorce guideline is an appropriate staring point for a judge to consider when assessing the claim of a surviving spouse. In *Re Bunning* the judge assessed that on divorce the applicant would have obtained an award of £36,000, but went on to award £60,000. The reason for this is that on divorce the court is forced to take the husband's as well as the wife's needs into account, whereas in these applications under the 1975 Act there is no such requirement. This clearly displays the point that the 'divorce guideline' may not be the best method of determining the spouse's claim. In *Re Krubert* [1996] 3 WLR 959 the Court of Appeal felt that there was no necessity for a court to take divorce as a starting point when determining the quantum of a claim. The Court emphasised the difference mentioned above between divorce proceedings and claims under the 1975 Act, and stated that it preferred the approach taken in *Re Besterman* to that of *Moody* v *Stevenson*. It is likely that future cases will adopt this approach.

The most recent application of *Re Besterman* is in *Adams* v *Lewis* LTL 6 February 2001 (unreported elsewhere). The claimant, Elizabeth Adams, married the deceased in 1937. They had 12 children and, aside from an 18-month separation in 1969, were married for 54 years. Under the terms of his will the testator gave his wife all his household goods and personal effects together with a legacy of £10,000, the residue to be divided amongst his children. The trustees of the estate allowed her to continue living in the matrimonial home, Gordon House. Three of her daughters objected to this. The wife made an application for reasonable financial provision out of the estate.

The High Court held that the legacy of £10,000, together with the household goods, was not a reasonable financial provision for the claimant. She had made a significant contribution to the welfare of the family by bringing up 12 children. In this type of case the court felt that the divorce guideline was most important, although not the only factor to be taken into account. In view of this, the matrimonial home, Gordon House, was ordered to be transferred to Elizabeth

Adams by way of specific legacy and her legacy of £10,000 was ordered to be reduced to £5,000.

The particular guidelines applicable to former spouses must be considered in the light of the standard of maintenance applicable in such cases. However the number of cases where a former spouse can make a successful application under the 1975 Act are limited and the following are probably the main ones.

1. Where the former spouse has not had time to bring proceedings for financial provision subsequent to a divorce or the court has not heard such proceedings before the deceased's death. In such circumstances the court may in its discretion apply the higher standard of financial provision in s1(2)(a). See s14(1).
2. Where provision made for the former spouse in the divorce proceedings is inadequate and the death of the deceased makes more money available for this purpose.

In *Re Fullard* [1981] 2 All ER 796 the Court of Appeal considered the position of former spouses who bring applications under the 1975 Act. Purchas J considered that where a former spouse had settled her claim for financial provision in divorce proceedings, with the assistance of legal advisers, it would require exceptional circumstances or conditions for the court to conclude that what was reasonable provision on the dissolution of the marriage was no longer reasonable at the date of death. However, he pointed out some exceptional cases where this could occur.

1. Where there has been a long period of time since the dissolution of the marriage in circumstances in which a continuing obligation to support the ex-spouse has been established by an order of the court, by consent or otherwise, under which periodical payments have been, and continue to be made up to the date of death.
2. Where the death itself unlocks a substantial capital sum of which the testator should have been aware, and from which had he made a will immediately before death, he ought to have made some provision, for example, an insurance policy.
3. Where the deceased accrued further wealth after the dissolution of marriage which would have made the court consider in a different light any application by the spouse on divorce.

In *Re Fullard* [1981] 2 All ER 796 (CA) the applicant and the deceased married in 1939 and were divorced in 1977. Both had worked throughout married life and had saved a total of £3,000 from low earnings. At the date of divorce both had old age pensions. The main family asset was a dwelling-house worth about £9,000 after deduction of outstanding mortgages. The parties settled their financial arrangements after the divorce by negotiations in which it was agreed that the applicant would pay the deceased £4,500 for his share of the house and the deceased would leave. The deceased moved out in 1977 and went to live with a lady friend. The deceased died in January 1978 and by his will left all his estate to the lady friend. The greater part of the deceased's £7,100 estate compromised the £4,500 paid to him by the applicant. The applicant claimed that reasonable financial provision had not been made for her.

Held: where awards had been made under the Matrimonial Causes Act 1973 it would be difficult for the former spouse to show that reasonable financial provision had not been made for her. Having regard to the deceased's assets and the arrangements he made with the applicant to settle their financial affairs, it was reasonable that he had not made any further financial provision for her in his will. The reasoning in *Fullard* was recently applied in *Barrass* v *Harding* [2001] 1 FLR 138.

In some cases where there has been a settlement of financial affairs on divorce, the settlement may contain a provision that either party shall not be entitled on the death of the other party to apply for provision under the 1975 Act. Such clauses are permissible but they must have the approval of the court. See s15(1).

Children

Where an application is made under s1(1)(c) only one particular guideline is relevant namely:

> 'The manner in which the applicant was being or in which he might expect to be educated or trained.' See s3(3).

Where an application is made under s1(1)(d) then, in addition to the guideline mentioned in (a), the court must have regard to the following.

1. Whether the deceased had assumed any responsibility for the applicant's maintenance and, if so, the extent to which and the basis upon which the deceased assumed that responsibility and the length of time for which the deceased discharged that responsibility.
2. Whether in assuming and discharging that responsibility the deceased did so knowing that the applicant was not his own child.
3. The liability of any other person to maintain the applicant.

Other dependants

Under s3(4) the court is required, in the case of applications under s1(1)(e), to have regard to:

> 'The extent to which and the basis upon which the deceased assumed responsibility for the maintenance of the applicant and to the length of time for which the deceased discharged that responsibility.'

This requirement was considered in detail by Megarry V-C in *Re Beaumont* [1980] Ch 444, who concluded that the use of the word 'assumed' indicated that there must be some act or acts which demonstrate an undertaking of responsibility, or the taking of responsibility on oneself, and that it was up to the applicant to show that the deceased had 'assumed' responsibility for his or her maintenance. He also stated that the bare fact of maintenance did not in itself raise a presumption that responsibility had been assumed. The Court of Appeal also considered these words in *Jelley* v *Iliffe* [1981] 2 All ER 29 and disagreed with this interpretation. In the course of his judgment, Stephenson LJ held that the bare fact that the applicant was being maintained by the deceased under an arrangement subsisting at the deceased's death was sufficient to, and generally did, raise a presumption that the deceased had assumed responsibility for his maintenance. Griffiths LJ considered that greater emphasis had been put upon the words 'assumed responsibility' than was necessary in *Re Beaumont* and pointed out that it was highly unlikely that any formal arrangements will have been made between the deceased and the applicant. He then said:

> 'Obvious examples are the elderly but impoverished relative or friend who is taken into the deceased's household and given free board and lodging and treated as a member of the family. Or a man living with a woman out of wedlock but supporting her as he would a wife. In such circumstances I would not as a general rule expect to find any formal declaration of assumption of responsibility but it cannot have been the intention that such cases should fail for want of some such formality.'

In *Jelley* v *Iliffe* [1981] 2 All ER 29 (CA) the applicant lived with the deceased from 1971 until the deceased's death in 1979. Both were pensioners. The deceased was the widow of the applicant's brother-in-law who lived alone in a house left to her in her late husband's will and she asked the applicant to live with her as she was lonely and frightened. The applicant and the deceased agreed to share the house and to pool their incomes to meet living expenses. The applicant provided some furniture, tended the garden and carried out some household jobs. The deceased provided the applicant with rent-free accommodation and did all his cooking and washing. When the deceased died in 1979 she left her estate, including the house, to her children, and made no provision for the applicant who applied under s1(1)(e) of the 1975 Act.

Held: the benefit of rent-free accommodation was a significant contribution to the reasonable needs of a person and, in the case of an old-age pensioner such as the applicant, it was a substantial contribution to his reasonable needs. As this had been provided over a period of eight years, this amounted to an assumption of responsibility for the applicant's maintenance. Therefore, unless the applicant's contributions equalled or outweighed the benefit of rent-free accommodation he would be treated as a dependant under s1(1)(e).

In *Bouette* v *Rose* [2000] 1 FLR 363 a mother who looked after her brain-damaged daughter from birth until her death at the age of 14, was regarded as a dependant for the purposes of the 1975 Act and as such was entitled to claim maintenance.

Mrs Bouette's daughter, Louise, was disabled at birth as a result of medical negligence. Louise was awarded £250,000. Part of the award was used to buy a house where Mrs Bouette could look after her daughter. The Court of Protection had made regular payments to Mrs Bouette as receiver of Louise's fund.

When Louise died, her estate was divisible between her parents, Mrs Bouette and Mr Rose. Her father, Mr Rose, had left shortly after her birth. Mr Rose argued that it was not possible for Louise as a minor of limited mental capacity to have assumed responsibility for her mother's maintenance under s3(4) and as such that Mrs Bouette should not be entitled to apply for provision under the Act.

The Court of Appeal found itself bound by *Jelley* v *Iliffe* in that it made clear that 'the mere fact of one person making a substantial contribution to another person's needs raises an inference of an assumption by the former of responsibility for the latter' – per Lord Justice Walker, who went on to say that 'Mrs Bouette's needs were Louise's needs, because Louise needed her mother's constant care, and because of Louise's need for that care, Mrs Bouette had to give up her business and had no other source of income (apart from social security benefits).' The Court of Appeal felt that the Act should be read as a whole and that Mrs Bouette should be entitled to make a claim on the estate.

In *Graham* v *Murphy* [1997] 1 FLR 860 the applicant cohabited with the deceased for 17 years. They first shared rented accommodation and then, from 1985, they lived in houses bought in the deceased's sole name. The deceased earned a high income which allowed the couple to enjoy a good standard of living. She paid for foreign holidays, meals in restaurants and bought a boat that the applicant used. The applicant on the other hand did not earn very much. In the early 1990s the deceased took ill and the applicant looked after her until she died in 1994. She died intestate and he claimed for provision out of her estate under s1(1)(e) of the 1975 Act. He could not bring his action as a cohabitee as she died before the Law Reform (Succession) Act 1995 came into force on 1 January 1996. As such he was required to prove his dependency.

The court held that the applicant had free accommodation from 1985 until 1994 and received substantial additional benefits which qualified him to make a claim as a dependant. No reasonable financial provision had been made for him as the deceased left no will and there was no entitlement under the intestacy rules. The court commented that reasonable financial provision in this context did not necessitate providing him with a very high standard of living for the rest of his life. The court awarded him a lump sum of £35,000 to assist in the purchase of a modest home or to supplement his income.

Had death occurred on or after 1 January 1996, the applicant would not have been required to prove dependency as they had cohabited for more than two years. However, the quantum of provision may still have been the same as the maintenance standard applies to cohabitees as it does to all other classes of applicants aside from the surviving spouse.

Foreign elements

In all cases under the Inheritance (Provision for Family and Dependants) proceedings under the 1975 Act the court only had jurisdiction where the deceased died domiciled in England and Wales.

The deceased's foreign wife or husband

Where the deceased's wife or husband is foreign the marriage must be one that is recognised in English law. In the case of *Re Sehota (deceased)*, *Kaur* v *Kaur* [1978] 1 WLR 1506; [1978] 3 All ER 385 referred to above it was held that a wife in a polygamous marriage can apply. See also *Nabi* v *Heaton* [1983] 1 WLR 626. This appears to be the current position.

The deceased's foreign former husband or former wife

The 1975 Act has been amended to allow the same rights to apply for provision to persons whose marriages are dissolved or annulled overseas to apply for provision as those persons whose marriages are dissolved under the Matrimonial Causes Act 1973; see s25(1) of the 1975 Act as amended by s25 of the Matrimonial and Family Proceedings Act 1984. It should be noted that the rights to apply are retrospective and that the position noted in section 12.2 above is therefore affected as a result of this amendment.

Foreign assets

1. Provided that the deceased had the power to dispose of his foreign assets by will they may be treated as part of the 'net estate' within the meaning of s25(1) of the 1975 Act (referred to in section 12.12 below).

   Where this is not the case, such as where the *lex situs* of immovables or the national law of a foreigner domiciled restricts testamentary power, then the foreign assets are not included. See, for example, *Re Ross (deceased)*, *Ross* v *Waterfield* [1930] 1 Ch 377; [1929] All ER Rep 456.

2. The jurisdiction of the court extends to overseas property in general but subject to the overriding consideration that there must be evidence that the order sought would be effective in a foreign court. See *Tallack* v *Tallack and Broekema* [1927] P 211; [1927] All ER Rep 6766; *Thornley and Goff* v *Goff* [1934] P 107; (1934) 103 LJ P 55.

   The court has held in relatively early judgments that its statutory power to vary settlements was not excluded by the fact that the property was in Scotland. See, for example, *Nunnely* v *Nunnely and Marrian* (1890) 12 PD 186; *Forsyth* v *Forsyth* [1891] P 367.

   This was seen more broadly in the recent case of *Hamlin* v *Hamlin* [1985] 3 WLR 629; [1985] 2 All ER 1037 (CA), as well as in the earlier case of *Razelos* v *Razelos (No 2)* [1970] 1 WLR 390. The latter case illustrates well the extension of the principle to jurisdictions that are further afield in a case which dealt with a summons under s17 of the Married Women's Property Act 1882.

   In *Razelos* v *Razelos* an American woman gave money to her Greek husband in Greece because she was under threat. Apparently, fraud was also involved. The husband used the money to purchase land in Greece. Subsequently they moved to England. While in England he used money from a trust of which his wife was sole beneficiary to open a savings account in London. This was used to purchase stocks and shares which were then maintained in the USA at the request of her husband.

Held: the court's jurisdiction extended to the property at issue. In its decision the court took into consideration that no evidence had been produced indicating that any order in respect of the land in Greece would be ineffective. The wife was entitled to an order in respect of that land declaring her ownership as well as ownership of other property claimed.

Foreign law

In an English court foreign law is a question of fact that must be adequately pleaded and proved by expert evidence. It has been established that any party seeking to rely upon and call evidence of a special or peculiar sense and construction of words in a foreign document must allege this in their pleadings. The same applies as regards matters of substantive foreign law. For authority on both points see *Ascherberg, Hopwood & Crew* v *Casa Musicale Sonzogono* [1971] 1 WLR 1128; [1971] 3 All ER 38 (CA).

12.8 Orders

The orders which the court can make in applications brought under the 1975 Act are set out in s2(1), and below.

Periodical payments

Under s2 such an order may take three forms:

1. a specified amount, for example, £60 per week or £3,500 per annum;
2. payments equal to the whole of the income of the net estate or of such proportion thereof as may be so specified, for example, the income from one-third of the net estate;
3. payments equal to the income of either the whole or such part of the net estate as is directed to be set aside for this purpose.

The court has wide powers under s2(2) in drawing up the terms on which these payments will be made and under s2(1)(a) the period for which the payments are to be made must be specified, for example, for life, or until remarriage, for 20 years, etc. Much will depend on the class of applicant. It would be uncommon to find periodical payments to a widow being for any period other than for life but in the case of other dependants the period will probably be limited.

Lump sum payments

The amount of the lump sum will be specified in the order. The sum can be paid in instalments under s7, the instalments being of such amount as the court orders. Section 7 also contains provisions allowing the court to vary either the amount payable in each instalment or the number of instalments. Lump sum payments are useful when the estate is small. In *Re Besterman* (*deceased*) [1984] 2 All ER 656 it was held that in making lump sum orders the absence of an opportunity for the applicant to return to court again for further relief should result in greater account being taken of contingencies and inflation than would be taken in the case of periodical payments.

Transfer of property

Under s2(1)(c) an order can be made for the transfer of property comprised in the deceased's estate, for example, a dwelling house. Such an order can often avoid the unnecessary sale of assets, something necessary in many cases where large lump sums are awarded.

Settlement of property

This power is useful in that the court has, under s2(4), wide powers to insert provisions in the order so that it can be given proper effect. Discretionary trusts may come in useful in the case of applicants who are unable to deal with their own financial affairs, while in the case of children use may be made of accumulation and maintenance settlements, thereby conferring tax advantages.

Acquisition of property for transfer or settlement

The deceased's estate may not comprise the type of property which is suitable for the applicant. There may be no house for a spouse, or it may be far too big for her. In these circumstances an order can be made to purchase for her a more suitable property.

Variation of marriage settlement

This type of order is likely to be restricted to spouses and children. Under it, the court can make such alteration as it deems appropriate to the marriage settlement in order to make reasonable financial provision.

Capital or life interest

In fact in two recent cases the court preferred not to grant outright awards of capital, but rather granted life interests only in the estates. These were the cases of *Davis* v *Lush* 15 January 1991 (CA) (still to be reported in the *Family Law Review*) and *Re Clarke* [1991] Fam Law 364.

In *Davis* v *Lush* 15 January 1991 (unreported) the applicant was the surviving spouse of a second marriage. She had owned a modest property prior to her marriage and she sought an outright transfer of the property which comprised part of the estate. She was living on this property.

Held: at first instance Thorpe J held that if the applicant was to have the use of the whole of the income from the estate she was not entitled to any outright award of capital or property. The applicant was granted a life interest in the whole of the deceased's estate but no capital except for the sum of £15,000 which the deceased had given to the applicant prior to his death. The Court of Appeal confirmed this decision, holding that there had been no application of a wrong principle at first instance.

In the case of *Re Clarke* [1991] Fam Law 364 again an application for capital provision was refused. The applicant was again a widow from a second marriage. Insufficient time had elapsed to enable her to consolidate the non-financial contributions of caring for the home or family under s32(a) and (b) of the 1975 Act. She applied for provision under the Act having been granted a life interest in the matrimonial home and a life interest in £25,000.

Held: the judge refused the application.

So far there is no reported case dealing with the question whether a life interest may be reasonable provision for a widow who has dependant children, and who had therefore built up maximum non-financial contributions. This type of applicant would have a meritorious claim for capital and property as a 'just share' of the deceased's estate.

Joint property

There have been two fairly recent decisions concerning property held on joint tenancy which illustrate an increasing tendency to treat the deceased's severable share of that property as part of the net estate following s9 of the 1975 Act, possibly in recognition of the amount of monies that the deceased may have tied up in property. These decisions, *Jessop* v *Jessop* [1992] 1 FLR 591 (referred to in section 12.7) and *Powell* v *Osbourne* (1992) The Times 3 December, demonstrate that it is worth looking beyond an apparently insolvent estate to the monies released as a result of the deceased's death.

The facts of *Powell* v *Osbourne* (1992) The Times 3 December are relevant while bearing in mind the decision of *Re McBroom (deceased)* [1992] 2 FLR 49 Family Division (Eastham J) regarding the timing of such an application: according to that decision an application can only be made after a grant has occurred.

In *Powell* v *Osbourne* (1992) The Times 3 December the deceased held property jointly. Its value was greatly enhanced by a life policy which redeemed the mortgage upon his death. What was the correct approach with regard to s9 which provides that the court may order that the deceased's severable share be taken 'at the value thereof immediately before his death' as being part of the net estate? At first instance the judge had considered that he was restricted by these words in s9 to deal only with the equity in the property prior to the policy monies redeeming the charge. In doing so the deceased's *prima facie* half share in the proceeds of the policy as applied to the mortgage could not be claimed by the applicant.

Held: the Court of Appeal held that the purpose of s9 was to make available, if appropriate, what could have been severed immediately before the date of his death. The last moment that severance can take place is immediately before death. The judge at first instance had treated the deceased's half share of the policy as, in effect, of no value at all. However, the Court of Appeal indicated that the imminence of the deceased's death meant that the value was in effect the same as the value upon death. Although, therefore, the building had been subject to a mortgage and it was a condition of that mortgage that half share of the policy monies were to be applied to it, it was held that the policy monies formed part of the net estate. As a result, the applicant received an increased capital sum.

Bona vacantia

A related issue is that of *bona vacantia* estates. It will be recalled that if a person dies intestate without being survived by any relatives entitled under the intestacy rules, the estate passes as *bona vacantia* to the Crown, the Duchy of Lancaster or to the Duchy of Cornwall for the time being under s46(1)(vi) of the Administration of Estates Act 1925. According to the intestacy rules, those entitled are a spouse, children or remote or direct descendants, parents, brothers and sisters (of either the half or the whole blood) or remoter direct descendants, grandparents, uncles or aunts (of either the half or the whole blood) or remoter direct descendants. While the list looks fairly comprehensive, in fact there are several groups that are not entitled such as step-children and other relatives by marriage, such as a brother's widow, a wife's sister, aunts or uncles, any of whom might well have been very close to the deceased. These relatives, and indeed close friends, may well have thought that they would be entitled in the event of the death of the deceased. This highlights the need for a will, of course.

Once it has been established that the deceased did not leave a valid will and that, *prima facie*, there are no relatives entitled to an estate, the first procedural step is to inform the appropriate *bona vacantia* authority. Usually this is the Treasury solicitor, but if the deceased lived in Cornwall it is the solicitor to the Duchy of Cornwall, and if in County Palatine of Lancaster, the solicitor for the affairs of the Duchy of Lancaster. There are certain procedural steps, including advertising, with regard to the administration of *bona vacantia* cases. This type of estate can be subject to the same difficulties and delays as an ordinary estate.

If the person believes that they are entitled legally, by virtue of the intestacy rules, to an estate which is being treated as a *bona vacantia* estate then the administering authority should be notified at the earliest possible opportunity. Again there are various steps, once evidence of the identity of the claimant has been established, to ensure that any costs prior to the date of the claim being accepted should be borne by the estate. Furthermore, the *bona vacantia* authorities have the power, as regards the whole or any part of the property devolving on them as *bona vacantia*, to provide 'in accordance with existing practice' for dependants, whether kindred or not, of the deceased and for other persons for whom he or she might reasonably have been expected to provide (s46(1)(vi)) of the Administration of Estates Act 1925). This is regarded as the power to make *ex gratia* payments from an estate. Such payments are entirely at the discretion of the appropriate authority and are considered at the end of the administration. These may be made to any person who was close to the deceased prior to their death, such as a relative by marriage or a friend who has provided support and services without payment over many years. Payments may also be made in accordance with the deceased's last known wishes if these can be clearly established.

The type of information that is required to support a request by any claimant would be the amount of contact that they had with the deceased over the years, particularly in the period immediately before the death of the deceased, the closeness of the friendship and any assistance provided. As a result of the discretionary nature of this power evidently those who are, instead, able to make family provision claims under the Inheritance (Provision for Family and Dependants) Act 1975 should use that route as in *Cameron* v *Treasury Solicitor* above.

12.9 Effect, duration and form of orders

When an order is made under s2, then the will or intestacy of the deceased or the combination of both will take effect subject to the order. See s19(1). Enactments relating to capital transfer tax are also subject to the order under s19(1). Thus, if the deceased left all his estate to his mistress, capital transfer tax would be payable if the estate was of a substantial size. If the court should award the deceased's wife half of the estate some capital transfer tax would be repayable, as generally all transfers of property between spouses are exempt from the tax.

When an order is made and the deceased has left his estate by will to several persons, the question often arises as to who should bear the heaviest burden in meeting the provisions of the order. Under s2(4)(b) the court has wide powers in this respect and can vary the disposition by the will or intestacy as it thinks fair and reasonable in the circumstances.

The duration of the order will normally be irrelevant in all cases except periodical payments under s2(1)(a). Section 19(2) contains special provisions as to the duration of periodical payments where the applicant was a former husband or wife of the deceased or where the applicant and deceased were judicially separated. In such cases the periodical payments will cease automatically on the remarriage of the applicant in so far as there are any arrears.

12.10 Variation and discharge of orders

The variation and discharge or orders is only applicable to periodical payments. Under s6(1) the court can, on an application, order that these be varied or discharged or that a provision in the original order be suspended or, if suspended, revived. Under s6(2) the court's power is widened in three respects in dealing with these applications:

1. to make periodical payments to any other person who made an application under the Act, whether or not he was successful, or who would have been entitled to apply but for the time-limits in s4;
2. to order the payment of a lump sum to any person, in receipt of periodical payments under the original order;
3. to order the transfer of property to any person or the original recipient.

The powers the court has under s6(2) are limited to 'relevant property'; this is the property which was originally set aside to make periodical payments. Therefore, the powers under s6(2) are somewhat limited when several dependants are receiving periodical payments because an application to increase payments being received by one party will, if successful, reduce those being received by another. To make provision by way of these under (1) above would have the same effect. It is only when the court is in a position to reduce the periodical payments of a party because of the merits of the case that any satisfactory conclusion can be reached between several applicants. One exceptional situation exists where the court may be able to increase the amount of periodical payments where several dependants are in receipt of these. Under s6(3) periodical payments may cease to be payable on the occurrence of an event specified in the order or on the expiration of a period specified. If an application is made within six months of the occurrence of the event specified in the order, then the court has the power to make further provision for the applicant out of the property affected. Thus, if a widow and a mistress were receiving periodical payments from a fund of £60,000 set aside for that purpose and it was ordered that these should cease in the case of either applicant on remarriage or marriage, then in the occurrence of the event in the case of the mistress, the widow could have her periodical payments increased or even receive a lump sum, provided she makes her application within six months of the occurrence of the event.

Applications for the variation or discharge of orders can be made by the following persons under s6(5):

1. any person who applied for an order under s2 or who would have applied but for s4 of the Act;
2. the personal representative of the deceased;
3. the trustees of any relevant property;
4. any beneficiary of the estate of the deceased.

12.11 Interim orders

Section 5 of the Act gives the court power to make interim orders. This power is necessary as it may well take 18 months to two years before the application can be heard by the court. Dependants may in some cases be unable to maintain themselves without receiving continuing support from the deceased's estate.

Two conditions must be fulfilled before the court can make an interim order:

1. that the applicant is in immediate need of financial assistance; and
2. that property forming part of the net estate of the deceased is, or can be, made available to meet the need of the applicant. See s5(1).

The court has wide powers under s5(1) as to imposing conditions and restrictions on the order, the amount of the payments and intervals between them and any determining events. In deciding whether to make an interim order the court is required to have regard to the matters set out in s3 of the Act. See s5(3).

Under s5(4) the court has wide powers in dealing with interim orders when it comes to making an order after the full hearing of the application. In some cases it may ignore these, for example, a surviving spouse, while in others it may consider that they have had the effect of making reasonable provision for the applicant. Thus if a child of the deceased applied for an interim order in order that he could continue his education, there would be little point in making any further order if by the time of the hearing he had completed his education and taken up employment.

12.12 Property available for financial provision

When the court makes an order under s2 for provision, that provision must come out of the deceased's net estate. The 'net estate' is defined by s25(1) as including:

First, all property which the deceased had power to dispose of by his will (otherwise than by virtue of a special power of appointment) less the amount of his funeral, testamentary and administration expenses, debts and liabilities including any capital transfer tax payable out of his estate on his death.

Second, any property in respect of which the deceased held a general power of appointment (not being a power exercisable by will) which has not been exercised. This refers to a property subject to a general power which has not been exercised. However, s25(1)(b) is concerned only with powers exercisable by deed. It does not apply to powers exercisable by will; these will come wthin s25(1)(a) whether exercised or not. If a general power has been exercised by deed then it may be possible to apply the anti-avoidance provisions in s10 so that an order can be met.

Third, any sum of money or other property which is treated for the purpose of this Act as part of the net estate of the deceased by virtue of s8(1) or (2) of this Act. Under s8(1) of the Act, money or property nominated by the deceased in favour of any person on his death, is treated as part of the net estate. However, should the court order that property nominated be made available to meet a claim, only the nominee will be liable to do this. Section 8(1) specifically states that any person paying the money to the nominee shall not be held liable for so doing. This is to ensure that prompt payment is not discouraged. Under s8(2) property received by a person under a *donatio mortis causa* is part of the net estate if the court orders it to be used to meet a claim. Again, as in s8(1), persons who pay over property to give effect to a *donatio mortis causa* are in no way liable for having done so.

Fourth, any property which is treated for the purposes of this Act as part of the net estate of the deceased by virtue of an order made under s9 of the Act. Under the 1938 Act property subject to a joint tenancy was never treated as part of the net estate. The deceased's share in a joint tenancy passed automatically to the surviving joint tenant(s) and was outside the Act. Section 9 reverses this position and such property can now be made available for an order under s2. But it should be noted that such property does not, under s9, automatically form part of the net estate. The court has a discretion in the matter and the property will only become part of the net estate when the court makes an order to that effect. Further, it is clear from s9 that the court can only make an order under s9 if the application is made within the time limit laid down in s4. The reason for this is to give the surviving joint tenant some certainty as to the position of the property as quickly as possible. A similar provision is, of course, unnecessary in the case of tenancies in common, as here the deceased's share will vest in his personal representatives on death.

Fifth, any sum of money or other property which is, by reason of a disposition or contract made by the deceased, ordered under ss10 or 11 of this Act to be provided for the purpose of making financial provision under this Act.

Sections 10 and 11 are dealt with below. They are anti-avoidance provisions.

Lastly, the decision of *Smith* v *Clerical Medical and General Life Assurance Society* [1993] 1 FLR 47 should be cited. The question was whether an endowment policy on the death of one policyholder could be dealt with under family provision.

The practical concern related to the policy money. Was it due to the other policyholder or to the personal representatives? Equity would not allow personal representatives to defeat the intention of the parties paying into an endowment policy whereby the mortgage debt could be discharged and on the basis of which they had entered into substantial financial commitments. The plaintiffs appealed against the first instance decision (where the judge had dismissed their claim on the ground that the intention of the parties with regard to the endowment mortgage had been deferred by the building society's decision to look to the proceeds of sale of the house rather than the proceeds of the policy).

Held: the plaintiff's appeal was allowed. The entire objective of the transaction was that the policy money should be used to discharge the mortgage so that the survivor would be left with an unencumbered property. If the building society elected not to demand the policy money as a means of discharging the mortgage there could be no ground upon which the personal representatives could claim to be beneficially entitled.

12.13 Anti-avoidance provisions

The main problem with the 1938 legislation was that it defined the net estate available to make financial provision in rather narrow terms. By s1 of the 1938 Act 'net estate' was no more than the deceased had to dispose of by his will less expenses and debts. As a result it was very easy to defeat an application by a dependant by disposing of property before death. So if the deceased did not wish his wife to have any of his property, all he had to do was to make *inter vivos* dispositions so that at his death he had nothing. Alternatively, if he wished to enjoy his property up until death he could make a contract to leave his property by will to a certain beneficiary. As the contract imposed a debt upon the estate it had to be deducted before ascertaining the net estate. The ease with which an application could be defeated led to the wide definition of 'net estate' contained in s25(1) of the 1975 Act. However, it is in ss10 and 11 of the 1975 Act that powers are given to the court to set aside transactions intended to defeat applications.

12.14 Dispositions intended to defeat applications: s10

Before the court can set aside a disposition intended to defeat an application, four conditions must be satisfied as laid down in s10(2).

First, there must be a disposition within six years of the date of death. For these purposes 'disposition' is defined by s10(7) as including almost any *inter vivos* transactions, that is, the payment of money (including premiums under a policy of assurance), a conveyance, assurance, appointment or gift of property, whether by instrument or otherwise. The disposition must be within six years of death and by s10(8) the provisions do not apply before the commencement of the Act, so the disposition must be after 1 April 1976. The moral for those who want to defeat possible applications is to give away their property well in advance.

Second, the disposition was made with the intention of defeating an application for financial provision. Section 12(1) deals with the issue of 'intention' and provides that such intention to defeat the application will be fulfilled if the court is satisfied that;

'... on a balance of probabiities, the intention of the deceased (though not necessarily his sole intention) in making the disposition or contract was to prevent an order for financial provision being made under this Act, or to reduce the amount of the provision which otherwise be granted.'

This requirement will not be easy to satisfy in many cases as it will necessitate the court looking at the evidence (if any) which shows that the deceased did not wish to live up to his obligations. If there is no such evidence, the requirement will be difficult to satisfy. However, it remains to be seen if the court will infer an intention to defeat an application from the size of the disposition or the donee's relationship with the deceased.

Third, full valuable consideration was not given. Under s25(1) valuable consideration does not include marriage or a promise of marriage.

Fourth, the exercise of the powers in s10 would facilitate the making of financial provision.

If the four conditions just mentioned have been satisfied then under s10(2);

> '... the court may order the donee (whether or not at the date of the order he holds any interest in the property disposed of to him or for his benefit by the deceased) to provide, for the purpose of the making of that financial provision, such sum of money or other property as may be specified in the order.'

It is to be noted that it is not essential that the donee still has the money or property. Therefore he cannot escape liability under s10 by disposing of the money or property. However, before any order is made under s10(2) the court must have regard to the matters mentioned in s10(6) of the Act. These are:

> 'The circumstances in which any disposition was made and any valuable consideration which was given therefor, and relationship, if any, of the donee to the deceased, the conduct and financial resources of the donee and all other circumstances of the case.'

Thus it would be most unlikely that the court would make any order under s10(2) if the donee was now bankrupt, or if he were the son of the deceased who was given business assets which he had helped the deceased to acquire.

When the court makes an order under s10(2) ordering a donee to return money or property in order that it can be used to make financial provision, the donee's liability will not be to pay back the full amount in every case. Under s10(3) if the donee received money he is not liable to pay back more than the net sum he received after deduction of tax.

It will be seen that the provisions in s10 can only be considered by the court if an application is made for this purpose. See s10(1). The applicant would normally be expected to identify the disposition which is to be subject of an s10(2) order. In some cases it may well be that the applicant cannot succeed in respect of the disposition he has identified. In such circumstances, if it becomes apparent in the course of the application that there are other dispositions not covered by the application which satisfy the conditions in s10(2), then the court can by virtue of s10(5) make an order under s10(2) in respect of those dispositions.

As yet there is little reported case law on the way in which the courts apply and interpret s10 of the Act. In *Re Dawkins (deceased)* [1986] 2 FLR 360 the deceased made no effective provision for his widow in his will and she applied under the Act for an order that the proceeds of sale from a previous matrimonial home owned by the deceased be applied in part for her benefit. Before his death the deceased had transferred the matrimonial home to his daughter for a nominal consideration of £100.00. The widow now argued that this transfer to the daughter was made with an intent to defeat the Inheritance Act and should therefore be set aside. It was held that the transfer had been made by the deceased with the intention of defeating the Act but bearing in mind the circumstances of the plaintiff widow she would be awarded £10,000 from the proceeds of sale (£27,000). The daughter was therefore ordered to pay the sum of £10,000 to the plaintiff.

In the more recent case of *Hanbury* v *Hanbury* [1999] 2 FLR 255 the county court applied ss9 and 10 of the 1975 Act to make provision for a disabled daughter by taking into account property subject to a joint tenancy. In this case the deceased has a physically and mentally disabled daughter by his first marriage. She lived with and was cared for by her mother. The deceased had no contact with her aside from making a payment of £900 per annum under a court order. By his will he left his daughter a legacy of £10,000 which was the bulk of his net estate. However, his second wife had capital of over £25,000 and a net income of £27,000 from investments and bank accounts. As most of his possessions were jointly owned his second wife inherited these under the survivorship rules. Evidence showed that the deceased had sought advice as to how he could frustrate any claim his daughter might make under the 1975 Act. He was advised to put his property in joint names with his second wife.

The court held that reasonable financial provision had not been made for the applicant. The £10,000 provided would not yield enough to care for her. The deceased and his second wife had deliberately taken steps to reduce his estate to minimise the applicant's claim. In view of this the court held that the estate would be taken to include a half share in the investments and bank accounts held in joint names or deliberately transferred with the intention to defeat a claim under the 1975 Act. The court took into account the fact that the applicant would require eventual residential care and as a result awarded her £39,000 to be held on a discretionary trust for her benefit.

12.15 Contracts to leave property by will: s11

Section 11 is concerned with contracts to leave property by will. It does not include contracts made to dispose of property *inter vivos* where the contract is for less than full valuable consideration; such cases fall under s10. Four requirements must be fulfilled before an application will be successful under s11.

1. A contract to leave property by will. There is no time limit imposed on this requirement. Contrast this with s10 where the disposition must be within six years of death. However, s11(6) makes it clear that the provision does not apply to contracts made before the commencement of the Act, that is, 1 April 1976.
2. A contract intended to defeat an application for financial provision. This requirement is give a similar interpretation to that just mentioned in s10, that is, the requirements in s12(1) apply. However a special rule is applied to contracts under seal under s12(2); in these cases there is a rebuttable presumption that such contracts are made to defeat an application. The onus of proof is on the recipient rather than the applicant.

3. Full valuable consideration was not given or promised. This requirement is similar to that in s10.
4. The exercise of the powers in s11 would facilitate the making of reasonable financial provision.

If the court decides to make an order under s11(2) because the above conditions have been satisfied then it must take into account the factors mentioned in s11(4), that is, the circumstances in which the contract was made, the relationship, if any, of the donee to the deceased, the conduct and financial resources of the donee and all other circumstances of the case.

The orders the court can make depend on whether the money or property has already been paid over to the donee. If it has, then the order will be that the donee pay over the money or property specified in the order for the purpose of making financial provision. If it has not been paid over, the court will make any payment or transfer of property or any further payment or transfer or direct the personal representative to make such payment or transfer as is specified in the order. Sometimes the personal representatives may not wish to make a payment under a contract because it is obvious that an application is going to be made under the 1975 Act. Under s20(3) if they consider that the deceased entered into the contract with the intention of defeating an application they may postpone payment under the contract until the six month period for bringing applications has expired or, if an application is made, until it is determined.

The donee's liability under a contract in respect of which an order has been made under s11 is limited to the extent of the gift element under the contract. Thus any consideration he has given will be taken into account and the property will be valued at the date of hearing. See s11(3).

The right of the donee to sue on the contract either for specific performance or for damages is restricted by s11(5). Such rights will be subject to the order of the court under s11(2).

12.16 Trusts and ss10 and 11

The provisions of ss10 and 11 apply to trustees but under s13 special provisions are set out defining their liability to return property to the estate.

Under s13(1)(b)(i), where under a disposition or contract money was paid to the trustees, any order against them to return money for the purposes of making an order under s2 will be limited to the amount of such money, or property which represents that money, which is in their hands at the date of the order, less any capital transfer tax payable. It would therefore appear that any money which the trustees have distributed either under a discretionary trust or to a person who is *sui juris* and absolutely entitled, cannot be recovered. Section 13(1)(b)(ii) has similar provisions which are applicable to other property given to trustees either by a disposition or a contract to give property by will.

Under s13(2) a trustee is not liable for failing to consider the possibility of an application under the 1975 Act when distributing money or other property. Thus it would seem that trustees receive preferential treatment.

12.17 Choice of court

The county court

Where the 'net estate' of the deceased does not exceed the limit of £30,000 the county court has jurisdiction to hear and determine applications under the 1975 Act. Again, if the court decides to order provision to be made for an applicant this order is made against the 'net estate' of the deceased.

Since the 'net estate' has a specific statutory definition this should be set out verbatim in accordance with the section, that is, s25 of the 1975 Inheritance Act:

'(1) In this Act ... "net estate", in relation to a deceased person, means:
(a) all property of which the deceased had power to dispose by his will (otherwise than by virtue of a special power of appointment) less the amount of his funeral, testamentary and administration expenses, debts and liabilities, including any inheritance tax payable out of his estate on death;
(b) any property in respect of which the deceased held a general power of appointment (not being a power exerciseable by will) which has not been exercised;
(c) any sum of money or other property which is treated for the purposes of this Act as part of the net estate of the deceased by virtue of s8(1) or (2) of this Act;
(d) any property which is treated for the purposes of this Act as part of the net estate of the deceased by virtue of an order made under s9 of the Act;
(e) any sum of money or other property which is, by reason of a disposition or contract made by the deceased, ordered under s10 or 11 of this Act to be provided for the purpose of the making of financial provision under this Act.'

While the meaning of s25(1) has been discussed in section 12.12 (above), a little further practical explanation of each subsection, should be noted here because close regard must be paid to the 'net estate' in order to make proper provision by court order, irrespective of the choice of court. More generally, of course, the meaning of net estate also affects the administration of the estate; this discussion occurs in later chapters.

Accordingly:

1. section 25(1)(a): this will evidently not include those insurance policies whose proceeds are payable direct to the beneficiary. In such a case the proceeds will not go to the policy holder's estate and therefore the deceased had no power to dispose of this property by will;
2. section 25(1)(b): here the power of appointment was exerciseable by will the property subject to the power falls into s25(1)(a) above irrespective of whether or not the deceased exercised it;
3. section 25(1)(c): this refers to any property nominated by the deceased to any

person under a statutory nomination or received by any person through a *donatio mortis causa* less any inheritance tax payable in respect of such property and borne by the nominee or donee. For an example of a statutory nomination: see *Re Cairnes* [1983] FLR 225;

4. section 25(1)(d): this only covers the deceased's severable share of a joint tenancy if the court so orders;
5. section 25(1)(e): this deals with that property which the court orders shall be available as a result of its anti-avoidance powers.

The Family or Chancery Division of the High Court

An application for an order under the 1975 Act may be made either in the Family Division or the Chancery Division of the High Court, whichever suits the applicant. There is a total freedom of choice which generally is governed only by his adviser's personal preference and experience.

There are circumstances, however, when one Division may be more advantageous than the other.

Family Division choice

Where an order has been made under the Matrimonial Causes Act 1973 (or former statutes) the Family Division is advantageous.

Chancery Division choice

Where there is a dispute regarding the validity of a will which is alleged not to have made reasonable financial provision for the applicant and where the true meaning of the will must first be determined under a construction summons or where complex accounts have to be taken, the Chancery Division is more appropriate.

In these circumstances the probate action can be heard by the same judge immediately before the family provision application. Therefore there can be a saving of time and expense.

12.18 Deed of variation

One should note that an Order made under the 1975 Act results in the alteration of the deceased's estate after the death. Such an alteration may achieve not only a more appropriate disposition of the estate but also a more satisfactory tax position. While there are a number of ways in which alterations after death can be effected, it is useful to consider briefly the deed of variation, a 'variation', which may be used quite efficiently in order to assist the family. To illustrate, a very recent case should be considered, which is also noteworthy insofar as the doctrine of rectification was discussed simultaneously.

The question concerned the validity of the deed of variation and whether rectification of the 'variation' was possible in the case of a clerical error. The document was a legitimate deed of variation designed to avoid tax under s142 of the Inheritance Tax Act 1984.

In *Lake* v *Lake* [1989] STC 865, Mervyn Davies J the testator had left a will whereby most of his estate passed to his widow for life, then to his children and grandchildren. Since she was independently wealthy, the widow wanted to avoid an aggregation of the two estates. A deed of variation was executed whereby additional sums were given to the children. Unfortunately, due to a clerical error the gifts were expressed to be 'free of tax'. Although a second corrective deed was made this was held to be ineffective. The family applied for rectification of the first deed of variation.

Held: rectification was granted. Since all the parties desired the Order rectification of the deed should not be refused where the sole purpose was to enable the parties to obtain an advantage which had been their common intention at the time of the document's execution.

13

Executors and Administrators

13.1 Appointment of executors

An executor is the person who is appointed by the testator in order to carry out his directions contained in the will. The appointment is normally made in the will by a clause such as:

> 'I appoint AB of (address and description) and CD of (address and description) to act as the executors of this Will.'

The appointment of the executor in the will may be absolute, that is, without restriction as to the testator's property or any limitation in point of time, or it may be qualified in one of the following ways.

1. As to time, so that the appointment shall only take effect at a specified time after the testator's death, for example, 'A to be my executor five years after my death', or 'I appoint my son, X, as my executor when he shall come to full age'. The

appointment may be for a limited period only, for example, 'I appoint AB to be my executor during the minority of my son'. See *Anon* (1675) Freem Ch 313.

2. As to subject matter, as where the testator appoints a literary executor to deal with his literary estate only (see *Re Orwell's Will Trusts* [1982] 3 All ER 177), or where general executors are appointed and, in addition, an executor or executors are appointed to deal with the testator's business assets, for example, 'I appoint AB to be the executor of this will in respect of my farming business carried on at (address)'. Under s22 of the Administration of Estates Act 1925 the testator may appoint 'special executors' to deal with settled land vested in him at his death. This is dealt with in further detail below.

3. As to place, if the testator has property in several countries he may appoint a separate executor to act in each country.

4. By a condition. The condition may be precedent, for example, 'I appoint my son, AB, to be my executor, if he shall have attained the age of majority at my death', or subsequent, as where AB is appointed executor if he proves the will within three calendar months of the testator's death. See *In b Day* (1850) 7 Notes of Cases 553.

An appointment of executors may contain substitutes. For example, 'I appoint AB to be my executor but if he cannot or will not act, then CD is to be my executor'. See *In b Betts* (1861) 30 LJPM & A 167. If AB, in the example, accepts office and afterwards dies intestate, CD could not accept office in his place unless the testator had shown a contrary intention because substitution is normally limited to the first appointment of executors. See *In b Foster* (1871) LR 2 P & D 304. Thus CD could only become executor if AB had died in the testator's lifetime or refused office.

If executors are appointed by the will this is referred to as an 'express appointment'. There may, however, be an 'implied appointment' of executors, this is also known as the appointment of 'an executor according to the tenor' of the will. An implied appointment arises where the testator has shown an intention that a person should act as executor by imposing on him some or all of the duties of an executor. The principal duties of an executor were described by Sir James Hannen P in *In b Adamson* (1875) LR 3 P & D 253 as: 'to collect in the assets of the deceased, to pay his funeral expenses and debts, and to discharge the legacies'.

Thus, in *In b Adamson* there was an implied appointment where the testator directed three persons to pay his debts and funeral expenses, and pay the balance of his estate to named trustees. There will also be an implied appointment where the testator appoints trustees of his will because, as Lord Penzance said in *In b Baylis* (1865) LR 1 P & D 21:

'The persons appointed trustees are to get in and receive the whole estate to pay the debts and to divide the residue. Now that is the very office of an executor, and therefore it is clear that the trustees are executors according to the tenor.'

However, an appointment by the testator of a trustee of his estate is not an implied appointment of an executor because the court cannot gather from this an intention to impose the duties of executor on the named person. See *In b Jones* (1861) 2 Sw & Tr 155.

The will may contain a combination of express and implied appointment of executors. In *In b Brown* (1877) 2 PD 110 the testator appointed his sister as executrix and then added a request that two named nephews should 'act for or with this dear sister'. There was an implied appointment of the nephews.

13.2 Transmission of office

The office of executor is, generally, for life or as Viscount Haldane LC said in *Attenborough* v *Solomon* [1913] AC 76: 'He is executor and remains executor for an indefinite time'. Normally, all the acts of administration will be carried out by the executor within a year or two of his appointment, but if property devolves on the testator's estate many years after his death, the executor will have to administer it. The office is one of personal trust and it cannot be assigned to anyone else. See *In the estate of Skinner* [1958] 1 WLR 1043.

If an executor dies shortly after taking office and/or before administration of the estate is complete, the question arises as to who should succeed him. This question is dealt with by s7 of the Administration of Estates Act 1925, which provides that the executor of an executor represents the original testator.

Consider the following example, which illustrates s7 diagrammatically.

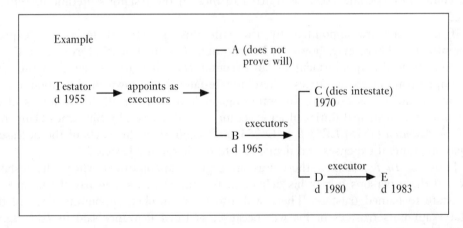

Under s7 an executor is not only executor of the testator by whose will he is expressly appointed but also 'executor by representation' of the will of any person of which the testator was executor. Thus, in the example, B is executor of the testator, on B's death C and D become B's executors and also the executors by representation of the testator. This chain of representation can continue indefinitely so that E would be executor of D and executor by representation of both B and the testator.

The chain of representation can only operate through proving executors. Section 7(1) provides that it shall not apply to an executor who does not prove the will. Thus in the example A did not prove the testator's will so he is ignored. However, if A proved the will after the death of B (when D would normally become executor by representation of the testator), then the chain of representation would not operate.

The chain of representation will be broken in three cases so that s7 is not applicable. These are:

1. intestacy; or
2. the failure of a testator to appoint an executor; or
3. the failure to obtain probate of a will (see s7(3)).

Thus in the example s7 would not apply if E died intestate, or without appointing executors, or without taking probate of D's will. In such circumstances an administrator would be appointed to E's estate under either r20 or r22 of the Non-Contentious Probate Rules 1987. This administrator could not represent the estates of D, B or the original testator. In respect of the estate of each of these, a grant of letters of administration *de bonis non* would be made. The persons who would be entitled to such a grant in each case are set out in r20 or r22 Non-Contentious Probate Rules 1987. If the court makes a temporary grant of administration to a testator's estate the chain of representation is not broken if probate is subsequently granted. Thus, for example, if there was a dispute over the validity of the will a grant of administration *pendente lite* may be made to protect the estate until the action is completed. If the will is declared valid the executors may take office in the usual way and the chain of representation will apply, if and when necessary.

Under s7(4) an executor by representation has the same rights and duties as the original executor had in respect of the estate he represents. Thus in the example E would have had the same rights and duties to B's estate as he has to D's estate.

13.3 Capacity to be an executor

As a general rule there is no restriction on who the testator may appoint as an executor but the following points should be noted.

Corporation

A corporation sole can be an executor eg a bishop. See *In b Haynes* (1842) 3 Curt 75. A trust corporation can act as an executor and take a grant of probate either solely or jointly with any other person named in the will as executor. See s115(1), Supreme Court Act 1981. However, s115(2) states that probate shall not be granted to any persons as nominee of the trust corporation. It appears from the decision in *Re*

Bigger [1977] 2 WLR 773 that probate can be granted to any trust corporation under the law of any member state of the EC. Prior to this, probate could only be granted to a trust corporation constituted under the law of the UK. See *Re Barlow* [1933] P 184. A corporation aggregate cannot take a grant of probate in its own name. See *Re Rankine* [1918] P 134. In such circumstances letters of administration with the will annexed may be granted to a nominee selected by it. See r36(1), (2) of the NCPR 1987.

Partnerships

The appointment of a firm of partners as executors is not valid because of the uncertainty as to which of the partners should take the office of executor. See *In b Fernie* (1849). However, the testator can make a valid appointment of the members of a firm by a suitable clause such as 'I appoint the partners at the date of my death in the firm of Smith & Co of (address) to be the executors and trustees of this my will'.

Infants

If an infant is appointed as an executor then under s118 of the Supreme Court Act 1981, the appointment shall not operate to vest in him the estate or any part of the estate of the testator or constitute him a personal representative for any purpose. In other words his appointment will be of no effect until he attains majority; but a grant for his use and benefit can be made to his parents or guardian until he attains the age of 18. See rr32 and 33 NCPR 1987.

Married women

At common law a married woman could not act as an executrix. This disability was removed by ss1(2) and 18 of the Married Women's Property Act 1882 and s170 of the Law of Property Act 1925 (now repealed by Statute Law (Repeals) Act 1969).

Criminals

The testator's estate will devolve on a criminal who is appointed executor in the same manner that it would devolve on any other person. However, the court may refuse to confirm the criminal as executor of the estate. This is dealt with in section 13.5, below.

Bankrupts

There is no restriction on appointing a bankrupt as executor but the court may refuse to confirm his position and grant probate to someone else. If an executor becomes insolvent after taking probate a receiver may be appointed. See *Bowen* v *Phillips* [1897] 1 Ch 174.

Mentally and physically incapable persons

The court will not grant probate to a person who is a mental patient or who is physically incapable. A grant may be made for the use and benefit of such a person under r35(2), (3), (4) of the NCPR 1987. This is dealt with below.

13.4 Number of executors

The maximum number of executors that may be appointed 'in respect of the same part of the estate of a deceased person' shall not exceed four, according to s114(1) of the Supreme Court Act 1981. Under s160(1) of the Judicature Act 1925 it was provided that probate could not be granted 'to more than four persons in respect of the same property'. In *In the estate of Holland* [1930] 3 All ER 13 Bucknill J construed this to mean 'the same estate', so that where the testator appointed four general executors and a literary executor, only the first four named could be appointed. The words of s114(1) differ from those of s160(1) and as the term 'the same part of the estate' is used, it appears that the decision in *In the estate of Holland* has been reversed. Where more than four executors have been appointed in respect of the same part of the estate and there is no agreement as to who should take probate, a district judge or registrar may resolve the matter: see r27(6) NCPR 1987.

There are no provisions requiring that a minimum number of executors be appointed but under s114 of the Supreme Court Act 1981 the court has power to appoint an additional personal representative to act with the executor where there is a minor of life interest under the will.

13.5 Passing over executors

Under s116 of the Supreme Court Act 1981 the court has power to pass over an executor:

> '... if by reason of any special circumstances, it appears ... to be necessary or expedient to appoint as administrator some person other than the person who, but for this section, would in accordance with the probate rules have been entitled to the grant'.

The court also has power under s116 to appoint such person as administrator as it thinks expedient and limit the grant in any way it thinks fit. See *Re Mathew* [1984] 2 All ER 396.

Matters which may cause the court to pass over an executor under s116 are where the executor is insolvent; incapable of acting in the office, as in *In the estate of S* [1968] P 302, where the person appointed was serving a term of life imprisonment for the manslaughter of the testator and was passed over as she could not carry out the office; is of bad character, see *In the estate of Potticary* [1927] P 202; refuses to act even though he has accepted office by intermeddling, see *In the estate of Biggs* [1966] P 118; or where he cannot be found as in *In b Wright* (1898) 79 LT 473, where the executor disappeared after a warrant for his arrest had been issued for embezzlement.

13.6 Renunciation of probate

A person who is appointed executor is not bound to accept the office. See s5 Administration of Estates Act 1925. Normally the testator will consult the person he wishes to appoint but even then he is not bound to accept it as Lord Redesdale said in *Doyle* v *Blake* (1804) 25 Sch & Lef 231:

> 'No man has the right to make another executor without his consent; and even if in the lifetime of the testator he has agreed to accept the office, it is still in his power to recede.'

If an executor wishes to renounce probate he should do so in writing, filing this at the probate registry. However, the renunciation is not effective until it is filed so that if he changes his mind before then he can still take probate. See *In b Morant* (1874) LR 3 P & D 151.

The effect of renunciation is as follows.

1. The whole of the rights and duties of the office of executor are lost. The executor cannot accept some of the duties of the office and renounce others. See *Brooke* v *Haymes* (1868) LR 6 Eq 25. Thus, for example, if A appoints B as his executor and B takes office but dies before the administration of A's estate has been completed appointing C as his executor, C cannot choose to take the executorship of B's estate and refuse the executorship by representation of A's estate. He can only accept both or refuse both. One exception exists to this principle under s23 of the Administration of Estates Act 1925, by which an executor may renounce probate to settled land without renouncing it to other property provided he was not a trustee of the settlement before the testator's death.

2. Where an executor renounces the office of executor he is not prevented from taking a grant to the deceased's estate in some other capacity, unless he has expressly renounced such right. Thus, if A appointed B his executor, C could renounce the executorship of B's estate (and thereby the executorship by representation of A's estate). However, if C wished to take a grant of administration to A's estate he would not be prevented from doing so by reason only of his renunciation of executorship. He would be able to take office as administrator of A's estate if he was entitled in priority to do so under r20 of the NCPR 1987.

Renunciation of executorship can be retracted under r37(3) of the NCPR 1987 but this is only permitted in 'exceptional circumstances' with leave of the court where a grant of administration has been made to some other person under r20 of the NCPR 1987. If a grant is made to a co-executor after renunciation, it is usually easier to retract renunciation. Thus, in *In b Stiles* [1898] P 12 retraction was allowed where the co-executor who took probate absconded.

An executor cannot renounce his office after he has accepted it. For these purposes the office will be deemed to have been accepted if he either:

1. takes probate. See *In b Veiga* (1862) 32 LJ PM & A9. Taking probate is signified by the court giving the executor the appropriate order so that it is still possible to renounce the office even where the executor's oath has been sworn. See *Jackson & Wallington* v *Whitehead* (1821) 3 Phill 577; or

2. acts as an executor. If the executor carries out any of the acts which are incident to his office, for example, collecting in the testator's assets or paying his debts, he is deemed to have accepted the office and cannot thereafter renounce. Thus, in *Re Stevens* [1897] 1 Ch 422, all the persons named as executors in the will signed a letter which was sent to an insurance company giving directions as to the payment of insurance monies. The monies were misapplied and after an action was begun against the executors one of them renounced. This was held ineffective; he had, by his conduct of signing the letter, accepted office. However, despite *Re Stevens*, it appears that the court is not prepared to consider trivial acts by the executor as amounting to acceptance. Thus, in *Holder* v *Holder* [1968] Ch 353 the Court of Appeal held that an executor could renounce probate where he had signed a few cheques for trivial sums and endorsed a few insurance policies but where he had never interfered in the administration of the estate.

Two citations are used in relation to renunication of executorship.

Citation to take probate

This is used where an executor has accepted office by intermeddling with the estate but not yet applied to the court for a grant of probate. Any person interested in the estate may apply for such a citation after six months from the death of the deceased, calling on the executor to show cause why he should not be ordered to take a grant. If the executor does not enter an appearance to the citation the citor may apply for an order that the executor take a grant within a specified time or for a grant to himself or some other person. If an order is made that the executor do take probate within a specified time, he will be liable to a fine or imprisonment for failing to do so. See r47 of the NCPR 1987.

Citation to accept or refuse probate

This is used to make an executor decide whether or not he will take probate in cases where he has not intermeddled with the estate. Any person who would be entitled to grant if the executor renounced his right thereto can apply for this citation. The executor will be called upon to enter an appearance and either accept or refuse probate. Should he fail to enter an appearance then a grant will be made to the person next entitled to a grant.

13.7 Appointment of administrators

An administrator is appointed by the court to administer a deceased's estate where the deceased either (1) died intestate; or (2) failed to appoint any executors in his will; or (3) where none of the executors appointed survived him; or (4) where the executors appointed died before completion of the administration of the estate, and the chain of representation under s7 of the Administration of Estates Act 1925 is broken.

The order of priority for obtaining a grant of letters of administration is set out in rr20 and 22 of the NCPR 1987. Rule 20 applies when the deceased left a will and r22 when the deceased died intestate.

The order of priority under r20 is:

1. the executor – an executor is entitled to a grant of probate but applicants in the later classes may only apply for a grant of administration with the will annexed;
2. any residuary legatee or devisee holding in trust for any person – a trustee of the residuary estate is very similar to an executor;
3. any other residuary legatee or devisee (including one for life) or where the residue is not wholly disposed of by the will, any person entitled to share in the undisposed of residue under the intestacy rules;
4. the personal representative of any residuary legatee or devisee (but not one for life, or one holding in trust for any other person), or of any person entitled to share in any residue not disposed of by the will;
5. any other legatee or devisee (including one for life or one holding in trust for any other person) or any creditor of the deceased – this class covers all other beneficiaries under of the will, for example, specific beneficiaries, recipients of pecuniary legacies;
6. the personal representative of any other legatee or devisee (but not one for life, or one holding in trust for any other person) or of any creditor of the deceased.

The order of priority under r22 follows the order for the administration of an intestate estate under s46 of the Administration of Estates Act. But in order to obtain a grant of administration under r22 it is necessary to have a beneficial interest in the estate. Thus, for example, if the deceased's children are entitled to all his estate under the intestacy rules, it would not be possible for the father or mother of the deceased or the brothers and sisters of the whole blood to apply for a grant. If there is no one in the above categories entitled to a grant then the deceased will have died intestate and *bona vacantia*, the Treasury Solicitor will then be entitled to a grant if he claims the estate on behalf of the Crown.

The personal representatives of a person beneficially entitled to a share in the deceased's intestate estate has the same right to a grant as the person whom he represents under r22(5). Further, creditors may apply for a grant of administration under r22, if all persons in the order of priority have been 'cleared off'.

Clearing off

This is the process which is used where a person who has a prior right to a grant shows no signs of taking the grant and another person of lower priority wishes to take the grant. The process applies to both rr20 and 22 but is usually met under r20. Clearing off requires citing those with a prior right to the grant to accept or refuse a grant.

Example

T leaves the residue of his estate to A and B on trust for his wife, C, for life with remainder to D and E. If C wishes to obtain a grant she must clear off the executors of T's estate, if any, and also A and B. This will, as stated, be done by citing them to accept or refuse a grant. If all of them refuse it, C can then have a grant.

In some cases persons may be entitled in the same degree to a grant. Thus, in the example above, D and E are entitled in the same degree. Under r25(1) a grant may be made to one person entitled in the same degree without giving notice to any other person in the same degree. Sometimes there may be disputes between such persons as to who should take the grant, then under r25(3) those who are living will be preferred to the personal representatives of a deceased person who was in the same degree and adults will be preferred to minors. If two adults are in dispute the court has power to determine the matter and usually makes a grant to the person most likely to administer the estate to the best advantage of all those interested therein. See *Warwick* v *Greville* (1809) 1 Phill 123.

13.8 Capacity to be an administrator

The rules on who can be an administrator are similar to those on who can be an executor. One difference which should be noted is that s118 Supreme Court Act 1981 does not apply to grants of administration but in both cases a grant for the use and benefit of the minor may be made to his parents or guardian until he attains 18. See r32 of the NCPR 1987.

13.9 Number of administrators

Under s114(1) of the Supreme Court Act 1981 administration shall not be granted to more than four persons 'in respect of the same part of the estate of a deceased person'. This rule is the same as that applicable to executors which was discussed above.

As a general rule there is no minimum number of administrators who must be appointed by the court. This is subject to the provisions of s114(2) of the Supreme Court Act 1981 which states that in the case of a minor or a life interest arising under a will or intestacy a grant must be made either to a trust corporation or to not less than two individuals unless it appears expedient in all the circumstances to appoint a sole administrator. If the number of administrators should fall below two at any one time then under s114(4) the court can, on the application of any interested person, parent or guardian, appoint an additional administrator.

13.10 Passing over administrators

The court has power to pass over a person entitled in priority to a grant of administration if it considers that he is unsuitable or unfit for the position. The principles are similar to those discussed in relation to executors.

13.11 Renunciation of administration

A person entitled in priority to a grant of administration is not bound to accept the grant and, like an executor, he can either accept or renounce. However, until he makes up his mind those who rank below him in the order of priority cannot obtain a grant. The course of action should be to cite him to accept or refuse a grant under r47 of the NCPR 1987. Delay in taking a grant may mean that in some cases persons entitled in the same degree will take the grant and thus no further application for a grant could be made.

A renunciation of the right to a grant of administration should be made in writing and filed in the probate registry. Renunciation of administration in one capacity destroys all rights to agrant in another capacity, if this is available. Thus, renunciation as residuary legatee would preclude the right to take as a specific devisee under r37 of the NCPR 1987. However, it appears that renunciation by a would-be administrator does not bind his personal representatives should he subsequently die.

13.12 Executors *de son tort*

An executor *de son tort* is one who, being neither an executor or administrator who has obtained a grant of probate or letters of administration in the deceased's estate, acts in some way as if he were an executor or administrator. Thus, if a complete stranger started to collect in the deceased's assets and pay off his debts he would be an executor *de son tort*. See *Sharland* v *Mildon* (1846) 5 Hare 469. The term is also applied to persons who are appointed executors in the will who begin administration before a grant of probate, and to persons entitled to a grant of administration who begin administration before grant, but in these cases it would appear that the grant divests them of their character as executors *de son tort*. See *Webster* v *Webster* (1804) 10 Ves 93.

Section 28 of the Administration of Estates Act 1925 sets out the acts which may make a person an executor *de son tort* and the consequence of this. It provides:

'If any person, to the defrauding of the creditors or without full valuable consideration, obtains, receives or holds any real or personal estate of a deceased person or effects the release of any debt or liability due to the estate of the deceased, he shall be charged as executor in his own wrong to the extent of the real and personal estate received or coming into his hands, or the debt or liability released after deducting –
a) any debt for valuable consideration and without fraud due to him from the deceased person at the time of his death; and
b) any payment made by him which might properly be made to a personal representative.'

Acts which have been held to make a person an executor *de son tort* in the past have included carrying on the deceased's business, *Hooper* v *Summersett* (1810) Wight 16; collecting in the deceased's debts, *Sharland* v *Mildon* (1848) 5 Hare 469 and *Long* v *Symes* (1832) 3 Hagg Ecc 771; and disposing of the deceased's goods, *Read's Case* (1604) 5 Co Rep 336; *New York Breweries Company Ltd* v *Att-Gen* [1899] AC 62. In the last mentioned case the House of Lords held that the company was an executor *de son tort* when it registered shares in the name of a person who was not the deceased's personal representative without requiring production of a grant of probate.

Not all acts of intermeddling with the deceased's estate will cause a person to be an executor *de son tort*, as where the acts are carried out in the interests of common humanity or out of necessity. Thus, collecting in a debt in order to pay for the deceased's funeral or taking possession of the deceased's assets to preserve them or feeding his cattle are not intermeddling. See *Peters* v *Leeder* (1878) 47 LJ QB 573. Moreover, as seen in *Pollard* v *Jackson* (1994) 67 P & CR 327, a tenant who merely cleared out the part of the property vacated by the death of his landlord and moved in has not been found to have done anything characteristic of an executor de son tort or constructive trustee. In this case in 1953 A and her mother left A's father and they had no more contact thereafter. The father owned a property; he let it in part to a tenant, B. In 1971 A's father died intestate and B remained in occupation of the property but, apart from burning some rubbish and cleaning the vacant part of the property into which he then moved, he did not take any further steps to install himself as an executor. B contacted solicitors some 12 years later, in 1983, and they traced A. A claimed that, subject to B's weekly tenancy, she was entitled to the property absolutely. B counter-claimed that he was entitled to the property. At first instance the court found that B had acted as an executor de son tort. As such, time could not run in his favour: he was a trustee and time cannot run in favour of a trustee against the beneficiary in such circumstances. B appealed.

Held: B's appeal was allowed. B had not done anything which could be considered characteristic of an executor. Accordingly B had not become a constructive trustee and was under no obligation to find A and notify her of the death of her father. B was therefore entitled to the property: a tenant who has not acted in any way as an executor will not be liable as an executor de son tort or a constructive trustee.

As s28 above states, an executor *de son tort* is liable 'to the extent of the real and personal estate received or coming into his hands'. However, he can deduct from these assets anything which was due to him or any payment made by him which could properly be made by a personal representative. See *Oxenham* v *Clapp* (1831) 2 B & Ad 309. As to the balance he must account for this to the duly appointed personal representatives; should he fail to do this they can take legal action against him. See *Coote* v *Whittington* (1873) LR 16 Eq 534.

Further, he may be liable to account for any capital transfer tax due on the property he intermeddled with under s25 of the Finance Act 1975. See *IRC* v *Stype Investments* [1982] 3 WLR 228. However, liability for capital transfer tax only extends to the value of the property in his hands.

It is not clear from s28 whether a defendant can be an executor *de son tort* in the event of his intermeddling in the estate but without actually receiving or otherwise dealing with the estate money. Although s28 refers to an 'obtaining, receiving or holding' of estate property it seems clear that on case law principles a defendant could be a constructive trustee of estate property without handling it. This would apply where the defendant knowingly assists a breach of trust by the ordinary executor but without actually touching the property as in *Eaves* v *Hickson* (1861) 54 ER 840.

14

Grants of Probate
and Administration

14.1 Distribution of probate business

14.2 Obtaining a grant in common form

14.3 Caveats and citations

14.4 Obtaining a grant in solemn form

14.1 Distribution of probate business

Under s61 of the Supreme Court Act 1981 the probate jurisdiction of the High Court is divided between the Chancery Division and the Family Division. Non-contentious probate or common form business is assigned to the Family Division while probate business, other than non-contentious or common form business, is assigned to the Chancery Division. See Schedule 1 of the SCA 1981.

Under s128 of the Supreme Court Act 1981, non-contentious or common form probate business means:

'The business of obtaining probate and administration where there is no contention as to the right thereto, including –
(a) the passing of probates and administrations through the High Court in contentious cases where the contest has been terminated;
(b) all business of a non-contentious nature in matters of testacy and intestacy not being proceedings in any action; and
(c) the business of lodging caveats against the grant of probate and administration.'

The great majority of grants of probate and letters of administration are non-contentious and are therefore made by the Family Division. An application for a grant may be made to either the Principal Registry of the Family Division or a district probate registry. See s105 of the Supreme Court Act 1981.

Contentious probate is, as stated above, dealt with by the Chancery Division, but the county court also has jurisdiction over probate business, including the construction of wills, where this is contentious, provided the value of the deceased's estate was at the time of death less than £30,000 after allowing for funeral expenses, debts and incumbrances.

245

14.2 Obtaining a grant in common form

A grant will normally be sought to the deceased's estate as soon as possible after death. This is in the interests of both the beneficiaries and the creditors. If the deceased left a will then it will be necessary for the executor appointed to apply for the grant. If the deceased died intestate, or without appointing executors in his will, then it will be necessary to refer to either r20 or r22 of the NCPR 1987 to decide who is entitled to the grant.

Under r6(2) of the NCPR 1987 it is provided that except with the leave of two registrars, no grant of probate or administration with the will annexed shall issue within seven days of the death of the deceased, and no grant of administration shall issue within fourteen days thereof. This minimum time appears to be based on the fact that the necessary documents needed to obtain probate could not be put together in that time. There is no maximum time limit for seeking a grant of probate but under the Stamp Act 1815 (as amended by the Finance Act 1975), a fine of £100 is imposed on any person who administers the estate without a grant after six months from the death of the deceased or, if the right to a grant was determined in contentious proceedings, after two months from the date on which the proceedings terminated.

The first step that will have to be taken before a grant is obtained, is to collect in and value the deceased's estate for capital transfer tax purposes. Under s25(5) of the Finance Act 1975 the personal representatives are liable for the capital transfer tax charged on the deceased's death on all 'free estate' which passes on his death, that is, property which was not comprised in a settlement or land in the UK which devolves on the personal representatives and which is not settled. The personal representatives must deliver an account giving all the relevant details of the deceased's property so that a proper assessment as to liability can be made. Under para 2 Schedule 4 of the Finance Act 1975, the account must be delivered to the Inland Revenue within twelve months after the end of the month in which the death occurred or, if later, three months from the date on which the personal representative first acted as personal representative. The tax payable is normally due on delivery of the account but special provisions are available to enable it to be paid by instalments if a very large sum is due.

Under s109 of the Supreme Court Act 1981, no grant will be made unless a capital transfer tax account is produced which contains either a receipt or certificate that capital transfer tax has been paid or that no such tax is payable. The section also provides that this can be dispensed with by arrangement between the President of the Family Division and the Commissioners of Inland Revenue. This is presumably to allow for a grant to be issued where it has been arranged that the tax be payable in instalments.

Documents needed in support of an application for a grant are as follows.

The oath

This is an affidavit sworn by the personal representative and the contents of it will vary according to whether there is a will or an intestacy. However, it should contain the following matters: (1) a date of the deceased's death, if known; (2) the deceased's domicile at death; (3) whether the deceased died testate or intestate (if the deceased died testate the personal representatives must swear that the document produced as the will is believed by him to be the last true will and testament of the deceased); (4) the title of the applicant to the grant (this will normally be that he is appointed executor by the will or showing his title under either r20 or r22 of the NCPR 1987); (5) whether there was land vested in the deceased which was settled prior to his death; (6) that the applicant will carry out his duties as a personal representative as set out in s25 of the Administration of Estates Act 1925, that is, (a) collect in estate and administer it according to the law, (b) when required exhibit on oath a full inventory of the estate to the court or render an account to the court, (c) deliver up the grant of probate or administration to the court when required to do so); (7) the gross value of the estate. See r8 of the NCPR 1987.

The will

This, of course, is only necessary where the deceased left a will. If the deceased left a will but it was lost or destroyed without being revoked by him it may be necessary to seek evidence of its contents. A registrar may make an order admitting to proof the will as contained in a copy, a completed draft, a reconstruction or other evidence of its contents. In such circumstances it will be necessary for the applicant for the grant to establish:

1. that the will was duly executed, for example, by evidence of the witnesses, if still alive; or evidence of other persons present at the execution of the will, for example, the deceased's solicitor;
2. the contents of the will, for example, by producing drafts or copies of the will.

In some cases it is impossible to decide whether the will was properly executed because witnesses who may have been present are dead also. In such cases the court may apply the maxim *omnia praesemuntur rite esse acta*, that is, all acts are presumed to have been done rightly and regularly. See *Re Webb* [1964] 1 WLR 509. In *Harris v Knight* (1890) 15 PD 170 Lindley LJ said of this maxim:

> 'The maxim expresses an inference which may reasonably be drawn when an intention to do some formal act is established; when the evidence is consistent with that intention having been carried into effect in a proper way; but where the actual observance of all due formalities can only be inferred as a matter of probability.'

As of 10 April 1995 a new *Practice Direction (Family Division) (Incorporation of Standard Forms and Clauses in Wills)* concering r14(3) NCPR 1987 enables the incorporation of standard forms or clauses without further production where the will has been previously lodged and accepted by a Senior District Judge. See Chapter 15, section 15.4.

Affidavits

In some cases it may be necessary to produce affidavits in addition to the oath. The following are the most important.

Affidavit as to knowledge and approval. The registrar may require an affidavit from any person he may think fit for the purpose of satisfying himself as to the manner in which the will was executed. This affidavit will normally be required where the testator was blind or illiterate or where there is some doubt as to whether the testator knew and approved of the contents of the will at the time of its execution.

Affidavit as to due execution. If the will does not contain an attestation clause or the attestation clause is insufficient or some irregularity appears as regards the signatures of the testator and the witnesses, an affidavit of due execution may be called for. Normally, the witnesses to the will would be asked to do this if still available but other persons present can be asked to swear such an affidavit also. If no affidavit can be obtained because there is nobody alive who can depose to the manner in which the will was executed, the court may apply the maxim *omnia praesumuntur rite esse acta*. If this is unsuitable then the will will most likely be refused probate.

Affidavit as to plight and condition. The registrar may call for an affidavit when the will contains any obliteration, interlineation or other alteration not authenticated in the manner laid down by s21 of the Wills Act 1837 or by re-execution of the will or execution of a codicil.

Surety's guarantee

Under s120 of the Supreme Court Act 1981 the court may, as a condition of granting administration to any person:

> '... require one or more sureties to guarantee that they will make good, within any limit imposed by the court on the total liability of the surety or sureties, any loss which any person interested in the administration of the estate of the deceased may suffer in consequence of a breach by the administrator of his duties at such'.

The requirement only applies to administrators not executors. The guarantee will only be demanded when the beneficiaries require special protection as when a creditor is administering the estate or where the grant is made to a person's attorney or for the use and benefit of a minor or a person incapable of managing his affairs. See *Harvell* v *Foster* [1954] 2 QB 367.

14.3 Caveats and citations

Caveats

In *Moran* v *Place* [1896] P 214 Lord Lindley LJ said:

'A caveat is not a notice to any opponent in particular. It is a notice to the registrar or officer of the court not to let anything be done by anybody in the matter of the will, or the goods of the deceased, without notice to the person who lodges the caveat.'

Under s108 of the Supreme Court Act 1981 a caveat against a grant of probate or administration may be entered in the Principal Probate Registry or in any district probate registry. If it is registered in a district probate registry then a copy will also be sent to the Principal Registry. The caveat will last for six months and it may be extended by further caveats being issued but an application for these must be made during the last month of the six month period. See r44 of the NCPR 1987.

The main purpose of entering a caveat is to stop the issue of a grant. This may be done for several reasons, for example, there is doubt as to the validity of the will or there are two wills and the caveator wishes to seek advice or in the case of administration to prevent someone entitled to a grant in the same degree. A caveat would not, however, be issued to stop a grant being issued where the only reason was for the caveator to find out when the grant is made so as to make an application under the Inheritance (Provision for Family and Dependants) Act 1975. In such circumstances a standing search for a grant would be entered. This entitles the party entering the standing search to notice of any grant made to the estate in the twelve months prior to the date of entry and the six months subsequent thereto. See *Practice Direction* [1975] 1 WLR 1301. It is submitted that a standing search is the appropriate procedure where an application for rectification of a will is in issue under s20 of the Administration of Justice Act 1982.

Where an applicant for a grant finds a caveat entered the appropriate course of action is to issue a warning to the caveator. The warning will state the interest of the applicant in the will or intestacy and give the caveator the alternative of either (1) entering an appearance stating his interest or (2) issuing a summons for direction where the aim is to prevent a grant being made to the applicant. If neither of these alternatives are taken by the caveator the caveat will cease to have effect and a grant may be made to the applicant.

Citations

These are normally used to speed up the process of a grant being issued to the estate. There are three types of citation.

Citation to take probate

This is issued when an executor has intermeddled with the deceased's estate in a manner by which he would be deemed to have accepted office. The citation requires the executor to show cause why he should not accept the grant. If he fails to do so then he will be ordered to take the grant. See r47 of the NCPR 1987 and s112 of the SCA 1981.

Citation to accept or refuse probate

If the executor has not intermeddled in the estate this citation can be used to force him to make up his mind as to whether he does or does not want to take the grant. The idea is to ensure that an executor or administrator is appointed so that the administration of the estate can be carried through. See r47 of the NCPR 1987 and s112 of the SCA 1981.

Citation to propound a will

This is mainly used where the validity of the will is in doubt. A person interested in the estate of the deceased as next of kin may cite either the executors or beneficiaries under an alleged will to propound it, or the executors of an alleged later will may be required to propound that will by the executors of the earlier will. The procedure is only appropriate where no grant has been issued to the deceased's estate. If a grant has been made it will be necessary to challenge the validity of the will. See *Re Jolley* [1964] P 262.

14.4 Obtaining a grant in solemn form

As stated above, contentious or solemn form probate matters are assigned to the Chancery Division. This will include the following.

1. Cases where the validity of the will is challenged because it is alleged that it is not, for example, properly executed, there was no knowledge and approval, the testator did not have testamentary capacity, or it is alleged that the will is revoked.
2. Claims as to the right of a particular person to take a grant, sometimes called 'interest actions'.
3. Applications for the revocation of a grant where, for example, it is claimed that a document being produced was a later will of the testator or, where it was thought the deceased died intestate, a will is produced and alleged to be that of the deceased.

If legal proceedings concerning the validity of the will of the deceased or for the recalling or revoking of a grant are pending then the court may, under s117 of the Supreme Court Act 1981, grant administration of the estate to an administrator pending suit. Such an administrator has all the rights powers and duties of a general administrator but he is subject to the immediate control of the court. The administrator pending suit must act under the direction of the court and he cannot distribute any part of the estate without the leave of the court. His office will usually come to an end when the proceedings have been determined.

An action to obtain probate in solemn form will take the same course as any other action with the exception of some peculiarities in the evidence rules. Since the case will be concerned almost entirely with issues of fact it will be a writ action. In many cases there will be disputes as to which of several documents form the will of the testator. Thus, for example, if there are two wills and several codicils thereto, claim and counterclaim may be made as to their validity. In order to ensure that these documents are in the safe custody of the court before the probate action begins, s123 of the Supreme Court Act 1981 empowers the High Court to issue a subpoena requiring any person who has in his possession any relevant testamentary document to bring it in.

Section 122 of the Supreme Court Act 1981 gives the court power to carry out an examination of persons who are believed to have knowledge of a testamentary document so that it can be obtained and brought into the custody of the court. The provisions of s122 give the court power to order any person believed to have knowledge of the document to attend for the purposes of being examined in open court, and:

1. require him to answer any question relating to the document concerned; and
2. if appropriate, order him to bring in the document.

A failure to comply with the orders of the court under s122 is contempt of court.

Where it is necessary to prove the due execution of a will in a probate action then it is essential to call at least one of the attesting witnesses to give evidence of due execution. See *Bowman* v *Hodgson* (1867) LR 1 P & D 362. If the attesting wintesses are available no other evidence can be called on this point; even evidence of other persons present at the execution is insufficient in such circumstances. However, if the attesting witnesses are unavailable this must be proved before the court, for example, that they are dead, beyond the jurisdiction or untraceable and then secondary evidence of attestation may be admitted. Secondary evidence of attestation takes the form of proving the handwriting of at least one of the witnesses. See *Clarke* v *Clarke* (1879) 5 LR Ir 47. If proof of handwriting is not available then, and only then, may evidence of other persons present at execution be admitted. An attesting witness is regarded as if he had been called by the court and he may, contrary to the general rule, be cross-examined by the party who called him to prove due execution. See *Re Webster* [1974] 1 WLR 1641. He cannot claim professional privilege in respect of previous statements to his solicitors concerning execution. See *In the estate of Fuld* [1965] P 405, and any other evidence may be given if he denies execution or refuses to testify. See *Bowman* v *Hodgson*.

Costs in a probate action normally follow the event so that the losing party must pay both his own costs and those of the successful party. However, it must be emphasised that in the matter of costs the court has an unfettered discretion so that the general rule just stated may not apply. Other orders as to costs may be made.

Costs out of the estate

The court may order that the costs be paid out of the estate where the ligitation was caused by the deceased. Thus, for example, if he failed to execute the will in the orthodox manner or left his testamentary documents in a state of disarray or there was serious doubt as to his testamentary capacity the costs would come out of the estate. See *Davis* v *Gregory* (1873) 3 P & D 28; *Re Cutliffe* [1959] P 6. Costs would also be ordered out of the estate if the litigation was caused by the residuary legatees as in such circumstances they will be the losers on distribution. Thus if they drew up the will in suspicious circumstances this rule would apply. See *Orton* v *Smith* (1873) LR 3 P & D 23.

No order as to costs

This order will normally be made where the facts of the case give rise to reasonable grounds for doubting the validity of the will bearing in mind the plaintiff's knowledge or means of knowledge. Thus, in *Tippett* v *Tippett* (1865) 1 P & D 54, no order as to costs was made when one attesting witness, who was a doctor, could not swear that the testator possessed the necessary testamentary capacity.

Costs for execution

Where an executor has had to propound a will he is, as a general rule, entitled to his costs and he does not need an order of the court for this purpose. See RSC O.62 r2. However, the court may order otherwise if the litigation was to some extent due to the fault of the executor as, for example, where he lost the will. See *Burls* v *Burls* (1868) 1 P & D 472. Where an executor fails to prove the will and the rule is that he may have to pay costs, the general rule that costs follow the event will apply unless the court orders otherwise. In such circumstances the executor ought to protect himself by seeking an indemnity from those who seek to have the will proved.

Notice to cross-examine

A party who requires the will to be proved in solemn form and who only intends to cross-examine the witnesses produced in support of the will, may give notice to this effect to the other side. Under RSC O.62 r6(1)(d) no order as to costs may be made that such a party pay the costs of the other side unless the court is of the opinion that it was unnecessary to have the will proved in solemn form. See *Spicer* v *Spicer* [1899] P 38. This procedure is normally used if there is doubt as to due execution, knowledge and approval or testamentary capacity. It cannot be used in cases where fraud or undue influence is alleged as the onus of proof is on the party who alleges these.

Administration of small estates

Under the Administration of Estates (Small Payments) Act 1965 certain types of estate may be administered without the necessity of obtaining any form of grant.

This will apply where the asset consists of property defined as suitable for such administration by the Act such as investments in Government securities like the Post Office. Where the Act applies, the payer is permitted to pay out the beneficiary out of the particular up to a maximum limit of £5,000.00 without the need for obtaining a grant. In addition to this Act there are other legislative provisions which permit payment out of designated funds by the personal representative without the need for a grant (for further details see Parry and Clark, *Law of Succession*, 8th edn, p166).

Consequences of not obtaining a grant

Except where statute specifically authorises a personal representative to dispense with obtaining a grant, any failure to obtain a grant may cause difficulties in the subsequent administration. This is seen in the recent case of *Chay Ching Hwa* v *Seah Mary* (1986) Sol Jo 860 (PC). Here a personal representative attempted to convey real property in the estate without a formal grant of administration. It was held that his purported conveyance was void. See also *Eastbourne Building Society* v *Hastings Corporation* [1965] 1 WLR 861.

15

Types of Grant

15.1 Introduction

15.2 Limited grants

15.3 Foreign grants; recognition and resealing of grants

15.4 Evidence in probate actions

15.1 Introduction

There are three main types of grant of representation.

1. Probate – made where an executor proves the will.
2. Letters of Administration with the Will Annexed – made where there is a will but a person other than the executor proves the will. See s119 of the SCA 1981.
3. 'Simple' Administration – made where the deceased died totally intestate.

Grants may be either general or limited in form. A general grant is one which is not limited in any way while a limited grant is one which is limited as to either property or time. The following matters should be noted in relation to general grants.

Double probate
This arises where the original grant of probate was made to only some of the executors appointed by the will and, later, a grant is made to one of those who was not included in the original grant. Thus, for example, if one of two executors appointed by will was an infant, the court would not grant him probate but would when granting probate to the other executor reserve power to the infant to take a grant on attaining majority. If the infant applies for a grant on attaining majority this grant is called 'double probate'; it is a general grant and will run concurrently with the original grant.

Cessate grant
Where a grant of probate or administration was limited in time, for example, a grant during the minority of an infant, at the termination of that grant the court may make a general grant so that the administration of the estate be completed. Such a grant is known as a cessate grant.

15.2 Limited grants

Under s113(1) of the Supreme Court Act 1981 it is provided that 'the High Court may grant probate or administration in respect of any part of the estate of a deceased person, limited in any way the court thinks fit'. Thus if the testator has appointed different persons to be executors for different parts of the estate, or if settled land is involved, the court can sever the grant as appropriate. However, under s113(2) it is provided that a grant to an insolvent estate cannot be severed in any way except as regards a trust estate in which the deceased had no beneficial interest. The types of limited grant are as follows.

Administration **de bonis non administratis** *(of goods not administered)*

This type of grant is made where the deceased's estate has not been fully administered and the personal representatives originally appointed are dead. In such cases two conditions have to be satisfied:

First, original grant made to a personal representative who has died. Thus, a grant *de bonis non administratis* would not be made where the original grant had terminated because it was limited in some way, for example, as to time; a cessate grant would be made here.

Second, the chain of representation under s7 of the Administration of Estates Act 1925 is broken. If an executor by representation can be found there is no need to make a grant *de bonis non administratis*. Thus, in *In the goods of Reid* [1896] P 129, a grant *de bonis non administratis* was refused after the death of the original executor because he had appointed an executor in his will who was executor by representation.

A grant *de bonis non administratis* may be issued where a previous grant has been revoked by the court. See *In the goods of Galbraith* [1951] P 422.

The persons entitled to receive a grant *de bonis administratis* are set out in rr20 and 22 of the NCPR 1987. Rule 20 will apply to cases where the grant is one with the will annexed and r22 will apply where the grant is one for simple administration.

Settled Land Act grant

Where the deceased's estate comprised of settled land and the land will continue to be settled land after his death, then a grant is made in respect of this to the deceased's 'special personal representatives'. See s22(1) of the Administration of Estates Act 1925. It must be emphasised that 'special personal representatives' are only needed where the settlement is continuing and they are unnecessary when the settlement comes to an end on the deceased's death. Thus, for example, if land was settled on A for life, remainder to B, remainder to C absolutely, on A's death the land would vest in the 'special personal representatives' as the settlement will continue. However, on B's death C becomes absolutely entitled, the settlement therefore comes to an end on B's death and no 'special personal representatives' are needed, B's general personal representatives will convey the land to C.

The 'special personal representatives' may be either 'special executors' or 'special administrators'. Section 22(1) of the Administration of Estates Act 1925 deals with special executors and provides that the testator may appoint the trustees of the settlement as his special executors and in default of an express appointment of them they shall be deemed to be appointed special executors. This means that if a testator should appoint A and B as his special executors when C and D are the trustees of the settlement, then the express appointment is of no effect and C and D will be deemed special executors under s22(1). Where the deceased left no will at his death then special administrators will be appointed. Rule 29 of the NCPR 1987 sets out provisions for their appointment.

Administration for the use and benefit of a minor

This is sometimes known as a grant *durante minor aetate* and it is made where the person appointed sole executor or entitled to a grant of administration is a minor. See s118 Supreme Court Act 1981. The grant will usually be limited in time, that is, until the minor attains 18 years. A grant for the use and benefit of a minor would not be made where one of two or more executors is a minor. In such circumstances the court would grant probate to the other executors and reserve power to the minor to take probate when he attains majority. The persons entitled to this type of grant are set out in r32(1) of the NCPR 1987. They are:

1. both parents of the minor jointly or the surviving parent or the minor's guardian;
2. elected guardians;
3. assigned guardians.

Administration during physical or mental incapacity

Where the registrar is satisfied that a person entitled to a grant is incapable of managing his affairs by reason of mental or physical incapacity then a grant for his use and benefit will be made, limited during his incapacity or in such other way as is appropriate.

This type of grant will be made in the following cases.

1. In the case of mental incapacity, to the person authorised by the Court of Protection to apply for the grant.
2. In the case of physical incapacity:
    a)   to the person entitled to the estate if the person who is physically incapable is appointed executor and has no interest in the estate;
    b)   if the executor appointed is incapable and has an interest in the residue, to the person who would take a grant if the executor had died intestate.

Administration ad colligenda bona defuncti

This is a grant to collect in the goods of the deceased. It will be made for the purpose of preserving the assets of the deceased where they are perishables and the person entitled to a grant cannot apply or has not applied. Thus, in *In the goods of Bolton* [1899] P 186, this type of grant was made where the deceased's next of kin lived in South America and the estate comprised a newsagents and tobacconists shop which would lose all its goodwill if closed down until the person entitled to administration arrived in England. The grant *ad colligenda bona* may confer whatever powers are needed to deal with the assets, for example, to sell them.

Administration pending suit

This will be made under s117 of the Supreme Court Act 1981 to ensure that the deceased's assets are collected in and safeguarded pending the outcome of litigation relating to the will or intestacy. The grant will usually be limited to the determination of the litigation.

This type of grant is normally made to someone who has no interest in the outcome of the litigation, such as an accountant, but it is open to the parties to agree to a particular appointment. The administrator pending suit is under the direct control of the court and must act under its direction; he must not distribute any part of the estate without the leave of the court. See s117(2).

15.3 Foreign grants; recognition and resealing of grants

It has been explained that the grant of representation enables the personal representatives of the deceased to deal with his property. This is the case for his property in England and Wales.

As regards his property and assets in another country, that country's probate requirements must be fulfilled. This usually means that a fresh grant will have to be taken out in that country. Likewise, in circumstances where a testator's will has already been proved in a foreign country generally it is not sufficient for the personal representative to produce the foreign grant. Usually, therefore, the will must be proved again and a fresh grant will have to be issued to the person entitled to deal with the testator's estate.

With the ever increasing movement of persons the position can be rather complex and there is a developing field of law relating to international wills as a result. It should also be noted that meanwhile an international convention, a Convention Concerning the International Administration of the Estates of Deceased, was signed in 1972. This Convention was intended to remove the duplication mentioned above through the introduction of an international certificate designating the person entitled to administer the deceased's estate. The certificate would be recognised by all contracting States. The United Kingdom has signed but not ratified this Convention.

The general rule has also been relaxed in England and Wales because of special links with certain countries. Relaxation has occurred in two instances as follows.

Recognition of Scottish confirmations and Northern Irish grants

Initially a Scottish confirmation and a Northern Irish grant, which are the equivalent to an English grant of probate or letters of administration, had to be resealed. The Administration of Estates Act 1971 relaxed the position so that where the deceased died domiciled in Scotland or Northern Ireland resealing was not necessary. Instead, the Scottish or Northern Irish grant became acceptable in England and Wales without any formality as described below.

Resealing of Commonwealth and colonial grants

Any foreign grants to which the Colonial Probates Act 1892 (as extended by the Colonial Probates (Protected States and Mandated Territories) Act 1927) applies are merely resealed as outlined below. They then are effective as if they had been granted in England and Wales. See also the Colonial Probates Act Application Order 1965 (SI 1965/1530). This legislation has extended to, in particular, all of the Australian States, most of the Canadian States, New Zealand, the Bahamas, Barbados, Bermuda, Botswana, the Falkland Islands, Fiji, Ghana, Gibraltar, Hong Kong, Jamaica, Kenya, Malawi, Malaysia, Nigeria, Singapore, Zimbabwe, Sri Lanka, Swaziland, Tanzania, Uganda and Zambia. See r39 of the NCPR 1987 for the procedure.

This process is used so that grants made in Commonwealth countries can be recognised. Under the Colonial Probates Act 1892 a grant made in any country to which this provision has been applied may be recognised in England and Wales if it is resealed with the seal of the Family Division. The court has a discretion to reseal and therefore such grants differ from Scottish and Northern Irish grants as these are entitled to automatic recognition.

15.4 Evidence in probate actions

Lodging of will

When the application for the grant is made the original will must be lodged and the general position is that, once it is lodged, it must be retained by the Registry. Where the will is not in the custody of the applicant and he cannot obtain the will he may obtain an order of the court requiring it to be lodged.

A photocopy of the will rather than the original is then available for public inspection.

Release for proof overseas

The question has arisen whether the will can ever be released from the Registry. In *Re White Todd's Estate* [1926] P 173 the applicant wished to prove the will overseas after it had been proved in England. The court held that it could be released for this purpose on the basis that a sealed copy was retained in the Registry. On the other hand in *Re Greer* (1929) 45 TLR 362 the court held that it did not have the power to permit the will to leave the jurisdiction for the purpose of foreign proceedings.

It has been suggested that the compromise solution would be that the will can only be sent abroad by court ruling where:

1. it is required to be proved abroad; and
2. the English court is satisfied that the foreign court will not accept a sealed copy.

Rule 54(2) of the NCPR 1987 provides that where a will is held abroad and cannot be brought here, for example where it has been proved in a foreign court and that court will not release it, probate can be granted of an authenticated copy of the foreign will.

Translation of foreign wills

Another point of evidence concerns a will that is written in a foreign language. Such a will is valid: a translation must be lodged, together with an affidavit by the translator verifying the translation (see the recent case of *Re Berger* [1989] 2 WLR 147 discussed in Chapter 1, section 1.3, above). The executor is sworn to the foreign will. However, the photocopy of the will attached to the probate is of the translation and not the original.

Loss of the will

Circumstances may arise where the will is not in existence or is lost, even though it has not been validly revoked in accordance with the provisions of the Wills Act 1837 (see Chapter 6).

Provided that the contents can be validly reconstructed probate will then be granted of the best documential evidence available. This is the case when considering a copy of the will, a draft of the will, and even a document which is a reconstruction from oral evidence.

Other general points of evidence to be noted have been made in Chapter 14, section 14.2, particularly in the discussion of affidavits.

Incorporation of standard forms and clauses in wills

The following *Practice Direction (Family Division) (Incorporation of Standard Forms and Clauses in Wills)* was issued by Gerald Angel, Senior District Judge, on 10 April 1995:

'Rule 14(3) of the Non-Contentious Probate Rules 1987 makes provision for the production to the Court of any document which is incorporated in a will. This provision extends to the incorporation of standard will forms and clauses, other than statutory will forms.

As from the date of this *Direction* when application is made to admit to proof a will which incorporates standard forms or clauses as contained in a published document, production of that document will not be required in any individual case, unless otherwise directed, if the published document containing the standard forms or clauses (together with as many copies as may be required) has been previously lodged with the Senior District Judge and accepted by him as sufficient lodgement for the purpose of this Direction.'

16

Revocation of Grants

16.1 Reasons for revocation

16.2 Effect of revocation

16.1 Reasons for revocation

Under s121(1) Supreme Court Act 1981 it is provided that:

> 'Where it appears to the High Court that a grant either ought not to have been made or contains an error, the court may call in the grant and, if satisfied that it would be revoked at the instance of a party interested, may revoke it.'

If the grant cannot be called in for revocation then under s121(2) the court may revoke the grant without calling it in.

Many reasons may exist for the revocation of a grant. The following is a summary of the main reasons.

Grant made to wrong person
The grant may have been wrongly made. Thus a grant of letters of administration simpliciter may have been made on the belief that the deceased died intestate but later a will is found and proved. It may be that a will is found which is later than that will to which probate was granted. See *Priestman* v *Thomas* (1884) 32 WR 842.

Where the grant was made as a result of a false statement
It may be that the statement was made with knowledge of its falsity. Thus, in *In the goods of Moore* (1845) 3 NC 601, the original grantee falsely claimed to be the deceased's wife. This ground will also apply if the statement was believed to be true. Thus, in *In the goods of Napier* (1809) 1 Phill 83, a grant was made to the deceased's estate in the belief that he had been left for dead on the battlefield. The grant was revoked when he appeared personally in court for such an application.

Where the grant contains a material irregularity
If the grant was made without giving proper notice to a caveator the court may revoke it. See *Trimblestown* v *Trimblestown* (1830) 3 Hag Ecc 243.

Grantee wishes to be relieved of his duties
If the grantee can show sound reasons why he should be relieved of the grant, it may be revoked. Thus, in *In the goods of Thacker* [1900] P 15, a grant to a receiver in bankruptcy was revoked after he had paid all the debts.

Grantee has left the country permanently or cannot be traced
In *In the goods of Loveday* [1900] P 154 the deceased's widow disappeared after obtaining the grant and it was revoked, while in *Re Thomas* [1912] P 177, the grantee emigrated to New Zealand to a known address but the grant was nevertheless revoked on evidence that he did not intend to return to England.

Grantee becomes incapable of acting
If the grantee should become incapable of acting through old age or physical or mental incapacity then the grant will be revoked. Thus, in *In the goods of Galbraith* [1951] P 422, a grant of probate was revoked where both grantees had become unable to act through physical and mental infirmity caused by old age.

Grantee commits a serious breach of duty
A grantee will not be removed from his office merely because he breaches his duty; the breach has to be serious. Thus, in *In the estate of Cope* [1954] 1 WLR 608, the court refused to revoke a grant of administration on the ground that the administrators had failed to submit an accurate estate duty account. It would appear that the grantee would have to commit some dishonest act. See *In the goods of Bradshaw* (1888) 13 PD 18, or act in a manner which is damaging to the interests of the beneficiaries, before the court would revoke the grant on this ground.

16.2 Effect of revocation

If a grant is revoked this may have a serious effect on all those who have dealt with the personal representative under the revoked grant. He may have sold assets from the deceased's estate, collected in debts and paid debts of the deceased and distributed assets to beneficiaries in accordance with the will by which he was appointed or under the intestacy rules. Statutory provisions provide protection for the personal representative whose grant is subsequently revoked, and for those who deal with him. These are as follows.

Section 27 of the Administration of Estates Act 1925

Under s27(1) the personal representative is given an indemnity in respect of payments and dispositions made in good faith by him. It states:

'Every person making or permitting to be made any payment or disposition in good faith under a representation shall be indemnified and protected in so doing, notwithstanding any defect or circumstances whatsoever affecting the validity of the representation.'

It is important that the personal representative should have acted in good faith. If he has doubts as to the validity of the grant and did not inform the court of his reasons, then he may be denied the protection of the section. See *In the estate of Bloch* (1959) The Times 2 July.

Section 27(2) protects those who in good faith made payments or dispositions to the personal representative whose grant is revoked, and permits the personal representative to re-imburse himself in respect of payments he made out of his own pocket provided the payments might properly have been made by the subsequent grantee. The section reads:

'Where a representation is revoked, all payments and dispositions made in good faith to a personal representative under the representation before the revocation thereof are a valid discharge to the person making the same; and the personal representative who acted under the revoked representation may retain and reimburse himself in respect of any payments or dispositions made by him which the person to whom representation is afterwards granted might properly have made.'

Section 37(1) of the Administration of Estates Act 1925

This section provides that the validity of a conveyance is not be affected by revocation of representation. It reads:

'All conveyances of any interest in real or personal estate made to a purchaser either before or after the commencement of this Act by a person to whom probate or letters of administration have been granted are valid, notwithstanding any subsequent revocation or variation, either before or after the commencement of this Act, of the probate or administration.'

'Conveyance' is defined by s55(1)(iii) as including:

'... a mortgage, charge by way of legal mortgage, lease, assent, vesting declaration, vesting instrument, disclaimer, release and every other assurance of property or of an interest therein by an instrument except a will, and "convey" has a corresponding meaning.'

The definition of conveyance in s55(1)(iii), does not cover transfers of property which take place without a written instrument such as the sale of chattels belonging to the deceased's estate. The decision in *Hewson* v *Shelley* [1914] 2 Ch 13 would apply in such cases and the purchaser will be protected so long as he acted in good faith. Although *Hewson* v *Shelley* was concerned with the purchase of land and given statutory blessing in this respect, the dicta in it is wide enough to cover the sale of chattels.

'Purchaser' is defined by s55(1)(xviii) as:

'... a lessee, mortgagee or other person who in good faith acquires an interest in property for valuable consideration, also an intending purchaser and "valuable consideration" includes marriage, but does not include a nominal consideration in money.'

Section 39(1)(iii) of the Administration of Estates Act 1925

This provision protects those who enter into a contract with a former personal representative and therefore it includes cases where the grant to the former personal representative was revoked. It reads:

> '... every contract entered into by a personal representative shall be binding on and be enforceable against and by the personal representative for the time being of the deceased, and may be carried into effect, or be varied or rescinded by him, and in the case of a contract entered into by a predecessor, as if it had been entered into by himself.'

Recovery of property from beneficiaries wrongly paid or over-paid

A beneficiary who has been wrongly paid or over-paid will have to return property after the revocation of a grant if the person rightfully entitled thereto, follows it into their hands to recover it. If following the property is not available because the property has been dissipated, then a personal action may be undertaken against the wrongly paid or over paid beneficiary. This is dealt with in Chapter 20, below.

17

Vesting, Collection and Realisation of Assets

17.1 Introduction: duties and liabilities of personal representatives

The administration of the estate of a deceased person is a three-stage process. First, the personal representatives must collect in and realise the assets of the estate. In this respect they must have regard to what assets actually vest in them for the purpose of administration. This is dealt with below. Second, they must pay all the debts and liabilities due from the deceased's estate according to the principles laid down in the Administration of Estates Act and Schedule 1. Third, when the above have been completed, they must distribute the remainder of the estate to those who are beneficially entitled thereto. These principles apply whether the deceased died testate or intestate.

As far as concerns the various duties of the personal representatives in connection with the administration of the deceased's estate, they must all be performed with 'due diligence'. While there is no absolute rule as to what is a reasonable time for the collection of assets or as to the steps that must be taken, the 'due diligence' principle means that the personal representatives should:

1. take reasonable steps to collect money due to the deceased, including taking proceedings if necessary; and
2. collect the assets of the estate as quickly as is practical.

In each case it is clear that the personal representatives will be liable for loss resulting from any failure to act only if they act unreasonably. This should be borne in mind when considering the aspects of the administration of the estate which are discussed in the following chapters.

It should also be noted that where there are several personal representatives each is liable for his own breach of duty but not for the breaches of any co-executor or co-administrator. This is subject to two provisos:

1. where a personal representative permits a breach of duty by another personal representative he will be liable since evidently he has failed to fulfil his own duty of safeguarding the deceased's estate; and
2. where a personal representative fails to attend to his duties and thereby allows a breach of a co-personal representative to go unnoticed then he may also be liable in negligence.

Brief mention should also be made of a practice direction whereby partners in a firm of solicitors are appointed executors in a will but are not individually named and not all the partners wish to apply for the grant:

1. it is sufficient for the oath to recite that the applicant(s) is/was/were partners at the appropriate date;
2. the oath must state that notice of the application has been given to the executors to whom power is to be reserved (r27(1) of the Non-Contentious Probate Rules 1987). It is sufficient for the oath in these circumstances to recite that notice has been given to all the other properties at the appropriate date without naming them.

17.2 Vesting of property

It is important for the personal representatives to know exactly what property belonging to the deceased actually vests in them on his death for several reasons.

1. They must know what property they are entitled to resort to in order to pay the debts and liabilities of the estate. Generally, all the property which vests in them will be available to meet debts and liabilities, if required. However, it must be emphasised that the property which is available for the payment of debts and liabilities is not limited to the assets which vest in the personal representatives as s32 of the Administration of Estates Act indicates. This is dealt with in further detail below.
2. If the personal representatives deal with property which has not vested in them

in the course of managing the deceased's estate they may be rendered liable in trespass or conversion.

What property vests in the personal representatives?

Before 1925 only the deceased's personalty vested in his personal representatives on his death; this was why they were called 'personal' representatives. The deceased's realty passed to his heir or the devisee under his will before 1925 and therefore never vested in the personal representatives.

Since 1925 the position of realty has been assimilated to that of personalty, with exceptions under s1 of the Administration of Estates Act 1925. Section 1(1) provides:

> 'Real estate to which a deceased person was entitled for an interest not ceasing on his death, shall on his death, and notwithstanding any testamentary disposition thereof, devolve from time to time on the personal representative of the deceased, in like manner as before the commencement of this Act chattels real devolved on the personal representatives from time to time of a deceased person.'

In short, realty belonging to the deceased is to devolve on the personal representatives after 1925 as chattels real did before 1926 (and still do), that is, immediately on the deceased's death.

'Chattels real' have not been defined by the Act, but mean leasehold and other interests in land which are less than freehold. For the purposes of s1(1) 'real estate' is defined by s3(1) as:

> '(i) chattels real, and land in possession, remainder or reversion, and every interest in or over land to which a deceased person was entitled at the time of his death; and
> (ii) real estate on trust (including settled land), or by way of mortgage or security, but not money secured or charged on land.'

Section 3(1)(ii) and trusts

Not all real estate held on trust devolves on the personal representatives of the deceased under s3(1)(ii). The following is a summary of the position.

Trusts. If the deceased was one of several trustees who held land on trust then on his death the land will vest in the surviving trustees. Because trustees hold the legal title as joint tenants, the surviving trustees take the title by the right of survivorship. Nothing will vest in the deceased's personal representatives. However, if the deceased was the last or sole trustee of a trust, then on his death the land will vest in his personal representatives under s3(1)(ii).

Settled land. If the deceased was the tenant for life of a Settled Land Act settlement, then whether the property vests in his personal representatives on his death depends on whether the settlement is to continue after his death. If the settlement is to continue, then the property will vest in the special personal representatives, who are normally the trustees of the settlement. However, if the deceased was the last tenant for life, then on his death the property would vest in his personal representatives. See *Re Bridgett and Hayes Contract* [1928] Ch 163. On the other hand, if the deceased was the trustee of a settled land settlement, his death would not affect the devolution of the settled land if the tenant for life and other trustees of the settlement survived him. However, if the deceased was the sole trustee of the settlement on the death of the life tenant, the property would vest in the personal representatives of the tenant for life. As the Trusts of Land and Appointment of Trustees Act 1996 is phasing out settled land, the need for settled land grants will reduce significantly.

Section 3(1)(ii) and mortgaged land
Where real estate has been conveyed to a mortgagee as security for a loan, on the death of the mortagagee the property will vest in the mortgagee's personal representatives under s3(1).

Under s3(2) real estate which the deceased appointed in his will under a general power of appointment will vest in his personal representatives. Thus, if T appointed Blackacre to X under his will, his personal representatives would hold the property to give effect to the appointment. However, it should be noted that where personalty is appointed under a general power by the will, the personalty does not vest in the personal representatives. See *O'Grady* v *Wilmot* [1916] 2 AC 231.

Under s3(3) an entailed interest will devolve on the personal representatives if it has been barred and disposed of by a gift in the will. If it has not been barred or disposed of by the will then it will not pass to the personal representatives but devolves according to the terms of the instrument creating it. See s176 of the LPA 1925.

Property which does not devolve on the personal representatives

There are six categories where property does not devolve on the deceased's personal representatives.

Property held by the deceased as a joint tenant
Under s3(4) of the Administration of Estates Act if the deceased had an interest under a joint tenancy and was survived by another joint tenant, then his interest would cease on death. This is in accordance with the right of survivorship. In such cases it is necessary to consider the interests of the deceased and his co-owner both at law and in equity.

At law and equity

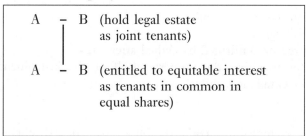

In the example above, if A dies then his interest in the property, both at law and in equity, will cease. B will become the sole owner of the property and the statutory trusts imposed on the property will cease. See *Re Cook* [1948] Ch 212.

At law only

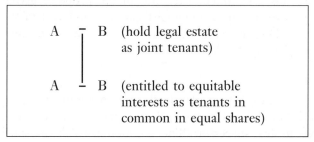

If A dies, then if he was only a joint tenant at law the legal estate would vest in B alone. However, as A and B were tenants in common in equity, there is no right of survivorship in relation to this, and A's equitable share will devolve on his personal representatives. However, this will devolve as personalty and not as realty on the personal representatives because of the statutory trust for sale which imports the doctrine of conversion here. See s3(1)(ii) of the AEA and *Re Kempthorne* [1930] 1 Ch 268.

Life interest ceases
Where the deceased had a life interest under a trust or settlement this will cease on his death, and property subject to the interest will devolve according to the terms of the trust instrument and not to the deceased's personal representatives.

Unbarred entails
Under s176 of the Law of Property Act 1925 an entail barred by will and disposed of by the will devolves on the deceased's personal representatives. This is only possible if four conditions have been satisfied; if not the entail will devolve according to the instrument creating it, and not upon the personal representatives.

The four conditions are:

1. the entail must be in possession, not in remainder;
2. the tenant in tail must be of full age;
3. the will must have been executed or confirmed by codicil after 1925;
4. the will must specifically refer to either the property itself or the instrument under which it was acquired or entails generally.

Statutory tenancy

A statutory tenancy is a status of irremovability conferred on a tenant of a dwelling-house by s2 of the Rent Act 1977 after the expiry of a contractual tenancy of the property. By s3(5) and Schedule 1 Part II of the Rent Act a statutory tenancy can be transmitted to the tenant's wife or a member of his family on his death. Transmission may occur twice. Where transmission of a statutory tenancy takes place the tenancy vests in the person entitled thereto and not in the personal representatives. However, if there was a contractual tenancy of the property giving rights to a statutory tenancy on its expiry, the contractual tenancy would vest in the personal representatives and vest in abeyance while the transmitted statutory tenancy is enjoyed. See *Moodie* v *Hosegood* [1952] AC 61.

Corporation sole

By s3(5) of the Administration of Estates Act, on the death of a corporator sole, for example, a bishop, his interest in the corporation's real and personal estate shall cease on his death and devolve to his successor. The corporator sole's personal representatives will have nothing to do with such property.

Donatio mortis causa

Where a testator makes a *donatio mortis causa*, a gift is delivered to the donee in anticipation of death. See *Jones* v *Selby* (1710) 2 Eq Cas Abr 573. The property is held on trust by the donee until the donor dies and at that time possession passes. The property does not devolve on the donor's personal representatives. See *Re Beaumont* [1902] 1 Ch 889.

The facts of *Sen* v *Headley* have already been described above (see Chapter 1, section 1.7) and, because of the importance of this decision, the finding of the court should be referred to again.

Accordingly, they held that land was capable of passing by way of *donatio mortis causa* subject to the general requirements in all such cases. Here the three general requirements for such a gift had been satisfied. (Note that the cases of *Snellgrove* v *Bailey* (1744) 3 Atk 213 and *Birch* v *Treasury Solicitor* [1951] CLY 4312 were also considered.) See also *Woodard* v *Woodard* (1991) The Times 15 March (CA).

Insurance policies

1. Any insurance policies on the life of the deceased taken out under the Married Women's Property Act 1882 or written in trust for third parties are not assets of the estate.

   These policies are payable on proof of death without need of the grant of representation. The personal representatives will not be involved in the payment of the proceeds unless there is no named trustee, in which case the proceeds will remain outside the estate for tax purposes.

2. Lump sum payments due under discretionary pension schemes are not part of the estate. The personal representatives are not concerned in their collection; the trustees of the scheme pay direct to the selected donees.

Nominations

One should be aware of nominations which do not devolve on the personal representative, such as pension/pension schemes whereby there may be a nomination of a person to receive benefits if the employee dies in service. There has been some question as to whether it constitutes a testamentary disposition, and, in this respect, one should note the case of *Baird* v *Baird* [1990] 2 WLR 1412; [1990] 2 All ER 300.

In *Baird*, a Trinidad oil company provided a contributory pension scheme whereby an employee was entitled to nominate a beneficiary to receive the death benefit payable on the employee's death before retirement. Nominations and revocations or alterations thereto were subject to the consent of the management committee of the scheme. In the absence of a nomination, the benefit was payable to the employee's widow or widower or to his or her estate. In this instance, an employee nominated his brother as beneficiary. Five years later he married, without revoking or varying the nomination. Two years afterwards he died while still in the company's employment. Both the brother and the widow claimed the death benefit. The High Court and Court of Appeal of Trinidad held that the brother was entitled. The widow appealed to the Privy Council contending that the nomination was a testamentary disposition which was only valid if executed with the formalities required for a will (discussed in Chapter 2, above).

The Judicial Committee (Lords Bridge of Harwich, Roskill, Brandon of Oakbrook and Oliver of Aylmerton and Sir Roger Ormrod) dismissed that appeal. It was held that the nomination was in essence no different from any other power of appointment, since it disposed of no property of the employee, who retained no proprietary interest in his contributions under the pension scheme. The nomination did not have to be executed as if it were a will. (*Re Danish Bacon Co Ltd Staff Pension Fund, Christensen* v *Arnett* [1971] 1 WLR 248 applied.)

Powers of appointment

The testamentary power of appointment was examined in *Re Beatty (deceased)* [1990] 1 WLR 1503. The testatrix had left an estate of £32 million. The testatrix had made a will in which she allocated her personal chattels and cash to her trustees to whom she also gave the power to distribute these 'among such person or persons (whether individual or corporate) as they think fit', and that any assets not distributed within two years after her death were to become part of her residuary estate.

The residuary beneficiaries brought proceedings against the trustees questioning the distributions made and their power to do so.

Held: Hoffmann J stated that the trustees had a fiduciary power and upheld the defendants' argument that these powers were not invalidated by the rule that a testator could not delegate the making of his will. The trustees only had to consider the wishes expressed by the testatrix.

The judge applied the case of *Re Park* [1932] 1 Ch 580. The powers being fiduciary, were not general powers, nor special powers but were intermediate or hybrid powers. In *Re Park* the court had upheld the validity of such an appointment and its powers so long as it was not delegated to a donee.

The plaintiffs argued that such a delegation amounted to the making of a will for a testator who had failed to do so. That was rejected and interpreted instead as:

'... giving effect to the testator's will and not making a will for a testator'. at p1507.

Such a power would be valid by deed and there is no rule prohibiting the delegation of testamentary power which would cause this will to be invalid or to forbid the actions taken here by the trustees.

17.3 Mode of vesting of property

Section 1(1) of the Administration of Estates Act states that the deceased's real estate shall 'devolve from time to time on the personal representative'. This means that the property is only vested in the personal representative while he holds office to carry out his duties of administration of the estate. Where there is a change of personal representative the property automatically devolves on the new personal representative to continue administration. Thus, for example, if X was appointed executor and obtained a grant of probate to the testator's estate and later his grant is revoked and Y appointed as an administrator, the property formerly vested in X as executor would vest automatically in Y on his appointment.

The time of vesting is important and occurs at different times with different consequences depending on whether the personal representative is an executor or an administrator.

Executor

1. If the executor is of full age the deceased's property will vest in him at the time of death whether it is personalty (see *Chetty* v *Chetty* [1916] 1 AC 603), or realty (see ss1 and 3 and AEA 1925). In *Attenborough* v *Solomon* [1913] AC 76 Lord

Haldane said:

> 'The position of the executor is a peculiar one; he is appointed by the will but then by virtue of his office by the operation of law and not under the bequest in the will, he takes a title to the personal property and not his realty, of the testator which vests in him with the *plenium dominium* over the testator's assets.'

2. An executor is entitled to do all acts which are incident to his office, except those for which he needs a grant, before obtaining probate. See *Re Stevens* [1897] 1 Ch 422. Thus, he may collect in assets and receive payment of debts owed to the estate, he may pay or take release of debts owed by the estate, sell any property belonging to the estate, and pay any legacies or transfer any property to persons entitled thereto under the will. Such acts are good even if the executor dies without ever having obtained probate. See *Wankford* v *Wankford* (1704) 1 Salk 299. However, if any question should arise as to his action, it would be necessary to produce a grant of probate in order to show that he was entitled to act as he did because probate is the authenticated evidence of the executor's title. In *Smith* v *Milles* (1786) 1 TR 475 Ashurst J said:

> 'So the executor has the right immediately on the death of the testator, and the right draws after it constructive possession. The probate is a mere ceremony but, when passed, the executor does not derive his title under the probate but under the will; the probate is only evidence of his right and is necessary to enable him to sue, but he may release etc, before probate.'

3. Because an executor derives his authority from the will he may commence litigation on behalf of the estate before obtaining probate and continue the litigation until such time as he needs to prove his title. See *Re Crowhurst Park* [1974] 1 WLR 583.

Administrator

1. In the case of an administrator s9 of the Administration of Estates Act provides:

> 'Where a person dies intestate, his real and personal estate, until administration is granted in respect thereof, shall vest in the Probate Judge ...' (that is, the President of the Family Division).

When the administrator is appointed by the court the deceased's property then vests in him in the same way as it vests in an executor on the testator's death. From this it can be seen that the administrator's source of authority to deal with the estate is the grant of administration. See *Chetty* v *Chetty* [1916] 1 AC 603.

2. Because the deceased's property does not vest in the administrator until he is appointed by the court, a doctrine of relation back has been applied by the courts to enable an administrator to protect the estate from injury in the period between death and his appointment. This doctrine is necessary because the vesting of the deceased's property in the President of the Family Division does not impose any duties on him in relation to that property. See *Re Deans* [1954] 1 WLR 332.

Under the doctrine the administrator may sue for trespass committed before the grant (see *Thorpe* v *Stallwood* (1843) 5 M & G 760), for the price of goods sold (see *Foster* v *Bates* (1843) 12 M & W 226), and where money belonging to the deceased, or due to him and paid in after his death, or proceeding from the sale of his assets after his death, has before the grant been applied by a stranger to the payment of the deceased's debts and funeral expenses, the administrator may recover it from such stranger, as money had and received to his use as administrator. See *Welchman* v *Sturgis* (1849) 13 QB 552. See also *Mills* v *Anderson* [1984] 2 All ER 538.

In *Foster* v *Bates* (1843) 12 M & W 226 the defendants were partners in a firm trading to the West Coast of Africa. Goods had been sent by the deceased to Africa for sale. After his death the defendants through their agent purchased the goods from the agent of the deceased there, who sold them for the benefit of the estate. After the sale, the plaintiff took out letters of administration to the estate of the deceased and brought an action for the price of the goods.

Held: the action was maintainable because (per Parke B):

> 'It is clear that the title of an admininstrator, though it does not exist until the grant of administration, relates back to the time of the death of the intestate; and he may recover against a wrong-doer who has seized or coverted the goods of the interest after the death, in an action of trespass or trover.'

3. An administrator has no authority to do any acts of administration before his grant. See *Chetty* v *Chetty* (above). In the period between death and obtaining a grant a receiver may be appointed to protect the assets of the deceased. See *Re Oakes* [1917] 1 Ch 230. However, in some cases it may be possible to obtain a grant of administration pendente lite and this may be preferable. See *Re Sutcliffe* [1942] Ch 453.

4. Unlike an executor, an administrator has no power to commence litigation on behalf of the estate until he has obtained a grant. Should he issue any proceedings before the grant they will be struck out because he has no title to sue; the doctrine of relation back will not apply to validate the proceedings.

In *Ingall* v *Moran* [1944] KB 160 (CA) the deceased died in a road accident. As he was intestate his father issued a writ 'as administrator of his son's estate' claiming damages against the other party involved in the accident for negligence. At the time the writ was issued the father did not have a grant of administration but he subsequently obtained one.

Held: the writ was issued at a time when the father had no title to sue and accordingly the action must fail.

Law of Property (Miscellaneous Provisions) Act 1994

Certain recent changes enacted by the Law of Property (Miscellaneous Provisions) Act 1994 should be noted. Mention has already made of s14 in the respect of intestacies (see Chapter 11, section 11.1). Under s14 the new authority of the Public

Trustee is extended to where there is a will but no executor with power to obtain a grant either at the date of death or later.

Section 15 validates the registration of a land charge under the Land Charges Act 1972 against a person who created a land charge even though he or she has since died. Before this a land charge could only be registered against an estate owner and nobody can be an estate owner after he or she has died.

Section 16 provides that all personal representatives, other than executors, who do not prove, must join in a contract for the sale of the land. Previously, it was not essential for all personal representatives to be a party to the contract so long as they joined in and executed the conveyance.

Section 17 of the enactment is concerned with provisions about notices. There are two situations which are covered. First, where the person serving the notice has no reason to believe the recipient is dead, the notice will be deemed to be properly served if served in a way which would have been effective if the recipient were still alive. For example, if the person who serves the notice has no reason to believe the recipient is dead, he or she can proceed in the usual way. This provision does not change what has to be done, but confirms the efficacy of the action.

If the person serving the notice has reason to believe that the recipient has died then, until a grant is filed in the principal probate registry, the notice must be addressed to 'The personal representatives of ...' and must be left at the last known address or residence or place of work. A copy of the notice, addressed in the same way, must also be sent to the public trustee.

The procedure applies both in respect of intestate persons and to testate persons before the issue of a grant of probate, until such time as a grant is filed in the principal registry. There may, in practice, be a delay after a grant is issued out of a district probate registry but there is one advantage: only one search is required to find out whether it still applies.

It is intended that the Public Trustee will keep a register of copy notices which are served on him, presumably by the name of deceased, and will make copies available. It is expected that regulations on this topic will soon be forthcoming.

17.4 Vesting of causes of action

Under s1(1) of the Law Reform (Miscellaneous Provisions) Act 1934 the general rule is that all causes of actions subsisting against or vested in the deceased on his death survive for the benefit of his estate and causes of actions subsisting against him survive against the estate. The deceased's personal representatives will sue or defend as appropriate.

The general rule in s1(1) is subject to some important limitations and exceptions. Under s1(2) damages recoverable in an action brought under s1(1) never includes exemplary damages, and damages will be calculated without reference to loss or gain to the estate as a result of the death of the deceased, except that a sum may be awarded for funeral expenses under s2(3). In some cases, especially tort, damage is an essential element of the cause of action, and the act or omission complained of might occur before death and the damage be suffered afterwards. In such circumstances there would be no cause of action subsisting and vested in the deceased at the time of death. This is dealt with by s1(4), which backdates the damage so as to produce a deemed cause of action vested in the deceased and subsisting at the time of death. See *Ronex Properties* v *John Laing* [1982] 3 All ER 961.

Contract

Generally, contracts entered into by the deceased before his death are enforceable by his personal representatives against the other party or enforceable against the personal representatives. See *Beswick* v *Beswick* [1968] AC 58. The usual remedies of damages, specific performance or injunction are available as appropriate. Thus, if the deceased entered into a contract with X, a builder, under which X was to build a house, the personal representatives could enforce the contract by claiming either damages, specific performance or injunction.

Contracts for personal services do not survive the deceased's death. In *Farrow* v *Wilson* (1869) LR 4 CP 744, Willes J said:

> 'Where, however, personal considerations are of the foundation of the contract, as in the cases of principal and agent, and master and servant, the death of either party puts an end to the relation and in respect of service after death the contract is dissolved unless there be a stipulation express or implied to the contrary.'

In *Farrow* v *Wilson*, it was held that a farm baliff's contract of employment terminated on his master's death by an implied condition. Similarly, in *Graves* v *Cohen* (1930) 46 TLR 121, a jockey's contract of employment was ended when his employer, a racehorse owner, died.

Tort

The general rule in s1(1) of the Law Reform (Miscellaneous Provisions) Act 1934 applies to causes of action in tort with the exception of defamation.

Claims under the Fatal Accidents Act 1976 should be distinguished from those under the Law Reform (Miscellaneous Provisions) Act. The former is concerned with claims by dependants of the deceased against a tortfeasor for the loss of financial support caused to them, while the latter is concerned with loss or damage to the estate. It should be noted that the right to damages for loss of expectation of life which existed under the 1934 Act was abolished under s1(1) of the Administration of Justice Act 1982.

17.5 Collection of assets

Under s25(a) of the Administration of Estates Act the personal representatives are under a duty to 'collect and get in the real and personal estate of the deceased'. Any assets on hire or loan from the deceased must be collected in within a reasonable time. Debts owed to the deceased will be an important matter here and they should be collected in whether they be arrears of rent or sums due on a promissory note.

So far as unsecured debts are concerned payment of these should be demanded by the personal representatives forthwith and, if necessary, legal proceedings commenced for their recovery. In *Powell* v *Evans* (1802) 5 Ves 839 it was said that 'debts due upon personal security are what executors without great reason ought not to permit to remain longer than is absolutely necessary'. Much will depend on the circumstances of each case as to how and when the debt should be collected but if payment could be made by the debtor the executor will be personally liable for failing to collect it in as soon as possible, as was illustrated in the following case.

In *Caney* v *Bond* (1843) 6 Beav 486 the testator had lent £500 to a friend on a promissory note. After the testator's death the executor did not call in the £500 loan because he believed the debtor was good for the money. £100 was paid voluntarily by the debtor and he would have paid the remainder if asked to do so. Two years after the testator's death the debtor died insolvent and the £400 was lost.

Held: the executor was personally liable for the loss; he had left the debt outstanding quite unnecessarily.

If a loan is secured there is no need for the personal representative to call it in, if he is satisfied that the security is adequate and an authorised investment under the deceased's will or the Trustee Investments Act 1961, unless it is needed for the payment of debts and liabilities. In cases where the security is inadequate the personal representative will have to choose whether to call in the loan, obtain more security or wait until a favourable time for realisation. So long as he acts honestly and with ordinary prudence in doing this, he will not be personally liable, as illustrated in *Re Chapman*.

In *Re Chapman* [1896] 2 Ch 763 (CA) the testator's estate comprised several mortgages on agricultural land. Because of an agricultural depression the value of the land decreased and at the testator's death was insufficient to cover the mortgages. The executors decided to retain the securities and wait for a more favourable time for realisation. The question arose whether they were liable for failing to call in the mortgages within 12 months of the testator's death.

Held: there was no rule of law that an honest executor is liable to make good loss sustained by retaining an authorised security in a falling market, provided he did so honestly and prudently.

Under s15 of the Trustee Act 1925 a personal representative has wide powers to compound liabilities or compromise claims. In particular the personal representatives may:

1. accept any property, real or personal, before the time at which it is transferrable or payable;
2. sever or apportion any blended trust funds or property;
3. pay or allow any debt or claim on any evidence that he or they think sufficient;
4. accept any composition or security real or personal, for any debt or for any property, real or personal, claimed;
5. allow any time of payment of any debt;
6. compromise, compound, abandon, submit to arbitration, or otherwise settle any debt, account, claim, or thing whatever relating to the testator's or intestate's estate.

These provisions give wide powers to settle claims for and against the estate. Thus, if a debt was owed to the estate the personal representatives could under s15 decide whether to release it because the debtor could not pay and was unlikely ever to pay, accept payment by instalments or an alternative to payment, or take security for the debt and leave it outstanding until a future time. The exercise of the discretion under s15 must be active rather than passive. Thus, if the personal representative has failed to collect in debt, he cannot rely on s15 if this has been due to negligence or carelessness rather than a mistaken but *bona fide* exercise by him of the powers in the section. See *Re Greenwood* (1911) 105 LT 509. The provisions in s15 also enable the personal representatives to settle disputes as to what the deceased did nor did not own by compromising claims as was done in the following case.

In *Re Earl of Strafford* [1980] Ch 28 (CA) the testator died in December 1951, two months after his wife in October 1951. The testator left his mansion house and all his chattels on a strict settlement while the testator's wife left all her estate to their two daughters equally. The testator and his wife owned many valuable works of art and chattels and after their deaths the two daughters, being the executors of the mother's will, reached decisions as to what works of art and chattels belonged to the estate of their mother and of their father, as no record had been kept of who owned what. The allocations they made were acted upon but subsequently evidence indicated that they had allocated chattels to the mother's estate which in fact belonged to the father's estate. The beneficiaries under the father's will, other than the two daughters, objected, and the power to compromise was eventually surrendered to the court because of the difficulties involved.

Held: the court would direct the trustees to implement the compromise made by the two daughters and, in deciding to compromise, the personal representatives were entitled to weigh the value of the assets recovered against the prospects of success in an action to recover them.

Under s26 of the Administration of Estates Act, the personal representatives are given statutory power to distrain for arrears of rent in the same manner as the deceased might have done if he had been living.

17.6 Inventory and account

Under s25(b) of the Administration of Estates Act the personal representative is under a duty to:

> 'When required to do so by the court, exhibit on oath in the court a full inventory of the estate and when so required render an account of the administration of the estate to the court.'

The inventory should contain a full and accurate description and valuation of the assets which have come into the hands of the personal representative. If a party interested in the estate wishes to know how it is being administered he can take out an originating summons for an order that the personal representative exhibit the inventory of the estate in court and the account also. Normally, such an order would be made during or shortly after administration. However, lapse of time is no bar to an application for an inventory and account, unless the period involved is extraordinarily long as in *Ritchie* v *Rees* (1822) 1 Add 144 where an application was refused 45 years after administration had been granted.

17.7 Realisation of the estate

In the course of the administration of the deceased's estate it will be necessary to find money to pay off debts and liabilities and to pay legacies. For these purposes the personal representatives must have a power to sell assets or mortgage them in order to meet these obligations. If the deceased died intestate as to either the whole or part of his estate s33 of the Administration of Estates Act 1925 will impose a statutory trust for sale on those assets as to which he died wholly intestate. This gives the personal representatives the right to sell those assets, if necessary. In some wills the deceased may have directed that his estate be held on an express trust for sale. However, where there is no trust for sale the personal representatives must rely on the powers of sale conferred upon them by the common law and by statute.

Powers of sale and mortgage

At common law and in equity, personal representatives have always had very wide powers of sale in respect of the deceased's personal estate for the purposes of administration. See *Nugent* v *Gifford* (1738) 1 Atk 463. The same wide powers of sale were conferred on personal representatives in respect of the deceased's real estate by s2(1) of the Administration of Estates Act 1925.

The personal representatives also have power at common law and in equity to raise money by way of mortgage or by pledging the deceased's personal estate. See *Mead* v *Orrery* (1745) 3 Atk 235; *Russell* v *Plaice* (1854) 18 Beav 21.

The provisions of s39 of the Administration of Estates Act 1925 also gives personal representatives wide powers to realise the deceased's estate; it states:

'In dealing with the real and personal estate of the deceased his personal representatives shall, for purposes of administration, or during a minority of any beneficiary or the subsistence of any life interest, or until the period of distribution arrives, have –
(i) the same powers and discretions, including the power to raise money by mortgage or charge (whether or not by deposit of documents), as a personal representative had before the commencement of the Act, with respect to the personal estate vested in him, and such power of raising money by mortgage may in the case of land be exercised by way of legal mortgage; and
(ii) all the powers, discretions and duties conferred on, imposed by law on trustees holding land upon an effectual trust for sale (including the power to overreach equitable interests and powers as if the same affected the proceeds of sale); and
(iii) all the powers conferred by statute on trusts for sale ...'

Section 39(1) confers on the personal representatives all the powers of trustees for sale of land. This means that s28(1) of the Law of Property Act 1925 also confers upon them all the powers of the tenant for life and the trustees of a Settled Land Act settlement. This gives the power to sell or exchange land or minerals separately. See *Re Chaplin and Staffordshire Potteries Waterworks Co Ltd Contract* [1922] 2 Ch 824, and the powers to lease or accept surrender of leases.

Protection of purchasers

Where the personal representatives have sold assets belonging to the deceased's estate, the purchasers thereof are given considerable protection by various provisions.

Propriety of disposition

1. The question here is whether a purchaser of property from a personal representative is bound to return his purchase to the deceased's estate if the disposition to him was not a proper one for the purposes of administration.
2. The position in respect of personalty (including leaseholds) has always been that a purchaser or mortgagee is entitled to presume that the sale of mortgage to him was for the purpose of administration. In *Re Venn & Furze's Contract* [1894] 2 Ch 101 the purchaser was entitled to rely on this presumption even though some 20 years had passed since the death of the deceased. However, before 1925 a purchaser could not rely on the presumption if he knew that the sale or mortgage was not made in the course of administration. See *Re Verrell's Contract* [1903] 1 Ch 65.
3. The rule in *Re Verrell's Contract* was altered by s36(8) of the Administration of Estates Act 1925 in respect of the sale and conveyance of a legal estate in land; this provides:

   'A conveyance of a legal estate by a personal representative to a purchaser shall not be invalidated by reason only that the purchaser may have notice that all the debts, liabilities, funeral and testamentary or administration expenses, duties and legacies of the deceased have been discharged or provided for.'

This provision applies to all conveyances of legal estates in land by personal representatives after 1925. However, it should be noted that the purchaser must be a purchaser for money or money's worth, who is acting in good faith in other respects. See *Re Spencer & Hauser's Contract* [1928] Ch 598 (obiter). The provisions in s36(8) only apply to legal estates in land; it would therefore appear that the rule in *Re Verrell's Contract* still applies to dispositions of personalty.

4. As stated above, a purchaser seeking to rely on s36(8) must have acted in good faith in making the purchase. This requirement applies to all purchases made from the deceased's personal representatives. Thus, if the personal representative sells the deceased's assets at a nominal price or at a fraudulent undervalue and the purchaser is in collusion with him, the sale will be set aside. See *Scott* v *Tyler* (1788) Dick 712. Thus, in *Rice* v *Gordon* (1848) 11 Beav 265, the court set aside the sale of a leasehold to the administrator's brother where it was at a fraudulent undervalue while in *Doe* v *Fallows* (1832) 2 Cr & J 481 a mortgage on the deceased's property to secure a personal debt of the administratrix was set aside as both parties to the mortgage knew it was a misapplication of the deceased's estate.

5. A purchaser has no duty to see that the money he pays over in the course of his purchase from the personal representative is correctly applied. This was the position at common law (see *Scott* v *Tyler* (1788) Dick 712) and is now provided for by s14(1) of the Trustee Act 1925 which states:

> 'The receipt in writing of a trustee for any money, securities or other personal property or effects payable, transferable or deliverable to him under any trust power shall be a sufficient discharge to the person paying transferring or delivering the same and shall effectively exonerate him from seeing to the application or being answerable for any loss or misapplication thereof.'

By s14(3) the deceased cannot exclude this provision by a direction in his will.

Previous assent

1. Before 1925 a purchaser did not get a good title from a personal representative if his purchase was made after the executor had assented to the property in favour of a devise or legatee. See *Attenborough* v *Solomon* [1913] AC 76 (below). In *Wise* v *Whitlawn* [1924] 1 Ch 460, Eve J said that the effect of the assent in such cases 'was to strip the executors of their titles'.

2. The position on previous assents has been altered by s36(6) of the Administration of Estates Act 1925 in cases concerning the purchase of a legal estate in land, it provides that:

> 'A statement in writing by a personal representative that he has not given or made an assent or conveyance in respect of a legal estate shall, in favour of a purchaser, but without prejudice to any previous disposition made in favour of another purchaser deriving title mediately or immediately under the personal representative, be sufficient evidence that an assent or conveyance has not yet been given or made in respect of the legal estate to which the statement relates, unless notice of a previous assent or

conveyance affecting that estate has been placed or annexed to the probate of administration.'

3. The position under s36(6) is best explained by an example. If X contracted to purchase Blackacre from Y who was selling in his capacity of personal representative, X could ask Y for a written statement that he, Y, had made no previous assents. Should X receive this, he can rely on it as 'sufficient evidence' that an assent has not been made or given provided there is no notice of an assent of conveyance placed on or annexed to the probate or letters of administration. The effect of s36(6) in such circumstances will be to:

> 'Operate to transfer or create the legal estate expressed to be conveyed in like manner as if no previous assent or conveyance had been made by the personal representative.'

4. It should be noted that s36(6) will only operate to vest the legal estate in a purchaser where the previous assent was made to the likes of a trustee or a beneficiary. It does not apply where there has been a previous assent in favour of another purchaser, hence the words in the section 'but without prejudice to any previous disposition made in favour of another purchaser'.

Revocation of grant

1. A grant to a personal representative may be revoked if it becomes clear that he should not have received it in the first place. It may be that a will is discovered where it was thought the deceased died intestate or a later will is discovered.
2. A purchaser from a personal representative whose grant is subsequently revoked will be protected by either s37 of the Administration of Estates Act 1925 or s204(1) of the Law of Property Act 1925. Section 37(1) provides that:

> 'All conveyances of any interest in real or personal estate made to a purchaser either before or after the commencement of this Act, by a person to whom probate or letters of administration have been granted are valid, notwithstanding any subsequent revocation or variation ... of the probate or administration.'

Purchaser for the purposes of s37 means a purchaser in good faith for valuable consideration, including marriage consideration. See s55(1)(xviii). Section 37 would, however, appear to be limited to cases where there has been a conveyance, that is, where a document has been used to transfer title. See s55(1)(ii). If the property is not conveyed, for example, where the purchaser bought chattels belonging to the deceased at an auction without a bill of sale, it would appear that reliance would have to be placed on the Court of Appeal decision in *Hewson* v *Shelley* [1914] 2 Ch 13; this case gives protection to all purchasers who take in good faith from personal representatives whose grant is subsequently revoked.

3. Section 204(1) of the LPA 1925 states:

> 'An order of the court under any statutory or other jurisdiction shall not, as against a purchaser, be invalidated on the ground of want of jurisdiction or of want of any concurrence, consent, notice or service, whether the purchaser has notice of any such want or not.'

Purchaser means a purchaser in good faith for valuable consideration. In such circumstances a purchaser can rely on the grant of probate under s204(1) as it is an order of the court. See *Re Bridgett & Hayes Contract* [1928] Ch 163.

Carrying on the deceased's business

The general rule is that the personal representatives have no authority to carry on the business of the deceased and they should normally cease trading and sell off the business assets. See *Kirkman* v *Booth* (1848) 11 Beav 273. The general rule is subject to two exceptions.

Realisation

The deceased's business may be carried on with a view to selling it in the course of administration as a going concern or in order to honour contracts entered into by the deceased in the business before his death. See *Dowse* v *Gorton* [1891] AC 190 and *Marshall* v *Broadhurst* (1831) 1 Cr & J 403. The authority for the former rests on the fact that it is expedient to continue the business until sale in order to obtain the best price therefor. The decision in *Marshall* v *Broadhurst* is to avoid involving the deceased's estate in liability for breach of contract and in that case it was said 'if a man makes half a wheelbarrow or half a pair of shoes and dies, the executors may complete them'. Realisation of the business should normally be effected within the executor's year but much will depend on the nature and circumstances of the business.

Direction in will

The deceased may give his personal representives express authority in his will to carry on his business or the will may by implication give them authority to do so. Thus, for example, if the deceased left his business on a trust for sale in his will giving the executors a power to postpone sale, they have by implication authority to carry on the business until such time as they decide to sell. In *Re Crowther* [1895] 2 Ch 56 the deceased left all his estate on trust for sale giving his trustees power to postpone sale 'for such period as to them shall seem expedient'. The trustees carried on two of the deceased's businesses for 22 years after his death in order to benefit his widow as life tenant. It was held by Chitty J that 'a power to postpone the sale of a business involves a power of continuing the business in the meantime'. If the will does contain a direction to carry on the business then the personal representatives are only entitled to use those assets in the business as the will directs. In the absence of such provision in the will they may only use the assets comprised in the business at the deceased's death in order to continue it. See *M'Neillie* v *Actan* (1853) 4 De GM & G 744.

If the personal representatives carry on the deceased's business without the necessary authority to do so they will be held personally liable for any losses which may occur.

They will also be personally liable for losses where they have employed more assets in the business than the will or the general law permitted them to do. In such cases the personal representatives should always seek the authority of the court under s57 of the Trustee Act 1925 or the consent of the beneficiaries (if all *sui juris*) before carrying on business where they have no authority.

If the business is carried on by the personal representatives either with a view to realisation or under a direction in the will they are personally liable for debts and liabilities which arise in the course of the business. In *Owen* v *Delamere* (1872) LR 15 Eq 134 it was said that a personal representative 'is liable for every shilling on every contract he enters into'. Creditors may obtain judgment against the personal representatives personally and it does not matter whether they entered the contract as personal representatives or in their own names. See *Labouchere* v *Tupper* (1857) 11 Moo PC 198.

However, despite this rule the personal representative may be entitled to an indemnity in two cases as follows.

Authority to carry on business

If the business was continued with a view to its proper realisation then the personal representative is entitled to an indemnity out of the estate for all liabilities incurred by him in doing so. This right of indemnity can be exercised against both creditors and beneficiaries. See *Dowse* v *Gorton* [1891] AC 190. The personal representative is also entitled to an indemnity if he carries on the business by the authority of the will. In such circumstances all the assets of the estate would normally be available for this purpose because the beneficiaries are bound by the directions in the will. But the creditors will only be bound if they have assented. See *Dowse* v *Gorton*. If the testator set aside particular assets to be used in the business, then the indemnity only extends to the value of those assets. See *Ex parte Garland* (1804) 10 Ves 110.

Creditor's assent

If a creditor assents to the carrying on of the deceased's business, regardless of whether the personal representative has authority to do so or not, the personal representative is entitled to be indemnified out of the assets of the deceased's estate in priority to that creditor. See *Dowse* v *Gorton*. But if a creditor has not assented to the business being carried on then he is entitled to be paid out of the deceased's assets in priority to the personal representative and no direction or authority in the will to carry on the business can affect this right. See *Re Oxley* [1914] 1 Ch 604. A creditor is only deemed to have assented to the continuance of the business if he has made a positive and definite indication to that end; mere acquiescence in the business continuing is not sufficient. See *Re Oxley*.

If the personal representative is entitled to an indemnity in respect of debts he incurs in carrying on the deceased's business the creditors who are owed those debts are entitled by subrogation to claim the right of indemnity. *Ex parte Garland* (above). Thus, if X as personal representative purchases £20,000 worth of goods from Y to carry on the deceased's retail business as directed by the will, then, in equity, Y is entitled to stand in the shoes of X and obtain payment out of the assets as against creditors and beneficiaries of the deceased. See *Ex parte Edmonds* (1862) 4 De GF & J 488. The right of subrogation is only available if the personal representative is entitled to an indemnity in the first place and it cannot give the creditor of the business any higher claim than the personal representative would have had for an indemnity. Thus, in *Re Evans* (1887) 34 Ch D 597, it was held that a seller of cement to an administratrix to carry on the deceased's business was only entitled to a claim for the price of the cement to the extent that the administratix could make such a claim and therefore could not insist on the actual proceeds of sale of the cement being used to meet his debt. The main purpose of subrogation here is to ensure that the creditor obtains payments if the personal representative becomes insolvent.

Leases held by the deceased

Where the deceased was the lessee of property, the leases devolve on his personal representatives by operation of law on his death. See *Parry* v *Harbert* (1539) 1 Dyer 456. They do not have to enter into possession for this to occur and covenants against assignments of the lease do not affect such devolution. See *Parry* v *Harbert*. The liability of the personal representative for the payment of rent and breaches of covenants in the lease depends very much on whether he has entered into possession or not. He will only be liable in his representative capacity if he has not entered into possession whereas if he has entered into possession he will be personally liable.

Representative liability

If the personal representative has not entered into possession, he is only liable to the extent of the deceased's assets for rent due and for other breaches of covenant. See *Wilson* v *Wigg* (1808) 10 East 315. Representative liability will last as long as the lease remains in the name of the personal representative. It therefore ends on the expiry of the lease but not necessarily by assigning it. If the deceased had taken the lease as an assignee, liability will end through assignment because there is only privity of estate between the head lessor and the assignor. See *Chancellor* v *Poole* (1781) 2 Doug KB 764. However, if the deceased was the original lessee, representative liability will endure for the whole term of the lease regardless of any assignment by the personal representative. See *Pitcher* v *Tovey* (1692) 4 Mod 71. This is because there was privity of contract between the head lessor and the deceased.

Where the deceased was the original lessee representative liability will not, as stated, end by assigning the lease. In these circumstances the personal representatives should consider either surrendering the lease to the landlord or, if this is not possible, relying on the provisions of s26 of the Trustee Act 1925. This lengthy section protects the personal representative in his representative capacity against future liability on the lease after conveyance to a purchaser, legatee, devisee or other person entitled to call for the same if he:

1. satisfies all liabilities under the lease which may have accrued and been claimed up to the date of the conveyance; and
2. where necessary sets apart a sufficient fund to answer any future claim that may be made in respect of any fixed and ascertained sum which the deceased agreed to lay out on the property, although the period for laying out the same may not have arrived.

In such circumstances he can then distribute the estate without making any futher provision for the lease and he will not be personally liable. However, s26(2) makes it clear that the right of the lessor to follow assets into the hands of those to whom they have been distributed is not affected.

Example
T died possessed of a leasehold property as original lessee with a term of 20 years still to run. At T's death there was £30,000 rent owed to the landlord and the lease provided for a payment of £10,000 by T on the expiry of the lease. X is willing to take an assignment of the lease from the executors. T's executors should obtain the protection of s26. To do this they must pay the outstanding rent and set aside a fund sufficient to meet the £10,000 on expiry. They will then be protected by s26 so that if X should default on payment of rent and become insolvent the lessor could not look to the executors for the unpaid rent.

Personal liability
A personal representative will become personally liable as an assignee of the deceased's leaseholds, if he enters into possession of the demised premises. Possession will be inferred not only from actual occupation or control of the premises but also from the acceptance of rent. See *Stratford-upon-Avon Corpn* v *Parker* [1914] 2 KB 562. Personal liability will exist for rent and any breaches of covenant so long as the lease remains vested in him, but this liability ends when he assigns the lease and he will not be personally liable for breaches committed thereafter. See *Whitehead* v *Palmer* [1908] 1 KB 151. Where he is personally liable the personal representative may, by proper pleading, limit his liability for rent to the annual value of the land. See *Rendall* v *Andreae* (1892) 61 LJ QB 630. This limit only applies to rent and not to other breaches of covenant. See *Rendall* v *Andreae*.

A personal representative who wishes to protect himself against personal liability cannot use s26 of the Trustee Act as this only gives protection against representative liability. See *Re Owers* [1941] Ch 389. Instead, he can either obtain an indemnity from the beneficiaries or set aside a fund for his protection. See *Re Owers*. The fund set aside will be distributable when all claims have been satisfied or been barred by lapse of time. See *Re Lewis* [1939] Ch 232.

17.8 Powers of personal representatives

Sole personal representative

A sole personal representative has the same powers in relation to the administration of the deceased's estate as two or more personal representatives. See s2(1) Administration of Estates Act 1925. Thus he may give a valid receipt for the proceeds of sale of land. See s18(1) SLA 1925 and s28(1) LPA 1925 and contrast the position of trustees.

Joint and several powers

Where there are two or more executors their powers in relation to pure personalty are joint and several. Therefore, one executor can sell or pledge or otherwise deal with personalty without the authority of his co-executors. See *Attenborough* v *Solomon* [1913] AC 76 (above). There is no clear authority that this rule applies to administrators also. See *Fountain Forestry* v *Edwards* [1975] 1 Ch 1.

Although these rules apply to all types of personalty it is probably inadvisable for one of several personal representatives to deal with stocks and shares alone as the company will probably insist on the share transfer certificate being executed by all.

One of several executors can enter into a contract for the sale of land, whether leasehold or freehold. However, it is necessary that all the executors join in the completion of the contract. See s2(2) of the Administration of Estates Act 1925 and *Fountain Forestry* v *Edwards*. This requirement only applies to executors who have proved the will and not to special personal representatives. See s2(2).

17.9 Trustees' powers of investment

Finally, it should be mentioned that trustees may not only have powers of investment under the terms of the trust as originally set out, but also may be granted an extension of these powers. A case that illustrates the possibilities, and highlights the importance of s57 of the Trustee Act 1925, was *Anker-Petersen* v *Anker-Petersen and Others* [1991] LSG 1 May.

The facts were that plaintiff was the tenant for life of a fund held on the trusts of his father's will. He applied for approval of the extension of the trustees' powers of investment, either under s57 of the Trustee Act 1925 or under s1 of the Variation of Trusts Act 1958. As the terms provided that moneys were to be invested as from time to time sanctioned by law for the investment of trust moneys they were governed by the Trustee Investments Act 1961. The proposed extensions would give power to the Trustee to (1) invest in assets of any kind as if they were beneficial owners; and (2) delegate to investment managers; and (3) hold investments through nominees; and (4) borrow money for any purpose. It should be noted that the proposals did not affect the beneficial interests under the will and that they were supported by all the defendants.

In the circumstances it was held that the proposals were approved. Judge Paul Baker QC said that it was preferable to bring an application for an extension of investment powers under s57 of the Trustee Act 1925 than under s1 of the Variation of Trusts Act 1958 where the beneficial interests under a will or settlement were unaffected. Doubt had occurred as to the applicability of s57 to the general enlargement of the power of investment because of the specific nature of the transactions which the section permitted. In his opinion there appeared to be no reason to adopt a restrictive view to the construction of the section: its manifest object was to enlarge the inherent administrative jurisdiction of the court – so far limited to cases of emergency – and there was a power 'either generally or in any particular instance' to effect a wide range of transactions, including investment. On the contrary, the terms of s1 of the 1958 Act, although general, did not appear to enlarge the scope of powers that the court could authorise.

In circumstances in which the beneficial interests were not affected s57 of the 1925 Act was more appropriate because: (1) the trustees were the natural persons to make the applications; (2) the consent of every adult beneficiary was not essential; and (3) the court was not required to give consent on behalf of every category of beneficiary separately but rather it would consider their interests in income and in capital collectively, which was more realistic. This meant that a less expensive application could be made without jeopardising the legitimate interests of the beneficiaries.

Another case that should be mentioned considered the duty of trustees in respect of investments. The focus for the case (*Harries and Others* v *The Church Commissioners for England and Another* (1991) 135 SJ(LB) 180) was the balance between financial criteria and non-financial criteria in the implementation of investment policy. The Church Commissioners, a charity, were the trustees of the Church of England funds and responsible for its investment policy. One of the Commissioners, the Bishop of Oxford, sought certain declarations in relation to this investment policy. He argued that in the implementation of their policy, undue importance was given by the Commissioners to financial considerations, and that they ought properly to bear in mind that the essential purpose for which they held the assets was the promotion of the Christian faith through the Church of England. Therefore, in his view, the Commissioners should take into account ethical considerations.

Held: Sir Donald Nicholls V–C held that where trustees held property as an investment to generate money, *prima facie*, the purpose of the trust would be best served by the trustees seeking to obtain the maximum financial return, whether by way of income or capital growth which was consistent with commercial prudence.

18

Payment of Debts and Liabilities

18.1 Duty to pay debts

18.2 Ascertaining debts payable

18.3 Funeral, testamentary and administration expenses

18.4 Insolvent estates

18.5 Solvent estates

18.6 Incidence of pecuniary legacies

18.1 Duty to pay debts

The debts owed by the deceased's estate should be paid by the personal representatives as quickly as is possible in the circumstances of the case. Much will depend on circumstances. The nature of this duty was explained by Uthwatt J in *Re Tankard* [1942] Ch 69:

> 'Apart from any provisions contained in the will of a testator which expressly or impliedly deal with the payment of debts, it is the duty of executors as a matter of due administration of the estate to pay the debts of their testator with due diligence having regard to the assets in their hands which are properly applicable for that purpose, and, in determining whether due diligence has been shown, regard must be had to all the circumstances of the case.
>
> It was contended by the defendants that this was a duty which was not owed to beneficiaries. In my opinion this contention is not correct. The duty is owed, not only to creditors, but also to beneficiaries, for the ultimate object of administration of an estate is to place the beneficiaries in possession of their interest, and that object cannot be fully achieved unless all debts are satisfied.'

The duty to pay debts 'with due diligence' applies both to debts which do not carry interest and interest-bearing debts. Cases where the duty may be considered as breached are (1) where the estate owes a debt bearing interest at 11 per cent whereas the assets in the estate applicable in the payment of this debt are only bearing interest at the rate of 7 per cent; (2) where a debt is not paid and the creditor brings proceedings for the recovery thereof, imposing legal costs on the estate in consequence. However, the question of whether there has been a loss to the estate is independent of the question of whether there has been a breach of the duty. Normally the court will make a declaration as to whether there has been a breach and, in cases where it has declared there is a breach, order an inquiry as to the extent of loss to the estate. See *Re Stevens* [1898] 1 Ch 162.

Uthwatt J also considered the time within which the personal representatives ought to pay the debts and said:

> 'With respect to the period within which debts should be paid, there is, in my opinion, no rule of law that it is the duty of executors to pay such debts within a year of the testator's death. The duty is to pay with due diligence. Due diligence may, indeed, require that payment should be made before the expiration of the year, and circumstances affecting the estate and the assets comprised in it may justify non-payment outside the year, but, if debts are not paid within the year, the onus is on the executors to justify the delay.'

Debts that may be regarded as requiring payment within the year are capital taxes which could bear a high rate of interest and penalties if not paid promptly. On the other hand, if a debt is interest free or bearing an unusually low rate of interest it may be regarded as improper if the executors sold off property from the deceased's estate to meet these immediately after death when it was clear cash would be available for this purpose within a few months of death.

The duty to pay debts may be modified by the will of the testator. However, this can only be done as against the beneficiaries and not against the creditors, because, as Uthwatt J explained:

> 'As against the creditors the provisions of the testator's will which relate to the realisation of his assets, or which otherwise bear upon the payment of debts, are irrelevant. As against the beneficiaries, the position is different. Beneficiaries take their interest under the will only upon the terms of the will. As respects them, full effect has to be given to any provisions which either in express terms or by implication modify the executors' duty of paying debts with due diligence.'

Having stated these principles in *Re Tankard* Uthwatt J concluded on the facts of the case that there had been no breach of the duty.

In *Re Tankard* [1942] Ch 69 T appointed the Midland Bank Trust Co as his executor and trustee and directed that his estate be held on trust for sale to pay his debts, funeral and testamentary expenses and then be divided into 14 shares for members of his family. At his death the deceased owed £9,147 to the bank and this debt carried interest at 1 per cent over the bank rate. The executor failed to sell sufficient assets to pay off this debt within the executor's year, and some shares which would have been properly applicable for the purpose fell in value in that time, so that more than necessary had to be sold to meet the debt.

Held: although loss had resulted to the estate, on the facts, this was not relevant as to whether there was a breach of duty to pay debts with due diligence because this duty arose out of the duty to administer the estate and not a duty to prevent avoidable loss. As the shares were of a speculative nature, and as the executor had properly exercised the express power to retain these shares given by the will because of poor market conditions caused by the war, the duty to pay debts had not been breached.

18.2 Ascertaining debts payable

In the administration of the majority of estates there will be little difficulty in ascertaining the creditors of the deceased as they will put forward their claims as soon as they have notice of the deceased's death. However, if the deceased had complex financial arrangements, all his creditors may not be known or traceable. This places the personal representatives in difficulty because they are personally liable for unpaid debts to the extent of assets which would have been properly applicable for that purpose, even if they had no notice of the debts. See *Knatchbull* v *Fearnhead* (1837) 3 My & Cr 122. Although they could rely on defences such as s61 of the Trustee Act 1925, that is, that they had acted honestly and reasonably, there is no guarantee that the court would allow the defence. The appropriate course in such a case is to advertise for creditors in accordance with the provisions of s27(1) Trustee Act 1925.

Section 27(1) provides:

'With a view to the conveyance to or distribution among the persons entitled to any real or personal property, the trustees of a settlement or of a disposition on trust for sale or personal representatives may give notice by advertisement in the Gazette, and in a newspaper circulating in the district in which the land is situated, and such other like notices, including notices elsewhere than in England and Wales as would, in any special case, have been directed by a court of competent jurisdiction in an action for administration, of their intention to make such conveyance or distribution as aforesaid, and requiring any person interested to send to the trustees or personal representatives within the time, not being less than two months, fixed in the notice or where more than one notice is given, in the last of the notices, particulars of his claim in respect of the property or any part thereof to which the notice relates.'

The requirements of s27(1) can be summarised thus:

1. advertisement in the Gazette;
2. if land is involved, an advertisement in a newspaper circulating in the district where the land is situated;
3. such other advertisements or notices as the court might direct;
4. at least two months from the date of the notice must be allowed for bringing claims.

In relation to (3), it is often advisable for the personal representatives to ask the court for directions as to what other advertisements should be made, especially if the estate is or is likely to be insolvent.

Under s27(2) it is provided that the personal representatives may:

'At the expiration of the time fixed by the notice ... convey or distribute the property or any part thereof to which the notice relates, to or among the persons entitled thereto having regard only to the claims, whether formal or not',

of which they then had notice.

It will be necessary to investigate the claims of the person who responded to the s27 advertisement. It is not uncommon to find bogus claims or claims which are doubtful. The personal representatives normally ask claimants to produce all deeds and documents necessary to substantiate their claims. If there is difficulty in deciding the validity of claims the personal representatives may ask the court to adjudicate on these.

The effect of s27 is that the personal representatives will not be liable to any person of whose claim they did not have notice at the time of the conveyance or distribution. Therefore if a creditor makes a claim after distribution he cannot sue the personal representatives for the loss. However, s27 only gives protection against claims after distribution, so that if a claim is made after the time for bringing in such claims has passed but before distribution, it should be adjudicated and, if valid, paid. The section does not give any protection against claims of which the personal representatives had notice even if the claimant did not respond to the advertisement. See *Re Land Credit Company of Ireland* (1872) 21 WR 1351.

A creditor who makes a claim after distribution has taken place in accordance with s27 is not without remedies. Under s27(2) it is provided that nothing in the section:

'... prejudices the right of any person to follow the property, or any property representing the same, into the hands of any person, other than a purchaser, who may have received it'.

Thus, the remedies of a refund from a person who has been wrongly paid or over-paid from the deceased's assets and of tracing and recovering property are available to the creditor. See *Re Diplock* [1948] Ch 465.

If there is any difficulty in advertising for claims under s27 then the personal representatives may apply to the court for leave to distribute on the footing that all the deceased's debts and liabilities have been ascertained. This may occur where there are lists of sums of money wich may be due but for which no claims have been received. In *Re Gess* [1942] Ch 37 the court allowed distribution on the footing that all the deceased's debts and liabilities had been ascertained where it was impossible to make advertisements under s27 because of wartime conditions.

18.3 Funeral, testamentary and administration expenses

Funeral expenses

The deceased's corpse must be disposed of after death. The personal representatives are entitled to custody and possession of it until it is buried or cremated and therefore they have the primary obligation to see that this is carried out. See *Rees* v *Hughes* [1946] KB 517. It may be that the deceased left directions that his body or part of it be used for medical education or research; the personal representatives are not bound to follow such directions and may not authorise the body to be used for these purposes. See s1(1) of the Human Tissue Act 1961. If no such directions were left the personal representatives can permit the deceased's body to be used for these purposes provided they have no reason to believe that he would have objected to the same. See s1(2) of the Human Tissue Act 1961.

As the personal representative has the primary obligation of disposing of the corpse he should order the funeral, but it may be that this does not always happen; the deceased's spouse or other relatives may order the funeral. The question arises as to who is liable to pay the undertaker for his services. The position is as follows.

1. Personal representative orders funeral: he is liable in contract to the undertaker for the price fixed by the contract or if no price is fixed for a reasonable price. See *Brice* v *Wilson* (1834) 8 Ad & E 349.
2. Someone other than personal representative orders funeral: the person ordering the funeral is liable in contract for the price if he was given credit by the undertaker. See *Brice* v *Wilson*.
3. If the personal representative did not order the funeral and no one else is liable for the price, then the personal representative is liable for the price thereof in quasi-contract. See *Rees* v *Hughes* [1946] KB 517.

The personal representative is entitled to an indemnity from the deceased's estate for the funeral expenses, and if any other person orders the funeral they may claim an indemnity from the deceased's estate through the personal representative. See *Green* v *Salmon* (1838) 8 Ad & E 348. The right to an indemnity only applies in so far as the funeral expenses are reasonable, reasonable being construed with reference to the deceased's circumstances and his station in life. See *Corner* v *Shaw* (1838) 3 M & W 350; *Goldstein* v *Salvation Army Assurance Society* [1917] 2 KB 291. Thus, the personal representatives must take into account the deceased's religious beliefs, the financial position of his estate and his position before death.

The rights and duties of the personal representatives in respect of funeral expenses are evident in the decision in *Re Grandison* (1989) The Times 10 July. The testator had come to England from Jamaica in 1960 and lived in England until his death in 1989. His executor maintained that the testator had said that he wished to be buried in Jamaica and this evidence was supported by other members of the family. However, his only daughter, who was entitled to a half share in his estate and who had been on close terms with her father, objected and sought an interlocutory injunction to restrain the executor from removing the body from the jurisdiction.

Held: the application would be dismissed. Vinelott J said that the testator, despite his long residence in this country, should want to be buried in Jamaica did not cause him any surprise. It was natural that he should discuss it with his executor – for it was the latter who would have to make the necessary arrangements. In his Lordship's judgment, on the facts of this case, the daughter did not come anywhere near establishing a ground for interference with the executor's discretion.

Where there is a dispute regarding burial the judge in *Ferris* v *Whitmore* [1999] 1 FLR 767 saw the situation as being akin to that of trustees bringing a dispute to the court for directions and not as a difficulty in the administration of the estate. In this case a dispute arose between divorced parents as to the final resting-place of the ashes of their deceased minor child.

Testamentary and administration expenses

There is no settled definition of 'testamentary' or 'administration' expenses and the court appears to be reluctant to draw a distinction between them. In *Re Taylor's Estate* [1969] 2 Ch 245 the will referred to 'testamentary expenses' and the question arose as to whether the costs of the action in court could be deducted from the estate as it might be more properly regarded as an administration expense. Chancellor Salt QC appears to have followed the pre-1926 view that no distinction should be drawn between these expenses and concluded 'that this court would be refining over much if it were to segregate testamentary expenses and administration expenses one from the other'.

The following items appear to be accepted as falling within the ambit of 'testamentary and administration expenses'.

1. Cost of obtaining probate or letters of administration whether in common form or in solemn form. See *Re Prince* [1898] 2 Ch 225.
2. Cost of legal advice obtained from solicitors or counsel in the course of administration of the estate. See *Sharp* v *Lush* (1879) 10 Ch D 468.
3. Cost of advertisements etc for the purpose of ascertaining the deceased's debts.
4. Cost of collecting and preserving the estate with the exception of the subject matter of specific bequests and devices. See *Re Sebba* [1959] Ch 166; *Re Rooke* [1933] Ch 970.
5. Costs of an administration action or other action to resolve any difficulty related to the administration of the estate. See *Sharp* v *Lush*.

18.4 Insolvent estates

Introduction

The deceased's estate will be considered to be insolvent where the assets are insufficient to meet all debts and liabilities including funeral, testamentary and administration expenses. In such circumstances the dispositions made by the will, if any, and the intestacy rules for distribution to next of kin will be irrelevant. The personal representatives will only be concerned with the payment of the deceased's creditors.

Whether the deceased's estate is or is not insolvent is a question of fact in each case. See *Re Pink* [1927] 1 Ch 237. An inquiry may be conducted by the court to determine this fact. See *George Lee & Sons* v *Olink* [1972] 1 WLR 214.

Creditors of the deceased will normally have to prove their debts to the personal representatives and for this purpose they should produce all deeds and documents necessary to substantiate their claims. If there is no written evidence of the debt it is permissible for the court to rely upon satisfactory oral evidence. The personal representatives should advertise for creditors under s27 of the Trustee Act 1925 where there is doubt as to whether all of them have been ascertained. Even if there is little doubt in this respect a s27 advertisement is still a prudent step.

The debts and liabilities will be proveable at their value against the deceased's estate and if there is any uncertainty as to the value of any of these then an estimate of value should be made. If it is not possible for an estimate to be agreed the court has power to fix a value. See *Re Bridges* (1881) 17 Ch D 342. All debts and liabilities, whether present or future, are proveable unless they are statute barred.

Administration of an insolvent estate can be carried out by one of three methods. Whichever method is chosen will depend largely on the state of the deceased's affairs at death. The methods are: (1) By the personal representative out of court. This will be used where the deceased's insolvency does not present any problems of fact or law. (2) By the court in an administration action. This is advisable if there are or are likely to be any difficulties in the administration of the estate because the personal representatives can protect themselves by acting on the orders of the court. (3) In bankruptcy, where an order in bankruptcy has been made against the deceased's estate under r5 of the Administration of Insolvent Estates of Deceased Persons Order 1986 (SI 1986/1999).

Administration of insolvent estates – practical procedures. In view of the recent increase in insolvencies and bankruptcies, it is important to understand the practical approach to the administration of an insolvent estate. As noted in (1) above, the after-death test of insolvency is similar to that *inter vivos*: will the estate, once realised, be sufficient to meet in full the debts and liabilities to which it is subject?

There are two courses available, depending upon whether or not there are bankruptcy proceedings.

No bankruptcy proceedings

Where the estate is found to be insolvent after death it is administered not for the beneficiaries under the will or intestacy but for the creditors until, as far as possible, if at all, the debts are paid.

Where the deceased left a will the executors take a grant and administer the estate. If the executors renounce or there is an intestacy a creditor may apply for letters of administration.

Just as in the case of bankruptcy during lifetime, an application can be made for an administration order in respect of the estate but an insolvency practitioner does not have to be appointed if there is no bankruptcy order made.

Bankruptcy proceedings

A petition is presented by either the personal representatives or the supervisor of any voluntary arrangement by the deceased before his death or any creditor. Generally there is a £750 minimum debt requirement in the latter case. The petition is for an insolvency administration order. Thereafter *inter vivos* bankruptcy procedures apply *mutatis mutandis*.

Order of payment of creditors

The administration of an insolvent estate is governed by the Insolvency Act of 1986 and the Administration of Insolvent Estates of Deceased Persons Order 1986 (SI 1986/1999). Under the combination of these two provisions the debts of an insolvent estate are to be paid in the following order of priority.

Under Schedule 6 of the Insolvency Act is set out the preferred debts which must be paid off first in priority to other debts owed by the insolvent estate. However, r2 of the 1986 Order lays down the additional rule that reasonable funeral testamentary and administration expenses shall have priority even over the preferred Schedule 6 debts of the insolvent estate.

Secured creditors

A secured creditor is one who has lent money or other property to the deceased by way of mortgage, charge or lien, the purpose of the security being to protect him in the event of insolvency. Thus, for example, if the deceased was loaned £20,000 by a building society before his death, in order to purchase a house worth £25,000, the building society could resort to the security of the mortgage, in the event of the deceased being insolvent, and sell the house to recover the money due to it. If this in fact occurs then the order of priority will not affect the secured creditor and, it seems, this will extend to funeral testamentary and administration expenses, which cannot be deducted from the value of the mortgaged property before the secured creditor has resorted thereto.

The most obvious course for the secured creditor is to realise his security and this will normally be the course taken where the security is sufficient to meet his debt. However, there are three other courses open to a secured creditor which are normally considered when the security is not sufficient to meet the debt.

1. To realise the security and prove for the balance of the debt. This will be the most expedient course if the security is inadequate.
2. To set a value on the security and prove for the balance of the debt. Valuation as opposed to sale of the security is appropriate if the security is only saleable with high expense of sale or where the secured creditor has decided to take over the security to keep it for himself.
3. To surrender the security and prove for the whole debt. This course of action is only advisable if the security has turned out to be worthless or where it would be a liability to the creditor. If a security has any value the creditor should normally realise it.

If a secured creditor has to prove for the balance of his debt after realising his security or for the whole of it because the security is worthless, then he will have to join in the order of payment of unsecured creditors. To that extent the payment of funeral testamentary and administration expenses will take priority over him.

Funeral, testamentary and administration expenses
These will take priority over all debts and liabilites owed to unsecured creditors but, as stated above, they do not take priority over secured debts. As between the funeral, testamentary and administration expenses themselves, it appears that the funeral expenses are entitled to priority. See *Re Walter* [1929] 1 Ch 647.

Specially preferred debts
Where the deceased held money or property belonging to a friendly society in the capacity of officer of the society or held money or property belonging to a trustee savings bank in the capacity of an officer or employee of the same, these will be regarded as specially preferred debts and take priority over all other debts, save funeral, testamentary and administration expenses, and secured debts. See *Re Eilbeck* [1910] 1 KB 136.

Preferred debts
These rank next in order and are:

Category 1: debts due to the Inland Revenue

1. Sums due at the relevant date from the debtor on account of deductions of income tax from emoluments paid during the period of 12 months next before that date.
    The deductions here referred to are those which the debtor was liable to make under s204 of the Income and Corporation Taxes Act 1970 (pay as you earn), less the amount of the repayments of income tax which the debtor was liable to make during that period.
2. Sums due at the relevant date from the debtor in respect of such deductions as are required to be made by the debtor for that period under s69 of the Finance (No 2) Act 1975 (sub-contractors in the construction industry).

Category 2: debts due to Customs and Excise

3. Any value added tax which is referable to the period of six months next before the relevant date (which period is referred to below as 'the six-month period'). For the purposes of this paragraph:
    a)   where the whole of the prescribed accounting period to which any value added tax is attributable falls within the six-month period, the whole amount of that tax is referable to that period; and
    b)   in any other case the amount of value added tax which is referable to the six-month period is the proportion of the tax which is equal to such proportion (if any) of the accounting reference period in question as falls within the six-month period;

and in sub-paragraph (a) 'prescribed' means prescribed by regulations under the Value Added Tax Act 1983.

4. The amount of any car tax which is due at the relevant date from the debtor and which became due within a period of 12 months next before that date.

5. Any amount which is due:
   a)   by way of general betting duty or bingo duty; or
   b)   under s12(1) of the Betting and Gaming Duties Act 1981 (general betting duty and pool betting duty recoverable from agent collecting stakes); or
   c)   under s14 of, or Schedule 2 to, that Act (gaming licence duty);
   from the debtor at the relevant date and which became due within the period of 12 months next before that date.

Category 3: Social Security contributions

6. All sums which on the relevant date are due from the debtor on account of Class 1 or Class 2 contributions under the Social Security Act 1975 or the Social Security (Northern Ireland) Act 1975 and which became due from the debtor in the 12 months next before the relevant date.

7. All sums which on the relevant date have been assessed on and are due from the debtor on account of Class 4 contributions under either of those Acts of 1975, being sums which:
   a)   are due to the Commissioners of Inland Revenue (rather than to the Secretary of State of a Northern Ireland department); and
   b)   are assessed on the debtor up to 5 April next before the relevant date;
   but not exceeding, in the whole, any one year's assessment.

Category 4: contributions to occupational pension schemes, etc

8. Any sum which is owed by the debtor and is a sum to which Schedule 3 to the Social Security Pensions Act 1975 applies (contributions to occupational pension schemes and state schemes premiums).

Category 5: remuneration, etc, of employees

9. So much of any amount which:
   a)   is owed by the debtor to a person who is or has been an employee of the debtor; and
   b)   is payable by way of remuneration in respect of the whole or any part of the period of 4 months next before the relevant date;
   as does not exceed so much as may be prescribed by order made by the Secretary of State. (At present £800.00).

10. An amount owed by way of accrued holiday remuneration, in respect of any period of employment before the relevant date, to a person whose employment by the debtor has been terminated, whether before, on or after that date.

11. So much of any sum owed in respect of money advanced for the purpose as has

been applied for the payment of a debt which, if it had not been paid, would have been a debt falling within paragraph 9 or 10.

12. So much of any amount which:
   a) is ordered (whether before or after the relevant date) to be paid by the debtor under the Reserve Forces (Safeguard of Employment) Act 1985; and
   b) is so ordered in respect of a default made by the debtor before that date in the discharge of his obligations under that Act;

   as does not exceed such amount as may be prescribed by order made by the Secretary of State.

All categories of preferred debts rank equally as between themselves, so that, if the assets are not sufficient to meet them in full, they will abate proportionately. See s328(2) Insolvency Act 1986.

Ordinary debts

This category includes all debts which are not within the categories mentioned above, that is, specially preferred or preferred, or the category below, that is, deferred debts. In practice the majority of debts owed by the deceased will fall within this category such as money he owed to traders and businessmen. The category also includes taxes, excise duties, VAT, National Insurance and wages which are not classified as preferred debts. Ordinary debts rank equally between themselves and if there are insufficient assets to meet them they will all abate proportionately. See s328(2) Insolvency Act 1986.

Deferred debts

These debts will only be paid if the claims of creditors falling within the categories set out above have been satisfied. They are listed below.

1. Loans to a spouse. Where one spouse lends money to another regardless of the purpose of the loan, the loan will rank as a deferred debt if the spouse to whom it was lent dies insolvent. See s329 of the Insolvency Act 1986. However, a loan by one spouse to another which is unconnected with business or trade will not rank as a deferred debt; unless secured, it will probably rank as an ordinary debt. Thus, in *Re Clark* [1898] 2 QB 330, a loan by a wife to her husband to meet household expenses was held to be an ordinary debt.

2. Money owed to the seller of the goodwill of the business who is taking a share of the profits. If X sold the stock in trade and goodwill of his hardware shop to the deceased under an agreement by which he was to receive a share of the profits of the business for a specified time in the future, the claim for such profits due to X would rank as a deferred debt. See s3 of the Partnership Act 1890.

3. Loan to the deceased with interest rate thereon varying with the deceased's business profits or where the lender is entitled to a share of the profits. See s3 of the Partnership Act 1890 and *Re Young* [1896] 2 QB 484.

Importance of order

The order of priority for payment of debts in an insolvent estatee is fixed by law and the deceased cannot vary it by directions in his will. See *Re Rothermere* [1943] 1 All ER 307. The personal representatives must follow the order strictly and should they fail to do so and, pay say, an ordinary creditor before a preferred creditor, leaving insufficient assets to pay the latter, either in full or at all, they will be personally liable to the preferred creditor for his loss. See *Britton* v *Batthurst* (1683) 3 Lev 113. This rule as to personal liability does not apply if advertisements have been made for creditors under either s27 of the Trustee Act or as directed by the court, or where the personal representatives had no notice of the preferred debt at the time of payment and had acted in good faith. See *Harman* v *Harman* (1686) 2 Shaw 492.

A personal representative who has doubts as to the solvency of the deceased's estate should normally administer it as if it were bankrupt. If it subsequently appears that it is, in fact, solvent then marshalling of the assets may be carried out so as to give effect to any benefits given by the will.

Section 10(2) of the Administration of Estates Act 1971 gives some protection to a personal representative who pays debts of the deceased without regard to the order of priority under the insolvency rules because at the time of payment he had no reason to believe that the deceased's estate was insolvent. Under this provision he will not be liable to account to creditors in the same class as the creditor(s) he paid, but it appears he would be personally liable to account to creditors in a superior class.

18.5 Solvent estates

An estate is solvent where there are sufficient assets to meet all the debts and liabilities of the deceased. In such circumstances all the debts will have to be paid and the only issue is how payment of these should affect the various dispositions in his will.

Under s34(3) and Part II of the First Schedule of the Administration of Estates Act 1925 a statutory order is laid down for the payment of the debts and liabilities. This order regulates the payment of the debts and liabilities according to the various kinds of dispositions which may occur on death, and places higher in the order those dispositions which a testator might be presumed to have wanted preserved until last in the payment of the debts and liabilities.

The statutory order

Section 34(3) of the Administration of Estates Act 1925 provides:

> 'Where the estate of a deceased person is solvent his real and personal estate shall, subject to rules of court and the provisions hereinafter contained as to charges on the property of the deceased, and to the provisions, if any, contained in his will, be applicable towards the discharge of the funeral, testamentary and administration expenses, debts and liabilities payable thereout in the order mentioned in Part II of the First Schedule to this Act.'

Under Part II of the First Schedule the prescribed order is:

1 'Property of the deceased undisposed of by will, subject to the retention thereout of a fund sufficient to meet any pecuniary legacies.'

Property 'undisposed of by will' includes not only property of which the deceased made no attempt to dispose by his will, for example, where there is no residuary gift in the will, but also property which the will has mentioned but not disposed of effectively. See *Re Lamb* [1929] 1 Ch 723. Thus, if T left his residuary estate to A, B and C in equal shares absolutely and A predeceased T causing his share to lapse, that share would be treated as property undisposed of under *Re Lamb*. A pecuniary legacy fund must also be retained out of the undisposed of property before it is resorted to for the payment of debts. This is dealt with below.

2 'Property of the deceased not specifically devised or bequeathed but included (either by a specific or general description) in a residuary gift, subject to the retention out of such property of a fund sufficient to meet any pecuniary legacies, so far as not provided for as aforesaid.'

This means that a residuary gift is second in the order to meet debts and liabilities. For these purposes a residuary gift will include a gift of 'all my real estate', even though all devises were regarded from their nature as specific before 1925. See *Re Wilson* [1967] Ch 53. Further, it was held in the same case that it was irrelevant whether a gift of 'all my real estate' was or was not preceded by other devises because as Pennycuick J said: 'in ordinary language today's lawyers would, I think, not inaptly describe such a gift as a residuary devise. They would certainly not describe it as a specific devise.'

3 'Property of the deceased specifically appropriated or devised or bequeathed (either by a specific or general description) for the payment of debts.'

The category would appear to include gifts such as 'I direct my executors to set aside £10,000 from my estate to pay all my debts.' One would have thought that a testator making such a direction in his will would have wanted the £10,000 to be used to pay his debts and expenses before any property in paragraphs (1) and (2) above. However, if this were so, then there would be no property to fall within paragraph (3). See *Re Kempthorne* [1930] 1 Ch 268.

4 'Property of the deceased charged with or devised or bequeathed (either by a specific or general description) subject to a charge for the payment of debts.'

This category appears to include gifts such as: 'I leave my house, Whiteacre, to X subject to the payment of all my debts and liabilities thereout.' Again, one would have thought that such a direction would have been intended to show that the debts and liabilities should fall on the property charged before any property in paragraphs (1) and (2) above, but for the reasons given above this is not so.

5 'The fund, if any, retained to meet the pecuniary legacies.'

Under paragraphs (1) and (2) the payment of the debts and liabilities from the undisposed of property and the residuary estate is subject to the retention of a pecuniary legacies fund. This means that the personal representatives must check through the will and find out how much is needed for this purpose. Under s55(1)(ix) of the Administration of Estates Act 1925 pecuniary legacy is defined as including 'an annuity, a general legacy, a demonstrative legacy so far as it is not discharged out of the designated property, and any other general direction by a testator for the payment of money'. Thus, if a testator left £10,000 to X in his will, among other gifts, the £10,000 needed to satisfy this legacy would have to be retained from the assets falling within paragraphs (1) and (2) and placed under paragraph (5) before payment of debts and liabilities commenced.

6   'Property specifically devised or bequeathed, rateably according to value.'

It should be noted that if the testator makes a specific devise or bequest of property which is 'charged' with the payment of debts, then this falls within paragraph (4) and not paragraph (6). The charge may be express, as in the example given in paragraph (4) above, or implied. Where specific gifts fall within paragraph (6) they will be liable 'rateably according to the value'. The value of the assets concerned is the probate value and not the value at which they are sold in order to meet unpaid debts. See *Re John* [1933] Ch 370. Further, if any specific devise or bequest is subject to a charge, the value of the property for the purposes of paragraph (6) is the probate value minus the charge. See *Re John*. Thus, if T left Blackacre to X, worth £50,000 but subject to a mortgage of £20,000 and Whiteacre to Y, worth £20,000 and free from mortgages or charges, and these were needed to pay debts of £10,000 the position would be as follows: the value of Blackacre is £30,000 for the purpose of paying the debts. Thus, the debt would be borne as to three-fifths from Blackacre, that is, £6,000 and as to two-fifths from Whiteacre, that is, £4,000.

7   'Property appointed by will under a general power, including the statutory power to dispose of entailed interests, rateably according to value.'

If a testator exercises a general power of appointment by will then under s32(1) of the Administration of Estates Act 1925 the property appointed will be available to meet debts and liabilities and will fall under paragraph (7). Under s1(1) of the Administration of Estates Act 1925 land appointed by will devolves on the personal representatives of the deceased but by an anomaly pure personalty does not. See *O'Grady* v *Wilmot* [1916] 2 AC 231. However, personalty can nevertheless be resorted to by the personal representatives to meet the debts and liabilities. See *O'Grady* v *Wilmot*. If the power is not exercised then the property will pass to the person in default, if any, or alternatively, it may devolve on the personal representatives if the testator had shown an intention to take the property out of the power and make it his own. See *Shaw* v *Marten* [1902] 1 Ch 314. If the power is not exercised then the property will form part of the testator's estate and, unless specifically disposed of, will form part of the residue or property undisposed of under either paragraphs (1) or (2) for the purpose of paying debts.

The statutory power to dispose of entails referred to in paragraph (7) arises under s176 of the Law of Property Act 1925. By this provision the testator can, if he was a tenant in tail, bar the entail by his will and dispose of the property by his will. In order to do this he must: (1) hold the entail in possession; (2) have executed his will after 1925; and (3) refer to the property concerned either specifically or generally, or to the instrument under which the property was acquired.

8. 'Property not mentioned in the Statutory Order.'

Certain assets do not fall within the Statutory Order even though they have been disposed of by the testator either in his will or otherwise. There are three main categories and as regards the order of priority between these *inter se* no settled authority exists on the point.

First, property appointed by deed under a general power: a creditor can in equity resort to property appointed by deed under a general power in order to meet his debt. See *Re Phillips* [1931] 1 Ch 347. In order that such property can be made available two conditions must be satisfied: (1) the appointment was made in favour of a volunteer; (2) the appointment took effect on the deceased's death and not immediately.

Second, options to purchase: a testator may give to a beneficiary an option to purchase certain property under his will at a price less than the market value. For example, T may by his will give X the option to purchase Blackacre at the price of £30,000 when it is worth £60,000 on the market. In such circumstances neither the option nor the difference between the option price and the market value is a specific gift under the statutory order and the property subject to the option comes last for the payment of debts. In *Re Eve* [1956] Ch 479 (Ch D) by his will a testator granted a beneficiary an option to acquire 1,000 ordinary shares in a company at a price of £1 per share, which was much less than the market value. The beneficiary gave notice of his intention to exercise the option. It was clear after the testator's death that the residuary estate was insufficient to meet the debts and liabilities in full, and the question arose whether the option amounted to a specific bequest, thus making it liable rateably with other specific gifts for the remainder to the debts.

Held: an option to purchase cannot be a specific bequest of shares and therefore the benefit conferred by the option, that is, the difference between the option price and the market value, did not rank with the other specific gifts to meet the debts and liabilities. It came last and did not fall anywhere within the statutory order.

In *Re Eve* Roxburgh J also explained how an option would be resorted to in order to meet the debts and liabilities. If the property which is the subject of the option is required for the payment of debts, the option over the property cannot be exercised. Thus, if X was given an option to purchase Blackacre, worth £60,000, for the sum of £30,000, his option would be destroyed if £50,000 of the value of Blackacre was needed to meet the debts and liabilities. However, if the purchase price stated in the will is, with other available assets, sufficient for the payment of debts, the option will not be destroyed as the debts will be paid out of the purchase price. Thus, in the example given, if only £20,000 were needed to pay the debts, the option would still be available.

Third, *donatio mortis causa*: a *donatio mortis causa* can be made available in the last resort for the payment of debts and liabilities. See *Re Korvine's Trust* [1921] 1 Ch 343 at p348.

In the majority of cases the debts and liabilities will be completely discharged from the residuary estate alone without the need to resort to property in other categories set out in Part II of the First Schedule. However, if the estate is heavily indebted and the testator has made many dispositions, the position will be different. The following example illustrates the operation of the statutory order:

T died recently and by his will made the following dispositions. His house Blackacre to A (worth £50,000), all his shares in X Co Ltd to B (worth £20,000), a legacy of £10,000 to C, a legacy of £20,000 to D and his residuary estate to E and F in equal shares. T also gave G an option to purchase Whiteacre for £20,000; the property is in fact worth £40,000. E predeceased T. In addition to the assets mentioned above, T had other assets worth £80,000. T's debts and liabilities amount to £62,000.

The first thing to do is to total the assets and the debts. This is important to ensure that the correct order of administration is used because an insolvent estate or an estate where solvency is doubtful should always be admininistered under the bankruptcy rules.

Debts	Assets		
£62,000	£50,000	=	Blackacre
	£20,000	=	Shares in X Co Ltd
	£40,000	=	Whiteacre
	£80,000	=	other assets
£62,000	£190,000	=	Total

The next thing to do is to set out the assets in the categories they fall within under Part II of the First Schedule. This will depend on how they have been disposed of by the will.

undisposed-of property	(1)	£40,000 (E's lapsed share of residue) minus £30,000 for the pecuniary legacy fund = £10,000
residuary gifts	(2)	£40,000 (F's share)
property given for paying debts	(3)	–
property charged with debts	(4)	–

pecuniary legacies fund	(5)	£10,000 to C; £20,000 to D= £30,000
specific gifts	(6)	Blackacre to A (£50,000);
		X Co Ltd shares to B (£20,000)
property appointed by will	(7)	–
property outside the order	(8)	Whiteacre (£40,000)

In paying the debts of £62,000 the first requirement is to take the pecuniary legacies fund out of the property in paragraph (1) and place it in paragraph (5). If paragraph (1) property is insufficient to meet this in any case then the property in paragraph (2) is resorted to. It will be noted that in this example E's share of residue lapsed and in accordance with *Re Lamb* it was placed in paragraph (1); after the pecuniary legacy fund is deducted from the undisposed of property it is worth £10,000. This £10,000 together with the £40,000 share of residue given to F will be needed to meet the debts and liabilities. As these amount to only £50,000, a further £12,000 will have to be taken from the pecuniary legacies fund. The pecuniary legacies will abate rateably and £4,000 of the £12,000 will come from E's £10,000 while the other £8,000 will come from D's legacy of £20,000. Thus C will receive £6,000 and D £12,000 when the estate is distributed. Other gifts will operate as the testator intended.

Variation of the statutory order

Under paragraph (8) of Part II of the First Schedule it is provided that 'the order of application may be varied by the will of the deceased'. The right to vary the statutory order arises because the testator is entitled to choose what order debts shall be paid in when there are sufficient assets to meet them. The variation is binding on the beneficiaries but not necessarily on the creditors. See *Re Tankard* [1942] Ch 69.

The statutory order may be varied as between paragraphs (1) and (2) of the order so as to throw the burden of debts and liabilities primarily on the residuary estate as a whole and not on undisposed of property. This type of variation is quite common as it is a widespread practice to deal with the payment of debts and liabilities in a well-drawn will by directing that they be paid out of the residuary estate. If the direction for the payment of debts and liabilities out of the residuary estate is to the effect that they be paid out of the residue as a whole so that property undisposed of is ascertained only after their payment, then the order has been varied. See *Re Harland-Peck* [1941] Ch 182.

Thus the following directions have been held to vary the statutory order.

1. 'All my leasehold property and all my personal estate and effects … subject to and after the payment of my funeral and testamentary expenses and debts.' See *Re Kempthorne* [1930] 1 Ch 268.
2. 'Subject to the payment of my funeral expenses and testamentary expenses death

duties ... and debts and legacies bequeathed by this will ... I devise and bequeath all the net and residue of my property to ...'. See *Re Harland-Peck* [1941] 1 Ch 182.

3. 'After all my debts and funeral and testamentary expenses are paid I give and bequeath all the residue of my estate in equal shares to ...'. See *Re Berrey's Will Trusts* [1959] 1 WLR 30.

4. 'My residuary real and personal estate to my trustees upon trust for sale and conversion and out of the proceeds to pay all my funeral and testamentary expenses and debts and legacies and to divide the balance between ...'. See *Re Petty* [1929] 1 Ch 726.

The effect of a variation of the statutory order as between paragraphs (1) and (2) is important as regards the next of kin, who take the undisposed of property falling within paragraph (1) in so far as it is not required for the payment of debts. If the order is varied then they may obtain benefits which would not come their way if the order was not varied, or greater benefits. The following example illustrates the position.

T leaves the residue of his estate to A, B and C in equal shares. The residuary estate is worth £30,000 and T's debts total £12,000. There are no pecuniary legacies given by the will. A predeceased the testator and his share of the residue has lapsed.

1. If the statutory order is not varied, that is, the gift is simply 'my residuary estate to A, B and C in equal shares absolutely', A's lapsed share will fall into paragraph (1) of the statutory order (worth £10,000) while the shares of B and C will fall within paragraph (2). See *Re Lamb*. The debts will be paid first from the property in paragraph (1); as they amount to £12,000 all of the undisposed property is used in their payment, so the next of kin on intestacy will receive nothing. The £2,000 needed to complete the payment of the debts will come from paragraph (2), that is, the shares of B and C worth £20,000 in total; B and C will receive £9,000 each.

2. If the statutory order is varied, that is, the residuary gift is 'my residuary estate subject to and after the payment of all my debts to A, B and C in equal shares' the £12,000 of debts must be deducted from the £30,000 forming the residuary estate before ascertaining beneficial interests. This leaves the residuary estate worth £18,000 after payment of debts. The shares of A, B and C are worth £6,000 each. B and C will take these amounts whilst A's lapsed share will pass to the next of kin on intestacy.

A mere direction to pay the debts and expenses out of the residue will not have the effect of varying the statutory order if it does not charge them on the residue as a whole so that it can only be ascertained after their payment. In *Re Lamb* the testator directed his executors to pay his debts and expenses after his death and then made some specific gifts in his will followed by a residuary gift to four named people in equal shares, one of whom predeceased the testator. It was held that the direction did not vary the statutory order. In *Re Sanger* [1939] Ch 238, Simonds J considered that it might be difficult to distinguish between cases where the statutory order had been varied and cases where it had not been varied.

The statutory order may be varied so as to make property which falls within either paragraphs (3) or (4) primarily liable for the payment of debts and liabilities. As stated earlier, it is curious that property which is specifically appropriated, devised or bequeathed for the payment of debts (paragraph 3) or devised or bequeathed subject to a charge for the payment of debts (paragraph 4) is not primarily liable for the payment of debts and liabilities. If a testator wishes to ensure that such property is to be primarily liable for the debts, he must show some indication that these funds are to be primarily liable either expressly or by showing an intention to exonerate some other fund. Thus, if the testator leaves 'my 10,000 £1 shares in X Co Ltd to be used to meet all my debts and expenses in preference to any other assets in my estate', then the statutory order will have been varied. It is clear that the property is not to fall within paragraph (3) of the statutory order. See *Re Kempthorne* [1930] 1 Ch 268 per Maugham J. Unfortunately, the words will not always be so clear and the decisions here often turn on the presence or absence of a residuary gift, as the following illustrate.

In *Re Meldrum* [1952] Ch 208 by his will a testator left to a beneficiary 'the sum of £500 for her immediate expenses ... and all moneys standing to the credit of my current account at Lloyds Bank at Dartmouth ... and also my War and National Savings Certificates and the residue of my deposit account at Lloyds Bank, Dartmouth, after all legacies, debts, funeral and other expenses have been liquidated but excluding death duties and testamentary expenses'. The testator then devised and bequeathed 'all the residue of my property to my trustees upon trust, after discharging death duties and testamentary expenses thereout, to pay the income to ...'

Held: the statutory order had been varied because the testator showed a clear intention to place the burden of some debts on the residuary estate and the burden of others on the deposit account. This indicated an intention on the part of the testator to exonerate the residuary estate from the payment of the legacies, debts, funeral and other expenses but not the death duties or testamentary expenses in so far as the deposit account was able to meet them.

In *Re Gordon* [1940] Ch 851 by her will made in 1939 a testatrix gave certain legacies and bequests and then gave her executors £50 upon trust to pay her debts and funeral and testamentary expenses thereout and pay the balance to the Rationalist Press Association Ltd. The will contained no residuary gift and the question arose whether the £50 was primarily for the debts or whether they should be paid out of the undisposed of property falling within paragraph (1) of the statutory order in the first instance.

Held: the statutory order had not been varied because the testatrix had not made a disposition of other property falling lower in the statutory order, so as to enable the court to conclude that she intended to exonerate such a fund by throwing the burden of the debts primarily on the £50. The mere fact that there was property undisposed of by the will did not justify the inference that the £50 was to be used in priority to it in the payment of the debts.

The decisions on paragraphs (3) and (4) leave many problems unresolved. From *Re Gordon* it is clear that where the testator makes a disposition falling within either of those paragraphs and fails to dispose of the residue, then the statutory order is not varied. However, it is not entirely clear if the court would have concluded the opposite if a residuary gift had been present. Following *Re Meldrum* it is suggested that the statutory order would be varied if there was a disposition within either paragraphs (3) or (4) and a residuary gift which was silent as to the payment of debts, or where the disposition within paragraphs (3) and (4) referred to the payment of some debts while others were directed to be paid out of the residue (as in *Re Meldrum*). But if the testator made a disposition falling within either paragraph (3) or (4) with a direction to pay debts in general terms and a disposition of the residue with a direction to pay debts thereout in general terms, it is suggested that the statutory order is not varied. See *Re Kempthorne* [1930] 1 Ch 268 at p278. See also *Re James* [1947] Ch 256; *Re Littlewood* [1931] 1 Ch 443.

Charges on property

Under s35 of the Administration of Estates Act 1925 special provisions deal with charges on the property of the deceased at his death. If the deceased devises his house, Blackacre, to X by his will and at his death there was a mortgage of £10,000 outstanding on the property, then the question is whether the beneficiary is primarily liable for the mortgage out of the value of Blackacre, or whether he is entitled to demand that the personal representatives pay the mortgage out of the general estate.

Originally the position was that the beneficiary was entitled to demand that a charge on property devised or bequeathed to him be paid out of the general estate of the deceased. This applied to both realty and personalty. See *Bartholomew* v *May* (1737) 1 Atk 487; *Bothamley* v *Sherson* (1875) LR 20 Eq 304. These rules were eroded prior to 1925 by a series of statutes known as Locke Kings Acts. In 1925 the Administration of Estates Act changed the position and made property charged with the payment of money at the deceased's death primarily liable for that charge. Section 35(1) provides:

> 'Where a person dies possessed of, or entitled to, or, under a general power of appointment (including the statutory power to dispose of entailed interests) by his will disposes of an interest in property, which at the time of his death is charged with the payment of money, whether by way of legal mortgage, equitable charge or otherwise (including a lien for unpaid purchase money), and the deceased has not by will, deed or other document signified a contrary or other intention, the interest so charged shall as between the different persons claiming through the deceased, be primarily liable for the payment of the charge; and every part of the said interest, according to its value, shall bear a proportionate part of the charge on the whole thereof.'

This provision is intended to regulate the position as between the beneficiaries; it does not affect the rights of any person entitled to the charge to obtain payment or satisfaction of the charge out of the other assets of the deceased or otherwise. See s35(3).

Effect of section 35(1)

The effect of s35(1) is to impose primary liability for the charge on the property charged. It does not impose any liability on the person taking the property. See *Syer v Gladstone* (1885) 30 Ch D 614. Thus, if T gives Blackacre to X, worth £30,000 but charged with a mortgage of £10,000, X will not have to meet the charge out of his own pocket; the property will have to be sold and X will receive the balance of the proceeds of sale after the mortgage has been discharged. However, X could, if he wished, take over the mortgage on the property or discharge it out of his personal assets and keep Blackacre.

If there are several mortgaged properties disposed of by the will to the same beneficiary, then under s35(1) each property will be liable for its own mortgage. The mere fact that they are given to the same beneficiary by separate and distinct gifts will not permit the mortgagee of one of the properties to resort to the other property if his security is inadequate. In such circumstances the shortfall will come out of the deceased's general estate. See *Re Holt* (1916) 115 LT 73. Thus, if T devised Blackacre and Whiteacre to X by separate devises and they were worth £40,000 and £50,000 respectively but mortgaged for £50,000 and £30,000 respectively, the mortgagee of Blackacre must look to the general estate for the balance of the money owed to him. However, if T made a single undivided gift of both properties to X, it appears that they will both be liable to meet the whole burden. See *Re Baron Kensington* [1902] 1 Ch 203.

A testator may give a single property charged with a mortgage to two or more beneficiaries. In such circumstances the beneficiaries will have to bear the charge proportionately according to the value of their interests unless a contrary intention appears by the will. See *Re Newmarch* (1878) 9 Ch D 12.

Sometimes two or more properties are charged together with the payment of money. If they are all primarily liable for the charge then it will be met proportionately from their values if they are given to different beneficiaries. See *Re Athill* (1880) 16 Ch D 211. If one is primarily liable for the charge and the other is merely a secondary security then they will be liable to meet the charge in that order. See *Re Athill*.

The provisions of s35(1) do not apply to property which is subject to an option to purchase given by the will. If T gives X an option to purchase Blackacre (worth £50,000) for the sum of £25,000 by his will and Blackacre is subject to a mortgage of £10,000 at T's death, then X is entitled to have the mortgage paid from T's general estate. See *Re Wilson* [1908] 1 Ch 839. This is because X will be claiming the property as a purchaser, not as a devisee, when he exercises the option. The fact that the purchase price is less than the value of the property is irrelevant. See *Re Fison's Will Trusts* [1950] Ch 394.

Charges falling within section 35(1)

The section clearly states that both legal and equitable mortgages come within its ambit. In addition judgment debts will come within the provisions where they have been charged on the property of the deceased at his death. See *Re Anthony* [1892] 1 Ch 450. A charge created by statute will come within the subsection such as a charge on property for estate duty (see *Re Bowerman* [1908] 2 Ch 340), or capital transfer tax, see Schedule 4 para 20 of the Finance Act 1975. An unpaid vendor's lien is a charge within the subsection. Thus in *Re Birmingham* [1959] Ch 523 where the testator had contracted to purchase a property for £3,500 having paid a deposit of £350 but died before the date for completion, it was held that the beneficiary took this property under the will subject to a charge on it for the balance of the purchase money.

The charge under s35(1) will also fall upon commercial property. If the testator owed money on shares at his death giving the company concerned a lien on them, then the beneficiary receiving these by the will takes them subject to the lien. See *Re Turner* [1938] Ch 593. Mortgages or charges on property belonging to the testator for the purpose of securing loans for a partnership should be noted. In such cases the debt will be regarded as a partnership debt and payable primarily out of the partnership assets. It is only if the partnership assets are insufficient to meet the debt in full that the mortgage can be called upon. This was held in the following case.

In *Re Ritson* [1899] 1 Ch 128 (CA) the testator carried on business in partnership with his brother. The testator mortgaged some of his own freehold property to secure a partnership debt owed to a bank. At his death the debt was unpaid and the partnership assets alone were insufficient to meet it. The question arose whether the debt was payable primarily from the mortgaged property or from the partnership assets.

Held: the partnership assets were primarily liable to satisfy the debt as this debt had been incurred in the course of the partnership business and not for the testator's personal use.

Contrary intention

The rule just discussed is applicable to property charged with the payment of debts unless the deceased has signified a contrary intention 'by will deed or other document'. Section 35(2) states that a contrary intention for these purposes is not signified:

> '(a) by a general direction for the payment of debts or of all the debts of the testator out of his personal estate, or his residuary real and personal estate, or his residuary real estate; or
> (b) by a charge of debts upon any such estate.'

It is necessary to have words which either expressly or by implication refer to all or some part of the charge.

Directions in a will, if they are to pass the burden of a charge from the property charged to the general estate, must be in clear terms so as to discharge the property charged. Thus if the testator directs payment of his debts out of the residue, 'including the mortgage debt on Blackacre', or 'including any mortgage debts', these would discharge the mortgage on the properties concerned. See *Re Fleck* (1888) 37 Ch D 677. However, a mere direction to 'pay all my debts' would not do. The disposition of the property charged may indicate that it is to pass free of the charge, for example, where T devises Blackacre to his wife, 'free of all mortgages or charges'. A direction in the will may by implication discharge the property charged as in *Re Valpy* [1906] 1 Ch 531, where the testator directed the payment of all his debts out of the residue 'except mortgage debts, if any charged on Blackacre'. It was held that this showed an intention to exonerate properties other than Blackacre from mortgages charged on them.

The will may direct the payment of debts from a special fund other than personal estate, residuary real and personal estate, or residuary real estate. See s35(2)(a). In such circumstances this may be regarded as showing an intention that mortgages or charges should be paid from the special fund also. In *Re Fegan* [1928] Ch 45 the testator left a specific gift of realty on trust for sale directing that the proceeds of sale be used to pay his debts. He also left the proceeds of insurance policies to his children but at his death these were subject to a £2,000 mortgage. It was held that the chidren could require the mortgage to be paid out of the special fund for the payment of debts, so far as it would go. If the special fund is not sufficient to meet the whole of the mortgage or charge then the property mortgaged or charged is liable for the balance. In *Re Birch* [1909] 1 Ch 787 a testator made a specific devise of realty which was subject to a mortgage of £500, and directed that the mortgage debt should be paid out of the proceeds of sale of other realty expressly mentioned in the will. The special fund for the payment of the mortgage only amounted to £285 in value and it was held that the property charged was primarily liable for the balance of the mortgage debt.

Section 35(1) states that a contrary intention may be shown in a deed or other document. If such a contrary intention is to be effective it appears that the deed or other document must indicate how the burden of the mortgage or charge is to be borne as between the beneficiaries under the testator's will. Thus, a letter from a testator to his solcitors directing that they should pay the balance of the proceeds of sale out of a cheque enclosed herewith will not discharge an unpaid vendor's lien on a property which the testator had contracted to buy but where he died before completion. This is because the letter and cheque only show an intention to discharge the lien in the testator's lifetime. See *Re Wakefield* [1943] 2 All ER 29. In *Re Birmingham* [1959] Ch 523 the testatrix contracted to buy a house before death and wrote to her solicitors directing them to execute a codicil leaving the house to her daughter 'free of all duties'. The testatrix died before the date of completion and it was held that the property passed to the daughter subject to the unpaid vendor's lien. The direction in the letter was insufficient.

It should also be noted that a direction in a will to pay mortgage debts does not extend to an unpaid vendor's lien. See *Re Beirnstein* [1925] Ch 12.

Example

T, who died recently, left a will containing the following dispositions: 'My house Whiteacre to A, my shares in ICI subject to the payment of all my debts to B, a legacy of £20,000 to C, my residuary estate to D.' Whiteacre is worth £60,00 but subject to a mortgage of £20,000, the shares are worth £40,000 and the rest of T's estate is worth £35,000. In addition to the mortgage debt, T had other liabilities of £25,000.

Payment of debts and liabilities will take effect as follows:

Assets	=	£135,000
Debts	=	£ 45,000

The gifts will fall within the statutory order as follows:

ICI shares worth £40,000

1) – undisposed of property – nil
2) – residue = £35,000
3) – nil
4) – nil
5) – pecuniary legacy £20,000
6) – specific devise of Whiteacre = £60,000 – £20,000 mortgage debt.

Variation of the statutory order. Normally a specific bequest of shares 'subject to the payment of all my debts' would be considered as falling within paragraph (4), as property bequeathed subject to a charge for the payment of debts. However, the statutory order has been varied in the present case so as to make the shares the primary fund to meet the debts. This is because T has disposed of his residuary estate and mentioned nothing in respect of debts being paid out of the residue. Therefore it can be inferred that the direction to pay debts out of the value of the shares is intended to exonerate the residue from the payment of debts in so far as the shares can do so. See *Re Gordon* and *Re Meldrum*. It should be noted that if T had failed to dispose of the residue in his will the position would have been similar to that in *Re Gordon* and the statutory order would not have been varied. However, if the residuary gift lapsed because D predeceased T, the statutory order would still be considered as varied. See *Re Gordon*.

Payment of the mortgage debt. This will fall to be paid from the proceeds of sale of Whiteacre under s35(1). The direction to pay debts out of the value of the ICI shares will not exonerate Whiteacre from this charge because under s35(1) a general direction to pay debts out of the testator's personal estate is not sufficient to show a contrary intention to the general rule in s35(1). However, it should be noted that if

T had left realty such as 'Blackacre subject to the payment of all my debts' then this would have shown a contrary intention to the rule in s35(1). This is because s35(2)(a) does not mention a general direction to pay debts out of real estate specifically or generally devised, it only refers to general directions to pay debts out of residuary real estate. See *Re Fegan*.

Payment of other debts. These will be paid out of the value of the ICI shares in the first instance. But before this can commence the pecuniary legacies fund must be deducted from the value of these shares and placed in paragraph (5). This will leave £20,000 from the proceeds of sale of the shares to meet the debts; as the debts amount to £25,000 it will be necessary to take £5,000 from the residuary estate to pay the debts in full. Therefore, on distribution of the estate B will receive nothing and the residue will be worth only £30,000 to D.

Marshalling of assets

The order under Part II of the First Schedule is intended to order the payment of debts according to the nature of the benefits given by the will. This order, as stated earlier, has no binding effect on the creditors and they may, and often do, resort to assets out of the statutory order in satisfaction of their claims. For example, a bank may sell a house specifically devised, and therefore falling under paragraph (6), in order to recover a mortgage debt thereon when it has been directed in the will that the mortgage be discharged out of the residuary estate. In order to ensure that the beneficiaries are given their interests in accordance with the proper order for the payment of debts, marshalling will operate in cases such as this. Accordingly, the devisee who should have received the house will be compensated out of the fund which was the proper fund for the payment of the mortgage debt, ie the residuary estate. See *Aldrich* v *Cooper* (1803) 8 Ves 382.

18.6 Incidence of pecuniary legacies

Introduction

This subject is concerned with the setting aside of the pecuniary legacies fund in the course of the administration of the deceased's estate. The issue which arises here is whether this fund is to be set aside out of personalty alone, realty alone, or both personalty and realty rateably. For example, if a testator leaves a £10,000 pecuniary legacy to A and his residuary realty to B and his residuary personalty to C, do the executors have to set aside the £10,000 needed to meet the pecuniary legacy from B's share or from C's share, or rateably from both?

Before 1926 the law on this subject was well settled and the pecuniary legacies were payable only out of the testator's general personal estate, that is, personalty which had not been specifically bequeathed by the will. A leading case on this point was *Robertson* v *Broadbent* (1883) 8 App Cas 812. A testator bequeathed pecuniary legacies totalling £49,200 and including £7,500 bequeathed to charities. He also gave 'all my personal estate and effects of which I shall die possessed, and which shall not consist of money, or securities for money to EAR'. He then gave and devised 'all the rest, residue and remainder of my estate, both real and personal, whatsoever and wheresoever' to his executors and trustees upon certain trusts. The personal estate was worth only £39,660. Some chattels had been delivered by the executors to EAR in partial discharge of the bequest to her. The executors took out a summons for redelivery of these to meet the pecuniary legacies fund. It was argued that the legacy to EAR was a specific legacy and also that the pecuniary legacies were payable only out of the residuary estate.

Held: the legacy to EAR was not a specific legacy, but was instead a part of the residuary personalty and therefore it was primarily liable for the payment of the pecuniary legacies.

Before 1926 the pecuniary legacies could not be paid out of the subject matter of specific bequests or out of the testator's realty. The testator could, however, use express words in his will charging the realty with the payment of the pecuniary legacies. In addition, two rules of construction were established by which the realty could be used to meet the pecuniary legacies, as shown below.

1. The rule in *Greville* v *Brown* (1859) 7 HLC 689. Under this rule the court held that the residuary realty was charged with the payment of the pecuniary legacies in aid of the residuary personalty where the testator made a gift of his residuary realty and residuary personalty as one mass. In order that the residuary realty and personalty could be regarded as being given in one mass the gift had to be something like 'all the rest, residue and remainder of any property I may die possessed of' or 'all my real and personal estate', or 'all my residuary estate'.
2. The rule in *Roberts* v *Walker* (1830) 1 R & My 752. Under this rule the pecuniary legacies are payable rateably out of the realty and personalty where the testator has directed payment of them out of a mixed fund of realty and personalty. Thus, if a testator left all his residuary real and personal estate upon trust for sale and conversion to pay all his funeral and testamentary expenses, debts and legacies thereout, then the pecuniary legacies would be paid out of the realty and personalty rateably according to their value. However, if the testator made no direction to pay the legacies out of the proceeds of sale then the rule in *Greville* v *Brown* would have applied instead.

Setting aside the pecuniary legacies fund under the statutory order

Under s34(3) of the Administration of Estates Act 1925 and Part II of the First Schedule it is provided that the primary fund for the payment of debts is the property undisposed of by will 'subject to the retention thereout of a fund sufficient to meet any pecuniary legacies', and the secondary fund is, in effect, the residuary estate 'subject to the retention out of such property of a fund sufficient to meet any pecuniary legacies, so far as not provided for as aforesaid'.

It is clear that under s34(3) the pecuniary legacies fund is to be set aside before the debts and liabilities are paid. However, despite the clarity of the provisions just mentioned they are in conflict with the provisions of s33 of the Administration of Estates Act 1925. Under s33(1) a statutory trust is imposed on all property which the deceased has not effectively disposed of by his will and which is therefore subject to the intestacy rules. See *Re McKee* [1931] 2 Ch 145. However, s33(2) then goes on to direct that the proceeds of sale must first be used to pay the debts and liabilities and the pecuniary legacies fund set aside afterwards. This provision and s34(3) must be examined in detail. As a result of the lack of clarity it is suggested that all wills contain express clauses to deal with the incidence of pecuniary legacies.

Section 33(2)

The application of the proceeds of sale of the trust is dealt with by s33(2) which states:

> 'Out of the net money to arise from the sale and conversion of such real and personal estate (after payment of costs), and out of the ready money of the deceased (so far as not disposed of by his will, if any), the personal representative shall pay all such funeral, testamentary and administration expenses, debts and other liabilities as are properly payable thereout having regard to the rules of administration contained in this Part of the Act, and out of the residue of the said money the personal representative shall set a fund sufficient to provide for any pecuniary legacies bequeathed by the will (if any) of the deceased.'

As can be seen s33(2) directs the payment of the debts and liabilities first and then the setting aside of the pecuniary legacies fund. This fund would include the proceeds of the sale of realty as well as personalty. This appears to alter the pre-1925 provisions regarding partial intestacy. It would appear that s33(2) is of limited application and is only intended to apply to cases where s33(1) imposes a statutory trust, as shown below.

1. Where there is a case of total intestacy. In these circumstances the whole of the deceased's estate will be subject to a statutory trust and it is easy to see why s33(2) directs payment of debts and liabilities first, because the next of kin will only be entitled to the balance of the deceased's estate after discharge of debts and liabilities. Further, in cases of total intestacy the beneficial interests (with the exception of the personal chattels which go to the surviving spouse, if any) are measured in terms of money so the application of the statutory order under Part II of Schedule One is irrelevant.

2. Where a testator dies wholly intestate as to a share of his residue. If the testator leaves his residuary estate to A and B in equal shares and A predeceases him, the

testator will be deemed to have died wholly intestate as regards the share of residue he attempted to give A. See *Re McKee*; *Re Worthington* [1933] Ch 771; *Re Berrey's Will Trusts* [1959] 1 WLR 30.

In *Re Worthington* [1933] Ch 771 (CA) the testatrix left a will which, after appointing a sole executor and bequeathing a number of pecuniary legacies, gave, devised and bequeathed all the residue of her estate both real and personal to ES and LMH in equal shares absolutely. ES died in the lifetime of the testatrix and her share lapsed and passed as on intestacy. The question arose as to how the debts, expenses and legacies should be paid.

Held: as there was nothing in the will to vary the statutory order the provisions of s33(2) applied in this case and the debts, funeral and testamentary expenses and the legacies were payable primarily out of the lapsed share of residue, without distinction between realty and personalty falling within that category.

If there is a statutory trust under s33(1), *Re Worthington* is clear authority that all undisposed property, whether realty or personalty, is to be available to meet debts and liabilities and the pecuniary legacies before the residue. However, if there is no statutory trust the position is unclear. The testator may direct that his residuary estate be held on an express trust for sale and that the proceeds of sale after payment of debts etc be given to A and B in equal shares. If A predeceased the testator, would s33(2) apply so that, on the authority of *Re Worthington*, the pecuniary legacies could be met out of both undisposed realty and personalty, that is, A's share? This question arose in the cases of *Re Beaumont's Will Trusts* [1950] Ch 462 and *Re Midgley* [1955] Ch 576; in the former the answer was no, while in the latter it was yes.

In *Re Beaumont's Will Trusts* [1950] Ch 462 the testatrix made a will in 1947 bequeathing specific articles and pecuniary legacies and then directing that her residue be held on trust for sale to pay debts etc and then to be divided between four named persons in equal shares. One of the four persons named as a residuary legatee predeceased the testatrix. The question arose, *inter alia*, whether the legacies were payable out of the residuary estate as a whole or primarily out of the undisposed share.

Held (per Danckwerts J): that the old rules as to the incidence of pecuniary legacies applied and as there was a trust for sale of the residue these should be paid out of the realty and personalty in proportion to their values. There was nothing in s34(3) which made the legacies payable out of the undisposed-of share and s33(2), the only provision which might have that effect was displaced by the express trust for sale.

In *Re Midgley* [1955] Ch 576 by her will the testatrix gave several pecuniary legacies and directed that the residue of her estate, both real and personal, be held on trust for sale to be divided among six persons. Subsequently, the testatrix executed a codicil to her will in which she revoked the gift of a share of residue to one of the six persons. However, no attempt was made to deal with this share, so that on the testatrix's death in 1951 it went as on intestacy. One of the questions which arose was whether the pecuniary legacies were payable primarily out of the undisposed of one-sixth share or out of the residue as a whole.

Held (per Harman J): the pecuniary legacies were payable primarily out of the undisposed of one-sixth share and not out of the residue as a whole.

The decision in *Re Beaumont* may be open to doubt. It is interesting to note that Danckwerts J did not have *Re Gillett's Will Trusts* [1950] Ch 102 cited to him in *Re Beaumont*; in that case Roxburgh J held that the pecuniary legacies were payable out of undisposed of income. Danckwerts J referred to his decision in *Re Beaumont* in *Re Berrey's Will Trusts* [1959] 1 WLR 30, and there are hints that he may have altered his views on the matter. Until the Court of Appeal rules on this matter there can only be uncertainty, but until then it is submitted that the decision in *Re Midgley* is to be preferred. Although it is clear that s33(1) cannot apply if there is an express trust for sale in the will, there is nothing in the wording of s33(2) which would enslave it to the provisions of s33(1).

Section 34(3)

It would appear that s34(3) must apply in the following cases.

1. Where the deceased died fully intestate, that is, there is no property undisposed of by his will, so that s33 cannot possibly have any bearing on the incidence of pecuniary legacies.
2. Where the deceased died partially intestate but s33(2) is not applicable because the deceased has disposed of some interest in the property concerned in his will, for example, where he has disposed of a life interest in property, and part of the remainder must be dealt with under the intestacy rules but is not subject to a statutory trust.
3. Where the deceased died partially intestate but the pecuniary legacies cannot be paid in full out of the undisposed of property falling under s33(2).

In (1) and (2) it is clear from s34(3) that the pecuniary legacies fund must be set aside before the debts and liabilities are paid. However, this cannot be the position in (3) because s33(2) will apply to the undisposed of property. In that case it would appear that the debts must be paid first from the undisposed of property but not first from residuary property. The following example illustrates the position:

(1)   Undisposed of property =   £10,000

(2)   Residuary estate   =   £20,000

T's debts = £6,000 and there are legacies of £10,000. Under s33(2) the £6,000 debts must be paid from (1) first, the £10,000 of legacies will then be deducted, £4,000 from (1) and £6,000 from (2).

T's debts = £12,000 and there are legacies of £10,000. Under s33(2) the debts should be paid first. But as the money in (1) is insufficient to meet these, only

£10,000 of debts will be paid under the provisions of s33(2). The other £2,000 of debts must be paid from (2), s33(2) does not apply and it would appear that the pecuniary legacies fund must be deducted from the £20,000 in (2) before the other £2,000 of debts are paid. See s34(3).

When s34(3) is applicable, there is considerable doubt as to whether the pecuniary legacies are payable from personalty only or from both realty and personalty. The decisions do not appear to be very helpful in some areas.

Deceased dies fully testate

If the deceased has effectively disposed of all his property by his will so that is no property in para (1) of the statutory order, the only issue is whether the pecuniary legacies are payable out of the residuary personalty alone or whether the residuary realty can be used also. As stated above, the rule before 1925 was that residuary realty could not be used to meet pecuniary legacies and they abated if the personalty was insufficient to meet them in full, unless the exception in *Greville* v *Browne* or *Roberts* v *Walker* applied. The decisions since 1925 suggest that the law, as it stood before 1926, has not been altered, so that realty cannot be used to meet pecuniary legacies unless one of the exceptions mentioned applies. These are *Re Thompson* [1936] Ch 676 and *Re Rowe* [1941] Ch 343. Other cases that support this view are *Re Beaumont* (above) and *Re Anstead* [1943] Ch 161.

In *Re Thompson* [1936] Ch 676 the testator left several pecuniary legacies by his will and then devised and bequeathed all his real and personal estate to certain hospitals. The net value of the personal estate was £11,809 after expenses. The legacies amounted to over £3,000. The question arose how the legacies should be borne as between the realty and personalty. It was argued that the law had been changed after 1925 and that they should be payable rateably from realty and personalty. Under the pre-1926 law the rule in *Greville* v *Browne* would have applied on the facts, making the realty liable only in aid of the personalty.

Held: the pre-1926 rules continued to apply; there was nothing in the Administration of Estates Act 1925 to indicate the contrary.

In referring to s34(3) and Schedule 1 Part II, para 2, Clauson J said:

> 'It is suggested that the effect of that provision is to alter the law and to provide that the fund which is to be retained out of the residuary realty and personalty in order to meet the pecuniary legacies is to be retained in this way, that a proportionate part is to be retained out of the realty and the personalty pro rata the amount of realty and personalty respectively. The provision does not say that. And the provision is not concerned with any such matter. The provision is concerned with the way in which funeral testamentary and administration expenses debts and liabilities are to be met. There is no indication that there is any intention to alter the law in regard to the rights of legatees as against those interested in the residuary real estate, and I can see no foundation for the suggestion that the provision has in any way altered the law'.

In *Re Rowe* [1941] Ch 343 the testator left pecuniary legacies by his will and then directed 'I devise all my real estate and bequeath all the residue of my personal estate to JPJ and JDP in equal shares'. The personalty was sufficient to pay all the pecuniary legacies and it was argued that they ought to be paid rateably out of the realty and the personalty.

Held: the law had not been changed after 1925 and, as the devise was specific, the rule in *Greville* v *Browne* did not apply and the legacies were to be paid out of the residuary personalty only. (See *Re Wilson* [1967] Ch 53 on whether the devise would now be regarded as specific.)

Farwell J considered the dictum of Clauson J (set out above) on whether the law had been changed and concluded that it had not.

Examples

By his will T leaves, *inter alia*, a pecuniary legacy of £20,000 to A, his residuary realty to B (worth £50,000) and his residuary personalty to C (worth £22,000). All of A, B and C survive T.

In this case the pecuniary legacy will have to be deducted from C's share alone, so C will only receive £2,000. If the residuary personalty was valued at £10,000, C would get nothing and A's legacy would abate. B's gift cannot be used to meet A's legacy as neither *Greville* v *Browne* nor *Roberts* v *Walker* are applicable to it on the facts.

By his will T leaves, *inter alia*, a £20,000 pecuniary legacy to A and all his residury estate to B and C in equal shares. The residue totals £72,000, that is, £60,000 of realty and £12,000 of personalty.

In this case the personalty is sufficient to meet the pecuniary legacy. Luckily for A it will not abate because the rule in *Greville* v *Browne* applies here and the realty can be used in aid of the personalty to meet the legacy. But C will get nothing.

Deceased dies partially intestate, section 33(2) not applicable

In this section the pecuniary legacies fund will be deducted from property in para (1) under s34(3) and Schedule 1 Part II before the payment of debts etc and, if this is insufficient to meet them in full, then from property in para (2). The words in paras (1) and (2) plainly support this. However, two issues arise here.

1. If the property in para (1) is sufficient to meet the pecuniary legacies fund, must undisposed of personalty be used before undisposed of realty for this purpose, or are they both liable rateably?

   Re Worthington is not an authority on this point because it only applies in cases covered by s33, that is, where there is a statutory trust for sale. There is no trust for sale in the present case imposed by statute or otherwise by the will. There are no authorities on this point and one can only speculate as to the outcome. The decisions in *Re Thompson* and *Re Rowe* (above) suggest that the pre-1926 rules would still apply and therefore the undisposed-of personalty only should be used.

2. If the pecuniary legacies have to be taken from property falling within both paras (1) and (2), should personalty in para (2) be used before realty in para (1)?

Again there is no answer to this question when there is no trust for sale imposed by statute or otherwise. The decisions in *Re Martin* [1955] Ch 698 and *Re Berrey* [1959] 1 WLR 30 (see below) are authority that the undisposed of realty must be used before residuary personalty if there is a statututory trust for sale. It is, however, doubtful if these authorities are of value in the present situation. The decision in *Re Thompson* probably applies.

Deceased dies partially intestate, s33(2) applicable, property in paras (1) and (2) needed to meet pecuniary legacies fund

If the property in para (1) was sufficient alone to meet the pecuniary legacies fund and s33(2) applied, then under *Re Worthington* both the realty and personalty falling within para (1) would be liable rateably to meet the pecuniary legacies fund. But when the property within para (1) is insufficient to meet the pecuniary legacies fund, the question is whether the realty falling within para (1) should be used before or after the personalty falling within para (2) in order to meet the pecuniary legacies fund. The answer to this question is clear on the case law and the undisposed realty must be used before the residuary personalty. The authorities are as follows.

Re Martin [1955] Ch 698. By his will, made in 1938, the testator gave several pecuniary legacies and then devised all his real estate to his daughter, Kathleen, absolutely. There then followed a gift of the residue of his personal estate to be held on trust for sale in equal shares for beneficiaries. In 1944 the testator made a codicil to his will revoking the devise to his daughter, but he made no attempt to dispose of the realty. On his death in 1953 the question arose whether the undisposed of real estate was primarily liable to meet the pecuniary legacies.

Held: under s33(1) the undisposed of realty was held on trust for sale and the provisions of s33(2) required the balance after payment of debts to be used to meet pecuniary legacies. Further, under para (1) of Part II of Schedule 1, there was a direction to set aside a fund to meet pecuniary legacies from the undisposed-of property. Therefore, the undisposed of property was the proper fund from which to meet these.

Re Berrey's Will Trusts [1959] 1 WLR 30. The testatrix left two pecuniary legacies of £500 each and then directed that the residue of her estate, after payment of debts and expenses, be divided among four named persons in equal shares. One of the four named residuary legatees predeceased the testatrix and one of the questions concerned what part of the estate was primarily liable to meet the pecuniary legacies fund.

Held: the pecuniary legacies were payable primarily out of the lapsed share of residue as the joint effect of ss33(1) and (2) was to require such a fund to be set aside and to require this fund to come out of the undisposed of property.

19

Distribution of Assets

19.1 Introduction

When the assets belonging to the deceased have been collected in and realised and all the debts and expenses either paid or provided for, then the personal representatives are in a position to distribute the assets to those entitled under either the deceased's will or intestacy.

The personal representatives have a duty to distribute the assets to those who are properly entitled thereto. See *Re Diplock* [1948] Ch 465. This may lead to detailed inquiries for beneficiaries or next of kin and is dealt with below. As to the time for distribution there are no time limits as to when they must distribute; instead s44 of the Administration of Estates Act 1925 provides:

'Subject to the foregoing provisions of this Act, a personal representative is not bound to distribute the estate of the deceased before the expiration of one year from the death.'

321

Thus a legatee cannot require the personal representatives to give him his legacy before the end of the year from death (often referred to as the 'executor's year'), even if the will has directed earlier payment. See *Brooke* v *Lewis* (1822) 6 Madd 358. However, it would appear from the dicta in *Re Tankard* [1942] Ch 69 that there is a duty on the executor to ensure that the administration of the estate is completed with 'due diligence'.

If the personal representatives are in a position to do so, they may distribute the estate within the executor's year. This is unusual as in most cases the obtaining of probate and settling of claims for inheritance tax will take at least one year. However, there is power for the personal representatives to distribute legacies or residuary gifts before the end of the executor's year. See *Pearson* v *Pearson* (1802) 1 Sch & Lef 10. Further, under s43(1) of the Administration of Estates Act 1925, the personal representatives may permit any person entitled to land to take possession of it before giving an assent or making a conveyance. This is subject to the personal representatives' right to resume possession if the land is needed for the administration of the estate.

19.2 Ascertaining the beneficiaries

The personal representatives must ascertain the persons who are entitled to take the deceased's estate whether under a will or under the intestacy rules. In the case of a will, few problems will arise in the majority of cases as the beneficiaries will be members of the deceased's family, such as his wife and children or named beneficiaries. However, intestacy may well present difficulties, if the deceased died at an advanced age and had little contact with his family. In such a case the personal representatives will have to make enquiries as to the whereabouts of the next of kin. If the next of kin are known then a pedigree should be prepared showing their relationship with the deceased. This should be done in conjunction with the known next of kin with birth, death and marriage certificates being produced, if available. In some cases it may be necessary to obtain information from the register of a parish church, if a pedigree has to be traced back before 1837, the date on which compulsory registration of births, deaths and marriages came into force in England and Wales.

If there are difficulties in ascertaining the beneficiaries, three courses of action are open to the personal representatives.

Section 27 advertisements

This section has already been mentioned in relation to ascertaining the creditors and is equally applicable to ascertaining the beneficiaries. See *Re Aldhous* [1955] 1 WLR 459. Therefore, if the provisions of the section are followed, the personal representatives will not be personally liable to any person of whose claim they did not have notice at the time of distribution. The provision does not prevent the unpaid beneficiary from recovering his share from the wrongly paid or over-paid beneficiaries. See *Re Diplock* [1948] Ch 465.

In *Re Aldhous* [1955] 1 WLR 459 the testatrix left a £100 legacy to her executor and his wife but made no other dispositions in her will and therefore died intestate as regards the remainder of her property. Her executor advertised in accordance with s27(1) of the Trustee Act and, having received no claims from next of kin, paid all the debts and liabilities and paid the balance to the Treasury Solicitor on the ground that the residue was *bona vacantia*. The plaintiff subsequently claimed to be the next of kin of the testatrix and claimed the money of the Treasury Solicitor. One question which arose was whether the s27 advertisement covered beneficiaries as well as creditors so as to protect the executor.

Held: the estate had been administered according to law; the advertisements applied to beneficiaries also. The plaintiff had a claim to recover the money from the Treasury Solicitor if she could prove that she was the next of kin.

'Benjamin order'

Section 27 advertisements are useful where the personal representatives have no idea who the beneficiaries are. Thus, if the deceased died intestate as to some or all of his property and his next of kin were brothers and sisters and their issue, a s27 advertisement would be appropriate to discover all of these persons where not even their names are known. If the names of the beneficiaries are known but they cannot be traced, however, s27 does not provide protection. Thus, if the testator left his estate to his children in equal shares and one son could not be traced, a s27 advertisement might bring a response from him but would not protect the personal representatives if there was no response.

In cases where the beneficiary is known but cannot be traced, the appropriate remedy is to apply to the court for a 'Benjamin order'. This form of order was first made in *Re Benjamin* [1902] 1 Ch 723 and it enables the personal representatives to distribute the estate on the footing set out in the order. It does not, however, amount to a declaration of rights and if the missing beneficiary appears at some subsequent date he is not prevented by reason of the order from recovering his share from the over-paid or wrongly paid beneficiaries. See *Hansell* v *Spink* [1943] Ch 396. See also *Re Green's Will Trusts* [1985] All ER 455.

In *Re Benjamin* [1902] 1 Ch 723 a son of the testator was entitled to receive a share of the residuary estate. The son disappeared in September 1892 and the testator died in June 1893. Advertisements and inquiries were made but the son could not be traced. On the evidence Joyce J was satisfied that the son was dead but did not wish to make a declaration to this effect in case he re-appeared or there was evidence that he had died after the testator. Accordingly, an order was made that the estate of the testator be distributed on the footing that the son had predeceased the father unmarried. His share of the residue could then be safely distributed by the executors.

Inquiry for next of kin

The personal representatives may be unable, in an intestacy, to ascertain the next of kin by means of their own inquiries among the deceased's relatives and friends or there may be difficulty in proving relationship with the deceased. In these cases the personal representatives may ask the court to conduct an inquiry for next of kin and protect themselves by means of court orders.

19.3 Rights of beneficiaries pending distribution

Prior to the distribution of the assets, ownership in them is vested in the personal representative. It is well established that he holds these assets on a limited type of trust, that is, to get in the estate and preserve it and administer the assets according to the law and the terms of the will. This was made clear in *Commissioner of Stamp Duties (Queensland)* v *Livingston* [1965] AC 694, where Viscount Radcliffe said:

> '... whatever property came to the executor *virtute officii* came to him full ownership, without distinction between legal and equitable interests. The whole property was his. He held it for the purpose of carrying out the functions and duties of administration, not for his own benefit ... Certainly, therefore, he was in a fiduciary position with regard to the assets that came to him in the right of his office, and for certain purposes and in some aspects he was treated by the court as a trustee.'

The trust Viscount Radcliffe referred to is limited in its scope. It does not as a general rule give beneficiaries under the will or intestacy an equitable interest in their entitlement in the same way as a beneficiary under an express trust has an equitable interest. On this point Viscount Radcliffe said:

> 'What equity did not do was recognise or create for residuary legatees a beneficial interest in the assets in the executor's hands in the course of administration ... It would have been a clumsy and unsatisfactory device from a practical point of view and indeed, it would have been in plain conflict with the basic conception of equity that to impose the fetters of a trust upon property, with the resulting creation of equitable interests in that property, there had to be specific subjects, identifiable as the trust fund. An unadministered estate was incapable of satisfying this requirement. The assets as a whole were in the hands of the executor, his property; and until administration was complete no one was in a position to say what items of property would need to be realised for the purposes of administration or of what the residue, when ascertained, would consist or what its value would be.'

The position of a beneficiary during the administration is therefore not as a beneficiary under a trust. Instead, pending distribution, the beneficiary has a chose in action to ensure that the estate is properly administered as is illustrated by the following case.

In *Commissioner of Stamp Duties (Queensland)* v *Livingston* [1965] AC 694 the testator, Livingston, left all his estate both real and personal to his wife absolutely. While his estate was still being administered, his wife died intestate. One question which arose was whether succession duty was payable by the wife's estate in respect of the property left to the wife by the testator's will. The relevant statute declared that succession duty was payable in respect of 'every devolution by law of any beneficial interest in property ... upon the death of any person'.

Held: no succession duty was payable. The testator's property had not passed to the wife at any time before his death and she did not have a beneficial interest under any trust prior to distribution; she only had a right or chose in action to see that the estate was properly administered.

The chose in action vested in the beneficiary to see that the estate is properly administered is assignable to him in the same manner as any other chose in action. This is illustrated by *Re Leigh's Will Trusts* [1970] Ch 277. By her will the testatrix bequeathed 'all shares which I hold and any other interest or assets which I may have' in S Ltd. The testatrix never possessed any shares or interest in S Ltd when she made her will, but at her death she was the sole administratix of her husband's unadministered estate which comprised shares in and a debt due from S Ltd.

The question arose whether these shares and the debt passed under the bequest.

Held (per Buckley J): the testatrix was able to transfer her right to require her husband's estate to be duly administered to her executors and eventually to the legatee under her will. Her interests in the company were sufficient to answer the description in the specific bequest and, therefore, to entitle the legatee to receive such of the shares and so much of the debt as in due administration of her husband's estate would fall into the possession of the testatrix.

It was pointed out by Buckley J that the assignment by the testatrix of her right to require her husband's estate to be properly administered could not fetter the new administrator of her husband's estate.

The decision in *Re Leigh* appears, on the face of it, to be perfectly acceptable. However, it may well be that some of the consequences which may flow from it were unforeseen at the time. It is difficult to see how the doctrine of ademption would operate if the shares had been sold at any time before the testatrix's death in order to administer her husband's estate. Further, it is unclear what the position would be if the testatrix had also owned shares in the company in her own name both at the date of the will and the date of her death. Would the gift in her will fail for uncertainty?

The rule that a beneficiary only has a right to ensure that the estate is properly administered applies to:

1. residuary legatees, as the *Livingston* case clearly indicates;
2. those entitled on intestacy – see *Lall* v *Lall* [1965] 3 All ER 330;
3. general legacies – see *Re Leigh's Will Trusts*.

There is, however, doubt as to whether the rule applies to a beneficiary entitled to a specific legacy or devise. In *IRC* v *Hawley* [1928] 1 KB 578 there are indications that the court considered a specific legatee as having a beneficial interest in the legacy from death. However, this case must be in doubt after the decision in the *Livingston* case and perhaps the better view is that specific legatees and devisees only have a chose in action as well.

The recent case of *Crowden* v *Aldridge* [1993] 1 WLR 433 should be mentioned. This involved in an administration of an estate, a variation of intention in memoranda expressing the legatees' intention; the question was whether this was effective in varying the distribution.

A testator had employed a housekeeper all of her working life. When he died the testator left £100 in his will to the housekeeper, with the remainder going to his 16 first cousins. Following the funeral the cousins agreed that £100 was inadequate for the housekeeper and each signed a memorandum to the effect that the will should be varied and that each was prepared to sign a deed accordingly. When the deed was prepared, four of the parties refused to sign.

The executors commenced proceedings to determine whether the testator's will had been effectively varied by the memoranda.

Held: the memoranda demonstrated the intention to create legal effect. In the absence of any grounds evidencing why the signatories did not intend the document to have legal effect the memoranda had effect to vary the estate as soon as communication was made to the executors. Accordingly, there was a declaration that the devolution of the estate of the testator had been varied.

19.4 Assents

When an executor or administrator assents to certain property passing in accordance with the terms of the will or the rules of intestacy, this indicates that he no longer needs the property for the purposes of administration and that it can pass to the beneficiary. Thus the assent represents the passing of title from the executor or administrator to the beneficiary.

At common law the power to assent existed in respect of pure personalty and leaseholds and it was extended to devises of realty by the Land Transfer Act 1897. However, the assimilation of the law between realty and personalty brought about in 1897 was broken by s36 of the Administration of Estates Act 1925 which lays down special requirements for an effective assent in respect of land. Therefore assents in respect of personalty and assents in respect of land are dealt with separately.

19.5 Assents to personalty

The common law rules still apply to assents to personalty and by these rules there is no prescribed form in which the assent has to be made; the only requirement is that the personal representative indicates that the property is no longer needed for the purposes of administration. Thus the assent may arise where the beneficiary is told either orally or by writing, for example, a letter, to take the chattels bequeathed to him, or from conduct, as where the executor allows a beneficiary to take his chattels. The leading case on this is *Attenborough* v *Solomon* [1913] AC 76 (HL).

In this case the testator died in 1878 leaving all his residuary estate to his two sons, AA Solomon and JD Solomon, as executors and trustees to hold the same on trust for sale and to divide the proceeds equally between all his children. The executors paid all the deceased's debts and liabilities within a year and the residuary accounts were passed but the estate was not distributed. In 1892 AA Solomon, one of the executors, pledged some silver forming part of the residuary estate with Attenborough, a pawnbroker, in order to secure a loan. AA Solomon died in 1907, when the matter came to light. The question arose whether Attenborough could claim any rights over the silver pledged. If the silver was pledged by AA Solomon as executor, then Attenborough had rights in it, as one executor can bind the others in this respect. However, if he pledged the silver as trustee, then Attenborough had no rights in it as the trustees' power of disposal is joint. Therefore it was vital to know if an assent had been made by the executors to transfer the property to themselves as trustees.

Held: the executors had assented to themselves as trustees. This could be inferred from the fact that the estate had been administered within one year of the testator's death and the estate accounts passed within that time. Further, the fact that no further acts of admininistration had taken place between that time and the date of the pledge strengthened this inference.

The assent has the effect of making the dispositions of the will become operative by vesting in the beneficiaries the property in the chattels bequeathed to them. See *Attenborough* v *Solomon* [1913] AC 76 per Viscount Haldane LC. However, the transfer of the property does not occur by reason of the assent by the executor, but by virtue of the dispositions of the will. The assent merely makes these dispositions operative.

Once an assent has been made in respect of personalty it has three important consequences.

Relates back to death
Because the assent makes a gift in the will operative, it relates back to death, giving the beneficiary the right to income and profits arising on the subject matter of the gift from death. Therefore, if an assent is made in favour of the wrong person because a later codicil or will is discovered, it nevertheless perfects the title of the person rightfully entitled because assents are to legacies and not to legatees. See *Re West* [1909] Ch 180.

In *Re West* [1909] Ch 180 the testator made a specific bequest of shares to a named beneficiary by a codicil to his will. The executors transferred the shares to that beneficiary in accordance with the terms of the codicil. Several years later a later codicil was found to the will which bequeathed the shares to a different person, who sued for the recovery of the shares and the dividends paid on them since the testator's death.

Held: both the shares and the dividends were recoverable because the beneficiary became entitled to these at the testator's death. The fact that the assent had been made in favour of the wrong person was irrelevant because the assent was to the bequest and not to the beneficiary.

Beneficiary becomes responsible for the subject matter

Since the assent vests the property in the beneficiary, he becomes responsible for it thereafter. One of the incidents of this is that the costs of transferring the property to the beneficiary must be paid by him and any transport or insurance costs must be paid by him also. In *Re Sivewright* [1922] WN 338 a legatee, it was held, must bear the costs of packing and delivering china and jewellery to her address after the assent had been made.

Legal action to recover bequest

A beneficiary is entitled to take legal proceedings to recover his bequest from either the executor or some other person after an assent has been made in his favour. See *Re West* (1909) (above). This right only exists in respect of specific bequests and not in respect of general legacies, residuary gifts or rights on intestacy. See *Deeks* v *Strutt* (1794) 5 TR 690; *Jones* v *Tanner* (1827) 7 B & C 542.

The title in the property in respect of which the assent has been made will pass on the assent being made. In the case of a chattel such as a vase or a piece of furniture, the title will pass immediately. However, if the personalty is in the form of a chose in action, then the effect of the assent may be to make the executors trustees of the property for the beneficiary when it is necessary to comply with other regulations for transfer. Thus, in *Re Grosvenor* [1916] 2 Ch 375, an assent by the executors to a specific legacy of shares did not vest the title in the beneficiary, as this could only occur by the execution of a share transfer certificate and the entering of the name of the beneficiary in the company's books. Therefore, the executors held the shares on trust for the beneficiary.

19.6 Assents to land

These are now governed by s36 of the Administration of Estates Act 1925. Under s36(1) the provisions apply to:

> '... any estate or interest in real estate in which the testator or intestate was entitled or over which he exercised a general power of appointment by his will, including the statutory power to dispose of entailed interests which devolved on the personal representative.'

It should be noted that s36(1) refers to land 'which devolved on the personal representative'. This means that if the land is conveyed to the personal representative after the deceased's death the provisions of s36(1) are not applicable and instead of an assent to transfer the land, a deed will be required. Thus, if the testator had contracted to purchase property and the same had not been conveyed to him at his death but was eventually conveyed to his personal representatives, the personal representatives would have to transfer the property to a devisee by deed rather than by an assent.

The authority on this is *Re Stirrup's Contract* [1961] 1 WLR 449. T died in 1908 and by his will he left his freehold house to his wife Jane for life, remainder to his daughter, Hannah, absolutely. Jane died in 1930 and appointed her son, Richard Stirrup, to be her sole executor. However, Hannah had died in 1925 appointing Richard Stirrup and her husband David Evans to be her executors. Richard Stirrup conveyed the freehold house to himself and David Evans to hold on the trusts for Hannah's will in 1932; they took the property in their capacity as personal representatives. Richard Stirrup died in 1943. David Evans died in 1957 appointing the National Provincial Bank as his executor. Therefore the bank became executor by representation of Hannah's estate under s7 of the Administration of Estates Act 1925. In 1958 the bank executed an assent under seal in favour of the person next entitled thereto under Hannah's will, one Ruth Jones, whose successor in title, Jane Helen Stirrup, sold the house to the Co-op. The Co-op objected to the title on the ground that the bank should have conveyed the house to Ruth Jones, rather than assenting in her favour, because the house had not devolved on Hannah's personal representatives on her death but was conveyed to them afterwards.

Held (per Wilberforce J): an assent was not available to pass the property in this case because under s36(1) this could only be used where the property had devolved on the personal representative. On the facts there had been a conveyance of the property by Richard Stirrup in 1932 and therefore a conveyance was required to pass the property. However, as the assent was under seal, it complied with s52(1) of the Law of Property Act 1925 and could be regarded as a deed.

The following are the main circumstances when an assent can be used:

1. to transfer the legal estate to a beneficiary in accordance with the terms of the will;
2. to transfer the legal estate to trustees under the terms of the will;
3. where a beneficiary has survived the testator but died before an assent can be made in his favour, an assent can be made to his personal representatives;
4. where a beneficiary has predeceased the testator but the devise does not fail, an assent can be made to his personal representatives;
5. where the deceased contracted to sell realty before his death but had not conveyed the property to the purchaser, the personal representatives may make an assent to the purchaser.

There is still uncertainty as to whether an assent can be made by the personal representatives to the purchaser from a beneficiary. For example, if X was left Blackacre in T's will and, before an assent was made in his favour, he contracted to sell the property to Y. Probably the safer course is for the personal representatives to make a conveyance by deed in accordance with s52(1) of the Law of Property Act 1925.

19.7 Form of assent

The provisions of s36(4) set out formal requirements for an assent. The provision states:

> 'An assent to the vesting of a legal estate shall be in writing, signed by the personal representative, and shall name the person in whose favour it is given and shall operate to vest in that person the legal estate to which it relates; and an assent not in writing or not in favour of a named person shall not be effectual to pass a legal estate.'

Assents are an exception to the basic rule that a conveyance must be used to transfer a legal estate and when made they relate back to the deceased's death. See s36(2). As s36(4) indicates, the assent must be in writing, signed by the personal representative, and name the person in whose favour it is given.

The requirement that an assent should be in writing has given rise to some problems in recent years. There is little doubt that an assent must be in writing where the personal representative is transferring the property to another. Section 36(4) plainly requires this because the legal estate is 'passing'. However, before 1964 it was thought that the provisions of s36(4) did not apply where the personal representative and the beneficiary were the same person because, in such circumstances it was said, there was no 'passing' of the legal estate, only a change in the capacity in which the estate was held. Thus, for example, if T appointed X as his sole executor and devised Blackacre to him, X already holds the legal estate in his name, albeit as personal representative, and when he has completed administration he merely changes from executor to beneficial owner *vis-à-vis* Blackacre. There is no 'passing' of the legal estate.

This theory was rejected in *Re King's Will Trusts* [1964] Ch 542. The testatrix appointed A, B and C as her executors, and A and B as trustees of certain trusts under her will. A and B proved the will and power was reserved to C to prove the will. On the death of A, B appointed C as a co-trustee of the trust property. On the death of B, X became executor of B's estate. C appointed the plaintiff by deed to be a co-trustee. C then died leaving the plaintiff as sole trustee. The question arose whether the legal estate in the trust property was vested in the plaintiff or in X as personal representative of the last surviving proving executor of the estate of the testatrix.

Held: since 1925, a written assent is essential to vest the legal estate in land in a trustee or beneficiary, even though the person holding the legal estate as personal representative is the same person as the trustee or beneficiary; as no effective assent has been made the legal estate was vested in X.

In rejecting the theory that a written assent was not needed if there was only a change in capacity, Pennycuick J said in *Re King*, in reference to the first sentence of s36(4), that it:

'Contemplates that for this purpose a person may assent vest in himself in another capacity, and such vesting, of course, necessarily implies that he is divesting himself of the estate in his original capacity. It seems to me impossible to regard the same operation as lying outside the negative provisions contained in the second sentence of the sub-section. To do so involves making a distinction between the operation of divesting and vesting the legal estate and that of passing the legal estate. I do not think that this highly artificial distinction is legitimate. On the contrary, the second sentence appears to be intended as an exact counterpart to the first.'

Thus Pennycuick J saw the matter as one of the executor divesting himself of the estate in one capacity and vesting himself in another capacity. But, to extend the word 'pass' in s36(4) to cases of change of capacity appears rather artificial.

Whatever criticisms may be made of *Re King's Will Trusts*, a written assent in accordance with s36(4) is still highly desirable in cases where the executor and beneficiary are the same person, because it provides documentary evidence of the title to the legal estate. However, *Re King* should be contrasted with *Re Cockburn's Will Trusts* [1957] Ch 438. In that case it was held that personal representatives having completed the administration of the estate, became trustees and could thereafter appoint new trustees of the will without the need for a vesting assent. If *Re King* is correct then it would appear to indicate that in future new trustees are unable to deal with the legal estate in land until an assent is executed in their favour. See below.

19.8 Effect of assent

The most important effect of an assent is stated in s36(4), namely, that it operates to vest the legal estate in the person in whose favour it is given. As stated earlier, under s36(2) the assent relates back to death.

Section 36 contains extensive provisions designed to protect purchasers in whose favour an assent is made. If the personal representatives have to sell any of the deceased's realty for the purposes of administration they are likely to want to use an assent in order to save stamp duty. From the purchaser's point of view, the following protection is given to him.

First, under s36(7):

'An assent or conveyance by a personal representative in respect of a legal estate shall, in favour of a purchaser, unless notice of a previous assent or conveyance affecting that legal estate has been placed on or annexed to the probate or administration, be taken as sufficient evidence that the person in whose favour the assent or conveyance is given or made is the person entitled to have the legal estate conveyed to him ...'

'Purchaser' for these purposes means a purchaser for money or money's worth. The provision states that an assent is 'sufficient' evidence that the purchaser in whose favour it is made is entitled to the legal estate. Thus, in *Re Duce and Boots etc*

Contract [1937] Ch 642, the assent contained a recital that the land was in fact settled but the document nevertheless purported to vest the property in the beneficiary absolutely. It was held that the purchaser was entitled to object to the beneficiary's title.

If the assent contains notice annexed to the probate or administration that an assent or conveyance has previously been affecting that legal estate then the provisions of s36(7) are no protection to the purchaser. He should refuse the property.

Second, under s36(8):

> 'A conveyance of a legal estate by a personal representative to a purchaser shall not be invalidated by reason only that the purchaser may have notice that all the debts, liabilities, funeral and testamentary and administration expenses, duties and legacies of the deceased have not been discharged or provided for.'

Note that this provision only applies where there has been a conveyance. As other subsections use the term 'assent or conveyance' it must be concluded that s36(8) is not applicable to assents. Therefore, a purchaser who has notice that all the debts, liabilities etc have not been paid, ought to request a conveyance rather than an assent. The provisions of s36(8) only apply to a purchaser in good faith for money or money's worth. See ss36(11) and 55(1)(viii). The main effect of s36(8) is that the purchaser does not have to inquire as to why the property is being sold if he has notice that the sale is not for the purposes of administration.

The provisions of s36(5) are intended to protect beneficiaries in whose favour an assent is made. They state that:

> 'Any person in whose favour an assent or conveyance of a legal estate is made by a personal representative may require that notice of the assent or conveyance be written or endorsed on or permanently annexed to the probate or letters of administration at the cost of the estate of the deceased, and that the probate or letters of administration be produced, at the like cost, to prove that the notice has been placed on or annexed to the probate or administration.'

This provision should always be taken advantage of by beneficiaries under the deceased's will or intestacy. If notice of the assent or conveyance is attached to the probate or letters of administration then the beneficiary's title will be protected in cases where the personal representatives subsequently try to sell the property. No purchaser would accept title from the personal representatives in such circumstances because the provisions of s36(7) (above) would not operate. However, if there is no notice of the assent or conveyance in accordance with s36(5), the beneficiary could lose the property to a purchaser, A purchaser should require the personal representatives, in such circumstances, to make a statement in writing that they have not made any previous assent or conveyance in respect of the legal estate, because under s36(6) such statement shall:

> '... operate to transfer or create the legal estate expressed to be conveyed in like manner as if no previous assent or conveyance had been made by the personal representatives'.

Example

V, as executor of T's estate, contracts to sell Blackacre to P. In perusing the title to Blackacre, P finds a notice annexed to V's grant of probate that V assented to Blackacre in favour of X. It is clear V cannot give P title. However, if P finds no such notice, he should ask V to give a statement in writing that he has not given an assent or conveyance in respect of a legal estate in Blackacre. If this is refused, P should refuse to accept title. If it is given, P can safely accept title from V and obtain the protection of s36(7).

The provisions of ss36(6) and 36(7) are a useful protection for purchasers against the claims of beneficiaries. But they provide no protection where the personal representative has already made an assent or conveyance in favour of a *bona fide* purchaser of the legal estate, because s36(6) operates:

'... without prejudice to any previous disposition made in favour of another purchaser deriving title mediately or immediately under the personal representative'.

The provisions of s36(10) protect the personal representatives who make the assent or conveyance. If the assent is made in favour of a beneficiary before all debts and liabilities have been paid the personal representative may:

'... require security for the discharge of any such duties, debts or liability, but shall not be entitled to postpone the giving of an assent merely by reason of the subsistence of any such duties, debts or liability, if reasonable arrangements have been made for discharging the same; and an assent may be given subject to any legal estate or charge by way of legal mortgage.'

Thus, if inheritance tax is payable in instalments, the personal representatives do not have to hold on to the property in the estate until the last instalments are paid. By s36(10) they should, and ought to, give assents subject to security for the discharge of unpaid inheritance tax. Should they fail to avail themselves of the protection of s36(10) they may have to bear the unpaid debts, liabilities and taxes themselves. In *Re Rosenthal* [1972] 1 WLR 1273 the executors assented to a house passing to a beneficiary without taking any security for unpaid estate duty thereon. The beneficiary sold the house and went abroad without paying the duty. It was held the executors must pay the duty themselves.

A personal representative may in some cases be slow to make an assent, or refuse to do so until he discharges the debts and liabilities. The remedy of a beneficiary in such circumstances is, under s43(2) of the Administration of Estates Act 1925, to apply to the court for directions and the court may make such order as it deems proper.

19.9 Appropriation

If a beneficiary has been left a large pecuniary legacy or a general legacy, for example, a new Rolls Royce motor car or 10,000 shares in ICI, it may be expensive and/or difficult for the executors to sell off assets to obtain the money to meet the pecuniary legacy or to find the property to satisfy the general legacy. In these cases the executors may exercise the power of appropriation under s41 of the Administration of Estates Act 1925 which states:

> 'The personal representative may appropriate any part of the real or personal estate, including things in action, of the deceased in the actual condition or state of investment thereof at the time of appropriation in or towards satisfaction of any legacy bequeathed by the deceased, or of any other interest or share in his property, whether settled or not, as to the personal representatives may seem just and reasonable, according to the respective rights of the persons interested in the property of the deceased.'

The power of appropriation is not unfettered; the personal representatives must observe the following matters. First, an appropriation must not be made under s41 so as to affect prejudicially any specific devise or bequest. See s41(1)(i). Thus the subject matter of a specific devise or bequest must not be appropriated to satisfy a pecuniary legacy.

Second, consents must be obtained to the appropriation from the following persons under s41(1)(ii).

1. Where a beneficiary is absolutely entitled, then no appropriation can be made without his consent. Thus, if Y was given 20,000 shares in ICI and the executors could not obtain these on the open market, they could not force X to take the cash equivalent or shares in some other company.
2. Where there is a settled interest, consent to the appropriation must be obtained either from the trustee thereof, if any (not being a personal representative), or the person who is for the time being entitled to the income.

If a person whose consent is required is incapable of giving consent, because he is an infant or a mental patient, then the consent must be given by his parents, guardian or receiver. If an infant has no parent or guardian the court will give consent on his behalf on the application of his next friend. No consents are necessary in the following cases in any circumstances.

1. On behalf of a person not yet born or who cannot be found or ascertained at the time of appropriation. See s41(1)(iii).
2. On behalf of a mental patient where there is no receiver acting for him and the appropriation is of an investment authorised, by law or by the will.
3. Where, in the case of a settled legacy, there is no trustee independent of the personal representative and no person of full age and capacity entitled to the income and the appropriation is of an authorised investment.

Third, the personal representatives should ascertain and fix a value of the parts of the estate to be affected by the appropriation. For this purpose they must employ a duly qualified valuer. The valuation for the purpose of appropriation is that relevant to the property at the date of appropriation rather than at the date of death. See s41(3) and *Re Collins* [1975] 1 WLR 309.

The effects of an appropriation, when made, are as follows.

1. The appropriation binds all persons interested in the property of the deceased whose consent was not necessary. See s41(4).
2. The property appropriated becomes the effective and binding substitute for the gift made to the beneficiary under the will. See s41(1) and (2).
3. If the appropriation was of real estate, then if the person to whom it was conveyed subsequently disposes of it in favour of a purchaser from him, the appropriation shall be deemed to have been made in accordance with s41 with all requisite consents being obtained. See s41(7).
4. The power of appropriation in s41 can be varied or modified or excluded by the testator's will and it therefore takes effect subject to the provisions in his will. See s41(6).

19.10 Power to set off legacies against debts

This power is sometimes referred to as the power to retain. It arises when a beneficiary under the testator's will or intestacy, who is entitled to money from the estate, owes money to the estate. The personal representative may set off or retain the money owed by the beneficiary against what is due to him. In *Re Rhodesia Goldfields Ltd* [1910] 1 Ch 239, it was said: 'the rule is of general application … where a fund is being distributed a party cannot take anything out of the fund until he has made good what he owes to the fund'. In *Re Akerman* [1891] 3 Ch 212, Kekewich J said:

> 'A person who owes an estate money, that is to say, who is bound to increase the general mass of the estate by a contribution of his own, cannot claim an aliquot share given to him out of that mass without first making the contribution that completes it.'

Thus, for example, if X is given a legacy of £10,000 by T's will and he owes T's estate a debt of £2,000, he must pay the £2,000 before he can obtain his legacy. Otherwise, the executors may deduct that figure from his legacy and only pay him the balance of £8,000.

The right of set-off or right to retain must be distinguished from 'retainer'. This right was closely connected with the right of preference which gave an executor the power to prefer one creditor to another creditor in the same degree. The right of 'retainer' was an aspect of preference, in that it referred to a case where an executor who was a creditor of the deceased preferred himself to another creditor of equal degree. These rights were abolished by s10(1) of the Administration of Estates Act 1971.

The right of set-off is not without its limitations; these spring from the general rule that the right is only exerciseable were there is 'money payable against money payable'.

Money must be payable to the beneficiary

The beneficiary must be entitled to receive a cash sum under the will or intestacy. If he is entitled to a legacy of chattels etc or a devise the right of set-off is not available. Thus, in *Re Savage* [1918] 2 Ch 146, the power could not be used where the beneficiary was entitled to colonial stock under the will, even though this could be easily sold.

Money must be owed by the beneficiary

The beneficiary must owe money and not something else, and the money he owes must be presently payable. If X owed money to the testator and it had been agreed this would be repaid by instalments, set-off is only available against instalments which have become due and not against future instalments. See *Re Abrahams* [1908] 2 Ch 69. The money must be owed by the beneficiary alone and not jointly with someone else such as a co-partner or co-director. Thus, in *Turner* v *Turner* [1911] 1 Ch 716, the right of set-off was not available where a debt was owed to the deceased by two partners jointly and one of the partners was entitled to a legacy under the will.

No application to derivative claims

The right of set-off cannot be used against a legacy given to a beneficiary who predeceased the deceased and whose benefit goes to someone else under the terms of the will or the rules of intestacy. Thus, in *Re Binns* [1929] 1 Ch 677, the court refused to allow the right to be exercised where children took their deceased father's share under the terms of the will. The personal representatives had to look to the father's estate for a debt owed by him to the testator and could not set off his debt against the shares his children took in his place.

The right of retainer gives the personal representatives the power to recover a debt without the need to incur expense in obtaining judgment for the debt. It even allows them to set-off against a statute barred debt. See *Courtenay* v *Williams* (1844) 3 Hare 539. However, if the beneficiary is bankrupt, the right to set-off depends on when his bankruptcy occurred. If it occurred before the deceased's death, the set-off is only available against the dividend due to the estate under the bankruptcy. No set-off is available against the debt because bankruptcy terminates the debt. See *Cherry* v *Boultbee* (1839) 4 My & Cr 442. If bankruptcy occurred after the deceased's death then the power of set-off is available, but it will be lost if the personal representatives prove in bankruptcy. See *Stammers* v *Elliot* (1868) 3 Ch App 195. Thus, if the legacy is greater than the net value of the bankrupt beneficiaries' estate, a claim should not be made in bankruptcy.

19.11 Transition from personal representative to trustee

The office of personal representative is one which lasts for life unless the grant was limited in time or is subsequently revoked. See *Harvell* v *Foster* [1954] 2 QB 367.

This is the position even if all the deceased's assets have been administered and distributed, because the office is independent of the property which originally devolved with it. However, in the course of the distribution of the deceased's assets, the personal representative may be directed by the will to hold certain property on trust or it may be that he cannot distribute because, for example, the beneficiary is an infant. The question arises whether in relation to the property concerned he remains a personal representative or whether he assumes the character of a trustee.

The general rule is that the personal representative holds the assets of the deceased during the course of administration as personal representative and not as a trustee. It is true that the definition of 'trustee' in s68(17) of the Trustee Act 1925 includes a personal representative but this is because he is a special type of trustee with special functions and duties. Thus he will not be regarded as a formal trustee of the legacies and devises prior to distribution. There are, however, three cases where the position of the personal representative deserves close attention.

Beneficiary an infant

If a testator leaves land or personalty to a person of full age and capacity, there is no trust on the personal representative. If the beneficiary is an infant the personal representative cannot transfer the property to him as an infant cannot give a valid receipt for it. But, even though distribution cannot be made to the infant, it appears that the personal representativee does not, on that fact alone, become a trustee of the infant's share. In *Harvell* v *Foster* (above), Sir Raymond Evershed MR touched on this point with reference to s42 of the Administration of Estates Act 1925 (which enables the personal representative to appoint a trust corporation or two or more trustees to hold the infant beneficiary's property and be discharged from further liability in respect thereof). He said:

> 'That provision seems to us to carry a necessary implication to the effect that until a personal representative having in his hands assets to which an infant is absolutely entitled either avails himself of the prescribed method of obtaining his discharge from further liability (scilicet as personal representatives) in respect of those assets, or accounts for them and pays them over to the infant on his or her attaining the age of (eighteen years) he remains liable for them in his capacity as personal representative.'

Intestacy

It appears that the principle in *Harvell* v *Foster* is also applicable in cases where the deceased died intestate and minority or life interests arise on intestacy, so that the administrator does not cease to act as such and assume the office of trustee. Some earlier decisions appear to indicate that the administrator did in fact become a trustee but these were criticised by the Court of Appeal in *Harvell* v *Foster*. In *Re Ponder* [1921] 2 Ch 59 the deceased died intestate leaving a widow and two infant sons. The widow was appointed administratrix of the estate and in due course she invested the beneficial interests of the two sons in her name. Sargant J appears to have decided that once the administratrix had cleared the estate and discharged all her functions other than those of trustee for the persons beneficially entitled to the residue she must be taken as having discharged herself from all her obligations as administratrix. This was regarded in *Harvell* v *Foster* as too wide. In addition Sargant J decided that an administrator of an intestate's estate could in due course of time assume the character and functions of trustee in the same way as one appointed by will as executor and trustee and could therefore invoke the statutory powers of appointing new or additional trustees. In *Re Yerburgh* [1928] WN 208 there are indications that Romer J may well have come to a similar conclusion as that in *Re Ponder* but the dicta on this point are rather vague.

The question as to whether an administrator can become a trustee of the estate on intestacy should not be confused with the imposition of statutory trusts under s33 of the Administration of Estates Act 1925. It would appear that these trusts are limited to the administration of the estate and have no relevance to the issue as to whether a formal trust arises when administration is complete *vis-à-vis* assets which remain in the hands of the administrator.

Formal trusteeship

A testator may create an express trust in his will such as 'the residue of my estate on trust for A for life, remainder to B', etc. In such circumstances he may have:

1. appointed the same persons to be executors of the will and trustees of the wills trust; or
2. made no appointment of trustees of the wills trust; or
3. appointed different persons to be executors and trustees.

In the third case the executors will have to transfer the assets subject to the trust to the trustees in the course of administration. If the property is personalty, an informal assent will be sufficient. See *Attenborough* v *Solomon* [1913] AC 76. But if it is land the provisions of s36 of the Administration of Estates Act must be complied with. In the second case the executors will be the proper persons to undertake the trusteeship. See *Re Cockburn* [1957] Ch 438.

In the first two cases above the executors will eventually change their capacity from that of executors to trustees of the property subject to the trusts. One question which arises is whether this change in capacity can be inferred from circumstances or whether some affirmative or declaratory act is necessary. If the trust comprises realty it is suggested that the wiser course is for the personal representative to make a written assent in favour of the executor, declaring in this that he now holds the property as trustee. But if the trust comprises pure personalty there is no need for formal assents or conveyances and the only issue is whether there is an automatic change in capacity from executor to administrator when the estate has been cleared.

The dicta of Danckwerts J in *Re Cockburn* appear to indicate that an automatic change in capacity from executor to trustee is possible. He said:

> 'I feel no doubt about the matter at all. Whether persons are executors or administrators, once they have completed the administration in due course, they become trustees holding for the beneficiaries, either on an intestacy or under the terms of the will, and are bound to carry out the duties of trustees.'

This dicta is far from conclusive as the decision was concerned with the appointment of new trustees rather than with the change in capacity. It remains to be decided whether some formality is needed for a change in capacity.

19.12 Income and interest from legacies and devises

The distribution of legacies and devises will frequently take place some years after the testator's death. Even if distribution is carried out efficiently there is bound to be an interval between the date of death and the date of distribution. The subject matter of the legacies, devises and other gifts, will continue to produce income in this period; for example, shares will be producing dividends and land rents and other profits. This section is concerned with the destination of this income. Further, if the property does not produce income it may be that interest is payable on it.

Specific bequests and devises

Immediate specific requests and devises

These gifts carry all income and profits which have accrued from the testator's death. Thus, in *Re West* [1909] 2 Ch 180, a specific legacy of company shares carried all dividends from the testatrix's death and the beneficiary was entitled to sue for both these and the shares themselves where they had been given to the wrong person by the executors.

The right to income on specific bequests and devises from the testator's death carries with it the burden of costs and expenses connected with the property concerned. Thus, the costs of insurance and upkeep of the property will be deducted from the actual income or, if necessary, the beneficiary will have to meet these expenses from his own resources if the actual income is insufficient. In *Re Rooke* [1933] Ch 970 it was held that a beneficiary to whom a house had been specifically devised was bound to meet the costs of preserving and maintaining the property. Maugham J considered that it would be difficult to justify the rule that the beneficiary was entitled to all the income from the testator's death if this did not carry with it the duty to meet costs and expenses on the property. In *Re Day's Will Trusts* [1962] 1 WLR 1419 a beneficiary who received property let to tenants was bound to meet the expenses involved in observing a landlord's covenant to keep the premises in repair between the testator's death and the date he received the property. However, a beneficiary under an immediate bequest or devise is not bound to meet the amount due on a contract entered into by the testator to effect improvements or repairs to the property. Thus, in *Re Rushbrook's Will Trusts* [1948] Ch 421 a devisee was not obliged to pay £550 for repairs to a house he received where the testator had entered into a contract with builders to have these executed. The cost of these was a burden on the general estate.

Sometimes the property devised or bequeathed will be producing income which is payable at stated intervals; for example, a leasehold property devised may be producing rent which is payable quarterly. In such circumstances it will be necessary to apportion the income between the devisee and the general estate if the testator dies in the middle of the period concerned. Therefore if rent was due for the quarter ending on 25 December and the testator died on 25 November, all rent due between 25 September and 24 November would belong to the general estate. This is provided for in s2 of the Apportionment Act 1870 which states:

> 'All rents, annuities, dividends and other periodical payments in the nature of income ... shall, like interest on money lent, be considered as accruing from day to day, and shall be apportionable in respect of time accordingly.'

This provision clearly applies to rents (see *Re Aspinall* [1961] Ch 526) and also dividends. See *Re Griffith* (1879) 12 Ch D 655. However, it will not apply if the income from an assent is deemed to accrue only on the final day of the period concerned; this appears to be the position in respect of many partnerships and other businesses. See *Re Robbins* [1941] Ch 434.

Future specific bequests and devises

Future gifts may be either contingent or deferred. A contingent gift is one which waits for and depends upon the happening of some event, or some condition being performed, by the beneficiary, for example, 'to X if he attains the age of 25'. A gift may also be deferred to a future date which must come, for example, 'to X after the death of my wife'.

Before 1925 the rules on income and interest on future gifts were rather complex. Some of these rules have been embodied in s175 of the Law of Property Act 1925 while others still depend for their authority upon pre-1926 decisions.

A contingent or future specific devise or bequest carries income from the death of the testator except insofar as it has been otherwise expressly disposed of. See s175 of the Law of Property Act 1925. Thus, if the testator left 'Blackacre to A when he attains 21' or 'Blackacre to A after the death of my wife' the gift will carry the intermediate income. However, the testator may direct that the income be paid to someone else in the intervening period, for example, he may direct 'Blackacre to A after the death of my wife, the income thereof to B until then'.

If a beneficiary is entitled to the income on a gift under s175 but is a minor then the income will be accumulated and added to the capital sum because he could not give a good receipt for the income. See s31 of the Trustee Act 1925. On attaining majority all income will be paid to him as it arises together with any accumulations of income, even if the gift is contingent or deferred. See s31 of the Trustee Act 1925.

General legacies

Immediate general legacies

An immediate general legacy only carries interest from the time at which it is payable, the current rates being 5 per cent per annum. See RSC O.44 r19. Thus, if X was left a pecuniary legacy of £10,000 he can only expect 5 per cent interest thereon. This rule applies to other general legacies such as stocks and shares. Thus, if X was left '10,000 shares in Marks and Spencer', this gift, being general in nature, will only carry 5 per cent interest even though the actual dividends on these shares may be much higher. See *Re Hall* [1951] 1 All ER 1073.

The time for the payment of a general legacy may be fixed by the testator himself so that interest may run from then; for example, he may leave his wife a legacy of £30,000 payable immediately on his death. See *Re Pollock* [1943] Ch 338. However, if no time for payment is fixed by the will, interest will, as a general rule, run from the end of one year after the testator's death, that is, the end of the executor's year. See *Wood* v *Penoyre* (1807) 13 Ves 325. This rule is based on the notion that it takes 12 months to administer the estate of a testator and that all legacies ought to be paid at the end of that period.

In several cases the interest on a general pecuniary legacy will run from the testator's death, contrary to the general rule just mentioned, and are as follows.

1. Where the legacy is charged on land. See *Pearson* v *Pearson* (1802) 1 Sch & Lef 10. This exception arises because of its different historical origin to the general rule. The ecclesiastical courts developed the rule that interest on general legacies was payable only from one year from the testator's death. This exception was developed by the Court of Chancery which had jurisdiction over matters relating to real property.
2. Satisfaction of a debt. If the testator left £100 to X in satisfaction of a debt of a similar or a lesser amount (but not a larger amount because there would not be satisfaction in such a case) the legacy will carry interest from death. See *Re Rattenbury* [1906] 1 Ch 667.
3. Where the legacy is given to an infant child of the testator or a child to whom he stands *in loco parentis* and there is no other fund for the child's maintenance. See *Re Bowlby* [1904] 2 Ch 685. The rule is based on the presumption that the testator also intended to provide for his children during their infancy. See *Harvey* v *Harvey* (1722) 2 P Wms 21. However, it appears that this rule will not apply if the legacy is not given directly to the child but is, for example, given to trustees to hold on trust for him. See *Re Pollock* [1943] Ch 338.
4. Where the legacy shows an intention to provide for the maintenance of an infant beneficiary. Thus if the legacy is left to an infant for his maintenance (see *Re*

West [1913] 2 Ch 345) or his education (see *Re Jones* [1932] 1 Ch 642), this rule will apply.

Future general legacies

Contingent or deferred general (or pecuniary) legacies do not carry income until they become payable. See *Re Raine* [1920] 1 Ch 716; *Rawlings* v *Rawlings* (1796) 2 Cox 425. Therefore the personal representatives do not have to make any special provision for the income arising from these gifts; such income will fall in and form part of the residuary personal estate. Thus, for example, if a testator left '£10,000 to X when he attains 21', or '£10,000 to X five years after my death', interest in each case would only run from when X attained 21 or five years after the testator's death.

The testator may direct that a contingent or deferred legacy is to be severed and set apart from the general estate for the beneficiary. If this is so the gift will carry income from the end of the executor's year. See *Re Medlock* (1886) 55 LJ Ch 738. Thus, for example, if the testator directed £20,000 to be held on trust for the benefit of X contingent upon him attaining the age of 25, interest will be payable from the end of the executor's year on the £20,000. However, if the direction to set aside the gift is not made for the benefit of the beneficiary but, instead, for administrative convenience, this rule will not apply. See *Re Inman* [1893] 3 Ch 518.

A testator is free to direct that interest on a contingent or deferred general legacy be paid from his death or some other specified time contrary to the general rule of law. Further, the exceptions mentioned above, in relation to legacies to infants or for maintenance, carry interest from death even if they are contingent or deferred. See *Re Bowlby* [1904] 2 Ch 685; *Re Jones* [1932] 1 Ch 642.

Residuary gifts

Immediate residuary gifts

An immediate residuary gift, like immediate devises and bequests, carries all income and profits accruing thereon from the date of the testator's death. It does not matter whether it comprises realty or personalty. See *Barrington* v *Tristram* (1801) 6 Ves 845.

Future residuary bequests

A contingent residuary bequest (which is not deferred in any way) will carry all income and profits arising thereon from the testator's death unless the testator has directed otherwise. See *Green* v *Ekins* (1742) 2 Atk 473. However, the income will not be paid directly to the residuary legatee if it is to pass with the gift. If he is an infant then the income will be available for his maintenance under s31 of the Trustee Act 1925 but otherwise it will be accumulated. If he is not an infant the income will be accumulated for so long as is permitted by the provisions in ss164–166 of the Law of Property Act 1925. Thus, for example, if the residuary personalty was left to X contingent upon him attaining 30 and X was 20 at the date of the testator's death, the income would be accumulated for the 10-year period. If, however, X was only five at the date of the testator's death, accumulations of income could only be made for a maximum period of 21 years and thereafter the income would pass to the next of kin on intestacy. See *Re Taylor* [1901] 2 Ch 134. See also *Re Geering* [1964] Ch 136.

A deferred residuary bequest only carries income from the date when it becomes payable; it does not carry any income between the testator's death and that date. See *Re Geering* [1964] Ch 136, where Cross J said:

> 'The very fact that a testator defers a gift of residue to a future date is itself, *prima facie*, an indication that he does not intend the legatee to have the income of the residue accruing before that date'.

This rule applies whether the gift is vested but deferred, for example 'to X after the death of my wife', or deferred and contingent, for example, 'to X after the death of my wife contingent upon him attaining 30'. See *Re Oliver* [1947] 2 All ER 162; *Re Geering* [1964] Ch 136.

Future residuary devises

A contingent residuary devise, like a contingent residuary bequest, carries income from the testator's death. Under s175 of the Law of Property Act 1925 it is provided that the income will pass whether the residuary devise is made directly to the devisee or to trustees upon trust for a beneficiary. The income from a contingent residuary devise will be dealt with in the same manner as that from a contingent residuary bequest.

A deferred residuary devise does not carry income until it becomes payable and any income arising between the testator's death and the date of payment will pass under the intestacy rules. See *Re Oliver* [1947] 2 All ER 162. It appears strange that such gifts were not mentioned in s175, especially as it dealt with contingent residuary devises. However, it has been suggested that since any deferred gift would now have to take effect behind a trust, the provisions of s175 that 'a specific or residuary devise of freehold land to trustees upon trust for persons whose interests are ... executory' shall carry income would mean that such a gift carried income in any event. See P V Baker (1963) 79 LQR 184. For these purposes 'executory' is construed as meaning 'deferred'. See *Re McGeorge* [1963] Ch 544.

The rule in Allhusen *v* Whittell

Where a testator leaves his residuary estate to one or more persons absolutely then they will receive what is left after the deduction of debts, expenses and legacies. However, if the testator leaves his residuary estate to A for life, remainder to B absolutely, then the life tenant, that is, A, may be entitled to all income arising from the date of the testator's death. This may result in A obtaining far more income in the first year or so than the actual residue may produce.

If, for example, the residuary estate was worth £200,000 before the payment of debts which amounted to £50,000, it would be inequitable to allow the life tenant to receive income on £200,000 until the debts were paid. In *Allhusen* v *Whittell* (1867) LR 4 Eq 295, Wood VC said:

> 'The tenant for life ought not to have the income arising from what is wanted for the payment of debts, because that never becomes residue in any way whatsoever.'

Under the rule in *Allhusen* v *Whittell* the true residue will be ascertained only by treating the legacies and debts as having been paid partly out of income and partly out of capital. This is to achieve equality between the life tenant and remainderman.

20

Remedies of Creditors
and Beneficiaries

20.1 Introduction

20.2 Administration by the court

20.3 Action for specific relief

20.4 Action against personal representatives

20.5 Action against recipient of assets

20.6 Bankrupt beneficiaries: the obligations and liabilities of personal representatives

20.7 Joint tenancies

20.1 Introduction

In the majority of cases it will be possible to carry out the administration of the deceased's estate without resorting to the court for assistance. However, problems may arise in the course of administration. The personal representatives may have difficulty in interpreting the will or have doubts as to the actual extent of the deceased's assets. The beneficiaries may have doubts as to whether the executors have collected in and distributed the assets correctly or why they are so slow in distributing. The creditors may wish to ascertain why there is a delay in payment of the debts owed to them. These problems and many more besides are dealt with in this section.

20.2 Administration by the court

Under s61 and Schedule 1 para 1 of the Supreme Court Act 1981 the administration of estates of deceased persons is a matter assigned to the Chancery Division. Any person interested in the estate of the deceased may issue proceedings for administration by the court; this includes creditors, beneficiaries under the estate and the personal representatives. The county court has a limited power to administer estates under s52 of the County Courts Act 1952, provided the value of the estate does not exceed £30,000.

An action for administration by the court may be commenced either by way of originating summons or by writ. If the matter is one of law the former method will be used, but in cases where there is a dispute of fact a writ should be issued. See RSC O.5.

An estate cannot be administered by the court unless there is a duly constituted personal representative. See *Rosewell* v *Morris* (1873) LR 17 Eq 20. This is because there must be somebody who can be made a defendant. An executor *de son tort* cannot be made a party to an administration action as his only duty is to account for what he received. See *Coote* v *Whittington* (1873) LR 16 Eq 534. In cases where no grant of representation has been made, creditors and beneficiaries interested in the estate may apply to the court for the appointment of a receiver to protect the estate pending the appointment of a personal representative. See *Re Sutcliffe* [1942] Ch 453. However, if there are proceedings pending in relation to the estate, it is better to apply to the court for the appointment of an administrator pending suit under s117 of the Supreme Court Act 1981.

An order for administration of the estate will not be made by the court unless it is of the view that such an order is necessary. Thus if the deceased's estate was bankrupt, the court may administer it if it is considered difficult for the personal representatives to do so. See *Re Bradley* [1956] Ch 615. However, if the problems of the estate are such that they could be dealt with by the executors out of court, then an order for administration will not be made. In *Re Stocken* (1888) 38 Ch D 319 the court refused to administer the estate merely because the testator directed his executors to have this done.

In many cases an action for administration of the estate by the court will have been brought by the creditors and/or the beneficiaries against the personal representatives on the ground that they have not fulfilled their functions properly. In such cases the court will normally make an order directing that certain accounts and inquiries be taken and made; these will include the following.

1. An account of the property which was not specifically devised or bequeathed and which came into the hands of the executor or the hands of any other person on behalf of the executor.
2. An account of the testator's debts and funeral and testamentary expenses or, alternatively, if the testator died more than six years ago, an inquiry as to whether any debts or funeral or testamentary expenses remain unpaid.
3. An account of the legacies.
4. An inquiry as to what parts of the testator's property, if any, are outstanding or undisposed of and whether any such property is subject to any, and if so what, incumbrances.

When the accounts and inquiries have been completed the Chancery Master will certify the result of these and then make an order for the payment of debts and/or distribution of the estate.

As stated, administration by the court is often a costly matter and the court may often take steps to avoid the necessity of such administration. This may be done by an order for limited accounts and inquiries on the issues directly in question only or, where the main problem has been the failure of the executors or administrators to render accounts, to make an order for accounts only. As an alternative to an order for limited accounts the court may appoint a person as judicial trustee to complete the administration of the estate. The judicial trustee is an officer of the court and he will act under its supervision, either alone or jointly with the personal representatives. Such appointments avoid the full expense of administration by the court. See Judicial Trustee Act 1906.

Administration by the court is only available so long as those who seek it have not had their claims barred by lapse of time under the Limitation Act 1980. In the case of creditors the limitation period is six years for a debt due under simple contract and the period runs from the date the right accrued. See s5 of the Limitation Act 1980. Where a judgment debt is due the limitation period is 12 years running from the date the judgment date became enforceable. See s24 Limitation Act 1980. However, in any of these cases the limitation period may be extended by acknowledgment of the debt by the executors either by part payment or an acknowledgment in writing. See Limitation Act 1980 ss29–31. In the case of beneficiaries the limitation period is 12 years running from the date the right to the beneficial interest accrued. See s22 of the Limitation Act 1980.

20.3 Action for specific relief

In many cases the personal representatives may be able to carry on administration of the estate out of court but still have problems on one or two matters. In such instances the appropriate remedy is to bring an action for specific relief on the relevant problems. Thus, for example, there may be difficulty on the meaning or construction of a certain clause in the will, or doubts as to the validity of a claim by a creditor or a beneficiary. In such circumstances the personal representatives may issue an originating summons asking the court questions relevant to their problems.

20.4 Action against personal representatives

If a personal representative commits any breach of duty in his office which results in a loss to either the creditors or beneficiaries of the estate he commits a devastavit. This is the equivalent in the law of succession of a breach of trust, although devastavit is a much older remedy. Sometimes the term breach of trust is used to cover a breach of duty by personal representatives, but these matters are essentially different. However, personal representatives may be appointed as trustees of property in the will, and should they breach this trust they will be liable for breach of trust.

Often it is difficult for a beneficiary to know whether a devastavit or breach of trust action is more appropriate against a defaulting personal representative. Even where the personal representative has not formally become a trustee of the property it may be more advantageous to argue that he has become a trustee by virtue of an inferred assent. This is seen in the case of *Attenborough* v *Solomon* [1913] AC 76. Here an executor wrongfully pledged the beneficiary's plate. If he were sued as a personal representative based on breach of executorship then the pledgee could plead that the pledge was valid due to the several authority possessed by executors. If the action was based on breach of trust the pledge would be void as the other personal representative had not concurred with the pledge. It was held that there was an inferred assent by the personal representatives to themselves as trustees. Accordingly the correct approach was to hold the pledge void as only one trustee had authorised it.

A devastavit will arise when the personal representative fails to collect in and preserve the deceased's assets correctly, pay the expenses and debts with due diligence, or distribute the estate to the beneficiaries properly entitled thereto. The following are examples of devastavit.

1. Failing to collect debts due to the deceased with due diligence and allowing them to become statute-barred. See *Hayward* v *Kinsey* (1701) 12 Mod Rep 568.
2. Failing to exercise due care in safeguarding the assets of the deceased so that they are lost or destroyed through carelessness. However, if the assets are accidentally destroyed by fire or stolen from the executor by a thief in circumstances where there was no carelessness on his part, he will not be liable. See *Crosse* v *Smith* (1806) 7 East 246; *Job* v *Job* (1877) 6 Ch D 562.
3. Selling assets belonging to the deceased's estate at an undervaluation. See *Rice* v *Gordon* (1848) 11 Beav 265.
4. Improperly converting the deceased's assets to his (the personal representative's) own use by, for example, using them to settle his own personal liabilities (see *Re Morgan* (1881) 18 Ch D 93) or giving away the deceased's assets without authority to do so. See *Marsden* v *Regan* [1954] 1 WLR 423.
5. Failing to pay the debts and expenses with due diligence by, for example, paying them out of the correct order. See *Re Tankard* [1942] Ch 69.
6. Paying legacies before debts so that insufficient is left to pay the debts in full. See *Wheatley* v *Lane* (1669) 1 Wms Saund 216.
7. Failing to protect the estate from unjustifiable claims by creditors such as unreasonably large funeral expenses (see *Stag* v *Punter* (1744) 3 Atk 119), or paying statute barred debts. See *Midgley* v *Midgley* [1893] 3 Ch 282.
8. Failing to distribute the assets to the persons properly entitled thereto. See *Re Diplock* [1948] Ch 465.

The recent decision in *Gray* v *Richards Butler* (1996) The Times 23 July should be noted. The plaintiff, Gray, sought recovery of sums paid to the defendants, Richards Butler, a firm of solicitors. The claim related to work done by a partner as executor of Gray's deceased mother's will, which was declared invalid after probate was granted. The two witnesses had not witnessed the will at the same time. As a result the judge pronounced in favour of an earlier will which made Gray the sole executor. Gray's claim was that the sums already paid to Richards Butler should be returned as the later will, including its charging clause, had already been declared invalid.

Held: the court found in favour of Gray. It held that three principles of law applied to the case:

1. money paid by personal representatives to those not entitled to it was recoverable by those entitled to the money provided the recipients were not bone fide purchasers;
2. any payments under a charging clause of a will amounted to bounty that should be dealt with in the same was as testamentary legacies; and
3. anyone who may be granted probate should be entitled to the powers of a personal representative until the grant of probate is revoked or determined.

On the facts of this case Richards Butler were in the same position as any other legatees under an invalid will. Since they were not third parties they could not rely on common law principles for protection.

Another interesting decision occurred in *Gough* v *Chivers & Jordan (a firm)* (1996) The Times 15 July. In this case the testator, A, died. In his will he left his estate to B as principal beneficiary and sole residuary legatee. In the will A had appointed two executors, one of whom was a partner in the defendant firm of solicitors which carried out the administration of the estate. The defendant's bill was submitted and approved by both executors. On 30 March 1993 a transfer of money in settlement of the bill was made from the estate account to the defendant's account. B objected to the way in which the estate had been administered. Lengthy correspondence continued over a period of time until 14 June 1994 when B issued a summons to refer the bill to taxation. The defendants issued a summons seeking a declaration that the court did not have jurisdiction to tax the bill since the application of taxation should have been made within twelve months of the time of settlement of the bill. The decision of the district judge was upheld and the defendant's application was refused. The defendants appealed.

Held: The appeal was allowed. The main issue was whether the transfer of money in settlement of the bill amounted to a 'payment'. If it did, then the time limit stipulated by s70(4) Solicitors Act 1974 applied. This time limit stated that there were 12 months in which an application could be made for taxation from the time of payment. Since the transfer had been made with the knowledge and consent of those who paid and who were the trustees, the fact that one of them was a partner in the firm whose bill was being paid was irrelevant. As a result time ran from the end of March 1993 – the time of the transfer – and the application for taxation was time-barred by the date on which B had made it.

A personal representative is personally liable for a devastavit and must replace the loss caused to the estate. However, he may raise certain defences in his favour.

Section 27 of the Trustee Act 1925
This has been dealt with already. In certain cases, especially intestacy or on distribution of a gift to a class of next of kin, it may be difficult for the personal representative to trace all the beneficiaries who may be entitled to a share on distribution. If the proper advertisements are made in accordance with s27 then the personal representative will be protected from personal liability to any unpaid beneficiary. See *Re Aldhous* [1955] 1 WLR 459. The same provision is also applicable to unknown creditors. However, unpaid beneficiaries or creditors may trace their interests into the hands of those who were wrongly paid.

Section 61 of the Trustee Act 1925
This provision permits the court, at its discretion, to excuse a beneficiary either wholly or partly from personal liability for a devastavit where it appears that he acted 'honestly and reasonably' and 'in all the circumstances ought fairly to be excused' for the breach. It is up to the personal representative to show that he acted 'honestly and reasonably' in the circumstances and much will depend on the facts of each case. See *Re Kay* [1897] 2 Ch 518.

Section 62 of the Trustee Act 1925
If a beneficiary or creditor instigated, requested or consented in writing to the breach of duty by the personal representative, then the court may indemnify the personal representative from liability for any loss caused by impounding the interest of the beneficiary or creditor concerned. This interest may give either a full or a partial indemnity.

Acquiescence
If either a creditor or a beneficiary was *sui juris* and had full knowledge of the facts, concurred or acquiesced in the breach, he cannot complain of the acts of the personal representative which he has himself authorised. However, the onus of proof in showing acquiescence will lie on the personal representative. See *Re Marsden* (1884) 26 ChD 783. Often a personal representative takes a 'release' from the beneficiary. This is done in the form of a deed in which the beneficiary covenants under seal to absolve the personal representative from any breaches of duty in the administration, whether they are past, present or future breaches. As a seal supplies its own consideration the deed will be binding on the beneficiary thereby affording a full defence to the personal representative. However it is open to the beneficiary to argue that the deed of release is ineffective due to fraud or undue influence.

Lapse of time

The Limitation Act 1980 lays down specific periods within which claims by creditors and beneficiaries must be made. These have already been dealt with above.

Plene administravit

A personal representative may plead *plene administravit* in defence to an action by either a creditor or a beneficiary. This means that he has administered all the assets of the deceased which have come into his hands. Thus, the personal representative may have administered an insolvent estate or a heavily indebted estate, and any creditor or beneficiary may find that a claim for his debt or interest is met with this plea. See *Taylor* v *Deputy Commissioner of Taxation* (1969) 123 CLR 206.

Plene administravit praeter

There is a claim by the personal representative that he has duly administered all the assets which have come into his hands, except assets of a stated value which are still in his hands. Where this defence is successful the creditor or beneficiary will obtain judgment only for the amount in the hands of the personal representative.

Section 48 of the Administration of Justice Act 1985

This provision enables a personal representative to rely on a barrister's opinion regarding any question of meaning or interpretation arising in respect of the will. Its purpose is to avoid the necessity of obtaining a judicial decision on a contentious point and the personal representative is allowed to act on the barrister's opinion without incurring liability for devastavit or breach of trust. However, before the section is relied on the barrister concerned must have at least ten years' standing, give the required opinion in writing and a court order must be obtained before this opinion is acted upon. This court order may be refused if in the court's opinion a dispute exists on the will which would make it inappropriate to act on the opinion without first hearing argument.

As a preliminary to an order that a personal representative replace any loss he has caused through a devastavit, the court may order an account upon the footing of wilful default. This account may be ordered in respect of the whole estate or in relation to a particular transaction only. If one act of wilful default has been proved the court has jurisdiction to order an account in respect of the whole estate. In *Re Tebbs* [1976] 1 WLR 924, Slade J held that the test as to whether the court should order an account in respect of the whole estate should be this:

> 'Is the past conduct of the trustees such as to give rise to a reasonable *prima facie* inference that other breaches of trust not yet known to the plaintiff or the court have occurred.'

20.5 Action against recipient of assets

A creditor or beneficiary seeking to recover his loss caused by a devastavit of the personal representative should attempt to recover this from the personal representative in the first instance. See *Re Diplock* [1948] Ch 465. If he is unable to recover the loss either at all or in full from the personal representative because of the latter's insolvency then two remedies are available:

First, a personal claim against those who have received the assets of the deceased either wrongly or in excess of their entitlement. See *Ministry of Health* v *Simpson* [1951] AC 251.

Second, a tracing action so that he can follow the assets into the hands of any person who has received them other than a *bona fide* purchaser for value without notice. See *Re Diplock* [1948] Ch 465.

The personal claim against recipients

This claim, like a personal claim against a personal representative, is only effective if the recipient of the assets is solvent. By it the unpaid or underpaid creditor, legatee or next of kin is entitled to recover from the recipient an amount equal to that which was wrongly paid to him. The claim does not depend on the recipient continuing to hold that which he received from the personal representatives as it is a personal claim. See *Ministry of Health* v *Simpson*.

The personal claim here is an equitable remedy. It was developed 'by the Court of Chancery in the administration of the assets of a deceased person to avoid the evil of allowing one man to retain money legally payable to another', per Lord Simonds in *Ministry of Health* v *Simpson*. See also *Harrison* v *Kirk* [1904] AC 1.

A tracing action

This form of action does not depend upon the solvency of the wrong recipient of the assets, unlike those remedies just mentioned. If the wrong recipient still has the asset which was given him by the personal representatives or something which represents it, it can be recovered from him in a tracing action. If the wrong recipient has given the property to another, other than a *bona fide* purchaser without notice, then tracing will be available against the holder of the property.

In order for a successful tracing action to take effect three conditions must be satisfied.

1. There must be an initial fiduciary relationship. This is never a problem in the case of personal representative *vis-à-vis* creditors and beneficiaries.
2. The property must still be in a traceable form. If it has been dissipated so that there is no longer anything to trace the remedy is not available. See *Borden (UK)* v *Scottish Timber Products* [1981] Ch 25; *Magneta Finance* v *Savings and Investment Bank* [1985] FLR 237. However, the mere fact that the recipient has

mixed that which he wrongly received with his own assets is no bar to tracing, as equity will allow the tracing party a charge on the property. See *Re Hallett's Estate* (1880) 13 Ch D 696.

3. It must not be inequitable to trace in the circumstances. In *Re Diplock* [1948] Ch 465 the Court of Appeal pointed to many of the injustices which might be caused to an innocent volunteer against whom a tracing action was brought. Thus, for example, it was said that no tracing would be permitted if an innocent volunteer used the property he wrongly received in order to improve assets he already possessed, as it would be impossible to decide which part of the property the charge ought to apply to. This problem stems mainly from the rule that the tracing party and the innocent volunteer rank *pari passu* in a tracing action.

4. The tracing claim must not be barred by lapse of time. As tracing is an equitable right the doctrine of Laches will bar the action. There is some doubt as to whether statutory limitation will bar a tracing action, but the old case of *March* v *Russell* (1837) 3 Myl & Cr 31 holds that tracing is not barred by limitation. This view is supported by Goff and Jones in their work *The Law of Restitution* (1978) p541.

20.6 Bankrupt beneficiaries: the obligations and liabilities of personal representatives

In view of the increasing number of bankruptcies more consideration has been given to the position of a personal representative who is called upon to distribute assets of a deceased estate to a beneficiary against whom a bankruptcy order has or may have been made.

Having regard to the topical nature of this problem it is as well to consider the law as far as possible on the subject. While it is unfortunately rather unclear, it seems possible that a personal representative could be at risk if he or she paid a sum or transferred assets due under a will or on an intestacy to a beneficiary who was or might be bankrupt without taking certain precautions if the beneficiary were then to dispose of the money or asset in such a way as to prevent the trustee in bankruptcy from gaining control of it or land.

The relevant statutory law is found in s307 of the Insolvency Act 1986 which deals with after acquired property. This section enables the trustee in bankruptcy to claim for the bankrupt's estate any property, with certain specified exceptions, which has been acquired by or has evolved upon the bankrupt since the start of the bankruptcy.

The start of the bankruptcy is the date of the making of the bankruptcy order. The trustee does this by way of a notice in writing. The section does not mention to whom the notice is to be given although a sub-section refers to 'the service on the bankrupt of a notice under this section' which possibly means that the notice procedure may only apply to the bankrupt.

Section 333 of the 1986 Act requires a bankrupt within the prescribed period of 21 days to give notice to the trustee of any property which is acquired by or devolved upon him or her after the commencement of the bankruptcy. In the absence of a reasonable excuse it is a contempt of court for the bankrupt to fail to do so.

Sections 353 and 354 of the Insolvency Act also provide that it is a criminal offence for a bankrupt to fail to disclose information about all the property comprised in his or her estate or fail to deliver up such property to the Official Receiver or trustee.

It would appear prudent for a personal representative, therefore, to refuse to pay any money or transfer any assets to the bankrupt until the beneficiary has produced evidence of having given notice to the trustee in compliance with s333 in order to avoid risk of becoming a party to or liable for any misconduct by the bankrupt beneficiary. This would almost certainly lead to the giving of a s307 Notice and the making a claim by the trustee for what was due to the beneficiary which the personal representative could then safely pay. The personal representative might also be advised to contact the trustee in bankruptcy him or herself, although she should simply not pay the trustee without insisting on the giving of a s307 Notice. A trustee cannot give a good receipt until he or she has given this notice as the after acquired property does not vest in him or her until he or she has done so.

Alternatively, the personal representative could pay the money into court under s63 of the Trustee Act 1925 or possibly by way of an inter-pleader. However, this should only be a procedure of last resort in view of the costs risk to the personal representative should the court decide that it was unnecessary to take such a step.

Another question is whether the personal representative can ever pay a beneficiary without taking steps to ensure that a bankruptcy order has not been made against him or her? The Insolvency Act provides specific protections for certain people in dealing with the bankrupt, but these do not include a personal representative or indeed anyone who pays money or transfers property to a person who turned out to be a bankrupt. This, and the limits to the protection given by advertisements in accordance with s27 of the Trustee Act 1925, may be an argument to suggest that a personal representative should make bankruptcy searches as a matter of course. Nevertheless, it seems unlikely that a court would be persuaded that a personal representative should be liable for assets removed by the bankrupt from the trustee's reach where he or she has paid them in good faith and without notice of the beneficiary's bankruptcy. The normal practice seems to be that payments are generally made without enquiries about the beneficiary's solvency. Of course, the situation could well be different if a personal representative had reason to suspect that a beneficiary might be bankrupt and had taken no or inadequate steps to enquire. Therefore, where there may be some doubt it might be advisable for a bankruptcy only search to be made under the Land Charges Act 1972. Such a search must be made with the exact details of the person's name in order to obtain a proper result. Alternatively, the insolvency service maintains a list of all bankruptcy orders made.

It should be noted that if a bankruptcy petition against the beneficiary has been presented but no order has yet been made there is nothing in the Insolvency Act which would jeopardise the personal respresentative since s307 only bites when a bankruptcy order has been made. Another aspect concerns whether a solicitor who has made a will for a client should consider whether he or she should advise the client to change the will, perhaps by way of codicil, should he or she discover that a beneficiary has been made bankrupt or that there is a possibility of this happening. One solution could be to leave whatever would otherwise have gone to the beneficiary on trust, possibly a discretionary trust, in order to safeguard the gift.

20.7 Joint tenancies

The special circumstances of joint tenancies were discussed recently in *Re Palmer (deceased) (A Debtor)* [1994] 3 WLR 420. In 1989 the deceased, a debtor, and his wife became joint tenants of a house. After the deceased's death in November 1990 large claims against his estate caused his executor to present a petition for an insolvency administration order. This was made in August of 1991. A trustee of the estate was appointed in October 1991. The trustee was granted a declaration pursuant to s283 of the Insolvency Act 1986 as modified by paragraph 12 of Part II of Schedule 1 to the Administration of Insolvent Estates of Deceased Persons Order 1986. The deceased's estate included a beneficial tenancy in common with his wife in the house prior to his death, thereby serving retrospectively the joint tenancy with his wife before the deceased's death. The widow's appeal was allowed. It was held that the power conferred did not enable the Order to extend the ordinary meaning of 'estate of a deceased person' so as to include within it property which would not otherwise have formed part of that estate. This was clearly a significant decision in the interests of common sense and fairness.

21

Taxation of Estates

21.1 Taxation of estates: the charge to tax on death and before

This chapter deals with the taxation of estates on death. Capital gains tax (see section 21.7 below) and income tax (see section 21.8) are considered only in outline, whilst the most significant tax on death, inheritance tax (IHT), is considered more fully. While the Finance Act 2000 also covers certain aspects of IHT, the provisions of IHT are governed by the Inheritance Tax Act (IHTA) 1984 and all statutory provision numbers in this chapter relate to this statute unless otherwise stated.

IHT acts as a tax on death and imposes a charge on the value of the deceased's estate and certain other property of which the deceased has not completely divested himself and on transfers made during his or her lifetime. The essential point is that when a person dies they are treated for IHT purposes as having made a transfer of value immediately before their death, the value transferred being the value of their estate immediately before death.

It should be noted that 'estate' has a particular meaning in this context. It is the aggregate of all the property to which a person is beneficially entitled, except that the estate of a person immediately before his death does not include excluded property (s5(a)).

IHT is charged on 'the value transferred by a chargeable transfer'. The term 'chargeable transfer' means 'a transfer of value made by an individual which is not exempt' (ss1 and 2). This charge may apply both to lifetime transfers and to transfers on death.

As regards lifetime transfers, the term 'transfer of value' is defined to mean any lifetime disposition made by a person ('the transferor') which reduces the value of his or her estate. Thus any lifetime gift falls within the definition. There are three types of lifetime transfers for the purpose of IHT:

1. exempt transfers such as gifts between spouses and gifts to charities or political parties (see further below);
2. chargeable transfers such as gifts to discretionary trusts or to companies; and
3. potentially exempt transfers (PETs) which become exempt transfers if the donor survives for seven years or more (s3A).

Example

On 1 March 1993 Jack, the transferor, gives £180,000 to Susan. Assume no lifetime exemptions apply. The gift is a PET – no IHT is chargeable at the date of the gift.

If Jack dies before 1 March 2000, ie within seven years, the PET becomes chargeable. Susan is then liable to pay IHT. If Jack survives until 1 March 2000 the PET becomes exempt. There will never be any IHT payable and it has no further significance for IHT purposes when valuing the estate.

21.2 Inheritance tax rates

IHT replaced capital transfer tax and was introduced with effect from 18 March 1986 when the threshold was £140,000. The threshold is raised from time to time. The threshold now stands at £234,000. Above that limit a flat rate of 40 per cent taxation applies, with regard being given to the transferor's cumulative total of transfers over the previous seven years. Below the threshold is a nil rate band.

Tapering relief

If death occurs within seven years of a PET or chargeable lifetime transfer tax is charged at the rates applicable at the time of death. However, a percentage reduction of the full tax charge may be available depending on the time at which the transfer was made. This is known as tapering relief and applies as follows:

Period of years before death	Percentage of tax payable %
Not more than three	100
More than three but not more than four	80
More than four but not more than five	60
More than five but not more than six	40
More than six but not more than seven	20

21.3 Reliefs and exemptions: tax planning in wills

Certain transfers of value will be entirely exempt from IHT. The main exemptions are important tax planning tools. They are set out below.

Exemptions applying to all transfers

1. Transfers between married couples domiciled in the United Kingdom are exempt without limit.
2. Certain gifts to charities or for national purposes, public benefit and the maintenance of historic buildings. The exemption also applies to gifts to political parties.
3. Gifts to employee trusts.
4. There is a death on active service exemption whereby the estate of someone who is killed whilst on active service, or who dies from wounds sustained whilst on active service, will be totally exempt from IHT.

Exemptions applying only to lifetime transfers

1. £3,000 annual exemption – up to £3,000 can be given away in any one tax year. Any unused allowance in one year may be carried forward to the next tax year so long as that year's exemption has been fully used. Thereafter it will be lost.
2. Small outright gifts exemption – outright gifts of up to £250 to any one beneficiary per tax year are exempt. This exemption cannot be used in conjunction with any other exemption so gifts in excess of £250 must be offset against the annual exemption above.
3. Normal expenditure out of income exemption – gifts made by an individual out of taxable income are exempt if made regularly and without affecting the standard of living. There is no monetary limit on such gifts provided they meet these conditions.
4. Gifts for the maintenance of the family – gifts made for the maintenance of a spouse, ex-spouse or dependent relative or for the maintenance, education or training of certain children will generally be exempt.

5. Gifts in consideration of marriage – gifts made to the bride or groom in consideration of their marriage are exempt as shown in the table below.

Gift made by	Maximum exemption £
Each parent	5,000
A grandparent	2,500
The bride or groom	2,500
Any other person	1,000

Such gifts must be conditional upon the marriage taking place and must be given on or before the date of marriage.

Partially exempt transfers

In some cases a transfer on death may be partly taxable and partly exempt because part only of the estate passes to an exempt beneficiary such as a spouse or a charity. In these circumstances s38 sets out how the IHT is to be calculated and how the burden of IHT falls. This can lead to a very complicated calculation depending upon the division of the non-exempt part and the exempt part of the estate. The position depends on whether or not the specific gifts bear their own tax.

Business property relief

This relief only applies to certain business assets, which must have been owned for at least two years to qualify. Investment and property dealing businesses are excluded. See ss103–114.

In addition, the asset must not be subject to a 'binding contract for sale', which briefly will be the case where a partnership agreement or a company articles of association contains a 'buy and sell agreement'.

The reliefs available are as follows.

Type of property	Relief available %
Interests in an unincorporated business, ie sole trader/partnership	100
Shareholdings of unquoted/unlisted companies and stock market listed companies:	
More than 25% of the votes	100
25% or less of the votes	50

For the purposes of establishing the size of the shareholding, the votes attached to any shares held by a spouse are taken into account.

Controlling shareholdings in a fully quoted company	50
Certain assets (for example buildings, plant machinery, etc) personally owned by a partner or controlling director and used by their business for the purpose of its trade	50
Trust property used by a life tenant (beneficiary with a life interest in a trust) in their own business	50

Agricultural property relief

Agricultural property relief (ss115–124A) applies to farmers who own their own farms and individuals who let land to tenant farmers. To qualify the property must have been occupied by the owner for the purposes of agriculture for at least seven years, or have been owned for seven years with others farming it.

Agricultural property includes agricultural land or pastures, ancillary woodlands, cottages, farm buildings and farm houses which are of an appropriate character and all of which are used for agricultural purposes.

The reliefs available are as follows.

Type of property	*Relief available* %
Land and buildings with vacant possession or the ability to achieve it within 12 months	100
Land and buildings which are tenanted	50

If an asset such as farm machinery, livestock, etc is not treated as agricultural property for this particular relief it may also qualify for business property relief.

As with business property relief, agricultural property will not be eligible for relief if it is subject to a 'binding contract for sale'.

There are further conditions for eligibility to business property or agricultural property relief in respect of PETs. Broadly speaking, the basic safeguard is that if the transferee retains the property for at least seven years from the date of the transfer, the relief should be available should the PET become chargeable.

Special considerations also apply to commercial woodlands on death whereby it is possible to defer IHT on the trees and underwood until they are sold or gifted by the transferee. (See ss125–130.) The timber relief is given simply by excluding the value of the growing timber from the IHT computation at death, thereby effectively reducing the IHT rate applicable to the rest of the estate.

Quick succession relief (s114)

This relief is available in the event that a person dies within five years of receiving a gift or inheritance on which IHT has already been paid. A percentage of the tax already paid is allowed as a credit against IHT due on the second death as follows:

1. 100 per cent if the death is within one year;
2. 80 per cent if more than one but not more than two years; and
3. 60 per cent if more than two but not more than three years.

The relief only applies where:

1. tax was paid on the transfer to the deceased; and
2. tax is payable on the deceased's estate.

However, it is important to note that this relief is not affected by the fact that the property may have been sold or given away before the second death.

'Excepted' estates

The Inland Revenue has introduced new rules for estates where death occurred on or after 6 April 1996. It has raised the limit for the excepted estates procedure from £145,000 to £180,000. In addition, the rules concerning foreign assets and life-time gifts have been relaxed.

Qualifying estates

Personal representatives – executors or administrators – of straightforward smaller estates (excepted estates) will not have to deliver an account to the Inland Revenue. An estate will qualify as an excepted estate only where the following conditions are met:

1. the deceased died domiciled in the United Kingdom;
2. the total gross value of the estate before deduction of any debts, together with the value of any life-time gifts referred to below, does not exceed £180,000;
3. the estate consists only of property which has been passed under the deceased's will or intestacy or by nomination, or beneficially by survivorship (the deceased's beneficial interest in joint property counts for the purposes of the £180,000 limit);
4. any estate assets outside the United Kingdom have a total value of £30,000; and
5. any taxable life-time transfers made within seven years of the deceased's death consisted only of cash, quoted shares or quoted securities with a total gross value not exceeding £50,000 (previously the excepted estates procedure would have been ruled out by such transfers).

Non-qualifying estates

The excepted estates procedure does not apply where the deceased had:

1. within seven years of the debt made a chargeable or potential exempt transfer other than transfers of cash, quoted shares or quoted securities, etc;
2. made a gift with reservation of benefit which continued until death or ceased within seven years before the death; or
3. enjoyed an interest in possession in settled property at, or within seven years before, the death.

Grants of representation

Where all the conditions for qualifying as an excepted estate are satisfied, an account of the estate need not be presented. This is true whether the grant of representation is the first made in respect of the deceased or whether the grant is limited in duration in respect of property or to any special purpose. The Lord Chancellor's department will not be making any changes to its non-contentious probate fees order as a result of the amendments to the excepted estate procedure.

21.4 Valuation

The basic valuation principle is that assets in the estate are valued for IHT purposes at 'the price which the property might reasonably be expected to fetch if sold in the open market' immediately before the death (s160).

This means that the value immediately before death of every asset forming part of the estate for IHT purposes must be assessed and reported to the Inland Revenue in the Inland Revenue Accounts in general. Some assets, such as bank and building society accounts and quoted shares, are easy to value. Others, such as land, may be more difficult. Negotiations may be required in order to reach an agreed valuation. The value of an asset agreed for IHT purposes is known as the 'probate value'.

This basic valuation principle may be modified under s171 which provides that where the death causes the value of an asset in the estate to increase or decrease that change in value should be taken into account.

In order to calculate the tax, therefore, the chargeable estate is evaluated by valuing all the assets, deducting liabilities and exemptions and by applying the reliefs. In addition to the above, a transferor who makes a lifetime gift must bear in mind that the value transferred will form part of his or her cumulative total for a period of seven years. As such, this could increase the tax payable on the estate upon death in that time. This will give the amount of property upon which tax should be paid and from this the nil rate band is deducted.

Application of valuation principles to particular assets

1. Bank and building society accounts – their value for IHT purposes is the balance on the account including interest up to the date of death.
2. Quoted shares – the value of quoted shares is taken from the Stock Exchange daily official list for the date of death (or the nearest trading day). The list quotes two prices. To value the shares for IHT, one quarter of the difference between the lower and higher price is taken and added to the lower price.
3. Unquoted shares – the value of unquoted shares is more complicated, although the basic principle of open market value still applies. Information about the company and its record will be required.
4. Land – if a deceased owned an interest in land, whether as tenant in common or joint tenant, that share is part of his or her estate for IHT purposes and must be valued. The usual method is to take the value of the whole property and divide it by the number of shares, but a discount is normally allowed of between 10 per cent and 15 per cent.
5. Debts owed to the deceased – if a debt is owed to the deceased, its value is part of his or her estate for IHT purposes. One of the duties of the personal representative is to ensure that the deceased's lifetime income tax position has been settled (see below). If the deceased has paid too much income tax during his or her lifetime, the overpayment will be reclaimed from the Inland Revenue. As a result, when the deceased died this amount was owed to him or her and should be included as part of the estate for IHT purposes.

Debts and expenses

Liabilities owed by the deceased at the time of death are deductible for IHT purposes providing that they were incurred for money or money's worth (s505). Therefore debts such as gas and telephone bills may be deducted. In addition, the deceased may not have paid enough income tax on the income he or she received before he or she died; this amount may also be deducted.

Reasonable funeral expenses are also deductible (s162).

Related property

The related property rules also modify the basic valuation principle. The rules apply to property owned by spouses where the items of property owned by husband and wife are worth more valued together than separately. Each spouse's property must be valued not in isolation but as a proportion of the whole.

Commorientes

The commorientes rule in s184 of the Law of Property Act 1925 (See Chapter 9, section 9.3) does not apply for the purposes of IHT payable on death. In circumstances where s184 would apply for succession purposes then, for IHT purposes, each person is assumed to have died at the same instant (s4(2)).

21.5 Liability and burden of inheritance tax: administrative provisions

Reporting lifetime gifts

Usually it is not necessary for lifetime gifts, other than chargeable transfers, to be reported to the Capital Taxes Office (CTO) of the Inland Revenue if they are covered by one of the exemptions or, in the case of PETs, if they total less than £10,000 during any tax year or less than £40,000 in the last seven years. However, it is recommended that all gifts are, in fact, documented by the transferor.

In general, chargeable transfers should be reported to the CTO within 12 months of the end of the month of transfer or death. This includes PETs that have become chargeable as a result of the transferor's death within seven years of the gift, whether any IHT is payable or not.

Any person who receives a gift which subsequently becomes chargeable as a result of the transferor's death or in which the transferor still reserves the benefit at the time of death must also report it within the same time scale.

Reporting by personal representatives

Personal representatives must complete a return accounting for all of the deceased's assets, together with valuations, and also include details of the non-exempt gifts made by the deceased in the seven years prior to the date of death, to enable the IHT liability to be assessed. If the precise value of some assets are difficult to ascertain a provisional return may be made which can subsequently be revised as appropriate.

Reporting by trustees

Trustees are required to deliver an account to the CTO whenever an event occurs which is not exempt from IHT.

Payment of IHT

IHT on the estate is payable by the personal representatives when they make an application for a grant of probate or letters of administration. Accordingly, the grant will not be given until the IHT is paid by the personal representatives (excluding the amount which they have the right to pay by instalments as mentioned below). This means that the personal representatives must raise the money, which can be done by:

1. the sale of stocks and shares and personal chattels where there are executors;
2. bank loans;
3. loans from the beneficiaries;
4. other sources such as national savings banks;
5. assets submitted to the Inland Revenue in kind.

The personal representatives are liable to pay the IHT on the 'free estate' to the Inland Revenue. The concept of burden concerns how that IHT is to be borne as between those who become entitled to the property, whether under the will or by intestacy or survivorship. Subject to a contrary intention in the will, IHT on the property which vests in the personal representatives is treated as part of the general testamentary and administration expenses of the estate (s211). Therefore, in order to decide where the burden of tax lies, it is necessary first to look at the will, if any.

Usually pecuniary and specific legacies are expressed to be made 'free of tax' and the gift of residue is expressed to be made subject to administrative and testamentary expenses. As a result all the IHT on the property passing by will is borne by the residue. Sometimes, however, a legacy may be given 'subject to tax' so that the beneficiary must bear the tax on the property which has been left to them (calculated according to the estate rate).

Where the will is silent, or if the deceased died intestate, tax is payable, like other testamentary expenses, according to the statutory order set out in the Administration of Estates Act 1925. This generally means that tax is borne by the residue.

Where the personal representatives are liable to pay IHT on the property which does not vest in them they are entitled, subject to a contrary intention in the will, to recover the tax from the persons in whom the property is vested (s211(3)). This provision is required because personal representatives are liable to pay IHT on the deceased's 'free estate' which includes property passing outside the will such as the deceased's interest in joint property passing by survivorship. It entitles the personal representatives to recover the tax that they have paid from the persons entitled to the property, ie the surviving joint tenant.

It should be noted that where the deceased was entitled to a life interest under a trust so that the trust fund is treated for IHT as part of the estate, the personal representatives are not concerned with liability for IHT or the burden of IHT. The trustees are liable to pay the tax and the burden falls on the trust fund.

Finally, where a gift is made with reservation of benefit the transferee of the gift is primarily liable for IHT. However, if tax remains unpaid for 12 months after the end of the month of death, the personal representatives become liable to the extent of the deceased's assets which they have actually received or would have received but for their neglect or default.

Payments by instalments

As noted above, the personal representatives may elect to pay IHT by way of instalments on certain property. However, this is not an automatic right and the personal representatives must elect to do so by informing the Inland Revenue. If they do elect for this option the tax will be paid in ten equal yearly instalments. This option is available on certain assets only, as follows:

1. land of any description;
2. a business or an interest in a business;
3. shares (quoted or unquoted) which immediately before death gave control of the company to the deceased; and
4. unquoted shares which do not give control if either:

   a) the holding is sufficiently large (a holding of at least 10 per cent of the nominal value of the company shares and worth £20,000 or more); or
   b) the Inland Revenue is satisfied that the tax cannot be paid in one sum without undue hardship; or
   c) the IHT attributable to the shares and any other instalment option property in the estate amounts to at least 20 per cent of the tax payable on the estate.

It should be noted that where the instalment option is exercised in relation to IHT on shares or any other business property or agricultural land, instalments carry interest only from the date when each instalment is payable. Therefore, no interest is due on the outstanding tax provided that each instalment is paid on the due date.

However, in the case of other land interest is payable with each instalment apart from the first on the amount of IHT which was outstanding for the previous year.

If the instalment option property is sold all outstanding tax and interest becomes payable.

It should be mentioned that the first instalment is payable six months after the end of the month of death. Therefore on delivery of the Inland Revenue Account before the expiry of the six-month period the personal representatives do not have to pay any IHT on instalment option property. If any of the property which falls under the instalment option category ceases to remain in this category IHT becomes payable immediately.

21.6 Accumulation and maintenance trusts

These are dealt with by s31 of the Trustee Act 1925 (see Chapter 19, section 19.12).

The requirements for IHT purposes are under s71 and cover the following:

1. age entitlement – the beneficiary must become entitled to an interest in possession or settled property on attaining a specified age (or before) not exceeding 25; and
2. there must not be any interests in possession subsisting in settled property; and
3. there should be an accumulation of income in as far as it has not been used for the maintenance, education or benefit of the beneficiary; and
4. the 25-year rule or common ground parent rule applies.

Under s31 of the Trustee Act 1925 income has to be used for the maintenance, education or benefit of the beneficiary. If it is not used in this manner it must be accumulated as part of the capital. The beneficiary, on attaining the age of 18, becomes entitled to income and this amounts to an interest in possession. The gift may vest at this stage, or may be subject to further contingency. However, it should be noted that this provision may be expressly excluded in the settlement. The accumulation and maintenance trust is given a special treatment for IHT purposes. Unlike the normal discretionary trust there is no ten-year charge to IHT and tax is not charged when the beneficiary becomes entitled to an interest in possession or the capital.

Additional gifts made into the accumulation and maintenance trust by the settlor are PETs. Therefore IHT may be avoided altogether if the gift is made seven years before death and there is also the potential for tapering relief.

Whereas trustees usually pay CGT at a rate equivalent to the basic rate, in the case of accumulation and maintenance trusts they pay an additional rate of CGT, currently 34 per cent, where:

1. income is being accumulated;
2. income is paid at the trustees' discretion.

Income tax on the trust income should be paid by the trustee at the rate of 35 per cent until the beneficiary obtains his or her specific interest. If the income is spent on maintenance, education or benefit tax will be payable on the gross equivalent and credit is given in respect of the tax paid by the trustee. The tax repayment claim may be made if appropriate. Finally, income paid to or spent on the minor unmarried child of the settlor will be treated as income of the settlor.

21.7 Capital gains tax

The Taxation of Chargeable Gains Act 1992 contains the main statutory provisions on capital gains tax (CGT). Capital gains tax is charged on capital gains made from the disposal of chargeable assets, a capital gain being the difference between the values at which an asset was acquired and disposed. Apart from in the very specific circumstances where property is settled, the death of an individual does not give rise to CGT liability. This is because death is not a 'disposal' for CGT purposes (s62(1)(a) Taxation of Chargeable Gains Act 1992). However, CGT needs to be considered by the personal representatives in connection with:

1. disposals made by the deceased up until death; and
2. disposals made by the personal representatives during the administration period.

Disposals made by the deceased up until death

Any liability of the deceased for CGT should be paid by their personal representatives as it is a debt owing by the deceased which may be deducted when calculating IHT due on the death. In addition, an overpayment of CGT will be regarded as an asset of the estate and increasing its size for IHT purposes.

Immediately after the deceased's death the personal representatives should submit a return of the capital gains, if any, of the deceased for the period commencing on 6th April before the death and ending with the date of death. If necessary an estimate figure for CGT liability should be included in the Inland Revenue Account.

Disposals made by the personal representatives during the administration

Despite the fact that there is no disposal of assets for CGT purposes on death the personal representatives may need to sell assets in order to pay debts and other liabilities while the estate is being administered. If they should do this they will be liable to CGT on any gains made after the deduction of any losses that they have incurred on disposals.

CGT is paid at a rate equivalent to the basic rate of income tax. The indexation allowance is available to the personal representatives in the same way as it is to individuals. Furthermore, incidental selling expenses and a proportion of the cost of valuing the estate for probate purposes can be deducted. The Inland Revenue publishes a scale of permitted deductions (SP7/81), but where the actual loss is greater more than these amounts can be claimed.

The personal representatives have rights to claim exemptions and reliefs but these are limited as follows:

1. the annual exemption is only available for the tax year of death and the two following years;
2. the only or main residence exemption does not apply, although if before and after death a residence has been used as the only or main residence by individuals who are entitled under a will or the rules of intestacy to the whole or substantially the whole of the proceeds of sale of the house either absolutely or for life the exemption can be claimed by the personal representatives (Inland Revenue concession D5).

21.8 Income tax

Income tax here is again being considered in the context of the period up to the deceased's death and the administration period.

Income of the deceased up to the date of death

Any liability to income tax must be paid by the personal representatives as it is regarded as a debt owing at death and as such is deductible in calculating the net estate for IHT purposes. Here again if a refund of income tax paid is obtained it is regarded as an asset which increases the size of the estate for IHT purposes.

The deceased's personal representative must make a return to the Inland Revenue of the income of the deceased for the period commencing on 6 April before the deceased's death and ending with the date of death as soon as possible after the death. This pre-death tax return should be submitted as soon as possible because it may take some time to assess how much income tax is due or is likely to be refunded and this will have some bearing upon the calculation of IHT liability. To avoid delay in obtaining a grant of representation the personal representatives may estimate the income tax liability of the deceased when completing the Inland Revenue Account and later submit a corrected account when the sum of tax due is agreed with the Revenue. The following should be noted.

1. The calculation of the deceased's income tax is done in the usual way by deducting any charges on income payable before death together with any reliefs or allowances. However, a full year's personal relief and allowances can be claimed regardless of the date of death.
2. Only income received or due before death is included in the return. Income receivable after death is income of the estate and is dealt with separately.

Income arising after death

The administration period begins on the day after the date of death and continues until the complete administration of the estate (s695 Income and Corporation Taxes Act 1988). The administration is regarded as complete on the date when the residue is ascertained for distribution.

For each income tax year (or part) during the administration period the personal representatives must submit a return to the Inland Revenue of the income they have received from the deceased's estate.

The personal representative cannot claim any of the reliefs available to individuals nor can they claim the lower rate of tax available to individuals. However, they can claim relief for interest paid on a loan to pay IHT. The personal representatives pay basic rate tax on the taxable income of the estate whatever the amount and type of income. There is a special rate for tax payable on dividends received by the personal representatives (20 per cent), although usually the personal representatives will have no income tax to pay on dividends received as basic rate tax has already been deducted at source.

21.9 Post-death variations

It should be mentioned briefly that the re-distribution of inherited property can be achieved by a beneficiary accepting the property and subsequently giving it to the intended transferee. If this were done there may be adverse taxation consequences. The beneficiary, as transferor, would be making a PET for IHT purposes and a disposal of assets for CGT purposes.

These effects can be avoided by taking advantage of provisions in the IHT and CGT legislation whereby beneficiaries under a will or an intestacy can alter, for tax purposes, the dispositions of a deceased's persons estate.

Where such conditions are satisfied the altered dispositions are 'read back' into the will or the distribution on intestacy and are treated as though made by the deceased person and taxed accordingly. The use of such provisions can often result in considerable savings of IHT. For example, a significant saving in IHT is possible where the nil rate band has not been fully used, such as where an entire estate has been left to a surviving spouse and is therefore exempt. Tax planning can assist to avoid a 'bunching of estates' in this instance as well as, more generally before death when preparing a will.

Index

Suggested Solutions to Past Examination Questions 1995–1999

The Suggested Solutions series provides examples of full answers to the questions set by examiners. Each suggested solution has been broken down into three stages: general comments, skeleton solution and suggested solution. The examination questions included within the text are taken from past examination papers set by London University. The full opinions and answers will not necessarily meet with the approval of examiners and may reflect examiners' opinions of the subject in question.

Only £6.95 Publication January 2001

Constitutional Law	Jurisprudence and Legal Theory
ISBN: 1 85836 040 6	ISBN: 1 85836 055 4
Contract Law	Land Law
ISBN: 1 85836 041 X	ISBN: 1 85836 052 X
Criminal Law	Law of Tort
ISBN: 1 85836 051 8	ISBN: 1 85836 054 6
English Legal System	Law of Trusts
ISBN: 1 85836 049 6	ISBN: 1 85836 056 2

Forthcoming titles of Suggested Solutions
1999–2000 due early December 2001

Company Law	Family Law
ISBN: 1 85836 122 0	ISBN: 1 85836 131 X
European Union Law	Public International Law
ISBN: 1 85836 123 9	ISBN: 1 85836 140 9
	Evidence
	ISBN: 1 85836 134 4

For further information on contents or to place an order, please contact:

Mail Order
Old Bailey Press
200 Greyhound Road
London
W14 9RY

Telephone No: 020 7385 3377
Fax No: 020 7381 3377
Website: www.oldbaileypress.co.uk

Suggested Solutions to Past Examination Questions 1998–1999

The Suggested Solutions series provides examples of full answers to the questions regularly set by examiners. Each suggested solution has been broken down into three stages: general comment, skeleton solution and suggested solution. The examination questions included within the text are taken from past examination papers set by the London University. The full opinion answers will undoubtedly assist you with your research and further your understanding and appreciation of the subject in question.

Only £6.95 Published January 2001

Constitutional Law
ISBN: 1 85836 389 6

Contract Law
ISBN: 1 85836 390 X

Criminal Law
ISBN: 1 85836 391 8

English Legal System
ISBN: 1 85836 392 6

Jurisprudence and Legal Theory
ISBN: 1 85836 393 4

Land Law
ISBN: 1 85836 394 2

Law of Tort
ISBN: 1 85836 395 0

Law of Trusts
ISBN: 1 85836 396 9

Forthcoming titles of Suggested Solutions 1999–2000 due early December 2001

Company Law
ISBN: 1 85836 442 6

European Union Law
ISBN: 1 85836 443 4

Evidence
ISBN: 1 85836 444 2

Family Law
ISBN: 1 85836 445 0

Public International Law
ISBN: 1 85836 446 9

For further information on contents or to place an order, please contact:
Mail Order
Old Bailey Press
200 Greyhound Road
London
W14 9RY

Telephone No: 020 7381 7407
Fax No: 020 7386 0952
Website: www.oldbaileypress.co.uk

Law Update 2001

Law Update 2002 edition – due February 2002

An annual review of the most recent developments in specific legal subject areas, useful for law students at degree and professional levels, others with law elements in their courses and also practitioners seeking a quick update.

Published around February every year, the Law Update summarises the major legal developments during the course of the previous year. In conjunction with Old Bailey Press textbooks it gives the student a significant advantage when revising for examinations.

Contents
Administrative Law • Civil and Criminal Procedure • Company Law • Conflict of Laws • Constitutional Law • Contract Law • Conveyancing • Criminal Law • Criminology • English Legal System • Equity and Trusts • European Union Law • Evidence • Family Law • Jurisprudence • Land Law • Law of International Trade • Public International Law • Revenue Law • Succession • Tort

For further information on contents or to place an order, please contact:

Mail Order
Old Bailey Press
200 Greyhound Road
London
W14 9RY

Telephone No: 020 7381 7407
Fax No: 020 7386 0952
Website: www.oldbaileypress.co.uk

ISBN 1 85836 385 3
Soft cover 246 x 175 mm
408 pages £9.95
Published March 2001

Old Bailey Press

The Old Bailey Press integrated student law library is tailor-made to help you at every stage of your studies from the preliminaries of each subject through to the final examination. The series of Textbooks, Revision WorkBooks, 150 Leading Cases/Casebooks and Cracknell's Statutes are interrelated to provide you with a comprehensive set of study materials.

You can buy Old Bailey Press books from your University Bookshop, your local Bookshop, direct using this form, or you can order a free catalogue of our titles from the address shown overleaf.

The following subjects each have a Textbook, 150 Leading Cases/Casebook, Revision WorkBook and Cracknell's Statutes unless otherwise stated.

Administrative Law
Commercial Law
Company Law
Conflict of Laws
Constitutional Law
Conveyancing (Textbook and Casebook)
Criminal Law
Criminology (Textbook and Sourcebook)
English and European Legal Systems
Equity and Trusts
Evidence
Family Law
Jurisprudence: The Philosophy of Law (Textbook, Sourcebook and
    Revision WorkBook)
Land: The Law of Real Property
Law of International Trade
Law of the European Union
Legal Skills and System
Obligations: Contract Law
Obligations: The Law of Tort
Public International Law
Revenue Law (Textbook,
    Sourcebook and Revision
    WorkBook)
Succession

Mail order prices:	
Textbook	£14.95
150 Leading Cases/Casebook	£9.95
Revision WorkBook	£7.95
Cracknell's Statutes	£9.95
Suggested Solutions 1998–1999	£6.95
Law Update 2001	£9.95

To complete your order, please fill in the form below:

Module	Books required	Quantity	Price	Cost
		Postage		
		TOTAL		

For Europe, add 15% postage and packing (£20 maximum).
For the rest of the world, add 40% for airmail.

ORDERING

By telephone to Mail Order at 020 7381 7407, with your credit card to hand.

By fax to 020 7386 0952 (giving your credit card details).

Website: www.oldbaileypress.co.uk

By post to: Mail Order, Old Bailey Press, 200 Greyhound Road, London W14 9RY.

When ordering by post, please enclose full payment by cheque or banker's draft, or complete the credit card details below. You may also order a free catalogue of our complete range of titles from this address.

We aim to despatch your books within 3 working days of receiving your order.

Name

Address

Postcode   Telephone

Total value of order, including postage: £

I enclose a cheque/banker's draft for the above sum, or

charge my   ☐ Access/Mastercard   ☐ Visa   ☐ American Express
Card number

☐☐☐☐ ☐☐☐☐ ☐☐☐☐ ☐☐☐☐

Expiry date   ☐☐☐☐

Signature: ....Date: ....

Learning Resources
Centre